Criminal Law and Procedure

CRIMINAL LAW AND PROCEDURE:

Text and Cases

George T. Felkenes

*University of Alabama
in Birmingham*

PRENTICE-HALL, INC., ENGLEWOOD CLIFFS, NEW JERSEY

Library of Congress Cataloging in Publication Data

FELKENES, GEORGE T   (date)
    Criminal law and procedure.

    (Prentice-Hall series in criminal justice)
    Includes index.
    1.–Criminal law—United States—Cases. 2.–Criminal procedure—United States—Cases. I.–Title.
KF9218.F4   345′.73′05   75-5735
ISBN   0-13-193441-4

Prentice-Hall Series in Criminal Justice
James D. Stinchcomb, *Editor*

Printed in the United States of America

10 9 8 7 6 5 4 3 2 1

PRENTICE-HALL INTERNATIONAL, INC., *London*
PRENTICE-HALL OF AUSTRALIA, PTY. LTD., *Sydney*
PRENTICE-HALL OF CANADA, LTD., *Toronto*
PRENTICE-HALL OF INDIA PRIVATE LIMITED, *New Delhi*
PRENTICE-HALL OF JAPAN, INC., *Tokyo*
PRENTICE-HALL OF SOUTHEAST ASIA (PTE.) LTD., *Singapore*

To My Wife
Sandra

Contents

Chapter 1

THE CRIMINAL PROCESS.
QUESTIONS OF LAW VERSUS QUESTIONS OF FACT.
THE TRIAL AND APPEAL.   STATE AND FEDERAL COURTS.
FUNCTIONARIES IN THE CRIMINAL PROCESS.   PRECEDENTS.
GENERAL TERMS.

Chapter 2

Chapter 3

Chapter 4

Chapter 5

Chapter 6

List of Cases

Selected Provisions:
The Constitution of the United States

Article I

Section 9

(2) The privilege of the Writ of Habeas Corpus shall not be suspended, unless when in Cases of Rebellion or Invasion the public Safety may require it.

(3) No Bill of Attainder or ex post facto Law shall be passed.

Article II

Section 2

(2) [The President] He shall have Power, by and with the Advice and Consent of the Senate to make Treaties, provided two thirds of the Senators present concur; and he shall nominate, and by and with the Advice and Consent of the Senate, shall appoint Ambassadors, other public Ministers and Consuls, Judges of the supreme Court, and all other Officers of the United States, whose Appointments are not herein otherwise provided for, and which shall be established by

Law; but the Congress may by Law vest the Appointment of such inferior Officers, as they think proper, in the President alone, in the Courts of Law, or in the Heads of Departments.

Article III

Section 1

The judicial Power of the United States, shall be vested in one supreme Court, and in such inferior Courts as the Congress may from time to time ordain and establish. The Judges, both of the supreme and inferior Courts, shall hold their Offices during good Behaviour, and shall, at stated Times, receive for their Services a Compensation, which shall not be diminished during their Continuance in Office.

Section 2

(1) The judicial Power shall extend to all Cases, in Law and Equity, arising under this Constitution, the Laws of the United States, and Treaties made, or which shall be made, under their Authority;—to all Cases affecting Ambassadors, other public Ministers and Consuls;—to all Cases of admiralty and maritime Jurisdiction;—to Controversies to which the United States shall be a Party;—to Controversies between two or more States;—between a State and Citizens of another State;—between Citizens of different States;—between Citizens of the same State claiming Lands under the Grants of different States, and between a State, or the Citizens thereof, and foreign States, Citizens or Subjects.

(2) In all Cases affecting Ambassadors, other public Ministers and Consuls, and those in which a State shall be a Party, the supreme Court shall have original Jurisdiction. In all the other Cases before mentioned, the supreme Court shall have appellate Jurisdiction, both as to Law and Fact, with such Exceptions, and under such Regulations as the Congress shall make.

(3) The trial of all Crimes, except in Cases of Impeachment, shall be by Jury; and such Trial shall be held in the State where the said Crimes shall have been committed; but when not committed within any State, the Trial shall be at such Place or Places as the Congress may by Law have directed.

Section 3

(1) Treason against the United States shall consist only in levying War against them, or, in adhering to their Enemies, giving them Aid and Comfort. No Person shall be convicted of Treason unless on the Testimony of two Witnesses to the same overt Act, or on Confession in open Court.

(2) The Congress shall have Power to declare the Punishment of Treason, but no Attainder of Treason shall work Corruption of Blood, or Forfeiture except during the life of the Person attainted.

AMENDMENT I (1791)

Congress shall make no law respecting an establishment of religion, or prohibiting the free exercise thereof; or abridging the freedom of speech, or of the press; or the right of the people peaceably to assemble, and to petition the Government for a redress of grievances.

AMENDMENT II (1791)

A well regulated Militia, being necessary to the security of a free State, the right of the people to keep and bear Arms, shall not be infringed.

AMENDMENT III (1791)

No Soldier shall, in time of peace be quartered in any house, without the consent of the Owner, nor in time of war, but in a manner to be prescribed by law.

AMENDMENT IV (1791)

The right of the people to be secure in their persons, houses, papers, and effects, against unreasonable searches and seizures, shall not be violated, and no Warrants shall issue, but upon probable cause, supported by

Oath or affirmation, and particularly describing the place to be searched, and the person or things to be seized.

AMENDMENT V (1791)

No person shall be held to answer for a capital, or otherwise infamous crime, unless on a presentment or indictment of a Grand Jury, except in cases arising in the land or naval forces, or in the Militia, when in actual service in time of War or public danger; nor shall any person be subject for the same offence to be twice put in jeopardy of life or limb; nor shall be compelled in any criminal case to be a witness against himself, nor be deprived of life, liberty, or property, without due process of law; nor shall private property be taken for public use, without just compensation.

AMENDMENT VI (1791)

In all criminal prosecutions, the accused shall enjoy the right to a speedy and public trial, by an impartial jury of the State and district wherein the crime shall have been committed, which district shall have been previously ascertained by law, and to be informed of the nature and cause of the accusation; to be confronted with the witnesses against him; to have compulsory process for obtaining witnesses in his favor, and to have the Assistance of Counsel for his defence.

AMENDMENT VII (1791)

In Suits at common law, where the value in controversy shall exceed twenty dollars, the right of trial by jury shall be preserved, and no fact tried by jury, shall be otherwise re-examined in any Court of the United States, than according to the rules of the common law.

AMENDMENT VIII (1791)

Excessive bail shall not be required, nor excessive fines imposed, nor cruel and unusual punishments inflicted.

AMENDMENT IX (1791)

The enumeration in the Constitution, of certain rights, shall not be construed to deny or disparage others retained by the people.

AMENDMENT X (1791)

The powers not delegated to the United States by the Constitution, nor prohibited by it to the States, are reserved to the States respectively, or to the people.

AMENDMENT XIV (1868)

Section 1

All persons born or naturalized in the United States, and subject to the jurisdiction thereof, are citizens of the United States and of the State wherein they reside. No State shall make or enforce any law which shall abridge the privileges or immunities of citizens of the United States; nor shall any State deprive any person of life, liberty, or property, without due process of law; nor deny to any person within its jurisdiction the equal protection of the laws.

Preface

\

We will appoint as justiciaries,
constables, sheriffs, or bailiffs
only such men as know the law of the
land and keep it well.

Magna Carta, Chapter 45 (1215)

The complex of agencies called the criminal justice system is to a great extent shaped by the opinions of the courts. Consequently, criminal law and procedure are taught in almost, if not every, criminal justice program in the country. This book is an attempt to present in a concise yet thorough form an approach to developing an understanding and appreciation of law and procedure as viewed through court decisions. The approach, however, is not geared to set forth the entire case opinion but rather the court decision in an abridged, case-brief format.

The traditional approaches to teaching legal subjects—casebook or text—just do not meet the needs of the criminal justice practitioner, whether he is a parole or probation officer, police officer, alcoholic beverage control functionary, criminalistics technician, or other system-related person. Thousands of preservice students studying in hundreds of institutions of higher education and in various criminal justice academies are in need of a new kind of textbook—a combination casebook/text. The author has attempted to accomplish this goal in the book.

There has been an effort to achieve a balance between a pedantic discussion of cases related to precedent and a bare-bones, general statement of a rule without illustrative, explanatory case examples. Cases are still one of the best methods of analyzing and understanding criminal law and procedure. However, rather than develop a casebook with case decisions of some eight to fifteen pages, much of which is superfluous to understanding the point of the case as it pertains to the law or procedure involved, this book contains extracts of landmark cases on a specific point or topic. The case extract presents to the student a point of departure for class discussion regarding the particular rule, rationale, and analysis of the case.

The presentation of each case leads to a sound basis for initiating class discussion and further explanation of related legal principles. The development of the overall guiding constitutional principles is followed from case to case. This approach also presents an ideal vehicle to indicate to the student how a particular state decision on law or procedure has been altered to fit into constitutional standards. The teaching possibilities are almost unlimited. Anyone using this book can easily change the order of the topics to fit his scheme of presentation. There is nothing sacrosanct about the arrangement.

I want to express my sincere appreciation to Mrs. Patricia Riley, who typed and edited the manuscript. Professors Calvin Swank and C. Allen Graves, University of Alabama in Birmingham, and Professor William Mathias, Georgia State University, were very helpful in the advice on various chapters. I thank them. Dr. George Passey, Dean, School of Social and Behavioral Sciences, University of Alabama in Birmingham, deserves recognition for his encouragement in this project. Also deserving a special note of appreciation are two of my graduate students, Sharon Vacarella and Burton Butler. My wife, Sandra, is probably one of the most patient and understanding persons in the world for having put up with the long nights and innumerable weekends that were devoted to the preparation of this work.

Criminal Law and Procedure

Chapter 1

General Procedural Considerations and Steps in the Criminal Process

THE CRIMINAL PROCESS

This text is about the criminal procedures which to a large degree determine the treatment that a person suspected, charged, or convicted of a criminal offense is accorded as he is processed through the criminal justice system. Because the fundamental nature of the procedures stems from the Constitution of the United States and decisions of the United States Supreme Court, this text will examine in detail what the basic law provides and how the various provisions involving the criminal process have been interpreted by the Supreme Court.

To begin, the Bill of Rights, the first ten amendments to the Constitution, was added to the Constitution to specifically tell the government what it could and could not do. Of primary interest to those in the criminal justice system are the Fourth, Fifth, Sixth, and Eighth Amendments which in theory limit law enforcement officials significantly in the way in which they perform their job: their powers to arrest, detain, and search persons suspected of a crime are circumscribed; guilt is to be determined by courts and juries in courtrooms in which specific procedures or safeguards are provided that guarantee to the accused certain personal rights that a government cannot transgress.

Enforcement of these provisions has proved to be quite difficult and often divisive in our society. The criminal process has come under a great deal of criticism during the past decade. For the first time in our history we have seen the concern with law and order become an issue in a presidential election. Entire segments of our society have become antagonistic toward the system of criminal justice, including the police, judges, corrections personnel, prosecutors, and the criminal law. A significant number of people have a suspicion about the structure of criminal prosecution in particular, and its fairness and impartiality. Because this is the situation let us see how a typical criminal prosecution begins.

Early in the morning an officer is cruising in his patrol car in a downtown business district when he observes Steve running down a dark alley. Steve apparently notices the patrol car and attempts to hide behind a couple of trash barrels. What should the officer do? What kind of police action should he take? In most situations he will try to determine why Steve is so bent on not being seen by the officer.

In his quick investigation the officer must act as a judge without a robe. He must decide whether to stop Steve, search him, detain him, question him, or take him to the police station, among various other considerations. When he is faced with these decisions, numerous thoughts, motives, and personal involvements pass through his mind: his own personality is important, as are his prejudices and biases; also influential is his knowledge of departmental policy; familiarity with the district attorney and the kinds of cases he prosecutes; and an understanding and knowledge of the various courts in the area with the possibility of conviction causes him some concern. The officer decides that Steve is acting in a strange and suspicious manner and will detain him for further investigation—or if the officer believes he has probable cause to believe a crime has been committed, he will arrest him. Steve is taken to the police station, booked, locked up, and/or questioned.

From this simple routine beginning, numerous potential constitutional problems are raised in the areas of search and seizure, arrest, actions at the stationhouse, and questioning of the suspect.

Search and Seizure.   Under the Fourth Amendment a search may be conducted if a search warrant is obtained. The search warrant is in effect a court order specifically listing all the items that the policeman is searching for and may confiscate. An arrest warrant only names the person who is to be seized. In this situation however, and as in most police arrest situations, there is no warrant; because of the urgency of the situation, it is impractical to secure one. In such an occurrence there are exceptions to the warrant requirement. The law permits an officer to search a person for concealed weapons to insure his own safety, to deprive the person of means of escape, to prevent the destruction of evidence, and to confiscate fruits of the crime. Of special constitutional interest are the rules that have developed regarding searches of automobiles. If the officer has reasonable cause to believe that the car contains illegal items such as drugs, illegal weapons, smuggled goods, or instruments of a crime, the car may be stopped, searched, items seized, and the person(s) arrested.

The Fourth Amendment provides:

> *The right of the people to be secure in their persons, houses, papers and effects, against unreasonable searches and seizures, shall not be violated, and no warrants shall issue, but upon probable cause, supported by oath or affirmation, and particularly describing the place to be searched and the persons or things to be seized.*

The policeman is directly confronted with a situation of constitutional import because of the two decisions he must make: (1) Is the search reasonable? and (2) Is there probable cause to make it?

In situations similar to the one in the hypothetical occurrence above, the policeman probably would have approached Steve with a drawn gun; Steve would have been asked some questions, and he probably would have been searched to ascertain whether or not he was carrying a weapon. In many states, carrying a concealed weapon is illegal. In those states and at the federal level, if a gun is found as a result of a search, it would not be admissible as evidence because it was obtained during an illegal detention prior to the search. Of course if it were established that the officer had a reasonable suspicion to detain, then the seizure of the weapon would be valid. However, the decision to detain and "pat down" certainly involves a potential constitutional problem.

Arrest. Suppose in the officer's search of Steve he found nothing, but still decided to take Steve to the stationhouse for further questioning, to check his identity, and/or to find out if any crimes had been reported in the neighborhood. Generally an arrest is not permitted unless there is probable cause to believe, based on reasonable information, that a person has committed a specific crime. Did the patrolman have probable cause to think Steve might have perpetrated some crime? Did the facts he had lead him reasonably to believe that Steve committed a crime? Once again, each of these questions leads directly to interpreting the constitutional requirements for reasonable or probable cause, which in turn leads to the legality of the subsequent search and seizure.

Actions at the Stationhouse. In most instances a person who is brought to the stationhouse is "booked." This means that a record is made that he was arrested and for what charges. In most cases "booking" also means that the person is photographed and fingerprinted. Booking takes place as soon as the individual is brought to the stationhouse; then he is taken before a magistrate without unnecessary delay to determine why he is being held.

It must be remembered that the typical arrest is made without a warrant. In this situation a delay may occur between the arrest and filing of the formal charge. A number of constitutional issues are raised right here. First, after the arrest but before the charge, are the police permitted to conduct an investigation to ascertain whether or not there is evidence to support the charge? Second, if so, what are the limitations on the conduct of the investigation and the length of the delay? Third, is there a type of detention that is less severe than an arrest to permit police questioning? Fourth, does the law permit the police to release a suspect when their investigation shows that he has done no wrong?

The police practice in arresting "on suspicion" or "for investigation" means that in most situations the person taken to the police station is never formally charged with a crime; only a small percentage of those arrested ever get into court for a full trial. If all persons who were arrested were brought to trial, the courts would be swamped and all but cease to function. Some of those arrested who would otherwise be released without a court record would be subjected to a preliminary hearing and the expense of an attorney before they secured their release. Still others who are guilty would go free because the police would not be able to conduct an investigation. On the other hand, an arrest can violate the basic constitutional rights: the right to habeas corpus, the right to refuse to incriminate oneself, the right to bail, and the right to counsel.

Questioning of the Suspect.   The privilege against self-incrimination contained in the Fifth Amendment states that "no person . . . shall be compelled in any criminal case to be a witness against himself." One of the problems plaguing law enforcement personnel involves the extent to which this privilege applies to on-the-street questioning and stationhouse interrogation. In other words, how long is a policeman permitted to question a suspect *before* bringing him before a judge to be formally charged with an offense? This problem is especially important and presents great difficulties for the police, who depend on questioning prior to filing a charge in order to obtain enough information to satisfy the judge that there is indeed probable cause to hold the suspect for a specific crime and to obtain admissions and confessions to be used to convict the suspect.

During the past decade the Supreme Court decisions have changed the ground rules for the admission of confessions in almost all situations to a much more restrictive policy. The ostensible reason is to encourage more professional police work by relying on other evidence than extracted confessions. Recent Supreme Court decisions have changed the test for admissibility from whether the confession was trustworthy to whether it was voluntary.

Under the "trustworthy" test, a confession supported by evidence such as a knife found in a particular place described in the confession would be admissible no matter how the confession was obtained. More recently, the decisions have required that confessions be voluntary. If they are not, then they are not admissible. Evidence developed from the confession is likewise not admissible because it is tainted with illegality. This doctrine, known as the "fruit of the poisoned tree," is based on the idea that the prosecution should not be permitted to benefit itself based on its own unlawful actions. One of the sticky problems in any police interrogation is whether a confession is or is not voluntary.

Closely connected with the Fifth Amendment privilege is the right to counsel contained in the Sixth Amendment, which states that "in all criminal prosecutions, the accused shall enjoy the right to have the Assistance of Counsel for his defense." When does this right take effect in the criminal process? This has been the issue in several cases that you will study in this book. You will be confronted with such issues as these:

1. If a suspect requests a lawyer during interrogation, should he be given one?

2. What if he does not request one—should one be provided anyway?

3. What can the lawyer do during the questioning?

4. Should a suspect be provided with an attorney at state expense if he cannot afford one and he desires to have one?

5. Would a suspect ever confess if his lawyer were present?

QUESTIONS OF LAW VERSUS QUESTIONS OF FACT

To start off, two questions arise: What is the difference between a question of law and a question of fact? Why is this important in considering constitutional questions?

Consider the following hypothetical case which comes before you as the student court judge in your school. Peter, an excellent student, complains to the student court that Daniel, another student, borrowed a library book from him and lost it. Peter has been billed by the library because the book was checked out to him. Peter told Daniel that he should pay for the book but Daniel refused. Daniel has been called before the student court and denied that he borrowed the book from Peter, or said that he returned it to Peter.

What kinds of questions are raised by this case? In any legal controversy two kinds of questions arise:

1. What is the law that applies to the case?
2. What are the facts in the case?

First, you as the judge of the court must decide whether or not a student who borrows a book from another student should be held responsible for it. How are you going to do this? Several avenues are open. You might (1) look at the rules and regulations of the student legislature to see if one applies; or (2) construe (interpret) one of these rules and regulations if it is unclear in its application to this case. For example, you might construe the following regulation to be applicable to the case before you: "Each student shall compensate another student whose property he has damaged, lost, or destroyed." You might also (3) look into past decisions of the court to determine if a similar situation had come before the court (precedents); (4) decide the fairest solution for Peter and Daniel; (5) determine the best solution for the entire student body, one that would encourage the fullest use of the library, produce respect for another's property, protect the library, and so on.

If you decide that Daniel was not responsible for the loss of the book, the case ends. However, if you decide that Daniel must pay for the lost book, a second problem arises: you must decide whether Daniel had lost or borrowed Peter's library book. Only then can you decide whether Daniel has to pay for the book. This decision by you must be made after you have heard from both sides and listened to the testimony of anyone else who had information about the case, such as someone who saw Daniel borrow the book from Peter.

In this example the question of whether a student is responsible when he borrows and loses a library book of another is a question of law. The question of *fact* is deciding whether Daniel borrowed Peter's library book in the first place.

THE TRIAL AND APPEAL

In the previous section our hypothetical student judge heard testimony from witnesses and decided questions of fact. He then applied the law as he saw it to the facts as he found them and reached a decision about whether or not Daniel had to pay for the lost book.

The *trial* involves both questions of law and questions of fact. Depending on the specific case involved, the question of finding the facts and finding the law is divided between different persons. The jury is the "trier of fact"—that is, it has the responsibility for finding what laws are applicable. Occasionally the judge becomes the "trier" when a jury trial is waived by the defendant or none is permitted by the state law.

In practice, the system operates in the following general way. The jury listens to witnesses who testify to "facts" as they perceive them to be in the situation in issue. The judge decides what the law to be applied is in the situation. He then "instructs" the jury, which means that he explains the laws to them. He tells them that if they believe certain facts are true they should enter a certain verdict, or if they believe other facts are true they should enter another verdict; this is a decision. Going back to the student court situation, if there had been a jury the judge would have instructed the jury in a manner similar to the following:

> *If you find that Daniel borrowed the book from Peter and if you further find that Daniel lost the book, then you must enter a verdict which holds Daniel responsible for paying for the library book.*

You can note that the trial is thus separated into two functional areas: fact finding (jury) and law instructing (judge).

Once the trial is over, another legal step becomes a possibility. The person who lost may believe that the trial court decision is incorrect and decide to appeal the decision to a higher court which has greater authority over certain aspects of the trial than the court that conducted the trial. The loser can ask the higher authority (appellate court) to correct any mistake that may have occurred during the trial. How is the appeals court going to go about deciding whether the witnesses told the truth? Will it call them into court again to cross-examine them? Only on rare occasions will this occur, because as a general rule, appellate courts only have authority over questions of law.

What is the proceeding called when a higher authority reviews the application of law by a trial court? It is called the *appeal,* and the court is called the *appeals* or *appellate* court. It must also be remembered that the decisions of an appellate court can sometimes be reviewed by a still higher authority. For example, most states and the federal system have intermediate level appeals courts from which further appeals may be taken to the state supreme court or the United States Supreme Court. Also, the decisions of the highest court of a state (usually the supreme court) may be appealed further to the United States Supreme Court.

There is a significant difference in the proceedings of an appellate court from a trial court because only one kind of issue is examined—

questions of law. In an appellate proceeding the lawyers make an attempt to try to convince the judge (the number of judges sitting in appellate proceedings varies from one appellate court to another, but there are usually more than one) that the law applied in the trial court was applied incorrectly, or in the alternative, that the incorrect law was applied by the judge. For example, in the student court case five different bases were given for ascertaining the correct law to be applied; the student judge chose one of the five. On an appeal, the losing party will likely claim that the judge chose the wrong alternative upon which he made his decision.

The procedure for arguing cases in an appellate court is different. The lawyers submit their arguments in writing; this written document is called the *legal brief*. Frequently the counsel for both sides are accorded the opportunity to appear in court and orally explain and defend their legal position in the case. The judges hearing the case very often ask questions which the attorneys for both sides answer. During the entire appellate process the often heated, flamboyant, and exciting atmosphere of the trial is missing and is replaced by a calm, serene setting in which points of law are argued in exacting detail.

STATE AND FEDERAL COURTS

Our society is primarily regulated by two legal systems—state and federal. Most of the laws regulating our conduct are state laws—that is, laws that are promulgated by state and local governments or state court decisions. Most of our social intercourse is involved with state laws: marriages, voting qualifications, school attendance, utility rates, and so on. Chances are that if a person is involved in a lawsuit because of a failure to pay a bill, an automobile accident, or a contractual dispute, the case will be tried in a state court and the result determined in accordance with state law. Federal law only becomes involved when the parties in disputes of this kind are citizens of different states. Even under this "diversity of citizenship" doctrine as specified in Article III of the United States Constitution, the federal court must apply the state law to the specific dispute even though it is believed to be wrong or even foolish. As a result the United States Supreme Court has no jurisdiction over most of the cases coming before courts in the United States.

The federal legal system is headed by the United States Supreme Court, which has original jurisdiction—the power to hear cases for the first time—and appellate jurisdiction—the power to review decisions of another court. Article III of the Constitution specifically states the Supreme Court's jurisdiction. Control over its jurisdiction is determined by Congress, however, which may restrict the Court's jurisdiction through legislation. In short, Congress has an extremely important check on the federal courts if it desires to exercise the grant of power that it has under the Constitution. Authorization to review on appeal some decisions of both state and federal courts has been given.

As a general rule, before the United States Supreme Court can review decisions in cases originated in state courts, the case must have been taken to the highest state court in which a decision under state law can be made on the matter. As a practical matter, this means the state supreme court. It must be remembered, however, that the state rule might permit a final appeal in the case to be decided by a lower state court. For example, a provision in the law of the state might be that a person convicted of a minor offense who is fined less than x dollars cannot appeal to any state court. A direct appeal to the United States Supreme Court will then be possible if there is an allegation that the defendant's constitutional rights have been violated.

May a state court hold a federal statute to be unconstitutional without any action by the federal courts? The Supreme Court must review the decision *if it is appealed* when a state court decides that a federal law or treaty is unconstitutional or upholds a state law against the challenge that it is in conflict with federal law. As can be surmised, there are large numbers of other cases involving federal questions outside of the kind just mentioned. In all other state cases involving a federal question, the person who lost may ask (petition) the Supreme Court to review the state court decision. If the Court then issues a writ of *certiorari*, it means that it has decided to hear the appeal and the issuance of the writ is an order compelling the state court to send all the records pertaining to the case to the United States Supreme Court.

How does the Court decide whether it desires to listen to an appeal from a state court? The Supreme Court justices meet to review cases sent to the Court which are judged to be worthy of consideration by the Court. If four of the justices believe that case is important enough to require their attention, a writ of certiorari is granted. Of the millions of cases tried in the United States each year and of the several hundred thousand which are appealed, only about 3,500 are taken to the Supreme Court, which then issues full written opinions on about 100 to 110 each year. So you can see that the choice of the cases to be heard is highly selective.

As noted above, many cases involving federal questions originate in state courts. Later in the book you will see the case of *Miranda* v. *Arizona* in which Miranda was convicted of violating certain criminal laws of

Arizona. It was Miranda's claim that during the time he was interrogated by the police he was denied some of his basic constitutional rights. The state courts in Arizona were asked by Miranda to reverse his conviction based on his claim, but the state courts, including the Arizona Supreme Court, refused to do so. He then appealed to the United States Supreme Court because he thought that the protections afforded him by the Bill of Rights had been violated. The California Supreme Court reached an opposite decision in a very similar case, *People* v. *Dorado,* 62 Cal. 2D 338, 398 P. 2D 361 (1965). We then have the highest courts in two states reaching opposite decisions interpreting the same section of the United States Constitution. Although many people in our country believe that the highest court in a state should interpret and apply the Federal Constitution, Congress gave the United States Supreme Court the power to review all state court decisions involving federal questions in the Judiciary Act of 1789.[1]

The Fourteenth Amendment has done much to increase the concept of Supreme Court review. Before the Thirteenth, Fourteenth, and Fifteenth Amendments were adopted after the Civil War, the Court interpreted the Bill of Rights as being applicable to the federal government. With the exception of the First Amendment, each of the Bill of Rights was written so that it could be applied to the states. However, in *Barron* v. *Mayor and City Council,* 32 U.S. (7 Peters) 243 (1822), Justice John Marshall ruled for a unanimous court that the Bill of Rights applied only to the federal government.

The Fourteenth Amendment states:

> *Nor shall any State deprive any person of life, liberty, or property, without due process of law. . . .*

As is immediately evident, the language is extremely broad, even vague, and is susceptible to various meanings by different people. Throughout its history, it has been given different interpretations. The issue of significant political and legal importance has been whether the clause means that all the provisions of the Bill of Rights apply to the states. The position taken by the United States Supreme Court of today is that the due process clause of the Fourteenth Amendment incorporates selected provisions of the Bill of Rights. This "selective incorporation" doctrine today has been interpreted so as to make most of the provisions of the Bill of Rights applicable in the states in the same way that they apply to the federal government.

---

[1] *Statutes at Large,* Chapter 20, Section 13.

FUNCTIONARIES IN THE CRIMINAL PROCESS

The attorney in a case has the primary responsibility of being an advocate for his side. By his advocacy he develops persuasive arguments regarding legal theories, defenses, and evidentiary interpretations which he hopes will convince the judge of the correctness of his side. In an appeal, the attorney presents his oral arguments to the court. His arguments are already in the hands of the judges in the form of his legal brief. The brief is an outline of the case and contains the major arguments that will be made on behalf of the client. The brief follows a format similar to the following: (1) the main facts in the case; (2) the main issues involved; (3) the relevant law pertaining to the issues; (4) the way the law applies to the facts in the case; and (5) what the decision of the court should be.

When the attorneys present their oral arguments, they are questioned, often incisively, by the appellate court justices. This questioning is possible because as we have noted, the justices have had the briefs for some time prior to coming to court.

The responsibility of the appellate court judge differs significantly from the trial court judge, as we noted earlier. The United States Supreme Court Justices are probably the most unique of all because of their isolated position at the apex of the court system. When deciding cases the appellate court judge must give reasons for his decision. This is called an *opinion*. In his opinion he states why he believes the decision of the lower court should stand or be changed. The format of the opinions varies, but it includes a statement of the facts, a brief history of the case, and a complete discussion of the legal doctrines that apply to the case in support of the judge's opinion regarding the case.

PRECEDENTS

Prior court decisions from which law comes are called *precedents*. The United States legal system is based on precedent because every court decision makes law for the future to some extent. In our legal system judges depend on written decisions on previous cases for reasons, hopefully, to give continuity in the law. For example, we can turn again to the student court example, in which it was noted that one of the sources to which the student judge might turn in reaching his decision was a possible prior decision in a similar case. In ascertaining whether the prior decision would be applicable to the current case to be decided, the factual similarities and distinction are evaluated. If the factual situations are identical or almost identical, the prior court decision is said to be authority and precedent and the case is probably decided the same as the prior one. The idea behind the concept of precedence is that of fairness—fairness because like cases should be decided alike.

In the United States precedents are binding until they are overruled. Consequently, precedent is an extremely important argument in support of a particular view. The question is raised often as to why precedents are overruled. To begin with, a precedent, to be binding, must be based upon an identical point—which means not only the factual situation but the reasons behind the decision itself. If a law or precedent is not clear in its application to a case, then the court must interpret or construe the law to apply to the case at hand.

Suppose the precedent is entirely applicable but the times and circumstances have changed so that the Court is of the opinion that the prior decision was made in a way that was unfair or that all of the facts were not considered. The court can decide to adopt another policy as the best solution for society in general as the conditions stand at the time of the decision. In this situation precedent may be overruled. As a general rule, courts have been quite reluctant to overrule precedent. However, in the area of constitutional rights the federal courts in particular have been less likely to follow precedent because of the rapidly changing standards and values in our society.

A serious problem often arises when precedent is overruled—is the new decision thus retroactive? How will the new decision affect those imprisoned under the old rules? Should they be freed or be kept in prison? Generally, the rule of thumb followed in determining retroactivity is whether the new decision came about because of the unfairness or uncertainty in the previous fact-finding process. If this is the situation the new decision is probably retroactive.

GENERAL TERMS

Throughout this book certain words and phrases will appear frequently. This short glossary will serve to orient the reader to their meaning as used by the author.

Accused—one who is charged with an offense.

Accusatorial system—a system in which the alleged criminal is publicly accused of a crime and tried in public by a judge who is not the prosecutor. In this system, the alleged criminal has the opportunity to defend himself or obtain help in doing so. This system follows the idea that a man is innocent until proven guilty beyond a reasonable doubt.

Accusatory stage—the point in the criminal process at which the investigation focuses on a person whom the police are questioning as part of their investigative process.

Affirm—to agree.

Appellate jurisdiction—the power of a court to review the decision of another court.

Arrest warrant—an order of a court setting forth the name of the person to be arrested and the crime which he allegedly committed.

Bail—an obligation undertaken by a defendant (usually involving the deposit of an amount of money) in order to be released from jail between the time of the arraignment or preliminary hearing and the trial. The purpose is to guarantee that the defendant will appear at the trial.

Booking—recording the name of the person arrested and the charges against him in a police register.

Capital offense—a crime that may be punishable by death.

Certiorari—a writ issued out of a superior court (the United States Supreme Court) which compels the records of an inferior court to be delivered to the higher court. This discretionary writ is issued when the superior court decides to hear an appeal.

Charge—an explanation given to a jury by a judge of the laws involved in the case.

Citation—the set of numbers following a case which indicates where the written text of the case may be found; i.e., 391 U.S. 673 (1968).

Civil case—a case between private parties in which one party accuses the other of violating his rights or of negligence or of breaching a contract.

Coercion—the use of force.

Counsel—an attorney or lawyer.

Criminal case—a case involving the violation of a law that is punishable by fine and/or imprisonment or both.

Custodial interrogation—the situation in which a person has been taken into custody or deprived of his freedom of action by the police and a process of questioning has been commenced.

Defendant—the person accused of a crime.

Detain—to stop a person for a period of time.

Diversity of citizenship—a concept whereby federal courts have jurisdiction under Article III of the United States Constitution when citizens of different states are involved in a law suit.

Due process—fair.

Exclusionary rule—a legal principle which excludes evidence because it was obtained illegally. It is normally associated with confessions.

Incommunicado—to hold a person by the police without contact with anyone.

Incriminate—to implicate or to accuse.

Indigent—a person without funds.

Inquisitorial system—a system of criminal procedure in which the judge acts as the prosecutor. The criminal process in this kind of system is characterized by the idea that the person is guilty and must answer questions.

Jurisdiction—the power or authority of a court.

Opinion—the written reasons for a judge's decision.

Original jurisdiction—the authority or power of a court to hear a case for the first time. Trial courts are an example in that they hear and decide cases in the first instance.

Petition—to ask an appellate court to review a decision of a lower court.

Petitioner—the person who asks the higher court to review a lower-court decision.

Plaintiff—the person who brings the case to court. In most criminal cases tried for the first time it will be the "People," the "State of _____," or the "Commonwealth of _____" because the citizens of the state accuse the person of some law violation.

Precedent—an earlier decision that deals with the issues similar to those in the case at hand.

Preliminary hearing—the stage before the trial when the accused is brought before a judicial officer, usually a judge, magistrate, or commissioner, evidence is presented that indicates the accused may be guilty of a crime, and the judicial officer decides whether or not there is sufficient evidence to have the accused stand trial. The preliminary hearing takes place before an indictment is sought from the grand jury or any information is filed by the prosecutor.

Prosecutor—the individual who represents the state in a trial. He is usually called the district attorney. Deputy district attorneys usually try the cases.

Respondent—the person who is called upon to answer the contentions of the petitioner in an appellate proceeding.

Search warrant—a court order specifically directing that listed items may be searched for and seized by police officers.

Verdict—decision in a case.

Waive—to relinquish a right.

Writ of habeas corpus—the order of a court which demands the release of an individual because he is not being legally held. For example, the accused may not have been informed of the charges against him within a specific time or he was not afforded the opportunity to have counsel.

QUESTIONS

1. What is the difference between a question of law and a question of fact? Why is this difference important when deciding constitutional questions?

2. What are the differences between a trial and an appeal? Whose job do you think is more difficult—that of the trial judge or the appellate judge?

3. In your opinion, does the trial attorney or the appellate attorney have the more difficult job? Why?

4. In a criminal case citation, how would the title of the case be cited?

5. What is the difference between a criminal and civil case? Who is always the plaintiff in a criminal case?

6. Why do you think the framers of the United States Constitution provided for federal courts to have jurisdiction over "diversity of citizenship" cases? Are there any disadvantages to an Alabamian being tried in a New York court if he is involved in a lawsuit in New York?

7. Why do you think that the first Congress gave the power of reviewing all state court decisions involving federal questions to the United States Supreme Court? Why do you think the Supreme Court was given the power to decide to which cases it wished to grant certiorari?

8. What is meant by "selective incorporation"? What kinds of problems might be created by this doctrine?

9. Do you think the advantages to the individual and to society should outweigh the disadvantages of an arrest "on suspicion" or "for investigation"?

10. What is the preliminary hearing? At what point in the criminal process is it found in states that follow the grand jury indictment procedure? the information procedure?

Chapter 2

Search and Seizure:
Fourth Amendment

Constitution of the United States, Fourth Amendment

The right of the people to be secure in their persons, houses, papers, and effects, against unreasonable searches and seizures shall not be violated, and no warrants shall issue, but upon probable cause, supported by oath or affirmation, and particularly describing the place to be searched and the persons or things to be seized.

GENERAL PROCEDURES

Weeks v. United States
232 U.S. 383, 34 S.Ct. 341, 58 L.Ed. 652 (1914)

SETTING: Weeks was arrested without a warrant and convicted of illegally using the mails to transport lottery coupons. While officers were arresting Weeks, other police officers had gone to his house, where a neighbor told them where a key was located. They found it; entered the house, searched it, and seized various papers which were turned over to the United States Marshal. Later the same day the police officers returned with the marshal, who thought additional evidence might be found. They were admitted by someone in the house, probably a boarder. The marshal

16

then searched the room and carried away some letters and envelopes found in a drawer. Neither the marshal nor the police officers had a search warrant.

PROCEDURAL PROBLEM: The seized papers, books, and other evidence were introduced into evidence at Weeks' subsequent federal trial over his objection that the papers had been obtained without a search warrant in violation of the Fourth Amendment of the United States Constitution.

THE ISSUE: In a federal prosecution, does the Fourth Amendment bar the use of evidence secured through an illegal search and seizure?

THE ANSWER: Yes.

DISCUSSION: According to the majority view, the effect of the Fourth Amendment is to put the United States courts and federal officials in the exercise of their power and authority under limitations and restraints as to the exercise of such power and authority and to secure forever the people, their persons, houses, papers, and effects against all unreasonable searches and seizures under the guise of law. According to Justice Day for the majority, "This protection reaches all alike, whether accused of a crime or not, and the duty of giving to it force and effect is obligatory upon all entrusted under our Federal system with the enforcement of the laws. The tendency of those who execute the criminal laws of the country to obtain conviction by means of unlawful seizures and enforced confessions, the latter often obtained after subjecting accused persons to unwarranted practices destructive of rights secured by the Federal Constitution, should find no sanction in the judgments of the courts, which are charged at all times with the support of the Constitution, and to which people of all conditions have a right to appeal for the maintenance of such fundamental rights."

The Court, in holding that the exclusionary rule applies in federal prosecutions, did not base its decision on the explicit requirements of the Fourth Amendment nor on any legislation expressing congressional policy in the enforcement of the Constitution. The decision was a matter of judicial implication.

> *The right of the court to deal with papers and documents in the possession of the district attorney and other officers of the court, and subject to its authority, [is] recognized. . . . That papers wrongfully seized should be turned over to the accused has been frequently recognized in the early as well as later decisions of the courts.*
>
> *We therefore reach the conclusion that the letters in question were*

taken from the house of the accused by an official of the United States, acting under color of his office, in direct violation of the constitutional rights of the defendant; that having made a reasonable application for their return, which was heard and passed upon by the court, there was involved in the order refusing the application a denial of the constitutional rights of the accused, and that the court should have restored these letters to the accused. In holding them and permitting their use upon the trial, we think prejudicial error was committed. As to the papers and property seized by the policemen, it does not appear that they acted under any claim of Federal authority such as would make the amendment applicable to such authorized seizures. The record shows that what they did by way of arrest and search and seizure was done before the finding of the indictment in the Federal court; under what supposed right of authority does not appear. What remedies the defendant may have against them we need not inquire, as the 4th Amendment is not directed to individual misconduct of such officials. Its limitations reach the Federal government and its agencies.

It results that the judgment of the court below must be reversed, and the case remanded for further proceedings in accordance with this opinion.

Reversed.

QUESTIONS

1. What is the ruling of the *Weeks* case?
2. Was the ruling based on the explicit requirements of the Constitution? legislation? judicial implication? Explain and discuss.
3. Does the *Weeks* holding prevent the use in federal courts of evidence illegally obtained by state officers?

Wolf v. *Colorado*
338 U.S. 25, 69 S.Ct. 1359, 93 L.Ed. 1782 (1949)

SETTING: The defendant was convicted in Colorado based on evidence that was obtained under circumstances that would have rendered it inadmissible in a federal prosecution because of a violation of the Fourth Amendment.

PROCEDURAL PROBLEM: As previously noted in *Weeks* v. *United States*, 232 U.S. 383 (1914), evidence that is secured as a result of an illegal search and seizure under the Fourth Amendment cannot be introduced into evidence in a federal trial for a violation of federal law. The evidence seized by Colorado authorities would not have been inadmissible in a federal court because of the *Weeks* decision. The argument of the defendant on appeal was that *Weeks* should be overruled and that under the due process clause of the Fourteenth Amendment, such illegally seized evidence should not be admissible in a state prosecution. The United States Supreme Court affirmed the defendant's conviction.

THE ISSUE: Does a conviction by a state court for a state offense deny the due process of law required by the Fourteenth Amendment, solely because evidence that was admitted at the trial was obtained under circumstances which would have rendered it inadmissible in a prosecution for violation of a federal law in a United States Court because there was an infraction of the Fourth Amendment as applied in *Weeks?*

THE ANSWER: No.

DISCUSSION: Justice Frankfurter for the majority wrote that unlike the specific requirements and restrictions placed by the Bill of Rights upon the administration of criminal justice by federal authority, the Fourteenth Amendment did not subject criminal justice in the states to specific limitations. "The notion that the 'due process of law' guaranteed by the Fourteenth Amendment is shorthand for the first eight amendments of the Constitution and thereby incorporates them has been rejected by this Court again and again, after impressive consideration."

The majority rejected the idea of total incorporation of the Bill of Rights. They were of the opinion that due process of the law conveys neither fixed nor narrow requirements. "To rely on a tidy formula for the easy determination of what is a fundamental right for the purposes of legal enforcement may satisfy a longing for certainty but ignores the movements of a free society. It belittles the concept of due process."

Frankfurter maintained that the security of one's privacy against arbitrary intrusion by the police, which is at the core of the Fourth Amendment, is basic to a free society. "It is therefore implicit in 'the concept of ordered liberty' and as such enforceable against the states through the Due Process Clause." Noting "recent history" amply explains the reasons for condemnation of the offensive use of police authority, which is inconsistent with the conception of human rights enshrined in the history and the basic constitutional documents of English-speaking peoples.

The majority was nevertheless reluctant to incorporate the Fourth Amendment safeguard against unreasonable searches and seizures. It noted that if a state were to "affirmatively sanction" offensive police invasions into a person's privacy it would be contrary to the protection of the Fourth Amendment. The Court based part of its reasoning on the fact that most of the English-speaking world does not regard as vital to such protection the exclusion of the evidence thus obtained. But checking the police conduct raises some questions as to how it is to be accomplished. How the conduct is to be stopped, the remedies to be afforded, the means by which the right is to be most effective are questions that the Court was not about to answer, especially because varying solutions may be available with the range of allowable judgment on issues within each state.

Thirty-one states rejected the *Weeks* doctrine and sixteen were in agreement with it at the time *Wolf* was decided. Not one of the ten jurisdictions within the United Kingdom and British Commonwealth of Nations which had passed on the question held that illegally seized evidence was inadmissible.

Holding that in a state prosecution for a state crime, the Fourteenth Amendment does not forbid the admission of evidence obtained by an unreasonable search and seizure, Justice Frankfurter emphasized the remedies that are available to a person who has had his right to security of privacy transgressed:

> *The jurisdictions which have rejected the* Weeks *doctrine have not left the right to privacy without other means of protection. Indeed, the exclusion of evidence is a remedy which directly serves only to protect those upon whose person or premises something incriminating has been found. We cannot, therefore, regard it as a departure from basic standards to remand such persons, together with those who emerge scatheless from a search, to the remedies of private action and such protection as the internal discipline of the police, under the eyes of an alert public opinion, may afford. Granting that in practice the exclusion of evidence may be an effective way of deterring unreasonable searches, it is not for this Court to condemn as falling below the minimal standards assured by the Due Process Clause a State's reliance upon other methods, which, if consistently enforced, would be equally effective. Weighty testimony against such an insistence on our own view is furnished by the opinion of Mr. Justice [then Judge] Cardozo in* People v. Defore, 242 N.Y. 13, 150 N.E. 585. *We cannot brush aside the experience of States which deem the incidence of such conduct by the police too slight to call for a deterrent remedy not by way of disciplinary measures but by overriding the relevant rules of evidence. There are, moreover, reasons for excluding evidence unreasonably obtained by the federal police which are less compelling in the case of police under State or local authority. The public opinion of a community can far more effectively be exerted against oppressive conduct on the part of police directly responsible to the community itself than can local opinion, sporadically aroused, be brought to bear upon remote authority pervasively exerted throughout the country.*

QUESTIONS

1. Distinguish the holding in *Weeks* from that in *Wolf*.
2. What reasons did Justice Frankfurter give for holding that the "due process of law" requirement in the Fourteenth Amendment did not include a total incorporation of the Bill of Rights?
3. If a state were to encourage lawlessness on the part of police officers in their seizure of evidence, would the decision in *Wolf* have been different? Discuss the majority's likely approach in this situation.

People v. *Cahan*
44 Cal. 2ᴰ 434, 282 P. 2ᴰ 905 (1955)

SETTING: Wooters, an officer attached to the intelligence unit of the Los Angeles Police Department testified that after securing the permission of the chief of police to make microphone installations at two places occupied by defendants, he, Sergeant Keller, and Officer Phillips one night at about 8:45 entered one house through the side window of the first floor, and that he directed the officers to place a listening device under a chest of drawers. Another officer made recordings and transcriptions of the conversations that came over wires from the listening device to receiving equipment installed in a nearby garage. About a month later, at Officer Wooters' direction, a similar device was surreptitiously installed in another house and receiving equipment was also set up in a nearby garage.

As a result of evidence so obtained, Cahan and numerous other persons were convicted of various gambling offenses. The California Supreme Court reversed the conviction.

PROCEDURAL PROBLEM: Most of the incriminating evidence introduced at the trial was obtained by the police officers in the manner discussed above. The evidence obtained from the microphones was not the only unconstitutionally obtained evidence introduced at the trial over the defendant's objections. There was a mass of evidence obtained by numerous forcible entries and seizures without search warrants.

The forcible entries and seizures were candidly admitted by the various officers. For example, Officer Fosnocht identified the evidence that he seized, and testified as to his means of entry: ". . . and how did you gain entrance to the particular place? I forced entry through the front door and Officer Farquarson through the rear door. You say you forced the front door? . . . Yes. And how? I kicked it open with my foot. . . ." Officer Schlocker testified that he entered the place where he seized evidence "through a window located I believe it was west of the front door . . . When you tried to force entry in other words, you tried to knock it [the door] down, is that right? We tried to knock it down, yes, sir. What with? A shoe, foot. Kick it? Tried to kick it in, yes. And then you moved over and broke the window to gain entrance, is that right? We did." Officer Scherrer testified that he gained entry into one of the places where he seized evidence by kicking the front door in. He also entered another place, accompanied by Officers Hilton and Horral, by breaking through a window. Officer Harris "just walked up and kicked the door in" to gain entry to the place assigned to him.

THE ISSUE: Is evidence seized in violation of the Fourth and Fourteenth Amendments, and also of applicable California constitutional and statutory provisions, excluded from being introduced into evidence in California courts?

THE ANSWER: Yes.

DISCUSSION: This was a state court decision which adopted for its own courts the exclusionary rule barring the use of evidence seized as a result of an unreasonable search and seizure. An essentially identical guarantee of personal privacy to that found in the Fourth Amendment of the United States Constitution is also set forth in the California Constitution. Thus both the United States and California Constitutions make it emphatically clear that, as important as efficient law enforcement may be, "it is more important that the right of privacy guaranteed by this constitutional provision be respected" (majority opinion of the California Supreme Court).

Justice Traynor for the majority noted that the constitutional provisions themselves do not expressly answer the question of whether evidence obtained in violation of the provisions is admissible in criminal cases. He noted that the federal courts and some states exclude such evidence. In reconsidering the California rule that the admissibility of evidence obtained by unconstitutional methods is not affected, the California Supreme Court concluded that it had "carefully weighed the various arguments that have been advanced for and against that rule. . . . Despite the persuasive force of the [arguments] we have concluded . . . that evidence obtained in violation of the constitutional guarantees is inadmissible. We have been compelled to reach that conclusion because other remedies have completely failed to secure compliance with the constitutional provisions on the part of police officers with the attendant result that the courts under the old rule have been constantly required to participate in, and in effect condone, the lawless activities of law enforcement officers."

What are some of the arguments that are used to support the rule of admission of evidence?

The rules of evidence are designed to enable courts to reach the truth and, in criminal cases, to secure a fair trial for those accused of crime. Evidence obtained by an illegal search and seizure is ordinarily just as true and reliable as evidence lawfully obtained. The court needs all reliable evidence material to the issue before it, and how such evidence is obtained is immaterial to that issue. It should not be excluded unless strong considerations of public policy demand it. There are no such considerations.

Exclusion of the evidence cannot be justified as affording protection or recompense to the defendant or punishment to the officers for the illegal search and seizure. It does not protect the defendant from the search and seizure, because that illegal act has already occurred. If he is innocent or if there is ample evidence to convict him without the illegally obtained evidence, exclusion of the evidence gives him no remedy at all. Thus the only defendants who benefit by the exclusionary rule are those criminals who could not be convicted without the illegally obtained evidence. Allowing such criminals to escape punishment is not appropriate recompense for the invasion of their constitutional rights; it does not punish the officers who violated the constitutional provisions; and it fails to protect society from known criminals who should not be left at large. For his crime the defendant should be punished. For his violation of the constitutional provisions the offending officer should be punished. As the exclusionary rule operates, however, the defendant's crime and the officer's flouting of constitutional guarantees both go unpunished. "The criminal is to go free because the constable has blundered," and "Society [is deprived] of its remedy against one lawbreaker because he has been pursued by another."

Opponents of the exclusionary rule also point out that it is inconsistent with the rule allowing private litigants to use illegally obtained evidence, and that as applied in the federal courts, it is capricious in its operation, either going too far or not far enough. So many exceptions to the exclusionary rule have been granted the judicial blessing as largely to destroy any value it might otherwise have had. Instead of adding to the security of legitimate individual rights, its principal contribution has been to add further technicalities to the law of criminal procedure. A district attorney who is willing to pay the price may easily circumvent its limitations. And the price to be paid is by no means high. Thus, the rule as applied in the federal courts has been held to protect only defendants whose own rights have been invaded by federal officers. If the illegal search and seizure have been conducted by a state officer or a private person not acting in cooperation with federal officers, or if the property seized is not defendant's, the rule does not apply.

Finally it has been pointed out that there is no convincing evidence that the exclusionary rule actually tends to prevent unreasonable searches and seizures and that the disciplinary or educational effect of the court's releasing the defendant for police misbehavior is so indirect as to be no more than a mild deterrent at best.

In concluding, the California court was still mindful of the criticism directed against the federal rule of exclusion. However, it stated:

> We are not unmindful of the contention that the federal exclusionary rule has been arbitrary in its application and has introduced needless confusion into the law of criminal procedure. The validity of this contention need not be considered now. Even if it is assumed that it is meritorious, it does not follow that the exclusionary rule should be rejected. In developing a rule of evidence applicable in the state courts, this court is not bound by the decisions that have applied the federal rule, and if it appears that those decisions have developed needless refinements and distinctions, this court need not follow them. Similarly, if the federal cases indicate needless limitations on the right to conduct reasonable searches and seizures or to secure warrants, this court is free to reject them. Under these circumstances the adoption of the exclusionary rule need not introduce confusion into the law of criminal procedure. Instead it opens the door to the development of workable rules governing searches and seizures and the issuance of warrants that will protect both the rights guaranteed by the constitutional provisions and the interest of society in the suppression of crime.

QUESTIONS

1. If the federal rule of exclusion were overruled today, would your state still have an exclusionary rule similar to the one in California? What is the name of the case or statutory decision. Discuss its rationale.
2. What reasons are frequently given for supporting the rule admitting evidence even though it was unconstitutionally seized? Discuss the reasons. Do you agree or disagree with them?
3. What was the holding of *Cahan?* In subsequent cases note how the California experience tends to creep into the United States Supreme Court holdings.

Ker v. California
374 U.S. 23, 83 S.Ct. 1623, 10 L.Ed. 2ᴰ 726 (1963)

SETTING: Narcotics officers received information that a large-scale seller of marijuana who was out on bail might be engaged in further sales. The seller, Murphy, was recognized from mug shots. While Murphy was under surveillance, he met and talked to Ker, observed by the officers. They could not state that anything passed from one to the other. The officers then attempted to follow Ker but lost him in traffic. They checked the automobile for Ker's name and address and then called the information to Officer Berman, who knew Ker. Berman also had received reliable information from an informer that Ker was purchasing marijuana from Murphy and had also received a mug shot of Ker.

Armed with the knowledge of the meeting between Ker and Murphy and with Berman's information as to Ker's dealings with Murphy, four officers proceeded immediately to the address which they had obtained through Ker's license number. They found the automobile they had been following—which they had learned was Ker's—in the parking lot of the multiple-apartment building and also ascertained that there was someone in the Kers' apartment. They then went to the office of the building manager and obtained from him a passkey to the apartment. Officer Markman was stationed outside the window to intercept any evidence that might be ejected, and the other three officers entered the apartment. Officer Berman unlocked and opened the door, proceeding quietly, he testified, in order to prevent the destruction of evidence, and found defendant George Ker sitting in the living room. Just as he identified himself, stating, "We are Sheriff's Narcotics Officers, conducting a narcotics investigation," Diane Ker emerged from the kitchen. Berman testified that he repeated his identification to her and immediately walked to the kitchen. Without entering, he observed through the open doorway a small scale atop the kitchen sink, upon which lay a "bricklike—brick-shaped package containing the green leafy substance" which he recognized as marijuana. He beckoned the defendants into the kitchen where, following their denial of knowledge of the contents of the $2\frac{2}{10}$-pound package and failure to answer a question as to its ownership, he placed them under arrest for suspicion of violating the state narcotic law. Officer Markman testified that he entered the apartment approximately "a minute, minute and a half" after the other officers, at which time Officer Berman was placing the defendants under arrest. As to this sequence of events,

Ker testified that his arrest took place immedately upon the officers' entry
and before they saw the brick of marijuana in the kitchen.

Subsequent to the arrests and Ker's denial of possession of any other
narcotics, the officers, proceeding without search warrants, found a half-
ounce package of marijuana in the kitchen cupboard and another atop
the bedroom dresser. Ker was asked if he had any automobile other than
the one observed by the officers and Ker replied in the negative, while
Diane Ker remained silent. On the next day, having learned that an automobile was registered in the name of Diane Ker, Officer Warthen searched
this car without a warrant, finding marijuana and marijuana seeds in the
glove compartment and under the rear seat. The marijuana found on the
kitchen scale, that found in the kitchen cupboard and in the bedroom,
and that found in Diane Ker's automobile were all introduced into evidence against the defendants.

PROCEDURAL PROBLEM: The California District Court of Appeal, in
affirming the convictions, found that there was probable cause for the
arrests; that the entry into the apartment was for the purpose of arrest
and was not unlawful; and that the search being incident to the arrests
was likewise lawful and its fruits admissible in evidence against petitioners. These conclusions were essential to the affirmation, since the California Supreme Court in 1955 had held that evidence obtained by means
of unlawful searches and seizures was inadmissible in criminal trials.
People v. *Cahan,* 44 Cal. 2ᴰ 434 (1955). The United States Supreme Court
affirmed the conviction.

THE ISSUE: Where police officers have reasonable cause to believe
that a suspect had committed or was committing a felony (possession of
marijuana in California) and where they enter his premises without a
warrant and without permission for the purpose of arresting him, using
a key furnished by the apartment manager, was the officers' search of the
apartment after entering and seeing some narcotics in plain view valid as
incidental to a legal arrest?

THE ANSWER: Yes.

DISCUSSION: In this 5–4 decision the Court ruled that evidence
obtained in an unannounced entry by state police could be used in a state
court where admissibility is governed by constitutional law, even though
such evidence might not be allowed in a federal prosecution because it
would violate a federal statute. Justice Clark noted that *Mapp* v. *Ohio,*
367 U.S. 643 (1961) declared that the Fourth Amendment is enforceable

against states by the same sanction of exclusion as is used against the federal government by the application of the same constitutional standard prohibiting unreasonable searches and seizures. Clark noted, however, that the test is not one of "fundamental fairness." The lawful arrest by state officers for state offenses is determined by state law as long as it does not violate the United States Constitution.

In discussing the *Mapp* meaning, Clark said that "*Mapp*, however, established no assumption by this Court of supervisory authority over state courts; and, consequently, it applied no total obliteration of state laws relating to arrests and searches in favor of federal law. . . . Second, *Mapp* did not attempt the impossible task of laying down a 'fixed formula' for the application in specific cases of the constitutional prohibition against unlawful searches and seizures; it recognized that we would be 'met with recurring questions of the reasonableness of searches,' and that, 'at any rate, reasonableness is in the first instance for the [trial court] to determine.'"

Based upon these two principles the Court upheld the Ker conviction.

In a separate consideration the Court rejected the argument that the lawfulness of the arrest was vitiated by the method of entry because of the officers' failure to demand admittance and explain their purpose before breaking into the apartment. The California law permits police officers to break into a dwelling for the purpose of arrest after making a demand to be admitted and explaining their purpose. Admittedly the officers did not comply with this requirement. However, the Court accepted the proposition that the circumstances of the case came within a judicial exception which had been engrafted upon the statute by numerous California decisions. The basis for the judicial exception to prevent the destruction of the evidence according to the Court was explained as follows:

> It must be borne in mind that the primary purpose of the constitutional guarantees is to prevent unreasonable invasions of the security of the people in their persons, houses, papers, and effects, and when an officer has reasonable cause to enter a dwelling to make an arrest and as an incident to that arrest is authorized to make a reasonable search, his entry and his search are not unreasonable. Suspects have no constitutional right to destroy or dispose of evidence, and no basic constitutional guarantees are violated because an officer succeeds in getting to a place where he is entitled to be more quickly than he would, had he complied with section 844. Moreover, since the demand and explanation requirements of section 844 are a codification of the common law, they may reasonably be interpreted as limited by the common law rules that compliance is not required if the officer's peril would have been increased or the

arrest frustrated had he demanded entrance and stated his purpose. With-
out the benefit of hindsight and ordinarily on the spur of the moment, the
officer must decide these questions in the first instance. Citing People *v.*
Maddox, 46 Cal. 2ᴰ 306, 294 P. 2ᴰ 6 (1956).

Here there were no exigent circumstances and the officers' failure
to give the notice was justifiable. Ker was in the possession of narcotics
which could be quickly destroyed. His furtive conduct was the basis for
a belief that he was attempting to elude the officers. On these considerations, the officers' decision to disregard the statutory mandate of notice
before breaking into the apartment was reasonable.

Justice Harlan in a separate concurring opinion judged state searches
and seizures by "the more flexible concept of 'fundamental fairness,' or
'rights basic to a free society' embodied in the Due Process Clause of the
Fourteenth Amendment." He also was of the opinion that the Court
should not extend its power any further over state criminal cases.

The dissenters in this case agreed that the Fourth Amendment is
enforceable against the states by the same exclusionary standard as is
used against the federal government. Their point of disagreement, however, was that the federal standard of reasonableness required by the
Fourth Amendment was violated in this case. They concluded that "even
on the premise that there was probable cause by federal standards for
the arrest . . . the [arrest was] nevertheless illegal, because the unannounced intrusion of the arresting officers violated the Fourth Amendment."

QUESTIONS

1. Is the seizure of items found in plain view predicated on a search?
   What does this concept mean?
2. Compare the argument for the standards to be applied to searches and
   seizures with that of the majority. Which makes more sense to you?
3. What were the exigent circumstances in this case which justified the
   unannounced entry of the officers?

Aguilar v. *Texas*
378 U.S. 108, 84 S.Ct. 1509, 12 L.Ed. 2ᴰ 723 (1964)

SETTING: Two Houston police officers applied to a local justice of
the peace for a warrant to search for narcotics in defendant's home. In

support of their application, the officers submitted an affidavit which, in relevant part, recited that

> *Affiants have received reliable information from a credible person and do believe that heroin, marijuana, barbiturates and other narcotics and narcotic paraphernalia are being kept at the above described premises for the purpose of sale and use contrary to the provision of the law.*

The search warrant was issued.

In executing the warrant, the local police, along with federal officers, announced at defendant's door that they were police with a warrant. Upon hearing a commotion within the house, the officers forced their way into the house and seized defendant in the act of attempting to dispose of a packet of narcotics.

At this trial in the state court, defendant, through his attorney, objected to the introduction of evidence obtained as a result of the execution of the warrant. The objections were overruled and the evidence admitted. Aguilar was convicted of illegal possession of heroin and sentenced to serve twenty years in the state penitentiary. On appeal the Texas Court of Criminal Appeals affirmed the conviction.

The United States Supreme Court reversed.

PROCEDURAL PROBLEM: The affidavit in support of the search warrant was challenged because, according to the defendant, it was issued by a magistrate without probable cause. The magistrate who issued the warrant was not informed of some of the underlying circumstances upon which the informant based his conclusions and some of the underlying circumstances from which the officer concluded that the informant, whose identity need not be disclosed, was credible or that his information was reliable.

THE ISSUE: Does the same standard for obtaining a search warrant for the federal government apply to the states?

THE ANSWER: Yes.

DISCUSSION: The United States Supreme Court decided on the issue in this case. Justice Goldberg for the majority said that the standard for obtaining a search warrant is the same under the Fourth and Fourteenth Amendments.

Goldberg emphasized that the vice of the affidavit in this case was the mere conclusion that the defendant possessed narcotics and was not that of the affiant himself. It was that of an unidentified informant. The affidavit contained no affirmative allegation that the affiant spoke with personal knowledge of the matters contained therein. It did not even contain an affirmative allegation that the affiant's informant spoke with personal knowledge. "For all that it appears, the source here merely suspected, believed, or concluded that there were narcotics in defendant's possession. The magistrate here certainly could not 'judge for himself the persuasiveness of the facts relied on . . . to show probable cause.' He necessarily accepted 'without question' the informant's 'suspicion,' 'belief,' or 'mere conclusion.'"

To approve this affidavit would open the door to easy circumvention. A police officer who arrived at the "suspicion," "belief," or "mere conclusion" that narcotics were in someone's possession could not obtain a warrant. But he could convey this conclusion to another police officer, who could then secure the warrant by swearing that he had "received reliable information from a credible person" that the narcotics were in someone's possession.

Goldberg also noted that there is nothing improper about basing an affidavit on hearsay. However, the magistrate must be informed of "some of the underlying circumstances from which the informant concluded that the narcotics were where he claimed they were, and some of the underlying circumstances from which the officer concluded that the informant, whose identity need not be disclosed, was 'credible' or his information 'reliable.' Otherwise the inferences from the facts which lead to the complaints will be drawn not 'by a neutral and detached magistrate,' as the Constitution requires, but instead, by a police officer 'engaged in the often competitive enterprise of ferreting out crime.'"

The majority thus concluded that the search warrant should not have been issued because the affidavit did not provide a sufficient basis for finding probable cause and that the evidence obtained as a result of issuance of the search warrant was inadmissible in the trial against the defendant.

QUESTIONS

1. Correct the affidavit in support of the search warrant in this case so that it meets the standards as required by the majority.
2. What is the holding in this case? Now write a minority opinion.
3. What is the purpose of the affidavit in support of a search warrant? What does the Court mean when it states that hearsay can be used as a basis for the affidavit in support of a search warrant?

Stoner v. California
376 U.S. 483, 84 S.Ct. 889, 11 L.Ed. 2ᴰ 856 (1964)

SETTING: A food store was robbed by two men, one of whom was wearing horn-rimmed glasses, a grey jacket, and carrying a gun. Soon after the robbery a checkbook belonging to Stoner was found in a lot next to the grocery and turned over to the police. Check stubs in the book indicated checks had been written to the order of the Mayfair Hotel in Pomona, California. The police checked Stoner's record and found a photograph and previous criminal history. Two witnesses identified Stoner from the photograph. On the basis of this information the day after the robbery officers went to the Mayfair Hotel. They had neither search nor arrest warrants.

The officers checked the records and found that Stoner was living in the hotel.

PROCEDURAL PROBLEM: The officers asked the hotel clerk if Stoner was in his room and received a negative reply. They then asked the clerk for permission to enter the room and gave as a reason they were going to make an arrest of a robbery suspect and they were concerned about the fact that he had a weapon. The clerk said that he would gladly give permission and then took the officers to the room. The officers entered and made a thorough search of the room and its contents. They found a grey jacket, horn-rimmed glasses, and a .45-caliber automatic pistol with a clip and several cartridges in a bureau drawer. Two days later Stoner was arrested in Las Vegas, waived extradiction, and returned to California where he subsequently stood trial and was convicted of the robbery. The articles seized in the search of his hotel room were all introduced into evidence against him at the trial over the objection of the defendant that the search was unreasonable and in violation of his rights under the Fourth and Fourteenth Amendments. The United States Supreme Court reversed the conviction.

THE ISSUE: Is a search of a defendant's hotel room without his consent and with neither a search nor arrest warrant a violation of his constitutional rights, although the permission of the hotel clerk was received?

THE ANSWER: Yes.

DISCUSSION: The search and seizure question in this case was disposed of in short order as the Court declared inadmissible the evidence obtained by police officers in the search of the hotel room without a warrant but with the hotel clerk's consent. Justice Stewart for the majority (only Justice Harlan dissented in part) noted in rejecting the arguments that the clerk had apparent authority to admit the officers to Stoner's room, and said, "Our decisions make clear that the rights protected by the Fourth Amendment are not to be eroded by strained applications of the law of agency or by unrealistic doctrines of 'apparent authority.'" Stewart then went on to emphasize that it was the defendant's constitutional rights that had to be protected not the clerk's nor the hotel's. "It was a right, therefore, which only the [defendant] could waive by word or deed, either directly or through an agent. It is true that the night clerk clearly and unambiguously consented to the search. But there is nothing in the record to indicate that the police had any basis whatsoever to believe that the night clerk had been authorized by the [defendant] to permit the police to search the [defendant's] room."

Justice Stewart was careful to draw a distinction between types of implied consent given when a person engages a hotel room. He noted that implied or express permission is given to such persons as "maid, janitors, or repairmen" to enter the room in the performance of their duties. But the conduct of the police and the night clerk is entirely different. In an analogy situation the Court had held that when an owner of a tenant's house authorized a search by police of the house occupied by the tenant in circumstance in which the owner had not only apparent authority but authority, the search nevertheless invaded the tenant's constitutional right. The Court said that to permit search for minor administrative purposes (the check for waste in this case) when the real purpose was to find other evidence "would leave tenants' homes secure only in the discretion of their landlords." *Chapman* v. *United States*, 365 U.S. 610 (1961).

In conclusion the majority held that "No less than a tenant of a house, or the occupant of a room in a boarding house, . . . a guest in a hotel room is entitled to constitutional protection against unreasonable searches and seizures. . . . That protection would disappear if it were left to depend upon the unfettered discretion of an employee of the hotel."

QUESTIONS

1. Can the joint user of a piece of property consent to a search and thereby make admissible against another evidence seized as a result of the search? See *Frazer* v. *Cupp*, 394 U.S. 731 (1969).

2. In light of the *Stoner* decision, what would constitute a valid consent by the hotel clerk in this case?

3. It has almost always been held that one spouse may give consent to search the residence if the police suspect the other. What reasons can you give for this consent? Examine them closely to see if they are persuasive.

United States v. Ventresca
380 U.S. 102, 85 S.Ct. 741, 13 L.Ed. 2ᴰ 684 (1965)

SETTING: Ventresca was convicted in a federal court of operating and possessing an illegal distillery. The United States Court of Appeals reversed on the ground that the affidavit in support of the search warrant did not establish probable cause. The United States Supreme Court reversed the Court of Appeals.

PROCEDURAL PROBLEM: The affidavit upon which the warrant was issued was made and submitted to a United States Commissioner on August 31, 1961, by Mazaka, an investigator for the Alcohol and Tobacco Tax Division of the Internal Revenue Service. It stated that he had reason to believe that an illegal distillery was in operation in Ventresca's house at 148½ Coburn Avenue in Worcester, Massachusetts. The grounds for this belief were set forth in detail in the affidavit, prefaced with the following statement:

> *Based upon observations made by me, and based upon information received officially from other Investigators attached to the Alcohol and Tobacco Tax Division assigned to this investigation, and reports orally made to me describing the results of their observations and investigation, this request for the issuance of a search warrant is made.*

The affidavit then described seven different occasions between July 28 and August 30, 1961, when a Pontiac car was driven into the yard to the rear of Ventresca's house. On four occasions the car carried loads of sugar in 60-pound bags; it made two trips loaded with empty tin cans; and once it was merely observed as being heavily laden. Garry, the car's owner, and Incardone, a passenger, were seen on several occasions loading the car at Ventresca's house and later unloading apparently full 5-gallon cans at Garry's house late in the evening. On August 28, after a delivery of empty tin cans to Ventresca's house, Garry and Incardone were observed carrying from the house cans which appeared to be filled and placing them in the trunk of Garry's car. The affidavit went on to state that at about 4 A.M. on August 18, and at about 4 A.M. on August 30, "investigators" smelled the odor of fermenting mash as they walked along the sidewalk in front of Ventresca's house. On August 18 they heard, "at or about the same time . . . certain metallic noises." On August 30, the day before the warrant was applied for, they heard (as they smelled the mash) "sounds similar to that of a motor or a pump coming from the direction of" Ventresca's house. The affidavit concluded: "The foregoing information is based upon personal knowledge and information which has been obtained from Investigators of the Alcohol and Tax Division, Internal Revenue Service, who had been assigned to this investigation."

The reason the Court held the warrant insufficient was because the affidavit did not specifically state that the information it contained was based upon the personal knowledge of Mazaka or other reliable investigators. The Court of Appeals reasoned that all the information recited in the affidavit might conceivably have been obtained by investigators other than Mazaka, and it could not be certain that the information of the other investigators was not in turn based upon hearsay received from unreliable informants rather than their own personal observations. For this reason the Court found that probable cause had not been established.

THE ISSUE: Where there is a good-faith effort on the part of police officers to secure a search warrant, should the affidavit in support of the warrant be read in an unduly technical and restrictive manner to determine the establishment of probable cause to issue the warrant?

THE ANSWER: No.

DISCUSSION: The majority, in a strongly worded opinion written by Justice Goldberg, held that the reading of an affidavit for a search warrant should not be done in an "unduly technical and restrictive manner" and that the examination of the affidavit as a whole must be considered. In this case a reading of the entire affidavit made it clear that all the observations referred to were made by "full-time investigators" and that the observations "of fellow officers of the Government engaged in a common investigation are plainly a reliable basis for a warrant applied for by one of their number." Justice Goldberg was not concerned by the use of hearsay evidence in obtaining a warrant nor by the unreasonableness of inferences drawn by the police from the facts available. In fostering the idea that police officers are always urged to secure a search warrant by submitting the facts to an independent evaluation by a magistrate, Goldberg quoted Justice Jackson in *Johnson* v. *United States,* 333 U.S. 10 (1948).

> *The point of the Fourth Amendment, which often is not grasped by zealous officers, is not that it denies law enforcement the support of the usual inferences which reasonable men draw from evidence. Its protection consists in requiring that those inferences be drawn by a neutral and detached magistrate instead of being judged by the officer engaged in the often competitive enterprise of ferreting out crime. Any assumption that evidence sufficient to support a magistrate's disinterested determination to issue a search warrant will justify the officers in making a search without a warrant would reduce the Amendment to a nullity and leave the people's homes secure only in the discretion of police officers.*

The *Ventresca* opinion is important, but not so much for the specific holding that the facts in the affidavit for the search warrant constituted probable cause, nor for the fact that it serves as a reminder to law enforcement officers to be more specific in drafting affidavits to avoid problems of interpretation of what ordinarily should be routine phraseology. The important point is Justice Goldberg's emphasis upon the fact that in this case the officers applied for and obtained a search warrant instead of searching without one, and the Court's obvious concern that officers who act in this manner should be encouraged by "commonsense" opinions construing the validity of such warrants. The following language in the opinion, it is fair to assume, was directed not only to lower federal and state courts but also to prosecutors and police officers:

> *[T]his Court strongly supporting the preference to be accorded searches under a warrant, [indicate] that in a doubtful or marginal case a search under a warrant may be sustainable where without one it would fall. . . . These decisions reflect the recognition that the Fourth Amendment's commands, like all constitutional requirements, are practical and not abstract. If the teachings of the Court's cases are to be followed and the constitutional policy served, affidavits for search warrants such as the one involved here, must be tested and interpreted by magistrates and courts in a commonsense and realistic fashion. They are normally drafted by non-lawyers in the midst and haste of a criminal investigation. Technical requirements of elaborate specificity once exacted under common law pleadings have no proper place in this area. A grudging or a negative attitude by reviewing courts toward warrants will tend to discourage police officers from submitting their evidence to a judicial officer before acting (emphasis added). . . .*
>
> *This Court is equally concerned to uphold the actions of law enforcement officers consistently following the proper constitutional course. This is no less important to the administration of justice than the invalidation of convictions because of disregard of individual rights or official overreaching. In our view the officers in this case did what the Constitution requires. . . . It is vital that having done so their actions should be sustained under a system of justice responsible both to the needs of individual liberty and the rights of the community.*

QUESTIONS

1. What responsibility that may be surmised from this case does the police officer have in preparing the affidavit in support of the search warrant?

2. What is meant by the statement, "This is not to say that probable cause can be made out by affidavits which are purely conclusory." Discuss the ramifications of following this rule when preparing affidavits in support of the search warrant.

3. Do Justice Goldberg's comments weaken or strengthen the position of a police officer when he seeks a warrant? What part does the prosecutor play in this decision?

Warden v. *Hayden*
387 U.S. 294, 87 S.Ct. 1642, 18 L.Ed. 2ᴰ 782 (1967)

SETTING: About 8:00 A.M. on March 17, 1962, an armed robber entered a cab company in Baltimore and took $363 and ran away. Two cab drivers in the vicinity attracted by shouts followed the man to 2111 Cocoa Lane. The cab company relayed information to the police that a Negro male about 5 feet 8 inches tall wearing a light cap and dark jacket had entered the Cocoa Lane address. Within a few minutes several patrol cars arrived at the address. An officer knocked and announced the presence of the officers. Mrs. Hayden was told that they believed a robber had entered her home and asked permission to search the house. Mrs. Hayden offered no objection.

PROCEDURAL PROBLEM: The officers found defendant Hayden in an upstairs bedroom feigning sleep. He was arrested. Meanwhile one of the officers was attracted to an adjoining bathroom by the sound of running water. He discovered a shotgun and a pistol in the flush tank. Another officer who was "searching the cellar for a man or the money" found in a washing machine a jacket and trousers of the type the robber was wearing. A clip of ammunition for the pistol and a cap were found under the mattress of Hayden's bed. Ammunition for the shotgun was found in a bureau drawer in Hayden's room.

At the defendant's trial all the items were introduced into evidence without the defendant's objection. He was convicted in the Maryland court. The conviction was affirmed by state appellate courts. He was denied federal habeas corpus relief by the federal district court for Maryland. The Court of Appeals, Fourth Circuit reversed and the United States Supreme Court reversed the Court of Appeals' decision.

THE ISSUE: Is there under the Fourth Amendment a distinction between merely evidentiary materials on one hand, which may not be seized either under the authority of a search warrant or during the course of a search incident to an arrest, and, on the other hand, those objects that may validly be seized including the instrumentalities and means by which the crime is committed, the fruits of the crime such as stolen property, weapons by which escape of the person arrested might be effected, and property the possession of which is a crime?

THE ANSWER: No.

DISCUSSION: The law governing the issue involved in this case was established by *Gouled* v. *United States*, 255 U.S. 298 (1921), in which the Supreme Court said that search warrants "may not be used as a means of gaining access to a man's house or office and papers solely for the purpose of making a search to secure evidence to be used against him in a criminal or penal proceeding." Justice Brennan for the majority in *Hayden* reexamined the proposition and came to the conclusion that the development of the law of search and seizure since *Gouled* is replete with examples of the transformation of the substantive law brought about through the interaction of the felt need to protect privacy from unreasonable invasions and the flexibility in rule making made possible by the remedy of exclusion.

The Court said that the dual, related premises upon which *Gouled* rested—(1) the right to search for and seize property depended upon the assertion by the government of a valid claim of superior interest, and (2) that it was not enough that the purpose of the search and seizure was to obtain evidence to use in apprehending and convicting criminals—were no longer valid.

Justice Brennan also stated that the premise in *Gouled* that the government may not seize evidence simply for the purpose of proving crime has likewise been discredited. "The requirement that the government assert in addition some property interest in material it seizes has long been a fiction, obscuring the reality that the government has an interest in solving crime." As Brennan noted, "The survival of the *Gouled* distinction is attributable more to chance than considered judgment."

As a practical matter the *Gouled* rule according to the majority was

of little significance because the "mere evidence" limitation has spawned
so many exceptions that "it is questionable whether it affords meaningful protection." But if its rejection does enlarge the area of meaningful
searches, the intrusions are nevertheless made after fulfilling the probable
cause and particularity requirements of the Fourteenth Amendment and
after the intervention of "a neutral and detached magistrate." The Court
concluded that because the Fourth Amendment permits invasions of
privacy under these circumstances, and there is no viable reason to distinguish intrusions to secure mere evidence, *Gouled* should be discarded
as a precedent.

Justice Fortas and the Chief Justice concurred that the Fourth
Amendment should not be held to require the exclusion of the evidence
found in the *Hayden* case but could not join the majority opinion in
repudiating the mere evidence rule. They would have gone no further
than to hold that the identifying clothing worn in the commission of the
crime and seized during "hot pursuit" is within "the spirit and intendment
of the 'hot pursuit' exception to the search warrant requirement. That is
because the clothing is pertinent to identification of the person hotly
pursued as being, in fact, the person whose pursuit was justified by connection with the crime. I would frankly place the ruling on that basis.
I would not drive an enormous and dangerous hole in the Fourth Amendment to accommodate a specific and, I think, reasonable exception."

Justice Douglas in dissenting said that striking down the mere
evidence rule "needlessly destroys, root and branch, a basic part of
liberty's heritage." He thought that the constitutional philosophy was
clear, "the personal effects and possessions of the individual (all contraband and the like excepted) are sacrosanct from any prying eyes, from
the long arm of the law, from any rummaging by the police. Privacy
involves the choice of the individual to disclose or to reveal what he
believes, what he thinks, what he possesses. The Framers, who were as
knowledgeable as we, knew what police surveillance meant and how the
practice of rummaging through one's personal effects could destroy
freedom."

QUESTIONS

1. What was the "mere evidence" rule as established by *Gouled?*
2. What items may be seized during a search incident to a lawful arrest?
   Give an example of each.
3. Distinguish the holding and reasons given in the majority opinion from
   the reasoning given by Justice Fortas in his concurring opinion. In
   your opinion, which position makes the most sense?

Bumper v. North Carolina
391 U.S. 543, 88 S.Ct. 1788, 20 L.Ed. 2ᴰ 797 (1968)

SETTING: Bumper, a Negro, lived with his grandmother, Mrs. Leath, in a rural area of North Carolina. Two days after an alleged rape took place, four white law enforcement officers went to the grandmother's home. One of the officers stated, "I have a search warrant to search your house." Mrs. Leath responded "Go ahead," and opened the door. In the kitchen, the officers found a rifle that was later introduced in evidence at Bumper's trial after Bumper's motion to suppress had been denied.

PROCEDURAL PROBLEM: Bumper's conviction was affirmed by the state courts. The United States Supreme Court on appeal reversed the conviction.

At the hearing on Bumper's motion to suppress, the prosecutor informed the court that he did not rely upon an arrest warrant to justify the search, but upon the consent of Mrs. Leath. Mrs. Leath testified at the hearing and stated:

> *Four of them came. I was busy about my work, and they walked into the house and one of them walked up and said, "I have a search warrant to search your house," and I walked out and told them to come on in.*
>   . . . *He just come on in and said he had a warrant to search the house, and he didn't read it to me or nothing. So, I just told him to come on in and go ahead and search, and I went on about my work. I wasn't concerned what he was about. I was just satisfied. He just told me he had a search warrant, but he didn't read it to me. He did tell me he had a search warrant.*
>   . . . *He said he was the law and had a search warrant to search the house, why I thought he could go ahead. I believed he had a search warrant. I took him at his word. . . . I just seen them out there in the yard. They got through the door when I opened it. At that time, I did not know my grandson had been charged with crime. Nobody told me anything. They didn't tell me anything, just picked it up like that. They didn't tell me nothing about my grandson.*

THE ISSUE: Can a search be justified as lawful on the basis of consent when that "consent" has been given only after the official conducting the search has asserted that he possesses a warrant?

THE ANSWER: No.

DISCUSSION: Justice Stewart, writing for the majority (two justices dissented), held that the search could not be sustained under the Fourth Amendment on the basis of consent granted only after the state official conducting the search said he had a warrant. Stewart made it clear that there can be no valid consent under such circumstances.

When a prosecutor seeks to rely upon consent to justify the lawfulness of the search he has the burden of proving the consent was freely and voluntarily given. This burden cannot be overcome by merely showing no more than acquiescence to a claim of lawful authority.

Stewart drew an analogy between a search conducted on the basis of an invalid warrant which cannot later be justified on the basis of consent and the Bumper facts. "The result can be no different when it turns out that the State does not even attempt to rely on the validity of the warrant, or fails to show that there was, in fact, any warrant at all." A law enforcement officer who claims authority to search a home under a warrant, in effect, announces that the occupant has no right to resist the search. "The situation is instinct with coercion—albeit colorably lawful coercion. Where there is coercion, there cannot be consent."

Justice Black in his dissent found that on the record the consent was freely given. Even assuming it was not, Black said that the introduction of the evidence constituted nothing more than harmless error. Justice White, the other dissenter, felt that the case should have been sent back for a determination of whether the officials did, in fact, possess a lawful warrant.

QUESTIONS

1. Is it a common practice to seek permission to search a home or office by the police? What reasons can you give for favoring "consent searches" by the police?
2. What factors can you cite that would help in determining whether consent was given freely and voluntarily?
3. What is the holding in *Bumper* as it pertains to securing consent by fraud or deceit on the part of law enforcement officials?

Schneckloth v. *Bustamonte*
412 U.S. 218, 93 S.Ct. 2041, 36 L.Ed. 2ᴰ 854 (1973)

SETTING: Officer Rand, while on routine patrol at about 2:40 A.M. stopped an automobile with one headlight and license plate light burned out. There were six men in the vehicle. Three men—Bustamonte, Alcala, and Gonzales, the driver—were in the front seat. Officer Rand asked for Gonzales' driver's license and he could not produce one. None of the other five persons could produce any identification. Only Alcala could produce a license, and that was his brother's. At Rand's request the occupants stepped from the car, and after two additional officers arrived, Officer Rand asked Alcala if he could search the car; Alcala replied in the affirmative.

PROCEDURAL PROBLEM: Prior to the search, no one was threatened with arrest. Officer Rand even testified that everything "was very congenial at this time." Gonzales testified that Alcala actually helped in the search by opening the trunk and glove compartment. During the search the police officers found three checks wadded up under the left rear seat. The checks had previously been stolen from a car wash.

The checks were subsequently admitted in evidence after denial of a motion to suppress at Bustamonte's trial for possessing a check with intent to defraud.

The defendant was convicted in the California court and the conviction was affirmed by the state appellate courts. The standard the state courts applied was that the question of fact to be determined in light of all the circumstances was whether in a particular case an apparent consent was in fact voluntarily given or was in submission to an express or implied assertion of authority.

In a habeas corpus proceeding, after denial of the writ by the federal district court, the Court of Appeals set aside the district court's order on the ground that a consent was a waiver of a person's Fourth and Fourteenth Amendment rights, and that the state was under an obligation to demonstrate not only that the consent had been uncoerced, but that it had been given with an understanding that it could be freely and effectively withheld. Consent, according to the Court of Appeals, could not be found solely from the absence of coercion and a verbal expression of consent. Because the district court had not determined that Alcala had known that his consent could be withheld and that he could have refused to have his vehicle searched, the Court of Appeals remanded the case.

The United States Supreme Court reversed the Court of Appeals and upheld the district court decision.

THE ISSUE: In determining whether or not a consent is voluntarily given, does the state have the initial burden of proving that the person knows that he has a right to refuse consent?

THE ANSWER: No.

DISCUSSION: Justice Stewart, writing for the majority, narrowly held that when the subject of a search is not in custody and the state attempts to justify a search on the basis of his consent, the Fourth and Fourteenth Amendments require that it demonstrate that the consent was in fact voluntarily given, and was not the result of duress or coercion, express or implied. Voluntariness is a question of fact to be determined from all the circumstances, and while the subject's knowledge of a right to refuse is a factor to be taken into account, the prosecution is not required to demonstrate such knowledge as a prerequisite to establishing a voluntary consent. In short, the Court rejected the Court of Appeals' position that it is an essential part of the state's case to prove that a person positively knows that he has a right to refuse to consent.

The concept of voluntariness was addressed in great detail by Justice Stewart. He noted that its definition is enigmatic and that it is not possible to apply a mechanical application to it, and it also involves a complex of values implicated in police questioning of a suspect. According to Stewart, the decisions of the Supreme Court reflect a recognition that the Constitution requires the sacrifice of neither security nor liberty. "The Due Process Clause does not mandate that the police forego all questioning nor that they be given carte blanche to extract what they can from a suspect."

Are there specific circumstances that determine voluntariness? Stewart concluded that in determining whether or not a defendant's will was overcome in a particular, it is the totality of circumstances that will be assessed. Some of these might be age of the accused, lack of advice as to constitutional rights, details of the interrogation, law intelligence, length of detention, use of punishment, and repeated and prolonged questioning. Of striking importance to the Court is that seldom if ever has a Court decision turned on the presence or absence of a single controlling criterion.

Stewart noted that if the Court of Appeals' holding that the state must affirmatively prove that the subject of the search knew he had a right to refuse consent were approved, there is a serious doubt that consent searches would continue to be conducted. The majority concluded that,

> [W]e cannot accept the position of the Court of Appeals in this case that proof of knowledge of the right to refuse consent is a necessary prerequisite demonstrating a "voluntary" consent. Rather, it is only by analyzing all the circumstances of an individual consent that it can be ascertained whether in fact it was voluntary or coerced. It is this careful

sifting of the unique facts and circumstances of each case that is evidenced in our decisions involving consent searches.

The Court also rejected the argument that a consent is a waiver of a person's Fourth and Fourteenth Amendment rights. The argument is that by allowing the police to conduct a search, a person "waives" whatever right he had to prevent the police from searching. Under the doctrine of *Johnson* v. *Zerbst*, 304, U.S. 458 (1938), to establish such a waiver the state must demonstrate that there has been a knowing relinquishment or abandonment of a known right or privilege. Stewart noted that the cases applying the *Zerbst* doctrine make clear that it would be next to impossible to apply to a consent search the standard of "an intentional relinquishment or abandonment of a known right or privilege." Further, Stewart stated that it would be unrealistic to expect in the informal, unstructured content of a consent search, a policeman, upon pain of tainting the evidence obtained "could make the detailed type of examination demanded by *Johnson*." In short, *Johnson* v. *Zerbst* does not justify or compel the "easy equation of a knowing waiver with a consent search. . . . We decline to follow what one judicial scholar has termed 'the domino method of constitutional adjudication . . . wherein every explanatory statement in a previous opinion is made the basis for extension to a wholly different situation.' "

The majority also rejected the argument that the failure to require the government to establish knowledge as a prerequisite to a valid consent will relegate the Fourth Amendment to the special province of "the sophisticated, the knowledgeable, and the privileged." As Stewart emphasized, "the traditional definition of voluntariness we accept today has always taken into account evidence of a minimal schooling, low intelligence, and the lack of any effective warnings to a person of his rights; and the voluntariness of any statement taken under those conditions has been carefully scrutinized to determine whether it was in fact voluntarily given."

Justice Marshall in dissent was of the opinion that a simple statement like Alcala's should not be sufficient to permit the police to search or act as a relinquishment of Alcala's right to exclude the police. In Marshall's view the Court had always scrutinized with great care claims that a person has relinquished a constitutional right. "I see no reason," he emphasized, "to give the claim that a person consented to a search any less rigorous scrutiny. Every case in this Court involving this kind of search has therefore spoken of consent as a waiver. . . . Perhaps one skilled in linguistics or epistomology can disregard those comments but I find them hard to ignore." Marshall could not understand why consent "cannot be taken literally to mean a 'knowing choice.' In fact, I have difficulty in comprehending how a decision made without knowledge of available alternatives can be treated as a choice at all."

QUESTIONS

1. How does Justice Marshall differ from the majority?
2. If the Court of Appeals' opinion had been upheld, what would have been the practical effect on the officer who seeks consent to a search?
3. Compare and distinguish the facts and holding in this case with *Bumper* v. *North Carolina, supra.* What test did the court apply to the consent given by Bumper's grandmother?

Harris v. *United States*
390 U.S. 234, 88 S.Ct. 992, 19 L.Ed. 2ᴰ 1067 (1968)

SETTING: Defendant's automobile has been seen leaving the site of a robbery. The car was traced and Harris was arrested as he was entering it near his home. After a cursory search of the car, the arresting officer took Harris to a police station.

PROCEDURAL PROBLEM: The police decided to impound the car as evidence, and a crane was called to tow it to the precinct. It reached the precinct about an hour and a quarter after Harris. At this moment, the windows of the car were open and the door unlocked. It had begun to rain.

A regulation of the Metropolitan Police Department requires the officer who takes an impounded vehicle in charge to search the vehicle thoroughly, to remove all valuables from it, and to attach to the vehicle a property tag listing certain information about the circumstances of the impounding. Pursuant to this regulation, and without a warrant, the arresting officer proceeded to the lot to which Harris' car had been towed, in order to search the vehicle, to place a property tag on it, to roll up the windows, and to lock the doors. The officer entered on the driver's side, searched the car, and tied a property tag on the steering wheel. Stepping out of the car, he rolled up an open window on one of the back doors. Proceeding to the front door on the passenger side, the officer opened the door in order to secure the window and door. He then saw the registration card, which lay face up on the metal stripping over which the door closes. The officer returned to the precinct, brought defendant to the car, and confronted him with the registration card. Harris disclaimed all knowledge of the card. The officer then seized the card and brought it into the precinct. Returning to the car, he searched the trunk, rolled up the windows, and locked the doors.

The defendant at his robbery trial sought to suppress the automobile registration card belonging to the robbery victim which the government sought to introduce into evidence. The trial court ruled that the card was admissible and the defendant was convicted. The United States Court of Appeals affirmed, holding that the card was legally seized. The United States Supreme Court on certiorari affirmed.

THE ISSUE: Was the registration card secured as a result of an illegal search?

THE ANSWER: No.

DISCUSSION: In a *per curiam* opinion the court invoked the "plain sight" rule which avoided the more difficult problem of deciding whether a police department regulation can authorize the warrantless search of a lawfully impounded vehicle. As the Court saw the case, the evidence was in plain view and was discovered by a policeman who was merely rolling up a window of an impounded vehicle to protect it from the weather. "The precise and detailed findings . . . were to the effect that the discovery of the card was not the result of a search of the car, but as a measure taken to protect the car while it was in police custody. Nothing in the Fourth Amendment requires the police to obtain a warrant in these narrow circumstances."

According to the Court, once the door had lawfully been opened, the registration card with the name of the robbery victim on it was plainly visible. The decision noted that "it has long been settled that objects falling in the plain view of an officer who has a right to be in the position to have that view are subject to seizure and may be introduced in evidence."

Justice Douglas in a concurrence assumed that *Preston* v. *United States*, 376 U.S. 364 (1964), survived the majority opinion. He noted that *Preston* was not mentioned even though in the present case the car was in lawful police custody and the police were responsible for protecting the vehicle, and while the officers were engaged in their duty to protect the car and not in search of it or conducting an inventory of the car, they came across the incriminating evidence. The *Preston* decision is found later in this section.

QUESTIONS

1. What is the inventory that is conducted on an automobile seized by the police?
2. Distinguish an inventory of an automobile from a search of the automobile.
3. What is the specific holding of this case? What is your opinion as to why the question of the inventory of an automobile presents a ticklish issue for the Court to decide?

Chimel v. California
395 U.S. 752, 89 S.Ct. 2034, 23 L.Ed. 2ᴰ 685 (1969)

SETTING: Three police officers went to Chimel's home with an arrest warrant authorizing his arrest for the burglary of a coin shop. One officer, after knocking on the door and being greeted by Chimel's wife, asked if they could "come inside" where they waited for about ten to fifteen minutes until Chimel returned home from work. As he entered the house, one of the officers handed him the warrant and asked if he could "look around." Chimel objected but was advised that on the basis of the lawful arrest, the officers would search nevertheless.

PROCEDURAL PROBLEM: The officers then conducted a search of the entire three-bedroom house including the garage, attic, and small workshop. The search was relatively cursory in some rooms—however, in the master bedroom and sewing room, the officers directed Chimel's wife, who accompanied them throughout the entire search, to open drawers and to physically move contents of the drawers from side to side so that they might view any items that would have come from the burglary. After completing the search, they seized numerous items—primarily coins, but also several medals, tokens, and a few other objects. The entire search took between forty-five minutes and an hour.

At a subsequent trial for burglary the items seized by the officers were admitted into evidence against Chimel over his objections that they were seized unconstitutionally. The California courts affirmed the conviction on the grounds that the search of the home was valid because it was incidental to a lawful arrest.

THE ISSUE: Was the search for and seizure of the coins beyond the permissible scope for a search of premises incident to a lawful arrest?

THE ANSWER: Yes.

DISCUSSION: The Court in this case swept aside some nineteen years of its own case law, disposing of the case on the narrow issue of the permissible *scope* of a search incident to a lawful arrest. The decision greatly narrowed the breadth of such searches and limited their purposes to specific circumstances.

Justice Stewart for the majority was of the opinion that *Chimel* was foreshadowed by numerous Fourth Amendment cases in the several years preceding this decision. He noted the numerous inconsistencies in the Court opinions on the permissible scope of searches incident to an arrest. The most liberal cases were *United States* v. *Rabinowitz*, 339 U.S. 56 (1950), and *Harris* v. *United States*, 331 U.S. 145 (1947). Specifically, Harris approved the search of an arrestee's entire four-room home including desk drawers. The holding in *Rabinowitz* was equally as broad. However, *Rabinowitz* was overruled by *Chimel* insofar as it stood for the propositions "that a warrantless search incident to a lawful arrest" may generally extend to the area that is considered to be in the possession or under the control of the persons arrested. According to Stewart, the search now must be limited to the area into which an arrestee might reach, obtain a weapon, or destroy evidence.

The majority noted that recent Court decisions emphasized that searches and seizures incident to an arrest are justified only by the need to seize weapons or prevent destruction of evidence. As a consequence the *Rabinowitz* rationale cannot withstand either historical or rational analysis.

Although it would have been possible to distinguish *Chimel* from *Harris* and *Rabinowitz* on their facts, the majority stated that such a distinction "would be highly artificial." Stewart then overruled *both* of them: "No consideration relevant to the Fourth Amendment suggests any point of rational limitation, once the search is allowed to go beyond the area from which the person arrested might obtain weapons or evidentiary items. The only reasoned distinction is one between a search of the person arrested and the area within his reach on the one hand, and more extensive searches on the other.

According to the Court, the rule for a search incident to an arrest which is to be followed is that:

> . . . *[I]t is reasonable for the arresting officer to search the person arrested in order to remove any weapons that [might be used] to resist*

> arrest or effect his escape. Otherwise, the officer's safety might well be endangered and the arrest itself frustrated. In addition, it is entirely reasonable for the arresting officer to search for and seize any evidence on the arrestee's person in order to prevent its concealment or destruction. And the area into which an arrestee might reach in order to grab a weapon or evidentiary items must, of course, be guided by a like rule. A gun on the table or in a drawer in front of one who is arrested can be as dangerous to the arresting officer as one concealed in the clothing of the person arrested. There is ample justification, therefore, for a search of the arrestee's person and the area "within his immediate control"—construing that phrase to mean the area from which he might gain possession of a weapon or destructible evidence.
>
> There is no comparable justification, however, for routinely searching rooms other than that in which an arrest occurs—or for that matter, for searching through all the desk drawers or other closed or concealed areas in the room itself. Such searches, in the absence of well-recognized exceptions may be made only under the authority of a search warrant.

What are the exceptions recognized by the above holding? First of all, hot pursuits are still outside the rule. *Warden* v. *Hayden*, 387 U.S. 294 (1968), *supra*. If during the course of the pursuit incriminating evidence is found such as a discarded weapon, part of the loot, discarded objects such as clothing, or discarded contraband, it is admissible against the defendant. Automobiles come under special rules and are covered in a separate discussion later in this chapter. See *Vehicles*.

Items in plain view are also another exception. Observations of things in plain view are not searches. If in effecting an arrest, evidence is seen in plain view, it may be seized ordinarily. For example, if a suspect opens a door and the officer sees a room full of silver and television sets, he may check several numbers or cross the area to check the silver. He may check outside window boxes if they contain plants resembling marijuana. However, the officer does not have a right to peer or peep through the house except for his initial safety.

A fourth exception involves situations that arise in which it will be impractical to obtain a warrant. Evidence secured in these exigent circumstances usually will be admissible. For example, an officer in a rural desolate area might have to drive fifty or sixty miles over ice-covered roads to secure a warrant to search a home from which a sniper has been shooting at passing cars, in order to seize some ammunition. The officer will sometimes find it immediately impractical to obtain a warrant and may have no other alternative but to act. However, the officer must show probable cause such as that the prolonged delay could either have created danger, resulted in escape, or permitted the destruction of evidence. In these circumstances, there is still no assurance that the evidence will be admitted.

Justice Harlan, in concurring with the result in the case, stressed the difficulties of the doctrine of incorporation. He was particularly concerned with the practical effects of the majority decision. He stated, "We simply do not know the extent to which cities and towns across the Nation are prepared to administer the greatly expanded warrant system which will be required by today's decision; nor can we say with assurance that in each and every local situation the warrant requirement plays an essential role in the protection of those fundamental liberties protected against infringement by the Fourteenth Amendment."

Justices White and Black dissented and strongly noted the "remarkable instability in this whole area," and that the majority opinion does nothing but add uncertainty. According to them, "The rule which has prevailed, but for very brief and doubtful periods of aberration, is that a search incident to a lawful arrest may extend to those areas under the control of the defendant and where items subject to constitutional seizure may be found. The justification for this rule must, under the language of the Fourth Amendment, be in the reasonableness of the rule." White, in support of this argument cited the exigent circumstances rule making reasonable searches beyond a defendant's immediate reach. Even beyond the exigent circumstances argument, White noted that "Congress has expressly authorized a wide range of officials to make arrests without any warrant in criminal cases."

Justice White agreed with the majority that an arrest alone permits no broader search than the decision states. But he went further and concluded that he "would hold that the fact of arrest supplies the exigent circumstances, since the police had lawfully gained entry to the premises to effect the arrest and since delaying the search to secure a warrant would have involved the risk of not receiving the fruits of the crime."

QUESTIONS

1. Discuss the holding of this case as it would apply to the arrest of a person in his private business office. Would the same rules apply?
2. What are considered to be the four general exceptions to the rule pronounced in this case? Give an example of each exception.
3. What was Justice Harlan emphasizing in his concurring opinion? Give some examples. Is his prognostication of the practical effects of the *Chimel* decision valid?

Spinelli v. *United States*
393 U.S. 410, 89 S.Ct. 584, 21 L.Ed. 2ᴰ 637 (1969)

SETTING: Spinelli was convicted of traveling from Illinois to Missouri to engage in gambling in violation of federal law. The defendant
challenged the issuance of the search warrant under which the FBI
search that uncovered the necessary evidence for his conviction was
authorized.

PROCEDURAL PROBLEM:

In essence, the affidavit . . . contained the following allegations:

*1. The FBI had kept track of Spinelli's movements on five days during the month of August 1965. On four of these occasions, Spinelli was
seen crossing one of two bridges leading from Illinois into St. Louis,
Missouri, between 11 A.M. and 12:15 P.M. On four of the five days,
Spinelli was also seen parking his car in a lot used by residents of an
apartment house at 1108 Indian Circle Drive in St. Louis, between 3:30
P.M. and 4:45 P.M. On one day, Spinelli was followed further and seen to
enter a particular apartment in the building.*

*2. An FBI check with the telephone company revealed that this
apartment contained two telephones listed under the name of Grace P.
Hagen, and carrying the numbers WYdown 4-0029 and WYdown 4-0136.*

*3. The application stated that "William Spinelli is known to this
affiant and to federal law enforcement agents and local law enforcement
agents as a bookmaker, an associate of bookmakers, a gambler, and an
associate of gamblers."*

*4. Finally, it was stated that the FBI "has been informed by a
confidential reliable informant that William Spinelli is operating a handbook and accepting wagers and disseminating wagering information by
means of the telephones which have been assigned the numbers WYdown
4-0029 and WYdown 4-0136."*

The United States Court of Appeals sustained defendant's conviction and the warrant as being issued based on probable cause. The government in its arguments supporting the warrant claimed that the FBI
affidavit in the current case was more ample than that in *Aguilar* v.
Texas, 378 U.S. 108 (1964), *supra*. Not only does this affidavit contain a
report from an anonymous informant, but it also contains a report of an
independent FBI investigation which, it was argued, tended to corrobo-

rate the informant's tip. The Supreme Court then set out to determine whether or not this affidavit could square with the two-pronged test in *Aguilar:* that there must be underlying circumstances to permit the magistrate to independently judge the validity of the conclusions of the informant, and that the affiants must support their claim that their informant was reliable.

THE ISSUE: Did the FBI affidavit establish probable cause to permit the magistrate to issue the search warrant under the two-pronged test in *Aguilar?*

THE ANSWER: No.

DISCUSSION: Justice Harlan sought to delineate the manner in which *Aguilar's* two tests were to be applied. Speaking for the majority, he found as insufficient the affidavit's mere allegation that a "confidential reliable informer" had supplied information that Spinelli was conducting gambling operations by means of the two telephones whose numbers the informant supplied. In seeking an answer to the issue at hand, Harlan first noted that an informer's report must be measured against *Aguilar's* standards if probative value can be assessed. If the report is found to be inadequate the other allegations which tend to support the information in the hearsay report must be considered. According to Harlan, "A magistrate cannot be said to have properly discharged his constitutional duty if he relies on an informer's tip which—even when partially corroborated —is not as reliable as one which passes *Aguilar's* requirements standing alone." The informer's tip then failed to furnish probable cause for the search warrant even though it was partially corroborated by the independent FBI investigation. In Harlan's opinion the agent's observation contributed no more to probable cause than the fact that Spinelli went into and out of the apartment where the telephone numbers supplied to the government by the informer were listed.

Those in the majority were further of the opinion that *Aguilar* requires a magistrate to ask himself, "Can it fairly be said that the tip, even when certain parts of it have been corroborated by independent sources, is as trustworthy a tip as would pass *Aguilar's* tests without independent corroboration?" In this case in disagreement with the Court of Appeals, the Court said there was nothing in the affidavit that would permit the suspicions engendered by the informant's report to ripen into a judgment that a crime was probably committed. The majority just did not find that the tip itself furnished adequate probable cause. Even though the affiant reported the informant to be "reliable," there was no reason in support of this conclusion by the affiant that the informer was reliable.

The Court was even more concerned about the affiant's failure to meet the second of the *Aguilar* tests: a sufficient statement of the underlying circumstances from which it could be concluded by the informer that Spinelli was operating a bookmaking operation. Harlan commented, "We are not told how the FBI's source received his information—it is not alleged that the informer personally observed Spinelli at work or that he had ever placed a bet with him. Moreover, if the informant came by the information indirectly, he did not explain why his sources were reliable." In the absence of a statement detailing the manner in which the information was gathered, it is especially important that the tip describe the accused's criminal activity in sufficient detail that the magistrate may know that he is relying on something more substantial than a casual rumor circulating in the underworld or an accusation based merely on an individual's general reputation.

Spinelli made reference to *Draper* v. *United States,* 358 U.S. 307, (1959) as furnishing a "suitable bench mark." In *Draper* the informant did not state the way he obtained the information, but he did describe in such detail that "a magistrate when confronted with such detail, could reasonably infer that the informant had gained his information in a reliable way." Harlan said that the report in Spinelli was so meager that it "could easily have been obtained from an offhand remark heard—at a neighborhood bar."

Justice Black, in a dissenting opinion (there were three), thought that the holding of the majority was revolutionary. In his estimation the Court improperly expanded *Aguilar* to "unbelievable proportions" by requiring more probable cause for a search warrant so that the only way to obtain a search warrant if *Spinelli* were followed would be "to prove beyond a reasonable doubt that a defendant is guilty."

In a concurring opinion by Justice White, the swing man in the four-man majority, he thought that the majority opinion should be interpreted very narrowly. He believed *Draper* should be confined to its factual setting. In his opinion, the main thrust of *Draper* related to the reliability of the informant—"because an informant is right about somethings, he is more probably right about other facts, usually the critical, unverified facts." Under the Court's approach in *Draper* a warrant would be justified in *Spinelli.* White also hit at the real difficulty with the holding in this case; "the tension between *Draper* and the *Nathanson-Aguilar* line of cases. . . . Pending full-scale reconsideration of [*Draper*] on the one hand, or of [*Aguilar*] on the other, I join the opinion of the Court and of the judgment of reversal, especially since a vote to affirm would produce an equally divided Court."

QUESTIONS

1. The holding in *United States* v. *Ventresca*, 380 U.S. 102 (1965), *supra*, might have application to this case. What is it? Discuss fully.
2. How much corroborating information is adequate to establish probable cause? This is an extremely difficult problem. Discuss.
3. Rewrite the affidavit by the FBI agent to bring it in line with the Court's holding in this case.

United States v. *Edwards*
414 U.S. ___, 94 S.Ct. 1234, 39 L.Ed. 2ᴰ 771 (1974)

SETTING: Shortly after 11 P.M. on May 31, 1970, Edwards was lawfully arrested on the streets of Lebanon, Ohio, and charged with attempting to break into that city's Post Office. He was taken to the local jail and placed in a cell. Contemporaneously or shortly thereafter, investigation at the scene revealed that the attempted entry had been made through a wooden window which apparently had been pried up with a pry bar, leaving paint chips on the windowsill and wire mesh screen.

PROCEDURAL PROBLEM: The next morning trousers and a T-shirt were purchased for Edwards to substitute for the clothing he had been wearing at the time of and since his arrest. His clothing was then taken from him and held as evidence. Examination of the clothing revealed paint chips matching the samples that had been taken from the window. This evidence and his clothing were received at trial over Edwards' objection that neither the clothing nor the results of its examination were admissible because the warrantless seizure of his clothing was invalid under the Fourth Amendment.

In reversing Edwards' conviction the Court of Appeals, Sixth Circuit held that although the arrest was lawful and probable cause existed to believe that paint chips would be discovered on the defendant's clothing, the warrantless seizure of the clothing carried out after the administrative process and the mechanics of the arrest came to a halt was nevertheless unlawful under the Fourth Amendment. The United States Supreme Court reversed.

THE ISSUE: Should the Fourth Amendment be extended to exclude from evidence the clothing taken from Edwards while he was in custody at the city jail approximately ten hours after his arrest?

THE ANSWER: No.

DISCUSSION: Justice White for the majority noted that there are certain exceptions to the rule that warrantless searches are not allowed. One of these permits warrantless searches incident to custodial arrests. A second permits searches at the time the accused arrives at the place of detention even though it could legally have been made at the spot of the arrest. In rejecting the holding of the Court of Appeals, White emphasized that

> [E]ven on these terms, it seems to us that the normal processes incident to arrest and custody had not been completed when Edwards was placed in his cell on the night of May 31. With or without probable cause, the authorities were entitled at that point in time not only to search Edwards' clothing but also to take it from him and keep it in official custody. There was testimony that this was the standard practice in this city. The police were also entitled to take from Edwards any evidence of the crime in his immediate possession, including his clothing. And the Court of Appeals acknowledged that contemporaneously with or shortly after the time Edwards went to his cell, the police had probable cause to believe that the articles of clothing he wore were themselves material evidence of the crime for which he had been arrested. But it was late at night; no substitute clothing was then available for Edwards to wear, and it would certainly have been unreasonable for the police to have stripped petitioner of his clothing and left him exposed in his cell throughout the night. When the substitutes were purchased the next morning, the clothing he had been wearing at the time of arrest was taken from him and subjected to laboratory analysis. This was no more than taking from petitioner the effects in his immediate possession that constituted evidence of crime. This was and is a normal incident of a custodial arrest, and reasonable delay in effectuating it does not change the fact that Edwards was no more imposed upon than he could have been at the time and place of the arrest or immediately upon arrival at the place of detention. The police did no more on June 1 than they were entitled to do incident to the usual custodial arrest and incarceration.

In summary Justice White reiterated that "In upholding this search and seizure, we do not conclude that the warrant clause of the Fourth Amendment is never applicable to postarrest seizures of the effects of the arrestee. But we do think that the Court of Appeals for the First Circuit captured the essence of situations like these when it said in *United States v. DeLeo*, 422 F. 2ᴰ at 493 . . . 'While the legal arrest of a person should not destroy the privacy of this premise, it does—for at least a reasonable time and to a reasonable extent—take his own privacy out of the realm of protection from police interest in weapons, means of escape and evidence.'"

Justices Stewart, Douglas, Brennan, and Marshall dissented, arguing that the majority completely ignored the Fourth Amendment's prohibition against warrantless searches except in exceptional circumstances. According to the dissenters, the ten-hour delay between the time of the arrest and normal administrative arrest processing had ended and the search therefore was not contemporaneous with the arrest. Accordingly, they saw "no justification for dispensing with the warrant requirement. The police had ample time to seek a warrant, and no exigent circumstances were present to excuse their failure to do so. Unless the exceptions to the warrant requirement are to be 'enthrowned into the rule', . . . this is precisely the sort of situation where the Fourth Amendment requires a magistrate's prior approval for a search."

QUESTIONS

1. Distinguish this case from *Chimel* v. *California* above.
2. What is the specific holding of the majority opinion?
3. In your estimation, does the dissenting opinion offer a strong basis for possibly overturning the majority opinion? Discuss the strong points of the dissenters thoroughly.

United States v. *Harris*
403 U.S. 573, 91 S.Ct. 2075, 29 L.Ed. 723 (1971)

SETTING: A federal tax investigator and a local constable entered Harris' premises pursuant to a search warrant issued by a federal magistrate and seized some jugs of whiskey on which the federal tax had not been paid. The warrant had been issued solely on the basis of the investigator's affidavit, which stated:

> *Roosevelt Harris has had a reputation with me for over 4 years as being a trafficker on nontaxpaid distilled spirits, and over this period I have received numerous information [sic] from all types of persons as to his activities. Constable Howard Johnson located a sizable stash of illicit whiskey in an abandoned house under Harris' control during this period of time. This date, I have received information from a person who fears for their [sic] life and property should their name be revealed. I have*

interviewed this person, found this person to be a prudent person, and have, under a sworn verbal statement, gained the following information: This person has personal knowledge of and has purchased illicit whiskey from within the residence described, for a period of more than 2 years, and most recently within the past 2 weeks, has knowledge of a person who purchased illicit whiskey within the past two days from the house, has personal knowledge that the illicit whiskey is consumed by purchasers in the outbuilding known as and utilized as the "dance hall," and has seen Roosevelt Harris go to the other outbuilding, located about 50 yards from the residence, on numerous occasions, to obtain the whiskey for this person and other persons.

PROCEDURAL PROBLEM: Harris was subsequently charged with the possession of nontaxed liquor. His motion to suppress the evidence in the trial court on the ground that the affidavit was insufficient to establish probable cause was overruled and he was convicted. The United States Court of Appeals reversed the conviction holding that the affidavit was insufficient to enable the magistrate to assess the informant's reliability and trustworthiness. The United States Supreme Court then reversed the Court of Appeals and reinstated the conviction.

THE ISSUE: Is an affidavit in support of a search warrant adequate to establish probable cause for a magistrate to issue a warrant where there is ample factual basis for believing the informant coupled with a knowledge of the respondent's background?

THE ANSWER: Yes.

DISCUSSION: In previous decisions the Court appeared to make it harder for law enforcement officials to justify searches without warrants. However, the Court in *Harris* eased the strict *Spinelli* v. *United States,* 393 U.S. 410 (1969), *supra*, requirements. In a five-man majority, the Court found the affidavit sufficient even though it was largely based on hearsay information from an informant who was described only as a "prudent person" who had recent "personal knowledge" of the whiskey sales by Harris. The informant also subjected himself to possible criminal prosecution by stating that he had made several purchases of moonshine from Harris. Chief Justice Burger, writing for the majority, stated that "while a bare statement by an affiant that he believed the informant to be truthful would not in itself, provide a factual basis for crediting the report of an unnamed informant, we conclude that the affidavit in the present case contains an ample factual basis for believing the informant which, when coupled with his own knowledge of the respondent's background, afforded a basis upon which a magistrate could reasonably issue a warrant. The accusation by the informant was plainly a declaration against interest since it could readily warrant a prosecution and could sustain a conviction against the informant himself."

The Chief Justice placed great emphasis on the informant's declaration against his penal interest by emphasizing that "people do not lightly admit a crime and place critical evidence in the hands of the police in the form of their own admissions. Admissions of crime, like admissions against property interests, carry their own indicia of credibilty—sufficient at least to support a finding of probable cause to search. That the informant must be paid or promised a 'break' does not eliminate the residual risk and opprobrium of having admitted criminal conduct."

The Court also held that the affiant's knowledge of Harris' reputation as a moonshiner was entitled to weight in determining probable cause. As Burger noted, "Trials are necessarily surrounded with evidentiary rules 'developed to safeguard men from dubious and unjust convictions.' But before the trial we deal only with probabilities that are not technical; they are the factual and practical considerations of everyday life on which reasonable and prudent men, not legal technicians, act." In *Spinelli* the idea that weight should be given to a gambler's reputation was rejected. The majority in *Harris* abandoned this position by stating that "To the extent that *Spinelli* prohibits the use of such probative information, it has no support in our prior cases, logic, or experience and we decline to apply it to preclude a magistrate from relying on a law enforcement officer's knowledge of a suspect's reputation."

Whether the informant's information was detailed and fresh enough to furnish probable cause was addressed by the Court. It strongly affirmed the holding in *Jones* v. *United States*, 362 U.S. 257 (1960) that an affidavit may be based entirely on hearsay.

Justice Harlan, writing for the four dissenters, was of the opinion that the knowledge attributed to the informant, if true, would have established probable cause and that it was likely that the agent truthfully related what the informant told to him. However, the dissenters were convinced that the affidavit gave insufficient information to believe that the informant, himself, was reliable. Harlan contended that the tip plus the affiant's assertion that the informant was "prudent" was nothing more than the assertion of credibility or reliability. As he emphasized, "It is not possible to argue that since certain information, if true, would be trustworthy, therefore, it must be true. This is why our cases require that there be a reasonable basis for crediting the accuracy of the observation related in the tip. In short, the requirement that the magistrate independently assess the probable credibility of the informant does not vanish where the source of the tip indicates that, if true, it is trustworthy."

Harlan conceded that there may be situations in which the informant relates highly detailed descriptions of criminal activities such that "perhaps a magistrate could conclude that where the confidant claimed to speak from personal knowledge it is somewhat less likely that the informant was falsifying his report because if the search yields no fruit, when called to account he would be unable to explain this away by impugning the veracity or reliability of his sources. However no such relationship is revealed in this case. . . . I do not believe, however, that in this instance the relatively meager allegations of this character are, standing alone, enough to satisfy the credibility requirement essential to the sufficiency of this probable-cause affidavit."

The dissenters also strongly disagreed with the majority view that reputation evidence of the kind present in this case could be considered by a magistrate.

QUESTIONS

1. In what respects does *Harris* relax the stringent probable-cause requirements to issue a search warrant on an informant's tip in *Spinelli?*
2. Is the hold in *Harris* more in line with the desires expressed by Justice Goldberg in *United States* v. *Ventresca*, 380 U.S. 102 (1965), *supra?* Why? Discuss and compare the case holdings.
3. Discuss the main areas of disagreement between the majority and minority in this case.

Vale v. *Louisiana*
399 U.S. 30, 90 S.Ct. 1969, 26 L.Ed. 2ᴰ 409 (1970)

SETTING: On April 24, 1967, police officers possessing two warrants for Vale's arrest and having information that he was residing at a specified address went to the address in an unmarked car and began to watch the house. What took place next is set forth by the Louisiana Supreme Court as follows:

> *After approximately 15 minutes the officers observed a green 1958 Chevrolet drive up and sound the horn and after backing into a parking place, again blew the horn. At this juncture Donald Vale, who was well known to Officer Brady having arrested him twice in the previous month, was seen coming out of the house and walk up to the passenger side of the Chevrolet where he had a close brief conversation with the driver; and after looking up and down the street returned inside of the house.*

Within a few minutes he reappeared on the porch, and again cautiously looked up and down the street before proceeding to the passenger side of the Chevrolet, leaning through the window. From this the officers were convinced a narcotics sale had taken place. They returned to their car and immediately drove toward Donald Vale, and as they reached within approximately three car lengths from the accused (Donald Vale) he looked up and, obviously recognizing the officers, turned around, walking quickly toward the house. At the same time the driver of the Chevrolet started to make his get-away when the car was blocked by the police vehicle. The three officers promptly alighted from the car, whereupon Officers Soule and Laumann called to Donald Vale to stop as he reached the front steps of the house, telling him he was under arrest. Officer Brady at the same time, seeing the driver of the Chevrolet, Arizzio Saucier, whom the officers knew to be a narcotic addict, place something hurriedly in his mouth, immediately placed him under arrest and joined his co-officers. Because of the transaction they had just observed they informed Donald Vale they were going to search the house, and thereupon advised him of his constitutional rights. After they all entered the front room, Officer Laumann made a cursory inspection of the house to ascertain if anyone else was present and within about three minutes Mrs. Vale and James Vale, mother and brother of Donald Vale, returned home carrying groceries and were informed of the arrest and impending search.

The search of a rear bedroom revealed a quantity of narcotics. At Vale's trial he sought unsuccessfully to suppress the evidence. The Louisiana Supreme Court held that the search of the house did not violate the Fourth Amendment because it occurred in the "immediate vicinity of the arrest" of Vale and was "substantially contemporaneous therewith." The United States Supreme Court reversed.

THE ISSUE: Should the warrantless search of a defendant's house incident to a warrantless narcotics arrest on the front steps of his home be permitted under the Fourth Amendment?

THE ANSWER: No.

DISCUSSION: Justice Stewart for the majority stated that there was "no precedent of this Court [to] sustain the constitutional validity of the search in the case before us." The majority noted that a search may be incident to an arrest "only if it is substantially contemporaneous with the arrest and is confined to the immediate vicinity of the arrest." If a search of a house is to be upheld, Stewart stated, "that arrest must take place *inside* the house . . . not somewhere outside—whether two blocks away, twenty feet away, or on the sidewalk near the front steps." A belief, no matter how well-founded, that an article sought is concealed in a dwelling house furnishes no justification for a search of a place without a warrant.

Stewart also rejected the State claim that the search was independently supported because it involved narcotics which could be easily removed, hidden, or destroyed. As he concluded, "our past decisions make clear that only in a 'few specifically established and well-delineated' situations may a warrantless search of a dwelling withstand constitutional scrutiny, even though the authorities have probable cause to conduct it. The burden rests on the State to show the existence of such an exceptional situation. And the record before us discloses none." The majority also noted that there was no suggestion that anyone consented to the search.

The Court, however, did not need to reach a major issue left unanswered by *Chimel* v. *California*, 395 U.S. 752 (1969), *supra*, regarding whether or not *Chimel* applied retroactively to hold pre-*Chimel* searches unlawful.

Justice Black and Chief Justice Burger saw nothing unreasonable about the search because the officers had interrupted a narcotics sale in progress. They had probable cause to believe there were narcotics in the house which could easily be destroyed and they did not know if someone else was in the house who could cause the destruction. For these reasons the dissenters thought that there were sufficient exigent circumstances to justify the warrantless search.

QUESTIONS

1. For what reasons do you think the majority was unpersuaded by the argument of the dissenters that the exigent circumstances could be used to justify the search?
2. What is meant by retrospective and prospective application of a court decision? What reasons can you give for the reluctance to reach the issue of retroactivity of *Chimel?*
3. Distinguish the factual situations in *Chimel* and *Vale*. What are the crucial differences?

VEHICLES

Carroll v. *United States*
267 U.S. 132, 45 S.Ct. 280, 69 L.Ed. 543 (1925)

SETTING: Federal agents during the time of prohibition stopped a vehicle stocked with illegal liquor on the usual illegal liquor transportation route between Grand Rapids and Detroit, Michigan.

The government agents, without grounds for an arrest, stopped and searched the defendants' car. They found sixty-eight bottles of illegal liquor behind the upholstery of the seats. After verifying that the contents were in fact whiskey and gin, the agents arrested Carroll and several others. The officers at the time of the stop and search were not anticipating that the defendants were coming along the highway at that particular time, but when they met the defendants whom they knew and believed were carrying liquor, they made the search, seizure, and arrest.

PROCEDURAL PROBLEM: In this case the officers had some cause to believe that the vehicle was being used to transport contraband and as a result of their suspicions stopped and searched the vehicle for the illegal items and then impounded the car and seized the liquor.

THE ISSUE: Is a warrantless search of a vehicle being operated on a highway upon probable cause that it contained contraband unreasonable under the Fourth Amendment?

THE ANSWER: No.

DISCUSSION: There is no general right to stop all travelers on a highway although law enforcement officials do have the power to stop a vehicle if they have probable cause to believe that the vehicle is being used to transport contraband. Chief Justice Taft said that the history of the Fourth Amendment emphasizes that it is only unreasonable searches and seizures that are condemned. He stated, "We have made a somewhat extended reference to these statutes to show that the guaranty of freedom from unreasonable searches and seizures by the Fourth Amendment has been construed, practically since the beginning of government, as recognizing a necessary difference between a search of a store, dwelling house or other structure in respect of which a proper official warrant readily may be obtained and a search of a ship, motor boat, wagon, or automobile for contraband goods, where it is not practical to secure a warrant, because the vehicle can be quickly moved out of the locality or jurisdiction in which the warrant must be sought."

The Chief Justice was specific in noting that not all vehicles on public highways may be stopped upon the whim of law enforcement officials.

> *Having thus established that contraband goods concealed and illegally transported in an automobile or other vehicle may be searched for without a warrant, we come now to consider under what circumstances such search may be made. It would be intolerable and unreasonable if a prohibition agent were authorized to stop every automobile on the chance of finding liquor, and thus subject all persons lawfully using*

the highways to the inconvenience and indignity of such a search. Travelers may be so stopped in crossing an international boundary because of national self-protection reasonably requiring one entering the country to identify himself as entitled to come in, and his belongings as effects which may be lawfully brought in. But those lawfully within the country, entitled to use the public highways, have a right to free passage without interruption or search unless there is known to a competent official, authorized to search, probable cause for believing that their vehicles are carrying contraband or illegal merchandise.

QUESTIONS

1. Given the holding in this case, what requirements must be met before a vehicle may be stopped on a highway and before it can be searched without a warrant for contraband?
2. What is meant by word "contraband"?
3. Based on the *Carroll* decision, do you believe that an officer's well-founded "belief" that an article is concealed in a dwelling house is justification to search the house without a warrant?

Preston v. *United States*
376 U.S. 364, 84 S.Ct. 881, 11 L.Ed. 2ᴰ 777 (1964)

SETTING: The police received a telephone complaint at 3 o'clock one morning that "three suspicious men acting suspiciously" had been seated in a car parked in a business district since 10 o'clock the evening before. Four policemen immediately went to the place where the car was parked and found Preston and two companions. The officers asked the three men why they were parked there, but the men gave answers which the officers testified were unsatisfactory and evasive. All three men admitted that they were unemployed; all of them together had only 25 cents. One of the men said that he had bought the car the day before (which later turned out to be true), but he could not produce any title. They said that their reason for being there was to meet a truck driver who would pass through Newport that night, but they could not identify the company he worked for, could not say what his truck looked like, and did not know what time he would arrive. The officers arrested the three men for vagrancy, searched them for weapons, and took them to police headquarters.

PROCEDURAL PROBLEM: The car, which had not been searched at the time of the arrest, was driven by an officer to the station, from which it was towed to a garage. Soon after the men had been booked at the station, some of the police officers went to the garage to search the car and found two loaded revolvers in the glove compartment. They were unable to open the trunk and returned to the station, where a detective told one of the officers to go back and try to get into the trunk. The officer did so, was able to enter the trunk through the back seat of the car, and in the trunk found caps, women's stockings (one with mouth and eye holes), rope, pillow slips, an illegally manufactured license plate equipped to be snapped over another plate, and other items. After the search one of the petitioner's companions confessed that he and two others—he did not name Preston—intended to rob a bank in Berry, Kentucky, a town about 51 miles from Newport. At this, the police called the Federal Bureau of Investigation into the case and turned over to the Bureau the articles found in the car.

Over the objection of Preston, the articles seized in the searches of the automobile were introduced into evidence. The defendant was convicted of conspiracy to rob a federally insured bank, the conviction having been based primarily on the above evidence. The federal Court of Appeals affirmed the conviction. On certiorari to the United States Supreme Court, the conviction was reversed, not because the arrest was illegal but because the search and seizure were defective.

THE ISSUE: Could the search and seizure of articles in the car which took place after the arrest under the facts and circumstances noted above be justified as incidental to a lawful arrest?

THE ANSWER: No.

DISCUSSION: It must be noted in this case that state authorities turned the seized articles over to federal authorities for prosecution. The Court made clear in its opinion that searches of motor vehicles must meet the test of reasonableness under the Fourth Amendment before seized articles are admissible. However, as Justice Black for the majority noted, "Common sense dictates, of course, that questions involving searches of motorcars or other things readily moved cannot be treated as identical to questions arising out of searches of fixed structures like houses. For this reason, what may be an unreasonable search of a house may be reasonable in the case of a motorcar."

The government's argument that the search and seizure were justified as being incidental to a lawful arrest was rejected by the Court, which held:

The rule allowing contemporaneous searches is justified, for example, by the need to seize weapons and other things which might be used to assault an officer or effect an arrest, as well as by the need to prevent the destruction of evidence of the crime—things which might easily happen where the weapon or evidence is on the accused's person or under his immediate control. But these justifications are absent where a search is remote in time or place from the arrest. Once an accused is in custody, then a search made at another place, without a warrant, is simply not incident to the arrest. . . .

The search of the car was not undertaken until [Preston] and his companions had been arrested and taken in custody to the police station and the car had been towed to the garage. At this point there was no danger that any of the men arrested could have used any weapons in the car or could have destroyed any evidence of a crime—assuming that there are articles which can be "fruits" or "implements" of the crime of vagrancy. Nor, since the men were under arrest at the police station and the car was in police custody at a garage, was there any danger that the car would be moved out of the locality or jurisdiction.

From this analysis Black concluded that the search was too remote in time or place to have been made as incidental to the arrest and therefore did not meet the reasonableness test under the Fourth Amendment.

QUESTIONS

1. What effect does *Chimel* v. *California*, 395 U.S. 752 (1969), *supra*, have on the holding in this case? Will the *Chimel* rule still permit a greater degree of flexibility when determining the reasonableness of vehicle searches? Discuss.
2. What procedure should the police have followed in this case in order to assure the admissibility of the seized articles?
3. Distinguish this case from *Carroll* v. *United States*, 267 U.S. 132 (1925), *supra*.

Chambers v. *Maroney*
399 U.S. 42, 90 S.Ct. 1975, 26 L.Ed. 419 (1970)

SETTING: Two men robbed a service station attendant at gunpoint, carrying off the currency from the cash register in a right-hand glove. One of the men was wearing a green sweater and the other a trench coat. Witnesses reported that they saw four men speed away from a nearby parking lot in a blue compact station wagon. Within an hour, a vehicle answering the description and carrying four men was stopped about two miles from the service station. Chambers, who was in the car, was wearing a green sweater and one of the other men had a trench coat with him. The occupants were placed under arrest but no search was conducted at the scene.

PROCEDURAL PROBLEM: The vehicle was taken to the police station where an immediate search took place without success. The officers later returned to the car for a second search, and, on this occasion, found two revolvers, a right-hand glove containing some small change, and credit cards taken from the victim. Chambers was indicted and convicted of robbery. The federal Court of Appeals affirmed, as did the United States Supreme Court.

THE ISSUE: Was the evidence seized from the automobile in which the defendant was riding, after the automobile was taken to a police station and searched there without a warrant, admissible in evidence at the defendant's trial?

THE ANSWER: Yes.

DISCUSSION: The search and seizure issue has always caused the Court problems concerning police authority in making warrantless searches of automobiles. As we have noted in the past few cases, different Supreme Court decisions seemed to expand and contract the police authority. In the *Chambers* case the Court upheld the search, noting that there is a constitutional difference between an automobile and a house or an office. Mr. Justice White for the Court put the decision squarely and solely within the *Carroll* v. *United States*, 267 U.S. 132 (1925), *supra*, doctrine. Policemen who have probable cause to search a car at the time and the place of arrest do not violate the Fourth Amendment by conducting a warrantless search at another time and place several hours after the arrest. In the opinion of the Court, if there is probable cause to search, "for constitutional purposes, we see no difference between on the one hand seizing and holding a car before presenting the probable cause issue to a magistrate and on the other hand carrying out an immediate search without a warrant. Given probable cause to search, either course is reasonable under the Fourth Amendment."

The search at the station was clearly too remote in time and place to be justified as incidental to the defendant's arrest. But according to White, the search of an automobile on probable cause is based on a theory "wholly different from that justifying the search incident to an arrest." Quoting from *Carroll*, White added that "The right to search and the validity of the seizure are not dependent on the right to arrest. They are dependent on the reasonable cause the seizing officer has for belief that the contents of the automobile offend the law."

White emphasized that when an automobile is immobilized as in this case until a warrant can be obtained is just as great an invasion of privacy as a warrantless search. However he went on to state, "Arguably, because of the preference for a magistrate's judgment only the immobilization of the car should be permitted until a search warrant is obtained; arguably, only the 'lesser' intrusion is permissible, until the magistrate authorizes the 'greater.' But which is the 'greater' and which the lesser intrusion is itself a debatable question and the answer may depend on a variety of circumstances."

Despite the broad language of the decision, the warrant requirement still remains for the search of automobiles. White emphasized that a warrant may indeed be necessary in some circumstances even though there is probable cause to search:

> *Neither* Carroll *nor other cases in this Court require or suggest that in every conceivable circumstance the search of an auto even with probable cause may be made without the extra protection that a warrant affords. But the circumstances that furnish probable cause to search a particular automobile for particular articles are most often unforeseeable; moreover, the opportunity to search is fleeting since a car is readily movable. Where this is true, as in Carroll, and the case before us now, if an effective search is to be made at any time, either the search must be made immediately without a warrant or the car itself must be seized and held without a warrant for whatever period is necessary to obtain a warrant for the search.*

Justice Harlan dissented from the majority, holding that the search was invalid. According to Harlan the majority abandoned the previous framework of its decision setting forth the scope of search that can be made without a warrant. As he stated:

> *Fidelity to this established principle requires that, where exceptions are made to accommodate the exigencies of particular situations, those exceptions be no brcader than necessitated by the circumstances presented. For example, the Court has recognized that an arrest creates an emergency situation justifying a warrantless search of the arrestee's person and of "the area from within which he might gain possession of a weapon or destructible evidence"; however, because the exigency giving use to this exception extends only that far, the search may go no further. Chimel v. California, 395 U.S. 752 (1969), supra. Similarily we held . . . that a warrantless search in a "stop and frisk" situation must "be strictly circumscribed by the exigencies which justify its initiation." Any intrusion beyond what is necessary for the personal safety of the officers or others nearby is forbidden. . . .*

The Court concedes that the police could prevent the removal of the evidence by temporarily seizing the car for the time necessary to obtain a warrant. It does not dispute that such a course would fully protect the interests of effective law enforcement; rather it states that temporary seizure is a "lesser" than warrantless search "is itself a debatable question and the answer may depend on a variety of circumstances." I believe it is clear that a warrantless search involves the greater sacrifice of Fourth Amendment values.

QUESTIONS

1. Why does the majority in *Chambers* see "no difference" for constitutional purposes between immediate search of the car without a warrant and holding the car until a warrant is obtained? What is Harlan's position?
2. Refer to *Vale v. Louisiana,* 399 U.S. 30 (1970), *supra.* In your estimation, was the need to search without first obtaining a warrant in *Chambers* greater or lesser than in *Vale?*
3. Assuming that there was probable cause to search a car under *Carroll* and *Chambers,* but the absence of grounds to search an occupant in the car, may the occupant of the car be searched if the items sought are of such a nature that they can be concealed on his person? *United States v. Di Re,* 332 U.S. 581 (1948) holds no that there is not. Research this case and discuss the Court's opinion.

Cooper v. California
386 U.S. 58, 87 S.Ct. 788, 17 L.Ed. 2ᴰ 730 (1967)

SETTING: Cooper was convicted in California of selling heroin to a police informant. The conviction partly rested on the introduction in evidence of a small brown paper sack taken by the police from the glove compartment of Cooper's car. The seizure occurred from a warrantless search of Cooper's car one week after Cooper's arrest while the car was impounded and held in a garage.

PROCEDURAL PROBLEM: The defendant appealed his conviction and the California appellate courts affirmed. The United States Supreme Court also affirmed. The defendant's argument in urging reversal was that the search and seizure were unreasonable and violated his Fourth Amendment rights under the guidelines set forth in *Preston v. United States,* 376 U.S. 364 (1964), *supra.*

THE ISSUE: Were the search and seizure of the automobile by police officers one week after the arrest while the car was impounded in a police garage unreasonable under the Fourth Amendment?

THE ANSWER: No.

DISCUSSION: *Preston* involved a warrantless search of an automobile after an accused had been arrested and placed in custody. Preston was arrested for vagrancy, and the custody of the car was totally unrelated to the vagrancy charge for which he was arrested. The search in *Preston* was sought to be justified on the ground that it was incidental and part of a lawful arrest. The Court rejected this argument, stating that once an "accused is under an arrest and in custody, then a search made at another place, without a warrant, is simply not incidental to the arrest." The situation in this case is different according to the majority.

Under a California statute, any officer making an arrest for a narcotics violation shall seize and deliver to the state division of narcotics enforcement any vehicle used to store, conceal, transport, sell, or facilitate the possession of narcotics, such vehicle "to be *held as evidence* until a forfeiture has been declared or a release ordered." (emphasis added) The defendant's vehicle came within the terms of the statute. The majority noted, however, that the question in this case was not whether the search was authorized by law, but whether it was reasonable under the Fourth Amendment. Justice Black, for the majority, conceded that "lawful custody of an automobile does not itself dispense with constitutional requirements of searches thereafter made of it," but concluded that the reason for the search and the nature of the custody may constitutionally justify it.

The five-man majority in this case pointed out in distinguishing *Preston* that the officers seized Cooper's car because they were required to do so by state law. They seized it because of the crime for which Cooper was arrested. They seized it to impound it and they had to safely keep it until forfeiture proceedings were concluded some four months later. Their subsequent search of the car, whether the state had legal title to it or not, was intimately related to the reason for the defendant's arrest, the reason the car was impounded, and the reason it was being retained. With this consideration in mind, the majority concluded that "it would be unreasonable to hold that the police, having to retain the car in their custody for such a length of time, had no right, even for their own protection, to search it. It is no answer to say that the police could have obtained a warrant for '[t]he relevant test is not whether it is reasonable to procure a search warrant but whether the search was reasonable.' . . . Under the circumstances of this case, we cannot hold unreasonable under the Fourth Amendment the examination or search of a car validly held by officers as evidence in a forfeiture proceeding."

The four dissenters, for whom Justice Douglas wrote, were of the opinion that this case could not be distinguished from *Preston* with the exception *Preston* was a federal case and this was a state case. He noted that the "Fourth Amendment . . . applies to the states as well as to the Federal Government."

The minority could see only two ways to explain the Court's opinion —one being that it overrules *Preston sub silento*. To this Douglas wrote that "unless the search is incident to a lawful arrest, I would insist that the police obtain a search warrant just as they must do when they search his home." The second way to explain the Court's decision is to "view that when the Bill of Rights is applied to the states by reason of the Fourteenth Amendment, a watered-down version is used. In that view 'due process' qualifies all provisions of the Bill of Rights. . . . But I also reject this view."

QUESTIONS

1. Distinguish this case carefully from *Preston*. Is Douglas in fact correct?
2. What is the specific holding in this case? Did this decision strengthen or weaken the position of law enforcement officers in conducting searches of vehicles some time after an arrest is made? What are the reasons for your opinion?
3. Does your state have a law similar to the one in California in this case? If so, have there been any state decisions interpreting it? Discuss the holding in light of *Cooper*.

Cady v. *Dombrowski*
413 U.S. 433, 93 S.Ct. 2523, 37 L.Ed. 2ᴰ 706 (1973)

SETTING: On September 9, 1969, Dombrowski was a member of the Chicago, Illinois, police force and either owned or possessed a 1960 Dodge automobile. That day he drove from Chicago to West Bend, Wisconsin, the county seat of Washington County located some hundred-odd miles northwest of Chicago. He was identified as having been in two taverns in the small town of Kewaskum, Wisconsin, seven miles north of West Bend, during the late evening of September 9th and the early morning of September 10th. The defendant's automobile became disabled, and he had it towed to a farm owned by his brother in Fond du Lac County, which adjoins Washington County on the north. Early that afternoon he drove back to Chicago with his brother in his brother's car.

Just before midnight of the same day, Dombrowski rented a maroon 1967 Ford Thunderbird at O'Hare Field outside Chicago and apparently drove back to Wisconsin early the next morning. A person on his brother's farm saw a car matching the description of the rented car pull alongside the disabled 1960 Dodge at approximately 4 A.M. At approximately 9:30 A.M. on September 11th Dombrowski purchased two towels, one light brown and the other blue, from a department store in Kewaskum.

From 7 to 10:15 P.M. of the 11th defendant was in a steak house or tavern in West Bend. He ate dinner and also drank, apparently quite heavily. He left the tavern and drove the 1967 Thunderbird in a direction away from West Bend toward his brother's farm. On the way, Dombrowski had an accident with the Thunderbird, breaking through a guard rail and crashing into a bridge abutment. A passing motorist drove him into Kewaskum and after being left there, Dombrowski teleponed the police. Two officers picked him up at a tavern and drove to the scene of the accident. On the way, the officers noticed that he appeared to be drunk; he offered three conflicting versions of how the accident occurred.

At the scene the police observed the 1967 Thunderbird and took various measurements relevant to the accident. Dombrowski was, in the opinion of the officers, drunk. He had informed them that he was a Chicago police officer. The Wisconsin policemen believed that Chicago police officers were required by regulation to carry their service revolvers at all times. After calling a towtruck to remove the disabled Thunderbird and not finding the revolver on his person, one of the officers looked into the front seat and glove compartment of that car for Dombrowski's service revolver. No revolver was found. The wrecker arrived and the Thunderbird was towed to a privately owned service station in Kewaskum, approximately seven miles from the West Bend police station. It was left outside by the wrecker, and no police guard was posted. At 11:33 P.M. on the 11th Dombrowski was taken directly to the West Bend police station from the accident scene, and, after being interviewed by an assistant district attorney, to whom he again stated he was a Chicago policeman, Dombrowski was formally arrested for drunken driving. He was "in a drunken condition" and "incoherent at times." Because of his injuries sustained in the accident, he was taken to a local hospital by the same two officers. He lapsed into an unexplained coma, and a doctor, fearing the possibility of complications, had Dombrowski hospitalized overnight for observation. One of the policemen remained at the hospital as a guard, and the other, Officer Weiss, drove at some time after 2 A.M. on the 12th to the garage to which the 1967 Thunderbird had been towed after the accident.

The purpose for going to the Thunderbird, as developed on the motion to suppress, was to again look for Dombrowski's service revolver. Weiss testified that Dombrowski did not have a revolver when he was arrested, and that the West Bend authorities were under the impression that Chicago police officers were required to carry their service revolvers at all times. He stated that the effort to find the revolver was "standard procedure in our department."

Weiss opened the door of the Thunderbird and found, on the floor of the car, a book of Chicago police regulations and, between the two front seats, a flashlight that appeared to have "a few spots of blood on it." He then opened the trunk of the car, which had been locked, and saw various items covered with what was later determined to be type O blood. These included a pair of police uniform trousers, a pair of gray trousers, a nightstick with the name "Dombrowski" stamped on it, a raincoat, a portion of a car floormat, and a towel. The blood on the car mat was moist. The officer took these items to the police station.

Later that day when Dombrowski was confronted with the condition of the items discovered in the trunk, he requested the presence of counsel before making any statement. After conferring with Dombrowski, a lawyer told the police, "[Dombrowski] authorized me to state he believed there was a body lying near the family picnic area at the north end of his brother's farm."

Fond du Lac County police went to the farm and found, in a dump, the body of a male, later identified as the decedent McKinney, clad only in a sportshirt. The deceased's head was bloody and a white sock was found near the body. In observing the area, one officer looked through the window of the disabled 1960 Dodge, located not far from where the body was found, and saw a pillowcase in the back seat and a briefcase covered with blood. Police officials obtained, on the evening of the 12th, returnable within 48 hours, warrants to search the 1960 Dodge and the 1967 Thunderbird, as well as orders to impound both automobiles. The 1960 Dodge was examined at the farm on the 12th and then towed to the police garage where it was held as evidence. On the 13th, criminologists came from the Wisconsin Crime Laboratory in Madison and searched the Dodge; they seized the back and front seats, a white sock covered with blood, a part of a bloody rear floor mat, a briefcase, and a front floormat. A return of the search warrant was filed in the county court on the 14th, but it did not recite that the sock and floor mat had been seized. At a hearing held on the 14th, the sheriff who executed the warrant did not specifically state that these two items had been seized.

At the trial, the State introduced testimony tending to establish that the deceased was first hit over the head and then shot with a .38 caliber gun, dying approximately an hour after the gunshot wound was inflicted; that death occurred at approximately 7 A.M. on the 11th, with a six-hour margin of error either way; that Dombrowski owned two .38 caliber guns; that Dombrowski had type A blood; that the deceased had type O blood; and that the bloodstains found in the 1960 Dodge and on the items found in the two cars were type O.

The prosecution introduced the nightstick discovered in the 1967 Thunderbird and testimony that it had traces of type O blood on it; the portion of the floormat found in the 1967 car with testimony that it matched the portion of the floormat found in the 1960 Dodge; the bloody towel found in the 1967 car with testimony that it was identical to one of the towels purchased by Dombrowski on the 11th; the police uniform trousers; the sock found in the 1960 Dodge with testimony that it was identical in composition and stitching to that found near the body of the deceased.

At Dombrowski's trial for murder at which the seized items were introduced as evidence, a conviction resulted. On habeas corpus to the United States Supreme Court the conviction of the state court was affirmed. In so doing, the Supreme Court reversed the judgment of the U. S. Court of Appeals which had held the search and seizure to be unreasonable.

PROCEDURAL PROBLEM: The United States Supreme Court received the above facts and addressed itself to the sole problem of whether the search of the trunk of the 1967 Ford was unreasonable only because the local police officer had not previously obtained a search warrant. If the Court decided that the search was not unreasonable, a decision then had to be made regarding whether or not it was nevertheless unreasonable under the Fourth and Fourteenth Amendments.

THE ISSUES: Was the search of the trunk unreasonable? If not, was it unreasonable under the Fourth and Fourteenth Amendments?

THE ANSWERS: No. No.

DISCUSSION: In rejecting the evidence, the United States Court of Appeals relied primarily on *Preston* v. *United States*, 376 U.S. 364 (1964).

In *Preston,* the search could not be justified as "incident to a lawful arrest." Justice Rehnquist for the majority citing *Harris* v. *United States,* 390 U.S. 234, (1968) and *Cooper* v. *California,* 386 U.S. 58 (1967) noted that:

> *These decisions, while not on all fours with the instant case, lead us to conclude that the intrusion into the trunk of the 1967 Thunderbird at the garage was not unreasonable within the meaning of the Fourth and Fourteenth Amendments solely because a warrant had not been obtained by Officer Weiss after he left the hospital. The police did not have actual, physical custody of the vehicle as in* Harris *and* Cooper, *but the vehicle had been towed there at the officers' directions. These officers in a rural area were simply reacting to the effects of an accident—one of the recurring practical situations that result from the operation of motor vehicles and with which local police officers must deal every day. The Thunderbird was not parked adjacent to the dwelling place of the owner as in* Coolidge, *supra nor simply momentarily unoccupied on a street. Rather, like an obviously abandoned vehicle, it represented a nuisance, and there is no suggestion in the record that the officers' action in exercising control over it by having it towed away was warranted either in terms of state law or sound police procedure.*

> *In* Harris *the justification for the initial intrusion into the vehicle was to safeguard the owner's property, and in* Cooper *it was to guarantee the safety of the custodians. Here the justification, while different, was as immediate and constitutionally reasonable as those in* Harris *and* Cooper: *concern for the safety of the general public who might be endangered if an intruder removed a revolver from the trunk of the vehicle. The record contains uncontradicted testimony to support the findings of the state courts and District Court. Furthermore, although there is no record basis for discrediting such testimony, it was corroborated by the circumstantial fact that at the time the search was conducted Officer Weiss was ignorant of the fact that a murder, or any other crime had been committed. While perhaps in a metropolitan area the responsibility to the general public might have been discharged by the posting of a police guard during the night, what might be normal police procedure in such an area may be neither normal nor possible in Kewaskum, Wisconsin. The fact that the protection of the public might, in the abstract, have been accomplished by such intrusive means does not, by itself render the search unreasonable.*

QUESTIONS

1. What is the specific holding of this case?
2. Compare and distinguish this case from *Harris* v. *United States* and *Cooper* v. *California.*
3. In your estimation does this case favor law enforcement or hinder its activities.

INVESTIGATION PROCEDURES

Davis v. *Mississippi*
394 U.S. 721, 89 S.Ct. 1394, 22 L.Ed. 2ᴰ 676 (1969)

SETTING: A rape occurred on the evening of December 2, 1965, at
the victim's home in Meridian, Mississippi. The only description given
by the victim was that the rapist was a Negro youth. The only other
lead to his identity were finger- and palmprints found on a windowsill
through which the assailant apparently entered the victim's home. Starting on the next day, December 3, for about ten days the Meridian police,
without warrants, took at least twenty-four Negro youths to police headquarters for brief questioning; these boys were fingerprinted and released
without charge. About forty or fifty other Negro youths were also questioned on the streets, at school, or in police headquarters.

PROCEDURAL PROBLEM: Davis, a 14-year-old who occasionally
worked for the victim as a yard boy, was brought in on December 3,
routinely questioned, fingerprinted, and released. He was also questioned
several times between December 3 and December 7, apparently about
other potential suspects. During this same time he was exhibited to the
victim in her hospital room. The officers testified that the reason for this
exhibition was to sharpen the victim's description of her assailant by
providing "a gauge to go on by size and color." The victim did not identify Davis as her assailant at any of these confrontations.
On December 12, Davis was driven by the police to Jackson, Mississippi, where he spent the night in jail. There was neither a warrant nor
probable cause for this arrest. On December 13, Davis, who had not
yet been advised of his right to counsel, took a polygraph test and signed
a statement. He was then returned to and confined in the Meridian jail.
He was fingerprinted a second time on December 14. This set of prints
along with those of twenty-three other suspects were sent to the FBI
for comparison with the latent prints taken from the victim's house. The
FBI reported that Davis' prints matched those taken from the window
ledge. Davis was subsequently indicted and convicted. Evidence of the
fingerprints was admitted into evidence over the defendant's objections
that they were secured as a result of an unlawful detention. The Mississippi Supreme Court affirmed. The United States Supreme Court reversed.

THE ISSUE: Does the Fourth Amendment apply to the investigatory arrest stage of a prosecution so that its prohibition against unreasonable searches and seizures is violated by the "investigatory arrest"—a detention without probable cause?

THE ANSWER: Yes.

DISCUSSION: Justice Brennan, writing for the majority, first of all rejected the Mississippi holding that fingerprint evidence because of its trustworthiness is not subject to the prescriptions of the Fourth and Fourteenth Amendments. He stated that "fingerprint evidence is no exception. . . . [A]ll evidence obtained by searches and seizures in violation of the Constitution [is] inadmissible in a state court."

Turning to the question of the detention during which the fingerprints were obtained, the majority emphasized that the Fourth Amendment is as applicable to the investigatory stage of the case as to any other stage of the criminal process. As Brennan held:

> It is true that at the time of the December 3 detention the police had no intention of charging [Davis] with the crime and were far from making him the primary focus of their investigation. But to argue that the Fourth Amendment does not apply to the investigatory stage is fundamentally to misconceive the purpose of the Fourth Amendment. Investigatory seizures would subject unlimited numbers of innocent persons to the harassment and ignominy incident to involuntary detention. Nothing is more clear than that the Fourth Amendment was meant to prevent wholesale intrusions upon the personal security of our citizenry whether these intrusions be termed "arrests" or "investigatory detentions."

The Court did acknowledge in concluding that fingerprinting and detention for the purpose of fingerprinting may, because of its nature and reliability, constitute a much less serious intrusion upon personal security than other kinds of police searches and detentions. "Fingerprinting involves none of the probing into an individual's private life and thoughts that marks an interrogation and search. Nor can fingerprint detention be employed repeatedly to harass any individual, since the police need only one set of each person's prints." However, in this case the Court found the detention of the youth was so unreasonable that it violated the proscription of the Fourth Amendment.

Justice Black indicated disagreement with the Court's remarks on investigative arrests. He argued that the majority decision was but one more of an ever-increasing list of cases "in which this court has been so widely blowing up the Fourth Amendment's scope that its original authors would be hard put to recognize their creation."

QUESTIONS

1. What is investigatory detention? It is any different from an arrest? See *Terry* v. *Ohio*, 392 U.S. 1 (1968), *infra*.
2. In your opinion, what importance can be attached to the Court's remarks regarding the reliability of fingerprint evidence? Does it recognize the possibility that in some cases fingerprints may be admissible even though a detention is technically unlawful?
3. The Court rejected the Mississippi holding that fingerprints are outside the scope of the Fourth and Fourteenth Amendments. Why? Do you agree with the Supreme Court or Mississippi? Give your reasons.

Cupp v. *Murphy*
412 U.S. 291, 93 S.Ct. 2000, 36 L.Ed. 2ᴰ 900 (1973)

SETTING: The victim died of strangulation. There were abrasions and lacerations around her neck. There was no sign of a break-in or robbery. The woman's estranged husband, Murphy, voluntarily went to the police for questioning. He met his attorney at the police station. The police noted a dark mark on his finger. Suspecting that the spot might be dried blood, knowing that skin or blood is often found under fingernails of an assailant, the police asked Murphy if they could take a sample of scrapings from his fingernails. He refused. The police proceeded to take a sample over his protest and without a warrant.

PROCEDURAL PROBLEM: The evidence turned out to be blood cells, skin traces, and fabric from the victim's nightgown. The incriminating evidence was admitted at his trial. He was convicted and appealed, claiming that the scrapings were secured as a result of an unconstitutional search under the Fourth Amendment.

The United States Supreme Court affirmed the conviction.

THE ISSUE: Was the seizure of the samplings a type of "severe, though brief intrusion upon cherished personal security" which violates the Fourth Amendment?

THE ANSWER: No.

DISCUSSION: Justice Stewart for the majority, while noting that Murphy was detained only long enough to obtain the sample and was not arrested until a month later, held that "the detention of [Murphy] against his will constituted a seizure of his person, and the Fourth Amendment guarantee of freedom from 'unreasonable searches and seizures' is clearly implicated." Citing *Davis* v. *Mississippi*, 394 U.S. 721 (1969), *supra*, Stewart continued that the Fourth Amendment was to prevent "wholesale intrusions upon the personal security of our citizenry whether these intrusions be termed 'arrests' or 'investigatory detentions.'" However, in this case the intrusion went beyond seizing voice or handwriting exemplars and general physical characteristics. Nethertheless, the Court believed this search was constitutionally permissible even though there was no formal arrest (the Court did, however, indicate that there was probable cause to arrest had the police done so). As Justice Stewart noted:

> At the time Murphy was being detained at the stationhouse, he was obviously aware of the detective's suspicions. Though he did not have the full warning of official suspicion that a formal arrest provides, Murphy was sufficiently appraised of his suspected role in the crime to motivate him to attempt to destroy what evidence he could without attracting further attention. Testimony at trial indicated that after he refused to consent to the taking of fingernail samples, he put his hands behind his back and appeared to rub them together. He then put his hands in his pockets, and a "metalic sound, such as keys or change rattling" was heard. The rationale of Chimel, in these circumstances, justified the police in subjecting him to the very limited search necessary to preserve the highly evanescent evidence they found under this fingernails.
>
> On the facts of this case, considering the existence of probable cause, the very limited intrusion undertaken incident to the stationhouse detention, and the ready destructability of the evidence, we cannot say this search violated the Fourth and Fourteenth Amendments.

QUESTIONS

1. Distinguish this case from *Davis* v. *Mississippi* and *United States* v. *Dionisio*. Was *Murphy* easier to decide than either *Davis* or *Dionisio?*
2. What is the holding of this case regarding the constitutionality of "investigatory detention"? Does the case really involve a search incidental to a lawful arrest? Discuss.
3. Compare this case with *Schmerber* v. *California, infra.* Distinguish the factual setting. In your opinion are the facts sufficiently different to justify a different holding in *Murphy?*

United States v. *Dionisio*
410 U.S. 1, 93 S.Ct. 764, 35 L.Ed. 2ᴰ 67 (1973)

SETTING: A special federal grand jury was convened in Illinois to investigate possible violations of federal gambling laws. The grand jury had as some evidence court-ordered voice recordings. It then subpoenaed some twenty persons, including the defendant, seeking to obtain voice exemplars for comparison with the recorded conversations already in evidence. The witnesses were told where to go to record their voices and that they could have their attorneys present when they made the recording. Dionisio and other witnesses refused to do so, asserting that the disclosures would violate their rights under the Fourth and Fifth Amendments.

PROCEDURAL PROBLEM: The government then filed petitions in the federal district court to compel the defendant to furnish the voice exemplars. Following a hearing, the district court judge rejected the defendant's contention and ordered him to comply with the grand jury's request because "voice exemplars, like handwriting exemplars or fingerprints, are not testimonial nor communicative evidence and that consequently the order to produce them would not compel the witness to testify against himself."

The district court judge also found that there would be no Fourth Amendment violation because the grand jury subpoena did not itself violate the subpeona and the order to produce the voice exemplars would involve no unreasonable search and seizure within the proscription of the Fourth Amendment.

Dionisio still refused and was held in civil contempt. On appeal, the Court of Appeals upheld the district court ruling on the Fifth Amendment argument but reversed on Fourth Amendment grounds because in their view the grand jury was using its subpoena powers to find probable cause where none existed. Also the Court of Appeals apparently thought that the wholesale roundup of persons in *Davis* v. *Mississippi*, 394 U.S. 721 (1969), *supra*, was comparable to subpoenaing the twenty witnesses in this case.

The main issue that caused the Court some trouble was where the Court of Appeals held that the Fourth Amendment requires a preliminary showing of reasonableness before a grand jury witness can be compelled to furnish a voice exemplar, and that in this case the proposed seizures of the voice exemplars would be unreasonable.

THE ISSUE: In the grand jury investigative function, does the Fourth Amendment require that the grand jury establish the reasonableness of its request for investigative evidence before the evidence need be supplied?

THE ANSWER: No.

DISCUSSION: Justice Stewart for the majority held that the compulsory production of voice exemplar evidence from a grand jury witness turns upon a dual inquiry: whether or not either the initial compulsion of the person to appear before the grand jury or the subsequent directive to make a voice recording is an unreasonable seizure within the Fourth Amendment.

Because the seizure of voice exemplars is not testimonial compulsion under *Schmerber* v. *California*, 384 U.S. 757 (1966), the issue is whether or not a subpoena to appear before a grand jury to give a voice recording is a seizure in the Fourth Amendment sense. The Court emphasized that it is not. Stewart noted that it has long been recognized that "citizens are generally not constitutionally immune from grand jury subpoenas." According to the majority, the compulsion exerted by the grand jury subpoena differs from the seizure effected by an arrest or even an investigative stop. The latter is abrupt, effected with force or the threat of force, is often demeaning, and involves a record and social stigma. The subpoena, however, is served in the same manner as legal processes, involves no stigma, requests appearance at a convenient time, and remains under the control and supervision of a court. "A grand jury subpoena to testify is not that kind of governmental intrusion on privacy against which the Fourth Amendment affords protection once the Fifth Amendment is satisfied." Justice Stewart emphasized that the Court was not faced with the constitutional problem that was faced in *Davis* v. *Mississippi*. The grand jury may well call numerous witnesses in the cause of an investigation and no witness is permitted to resist the subpoena because too many witnesses have been called.

Dionisio's second argument was that the grand jury's subsequent directive to make voice recordings was itself an infringement of his rights under the Fourth Amendment. Stewart rejected this argument, stating that the required disclosure of a person's voice is immeasurably further removed from "the Fourth Amendment protection than was the intrusion into the body effected by the blood extraction in *Schmerber*." Similarly, a seizure of voice exemplars does not involve the "severe, though brief intrusion upon cherished personal security" effected by the patdown in *Terry*, "surely an annoying, frightening, and perhaps humiliating experience." Stewart then compared the voice exemplar to the fingerprinting in *Davis* v. *Mississippi*, where though the initial dragnet detentions were constitutionally impermissible, the Court held that fingerprinting itself "involves none of the probing into an individual's private life and thoughts that marks an interrogation or search."

In concluding, Stewart noted that "since neither the summons to appear before the grand jury, nor its directive to make a voice recording infringed on any interest protected by the Fourth Amendment, there was no justification for requiring the grand jury to satisfy even the minimal requirement of reasonableness. . . ."

Justice Marshall in dissent could not agree with the majority because he felt that the burden of showing reasonableness by a grand jury when it seeks to secure physical evidence is not too great a task; it has always been required of law enforcement officials. He stated that "the essence of the requirement would be nothing more than a showing that the evidence sought is relevant to the purpose of the investigation and that the particular grand jury is not the subject of prosecutorial abuse— a showing that the Government should have little difficulty making, unless it is in fact acting improperly. The 'reasonableness' requirement would do no more in the context of the cases than the Constitution compels—protect the citizen from the unreasonable and arbitrary governmental interference, and insure that the broad subpoena powers of the grand jury which the Court now recognizes are not turned into a tool of prosecutorial oppression."

QUESTIONS

1. What is the specific holding in this case in regard to the investigative powers of the grand jury? Do you agree?
2. The thrust of Justice Marshall's dissent is based on his fear of what? How would it be likely that his fears would be realized?
3. Compare the holding in this case with that in *Davis* v. *Mississippi*. Upon what grounds did the majority in *Dionisio* see significant differences?

ADMINISTRATIVE SEARCHES

Frank v. *Maryland*
359 U.S. 360, 79 S.Ct. 804, 3 L.Ed. 2ᴰ 877 (1959)

SETTING: Acting on a complaint from a resident on Reisterstown Road, Baltimore, Maryland, that there were rats in her basement, Gentry, an inspector of the Baltimore City Health Department, began an inspection of the houses in the vicinity looking for the source of the rats. In the middle of the afternoon of February 27, 1958, Gentry knocked on the door of Frank's detached frame house at 4335 Reisterstown Road. After receiving no response he proceeded to inspect the area outside the house. This inspection revealed that the house was in an "extreme state of decay," and that in the rear of the house there was a pile later identified as "rodent feces mixed with straw and trash and debris to approximately half a ton." During this inspection Frank came around the side of the house and asked Gentry to explain his presence. Gentry responded that he had evidence of rodent infestation and asked Frank for permission to inspect the basement area. He refused. At no time did Gentry have a warrant authorizing him to enter. The next forenoon Gentry, in the company of two police officers, returned to Frank's house. After receiving no response to his knock, he reinspected the exterior of the premises. He then swore out a warrant for Frank's arrest alleging a violation of Article 12 of the Baltimore City Code, which provides:

> *Whenever the Commissioner of Health shall have cause to suspect that a nuisance exists in any house, cellar or enclosure, he may demand entry therein in the day time, and if the owner or occupier shall refuse or delay to open the same and admit a free examination, he shall forfeit and pay for every such refusal the sum of Twenty Dollars.*

PROCEDURAL PROBLEM: Frank was arrested on March 5, and the next day was found guilty of the offense alleged in the warrant and fined twenty dollars. On appeal, Frank was also found guilty. The Maryland Court of Appeals denied certiorari. The United States Supreme Court affirmed.

THE ISSUE: Are administrative searches permissible under the provisions of the Fourth Amendment?

THE ANSWER: Yes.

DISCUSSION: Justice Frankfurter, who wrote the majority opinion, stated that giving the fullest scope to the constitutional right of privacy, "its protection cannot be here invoked." According to him the attempted inspection of Frank's home was merely to ascertain whether conditions existed which are proscribed by the Baltimore health code. In a case in which they do, then the person in violation is notified to correct the conditions. No evidence for criminal prosecution is sought to be seized. He is simply required to act in conformance with the minimum community standards of health and well being. Frankfurter emphasized the noncoercive nature of the statute by stating that there "was no midnight knock on the door, but an orderly visit in the middle of the afternoon with no suggestion that the hour was inconvenient. Moreover, the inspector has no power to force entry and did not attempt it. A fine is imposed for resistance, but the officials are not authorized to break past the unwilling occupant."

According to the majority the inspection only touches on the periphery "of the important interests safeguarded by the Fourteenth Amendment's protection against official intrusion, but it is hedged about with safeguards designed to make the least possible demand on the individual occupant and to cause only the slightest restriction on his claims of privacy." In this situation, then, the demands of the Fourteenth Amendment must be assessed in the light of the needs that have produced it.

Stressing historical precedent that concerned the health and safety needs of the community, the majority emphasized that the nature of our society has not vitiated the need for inspections, nor, in their view, has there been any abuse or inroad in freedom in meeting this need. In light of the long history of inspections of the kind in this case and of modern needs, the Court said that the carefully circumscribed demand which the Maryland statute makes upon a citizen's freedom does not violate due process.

Justice Harlan's concurring opinion stated that the health inspector's request for permission to enter Frank's premises for the sole purpose of locating a community health hazard was not an unreasonable search under the Fourth Amendment.

QUESTIONS

1. What is an administrative search?
2. What is the rationale of the majority for the holding in this case? Is it a theoretical or practical rationale?
3. Prepare a dissenting opinion to this case prior to reading the case that follows.

Camara v. Municipal Court of San Francisco
387 U.S. 523, 87 S.Ct. 1727, 18 L.Ed. 2ᴰ 930 (1967)

SETTING: On November 6, 1963, an inspector of the Division of Housing Inspection of the San Francisco Department of Public Health entered an apartment building to make a routine annual inspection for possible violations of the city's housing code. The building's manager informed the inspector that Camara, a lessee of the ground floor, was using the rear of his leasehold as a personal residence. Claiming that the building's occupancy permit did not allow residential use of the ground floor, the inspector confronted Camara and demanded that he permit an inspection of the premises. Camara refused to allow this because the inspector lacked a search warrant.

The inspector returned on November 8, again without a warrant, and was again refused permission to inspect. A citation was then mailed ordering Camara to appear at the district attorney's office. When he failed to appear, two inspectors returned to his apartment on November 22. They informed appellant that he was required by law to permit an inspection.

PROCEDURAL PROBLEM: Camara still refused the inspectors access to his apartment without a search warrant. Thereafter, a complaint was filed charging him with unlawfully refusing to permit a lawful inspection of his home pursuant to section 503 of the San Francisco *Housing Code:*

> *Sec. 503. RIGHT TO ENTER BUILDING. Authorized employees of the City departments or City agencies, so far as may be necessary for the performance of their duties, shall upon presentation of proper credentials, have the right to enter, at reasonable times, any building, structure, or premises in the City to perform any duty imposed upon them by the Municipal Code.*

THE ISSUE: Should *Frank v. Maryland*, 359 U.S. 360 (1969), *supra* be overruled to require health and fire inspectors to have warrants to search a home or business?

THE ANSWER: Yes.

DISCUSSION: Justice White, for a six-man majority, found it somewhat contradictory to say that an individual and his private property are protected by the Fourth Amendment only when the individual is suspected of criminal behavior. The majority therefore held that "administrative searches of the kind at issue here are significant intrusions upon the interests protected by the Fourth Amendment, and that such searches when authorized and conducted without a warrant procedure lack the traditional safeguards which the Fourth Amendment guarantees to an individual."

The reasons put forth in *Frank v. Maryland*, according to Justice White, are insufficient to justify the gross weakening of the Fourth Amendment's protections. The searches authorized by *Frank* were authorized and conducted without a warrant procedure like the safeguards mandated by the Fourth Amendment. The *Frank* decision was therefore overruled.

The majority, however, did recognize the necessity of having reasonable inspections as benefiting the public interest. Consequently a special probable cause standard was devised for administrative searches. As Justice White concluded:

> [I]t is obvious that "probable cause" to issue a warrant to inspect must exist if reasonable legislative or administrative standards for conducting an area inspection are satisfied with respect to a particular dwelling. Such standards, which will vary with the municipal program being enforced, may be based upon the passage of time, the nature of the building (e.g., a multi-family apartment house), or the condition of the entire area, but they will not necessarily depend upon specific knowledge of the condition of the particular dwelling. It has been suggested that so to vary the probable cause test from the standard applied in criminal cases would be to authorize a "synthetic search warrant" and thereby to lessen the overall protections of the Fourth Amendment. But we do not agree. The warrant procedure is designed to guarantee that a decision to search private property is justified by a reasonable governmental interest. But reasonableness is still the ultimate standard. If a valid public interest justifies the intrusion contemplated, then there is probable cause to issue a suitably restricted search warrant.
>   . . . Such an approach neither endangers time-honored doctrines applicable to criminal investigations nor makes a nullity of the probable cause requirement in this area. It merely gives full recognition to the competing public and private interests here at stake and, in so doing, best fulfills the historic purpose behind the constitutional right to be free from unreasonable government invasions of privacy.

QUESTIONS

1. What reasons did the majority give for distinguishing the reasons for *Frank* from *Camara?*
2. In your opinion, is an administrative inspection such as the one in this case a search? Would it make any difference if immunity from criminal prosecution were given prior to any administrative search? Discuss.
3. In your estimation, is there a likelihood that the fears of the three dissenters will come about?

Colonnade Catering Corporation v. United States
397 U.S. 72, 90 S.Ct. 774, 25 L.Ed. 2ᴰ 60 (1970)

SETTING: The defendant company operated a catering business in New York. A federal agent who was an employee of the Internal Revenue

Service's Alcohol and Tobacco Tax Division was a guest at a party held on the defendant's premises and noted a possible federal excise tax law violation. Later federal agents visited the place while another party was in progress. They inspected the cellar without the manager's consent. The manager was asked to open the locked liquor storeroom and he answered that only the defendant company's president could do so. Later the president came to the premises upon request and refused to open the storeroom. When asked for a warrant, the federal agents stated that they did not need one. After the president's continued refusal, the agents broke the lock to the room and entered. They removed some bottles of liquor.

PROCEDURAL PROBLEMS: At a subsequent trial the defendant sought to suppress the evidence and return of the seized evidence. The federal statute, 26 U.S.C. 7342, in question provides:

> Any owner of any building or place, or person having the agency or superintendent of the same, who refuses to admit any officer or employee of the Treasury Department acting under the authority of section 7606 (relating to entry of premises for examination of taxable articles) or refuses to permit him to examine such article or articles, shall, for every such refusal, forfeit $500.

The federal district court granted the requested relief—however, the Court of Appeals reversed. The United States Supreme Court in turn reversed the Court of Appeals and upheld the district court.

THE ISSUE: Is the imposition of a fine for refusal to permit entry, with the attendant consequences that violation of inspection laws may have in the loosely regulated alcoholic beverages industry, the exclusive sanction under the above federal statute, in the absence of a warrant to break and enter?

THE ANSWER: Yes.

DISCUSSION: Justice Douglas for the majority initially noted that *Camara* v. *Municipal*, 387 U.S. 523, (1967) *supra*, overruled *Frank* v. *Maryland*, 359 U.S. 360 (1959), *supra*, insofar as it permitted warrantless searches or inspections under municipal fire, health, and housing codes. Dictum in *Camara* mentioned that the provision for a fine for refusal to permit inspection made the use of force improper when there was no warrant. This case now tests whether the dictum presents a controlling principle.

Douglas and the Court conceded that Congress has broad powers of inspection under the federal liquor laws to meet the various evils that may exist. Citing *See* v. *City of Seattle*, 387 U.S. 541 (1967), the majority noted that the ruling regarding "administrative entry, without consent, upon the portions of commercial premises which are not open to the public may only be compelled through prosecution of physical force within the framework of the warrant procedure," is not applicable in this case. Congress has authorized inspection but has made no rules governing what procedures must be followed. Therefore, the various restrictive rules of the Fourth Amendment apply. Douglas then emphasized that the businessman has a constitutional right to go about his business free from unreasonable searches upon the private commercial parts of his property. This guarantee is breached if an inspector enters to inspect for various violations of regulatory law without official authority evidenced by a warrant.

The Court in concluding held that:

> *We deal here with the liquor industry long subject to close supervision and inspection. As respects that industry, and its various branches including retailers, Congress has broad authority to fashion standards of reasonableness for searches and seizures. Under the existing statutes, Congress selected a standard that does not include forcible entries without a warrant. It resolved the issue, not by authorizing forcible, warrantless entries, but by making it an offense for a licensee to refuse admission to the inspector.*

Chief Justice Burger in dissent was of the opinion that the agents needed neither a warrant nor the statute to secure entry to the defendant's premises because it was as open as any business establishment that seeks to sell goods and services to the public. In Burger's view Congress went beyond mere entry and authorized inspections. "Inspection authorization would be meaningless if the agents could not open lockers, cabinets, closets, and storerooms and indeed pry open cases of liquor to see the contents."

The Chief Justice also was of the opinion that the majority needlessly muddled a comparatively simple issue of statutory construction by improperly interjecting the undertone of constitutionally limited searches. He stated, "Congress having prescribed this [inspection of spirits locked or stored] as a reasonable means of enforcing the inspection necessary to tax collection, I can see no basis for any court to say it cannot be done."

Justice Black, in another dissenting opinion, took the majority members to task by stating that they did not find the search in this case unreasonable at all—only that it was not authorized by the federal statute.

Therefore, because Black could find no unreasonableness in the search and because the search was carried out in conformity with the statute, he believed the Court of Appeals was correct.

QUESTIONS

1. What is the specific holding in this case?
2. Chief Justice Burger in his dissent takes a position that the case involved an issue of statutory construction. What does he mean? Discuss.
3. In your opinion, does the holding in this case cripple the legitimate governmental interest in regulating the sale and possession of alcoholic beverages?

STOP AND FRISK—DETENTIONS

Terry v. *Ohio*
392 U.S. 1, 88 S.Ct. 1868, 20 L.Ed. 889 (1968)

SETTING: Detective McFadden of the Cleveland, Ohio Police Department observed three men who appeared to be "casing" a store. He had never seen the two men before and was unable to say precisely what first drew his attention to them. He had been a police officer for thirty-nine years, a detective for thirty-five, and had been assigned to patrol this area in question in plain clothes for thirty years for pickpockets and shoplifters. As he explained at the trial, he had developed routine observation habits for watching people. According to him the three men "didn't look right to me at the time."

He observed Terry and the other two men for about "10 to 12 minutes" in their activities of "casing the job for a stick-up." He then "considered it his duty as a police officer to investigate further." McFadden approached the three men, identified himself, and asked for their names. He also testified that he feared "they may have a gun."

PROCEDURAL PROBLEM: Upon receiving no answer to his question other than a few mumbled sounds, McFadden grabbed Terry, spun him around so he was facing the other two, and patted down the outside of his clothing. In the left breast pocket of Terry's overcoat, Officer McFadden felt what he thought was a pistol. He reached inside the overcoat but was unable to remove the gun. He ordered the three inside the store he thought they were "casing." He removed Terry's coat and found a .38-caliber pistol in the pocket. Officer McFadden proceeded to pat down the other two men and found a revolver on one and nothing on the third man.

McFadden later testified that he only patted the men down to see whether they had weapons and that he did not put his hands beneath the outer garments until he felt what appeared to be a weapon.

At a subsequent trial Terry was convicted of carrying a concealed weapon. The weapon and bullets taken from Terry were admitted in evidence over Terry's objection. His conviction was affirmed in the state courts, which held that it "would be stretching the facts beyond reasonable comprehension" to find that Officer McFadden had reasonable cause to arrest. But he did have reasonable cause to believe that Terry and the two men were conducting themselves suspiciously and some interrogation should be made of their actions. The state courts distinguished an investigatory stop and an arrest and a "frisk" or "patdown" from a full-blown search for evidence of a crime. The "frisk," the state courts held, was absolutely necessary for the proper performance of the officer's investigative function, for without it "the answer to a police officer may be a bullet, and a loaded pistol discovered during the frisk is admissible."

The United States Supreme Court affirmed Terry's conviction.

THE ISSUE: Did the seizure of the evidence as a result of the temporary detention and frisk violate the defendant's rights under the Fourth Amendment made applicable to the states by the Fourteenth?

THE ANSWER: No.

DISCUSSION: The Supreme Court in the case broke new constitutional ground—on less than probable cause to arrest, the police can constitutionally pat down a suspicious person who they believe presents a danger to themselves or others.

The point of departure involved the contention that a stop or temporary detention is distinguished from an arrest and a frisk is distinguishable from a search. The Court totally rejected this claim by holding that "it must be recognized that whenever a police officer accosts an individual and restrains his freedom to walk away, he has seized that person. And it is nothing less than sheer torture of the English language to suggest that a careful exploration of the outer surfaces of a person's clothing all over his or her body in an attempt to find weapons is not a 'search.' Moreover, it is simply fantastic to urge that such a procedure performed in public by a policeman while the citizen stands helpless, perhaps facing a wall with his hands raised, is a 'petty indignity.' It is a serious intrusion upon the sanctity of the person, which may inflict great indignity and arouse strong resentment, and it is not to be undertaken lightly."

The authority of the police is limited based on the Fourth Amendment's proscription against unreasonable searches and seizures. As a consequence the frisk or patdown is permissible where a police officer observes unusual conduct that leads him reasonably to conclude in light of his experience that criminal activities may be afoot and that the persons with whom he is dealing may be armed and presently dangerous. "[W]here in the cause of investigating this behavior he identifies himself as a policeman and makes reasonable inquiries, and where nothing in the initial stage of the encounter serves to dispel his reasonable fear for his own or others' safety, he is entitled for the protection of himself or others in the area to conduct a carefully limited search of the outer clothing of such persons in an attempt to discover weapons which might be used to assault him."

A question frequently arises whether seized evidence other than weapons is admissible. The Court did not decide this point, but Chief Justice Warren, writing for the majority, did say that the "exclusionary rule has its limitations, however, as a tool of judicial control." The exclusionary rule may be effective where obtaining convictions is an important objective of the police. However, "a stern refusal by this Court to condone such activity does not necessarily render it responsive to the exclusionary rule. Regardless of how effective the rule may be where obtaining convictions is an important objective of the police, it is powerless to deter invasions of constitutionally guaranteed rights where the police either have no interest in prosecuting or are willing to forego successful prosecution in the interest of serving some other goal." Warren went on and stated that when police misconduct is identified, it must be condemned by the judiciary and its fruits excluded from criminal trials. "And, of course, our approval of legitimate and restrained investigative conduct undertaken on the basis of ample factual justification should in no way discourage the employment of other remedies than the exclusionary rule to curtail abuses for which that sanction may prove inappropriate."

Is there a standard of reasonableness still imposed on an officer in reaching the decision to conduct the patdown search?

When an officer is justified in believing that the individual whose suspicious behavior he is investigating at close range is armed and presently dangerous to the officer or to others, it would appear to be clearly unreasonable to deny the officer the power to take necessary measures to determine whether the person in fact is carrying a weapon and to neutralize the threat of physical harm.

In making a decision, Warren emphasized that it is imperative that the "facts be judged against an objective standard: would the facts available to the officer at the moment of the seizure or search 'warrant a man of reasonable caution and belief' that the action taken was appropriate?" Anything less would invite intrusions on "inarticulate hunches." Warren also held that "good faith on the part of the arresting officer is not enough." According to him, "If subjective good faith alone were the test, the protection of the Fourth Amendment would evaporate and the people would be 'secure in their persons, houses, papers, and effects' only in the discretion of the police."

What other limitations does the Fourth Amendment place upon protective seizures and searches? The majority stated that *Terry* is not a terminal decision, but "limitations will have to be developed in the concrete factual circumstances of individual cases. . . . The sole justification for the search in the present situation is the protection of the police officer and others nearby, and it must therefore be confined in scope to an intrusion reasonably designed to discover guns, knives, clubs, or other hidden instruments for the assault of the police officer."

Justice Harlan in a concurring opinion "would make it perfectly clear that the right to frisk in this case depends upon the reasonableness of a forcible stop to investigate a suspected crime." However, the right to frisk must be "immediate and automatic if the reason for the stop is, as here, an articulable suspicion of a crime of violence." According to Harlan, the facts in this case are illustrative of a proper stop and an incidental frisk. Officer McFadden's justifiable suspicion offered a proper constitutional basis for accosting Terry, restraining his freedom of movement briefly, and asking him questions. Harlan maintained that once McFadden had reasons to invade Terry's privacy based on the circumstances, "the forced encounter was justified [and] the officer's right to take suitable measures for his own safety followed automatically."

Justice Douglas, the lone dissenter, insisted that a search and seizure can take place only if reasonable under the Fourth Amendment. Therefore he did not see how the majority held that a "stop and frisk" could be judged by less than constitutional standards. According to Douglas, the police have greater authority to conduct a search and seizure than a judge has when authorizing such action. He thought that by giving the police this excessive amount of power the Court took a step to authorize a totalitarian form of government. The choice, if it is taken, should be by the people by a constitutional amendment.

QUESTIONS

1. How did the majority answer the question that there is a distinction between a full search and a frisk and between a temporary stop and an arrest?
2. What is the scope of the frisk as set out by this case?
3. In determining whether or not there is reasonable cause to detain and frisk, what standard is used? Explain.

Sibron v. New York
392 U.S. 40, 88 S.Ct. 1889, 20 L.Ed. 2ᴰ 917 (1968)

SETTING: Officer Martin testified that while he was patrolling his beat in uniform on March 9, 1965, he observed Sibron "continually from the hours of 4:00 P.M. to 12:00 midnight . . . in the vicinity of 742 Broadway." He stated that during this period of time he saw Sibron in conversation with six or eight persons whom he (Patrolman Martin) knew from past experience to be narcotics addicts. The officer testified that he did not overhear any of these conversations and that he did not see anything pass between Sibron and any of the others. Late in the evening Sibron entered a restaurant. Patrolman Martin saw Sibron speak with three more known addicts inside the restaurant. Once again, nothing was overheard and nothing was seen to pass between Sibron and the addicts. Sibron sat down and ordered pie and coffee, and as he was eating, Patrolman Martin approached him and told him to come outside. Once outside, the officer said to Sibron, "You know what I am after." According to the officer, Sibron "mumbled something and reached into his pocket." Simultaneously, Patrolman Martin thrust his hand into the same pocket, discovering several glassine envelopes, which, it turned out, contained heroin.

PROCEDURAL PROBLEM: Sibron was convicted on the basis of the seized evidence. The New York appellate courts upheld the conviction. The United States Supreme Court reversed.

THE ISSUE: Was the search reasonable under the Fourth Amendment?

THE ANSWER: No.

DISCUSSION: Chief Justice Warren, speaking for the majority, said "It is clear that the heroin was inadmissible in evidence against [Sibron]." The mere act of talking with a number of known narcotics addicts over an eight-hour period of time gave no rise to probable cause of life or limb (*Terry v. Ohio,* 392 U.S. 1 (1968), *supra*) on the part of the officer, let alone as a justification for an arrest for committing a crime. As Warren noted, "Patrolman Martin was completely ignorant regarding the content of these conversations, and that he saw nothing pass between Sibron and the addicts. So far as he knew, they might indeed have been talking about the World Series." Nothing resembling probable cause existed until the envelopes of heroin were discovered. And they were not discovered incident to a lawful arrest.

The seizure of the heroin might still have been jusitfied because of a reasonable fear of Officer Martin that his life was in danger. However, Martin's testimony revealed no facts pointing to the apprehension, when Sibron put his hand in his pocket, that he was in fear that Sibron was going for a weapon. Martin's statement, "You know what I am after," made clear that he was looking for narcotics, not a weapon.

The Court assumed *arguendo* that if there were adequate grounds for believing that Sibron was armed, *Terry* restricted the frisk to a pat-down of the outer clothing. According to the Chief Justice, the search was not reasonably limited in scope to the accomplishment of the only goal which might conceivably have justified its inception—the protection of the officer by disarming a potentially dangerous man. Therefore, finding the narcotics was the result of an unreasonable search.

New York has a statute which authorized a stop and frisk (New York: *Code of Criminal Procedure,* section 180-2). The statute provides that

> *1. A police officer may stop any person abroad in a public place whom he reasonably suspects is committing a felony . . . and may demand of him his name, address, and an explanation of his actions.*
>
> *2. When a police officer has stopped a person for questioning pursuant to this section and reasonably suspects that he is in danger of life or limb, he may search such person for a dangerous weapon. If the police officer finds such a weapon or any other thing the possession of which may constitute a crime, he may take and keep it until the completion of the questioning, at which time he shall either return it, if lawfully possessed, or arrest such person.*

Chief Justice Warren found that it was unnecessary to decide whether this statute was or was not constitutional on its face. He stated,

"We decline . . . to be drawn into what we view as the abstract and unproductive exercise of laying the extraordinary elastic categories of the [New York statute] next to the categories of the Fourth Amendment in an effort to determine whether the two are in some sense compatible." The question on review, as the Court pointed out, is not whether the search and seizure was authorized by law but whether the search was reasonable under the Fourth Amendment.

Justice Harlan, in a concurring opinion, took the majority to task for not deciding on the facial constitutionality of the New York statute. Because New York had made an effort to comply with *Terry* v. *Ohio*, and on-the-street police work, he would have decided the facial constitutionality issue.

Mr. Justice Black, in dissenting, thought there was probable cause for Officer Martin to believe that when Sibron reached into his coat pocket, he had a dangerous weapon that might be used if not taken away. The majority, according to Black, "is hardly at this distance from the place and atmosphere of the trial in a position to overturn the trial and appellate courts on its own independent findings of an unspoken 'premise' of the officer's inner thoughts."

QUESTIONS

1. Distinguish the factual situation in this case from *Terry* v. *Ohio*.
2. What was the specific holding in this case?
3. What reasons did the Court give for indicating that Officer Martin lacked probable cause to arrest?

Adams v. *Williams*
407 U.S. 143, 92 S.Ct. 1921, 32 L.Ed. 2ᴰ 612 (1972)

SETTING: Sergeant Connolly was sitting alone in his patrol car early one morning in a high-crime area in Bridgeport, Connecticut. At about 2:15 A.M. a person Connolly knew came up to the patrol car and told him that a person seated in a nearby car was carrying narcotics and had a gun at his waist. Connolly called for assistance and then approached the car to investigate the informer's tip. Connolly tapped on the car window and asked Williams, the occupant, to open the door. Williams rolled down the window instead. Connolly reached into the car through the open window and removed a loaded revolver from Williams' waistband.

The gun was not visible from outside the car but was where the informant told Connolly it would be. Connolly then arrested Williams for illegal possession of the gun. After assistance arrived, a search incident to the arrest was conducted of the car. Substantial amounts of narcotics were found on Williams and in the car. In addition, a second revolver and a machete were found hidden in the automobile.

PROCEDURAL PROBLEM: Williams was convicted in Connecticut of unlawfully possessing a handgun and possession of heroin based on the seizure during the stop and frisk. The defendant objected to the introduction of the evidence as being unconstitutionally seized. He claimed that because of the absence of a more reliable informant or some corroboration of the tip, the actions of Sergeant Connolly were unreasonable. The United States Supreme Court affirmed the Connecticut conviction of Williams.

THE ISSUE: Did the officer have specific information to go on, even if not from his own personal observation, to frisk the defendant for weapons?

THE ANSWER: Yes.

DISCUSSION: *Terry* v. *Ohio*, 392 U.S. 1 (1968), *supra*, said that an officer must have something to go on prior to acting, but could the reason be something other than his own observation? As Justice Rehnquist wrote for the majority, "Applying [*Terry's*] principles to the present case we believe that Sergeant Connolly acted justifiably in responding to his informant's tip." Rehnquist stated while past decisions of the Court indicate that the informer's tip may have been insufficient for a narcotics arrest or search warrant, "the information carried enough indicia of reliability to justify the officer's forcible stop of Williams." The informer here was not an anonymous informer but was personally known to Sergeant Connolly. She had also provided him with information in the past. The information was immediately verifiable at the scene. In addition, under Connecticut law the informant might have been subject to immediate arrest for giving a false complaint, had Connolly's investigation revealed she gave incorrect information.

Did Sergeant Connolly have reason to fear for his safety in order to conduct the frisk as required by *Terry?* As Justice Rehnquist emphasized, "while properly investigating the activity of a person who was reported to be carrying narcotics and a concealed weapon and who was sitting alone in a car in a high crime area at 2:15 in the morning, Sergeant Connolly had ample reason to fear for his safety." The loaded gun was therefore admissible at Williams' trial.

Once the officer found the gun exactly where the informant said it would be, he had probable cause to arrest the defendant for illegal possession of the weapon, and the seizure of the narcotics was lawful as incident to the arrest.

The three dissenters wrote separate opinions, but all agreed with the decision of the Court of Appeals that *Terry* v. *Ohio* should not be applied to mere possessory offenses. Judge Frieraly for the Court of Appeals wrote that

> *Terry v. Ohio was intended to free a police officer from the rigidity of a rule that would prevent his doing anything to a man reasonably suspected of being about to commit a crime or having just committed a crime of violence, no matter how grave the problem or impelling the need for swift action, unless the officer had what a court would later determine to be probable cause for the arrest. It was meant for the serious cases of imminent danger or of harm recently perpetrated to persons or property, not the conventional ones of possessory offenses. If it is to be extended to the latter at all, this should be only where observation by the officer himself or well authenticated information shows "that criminal activity may be afoot." . . . I greatly fear that if the [contrary view] should be followed, Terry will have opened the sluicegate for serious and unintended erosion of the protection of the Fourth Amendment.*

QUESTIONS

1. Compare *Terry* v. *Ohio, supra,* with this case. What are the factual differences?
2. Do you agree with the analysis of Judge Frieraly, as quoted in the above dissenting statement?
3. What does the dissent mean when it states that mere "possessory offenses" should not be within the *Terry* doctrine? Why do you think that the dissent was concerned with this kind of offense in the content of the stop and frisk situation?

United States v. *Robinson*
414 U.S. 218, 94 S.Ct. 467, 38 L.Ed. 2ᴰ 427 (1973)

SETTING: On April 23, 1968, at approximately 11 P.M., Officer Jenks, a fifteen-year veteran of the District of Columbia Metropolitan Police Department, observed Robinson driving a 1965 Cadillac. Jenks, as a result of an investigation following a check of Robinson's operator's permit four days earlier, determined there was reason to believe that he was operating a motor vehicle after the revocation of his operator's permit.

Jenks signalled Robinson to stop the automobile, which he did, and all three of the occupants emerged from the car. At that point Jenks informed Robinson that he was under arrest for "operating after revoca-iton and obtaining a permit by misrepresentation." It was assumed by the majority of the Court of Appeals, and conceded by Robinson in his appeal to the United States Supreme Court, that Jenks had probable cause to arrest him, and that he effected a full-custody arrest.

PROCEDURAL PROBLEM: In accordance with procedures prescribed in police department instructions, Jenks then began to search Robinson. He explained at a subsequent hearing that he was "face to face" with Robinson and proceeded to pat him down. During this patdown, Jenks felt an object in the left breastpocket of the heavy coat Robinson was wearing, but testified that he could not tell what it was and also that he couldn't actually tell the size of it. Jenks then reached into the pocket and pulled out the object, which turned out to be a crumpled-up cigarette package. Jenks testified that at this point he still did not know what was in the package.

The officer then opened the cigarette pack and found fourteen gelatin capsules of white powder which he thought to be, and which later analysis proved to be, heroin. Jenks then continued his search of Robinson to completion, feeling around his waist and trouser legs, and examining the remaining pockets. The heroin seized from Robinson was admitted into evidence at the trial which resulted in his conviction in the district court. The Court of Appeals reversed. The United States Supreme Court reversed the Court of Appeals and upheld the district court.

THE ISSUE: Was the search of Robinson reasonable under the Fourth Amendment?

THE ANSWER: Yes.

DISCUSSION: Justice Rehnquist delivered the opinion of the Court. He first noted that there is a traditional exception to the warrant requirement of the Fourth Amendment and that the exception has historically been formulated into two distinct pronouncements. "The first is that a search may be made of the person of the arrestee by virtue of a lawful arrest. The second is that a search may be made of the area within the control of the arrestee."

In alluding to the decision by the Court of Appeals in which it was decided that even after an officer lawfully places a suspect under arrest for the purpose of taking him into custody, he may not ordinarily proceed to search the prisoner. He must instead conduct a limited frisk of the outer clothing and remove such weapons as he may, as a result of the frisk, reasonably believe the suspect has in his possession. In the type of crime for which Robinson was arrested there is no evidence or fruits of the crime to be searched for and the Court of Appeals held that the protective search had to be limited to the frisk.

The majority decided that the stop and frisk situation found in *Terry* v. *Ohio*, 392 U.S. 1 (1968), *supra*, afforded no basis to carry *Terry's* rationale over to a probable-cause arrest. In further disagreement within the holding of the Court of Appeals, Rehnquist emphasized that apart from the seizure of evidence, "the justification or reason for the authority to search incident to a lawful arrest rests quite as much on the need to disarm the subject in order to take him into custody as it does on the need to preserve evidence on his person for later use at trial."

The majority was reluctant to qualify the breadth of the search after there has been a lawful arrest. As Justice Rehnquist maintained:

> A police officer's determination as to how and where to search the person of a suspect whom he has arrested is necessarily a quick ad hoc judgment which the Fourth Amendment does not require to be broken down in each instance into an analysis of each step in the search. The authority to search the person incident to a lawful custodial arrest, while based upon the need to disarm and to discover evidence, does not depend on what a court may later decide was the probability in a particular arrest situation that weapons or evidence would in fact be found upon the person of the suspect. A custodial arrest of a suspect based on probable cause is a reasonable intrusion under the Fourth Amendment; that intrusion being lawful, a search incident to the arrest requires no additional justification. It is the fact of the lawful arrest which establishes the authority to search, and we hold that in the case of a lawful custodial arrest, a full search of the person is not only an exception to the warrant requirement of the Fourth Amendment, but is also a "reasonable" search under that Amendment.

Because the offense in this case for which the defendant was arrested involved taking him into custody and transporting him to the stationhouse for booking, the officer was required by department regulations to make a full-field search of Robinson's person incident to the arrest. A full-field search is a thorough search of the arrestee's clothing and person.

In another significant pronouncement, Justice Rehnquist stated that the United States Supreme Court should not be analyzing the search and seizure cases on a case-by-case basis. Justice Marshall, joined by Justices Douglas and Brennan in dissent, took strong issue with this position. Justice Marshall emphasized that certain fundamental principles have char-

acterized the Court's interpretation of the Fourth Amendment over the
years. He noted:

> And the intensive, at times painstaking, case-by-case analysis char-
> acteristic of our Fourth Amendment decisions bespeaks our "jealous re-
> gard for maintaining the integrity of individual rights." . . . The majority
> turns its back on these principles, holding that "the fact of the lawful
> arrest" always establishes the authority to conduct a full search of the
> arrestee's person, regardless of whether in a particular case "there was
> present one of the reasons supporting the authority for a search of the
> person incident to a lawful arrest." . . . The majority's approach repre-
> sents a clear and marked departure from our long tradition in case-by-
> case adjudication of the reasonableness of searches and seizures under
> the Fourth Amendment.
>   I continue to believe that "the scheme of the Fourth Amendment
> becomes meaningful only when it is assured that at some point the con-
> duct of those charged with enforcing the laws can be subjected to the
> more detached, neutral scrutiny of a judge who must evaluate the reason-
> ableness of a particular search or seizure in light of the particular circum-
> stances." . . .
>   The requirement that the police seek prior approval of a search
> from a judicial officer is, no doubt, subject to "a few specifically estab-
> lished and well-delineated exceptions." . . . But because an exception
> is invoked to justify a search without a warrant does not preclude further
> judicial inquiry into the reasonableness of that search. It is the role of the
> judiciary, not of police officers, to delimit the scope of exceptions to the
> warrant requirements. "The general requirement that a search warrant
> be obtained is not likely to be dispensed with, and 'the burden is on those
> seeking an exemption from the requirement to show the need for it. . . .'"

In concluding, Marshall stated that the search conducted by Officer
Jenks went far beyond what was reasonably necessary to protect him
from harm. Therefore it fell outside the scope of a properly drawn search
incidental to an arrest under the Fourth Amendment.

In a companion case decided the same day as *Robinson*, the Supreme
Court held that, contrary to the factual situation in *Robinson*, police department regulations requiring an officer to take the arrested person into
custody or to make a full body search were not required to justify a
complete in-custody search. "It is sufficient that the officer had probable
cause to arrest the [defendant] and that he lawfully effectuated the arrest
and placed the [defendant] in custody." *Gustafson* v. *Florida*, 414 U.S.
260, 94 S.Ct. 488, 38 L.Ed 2ᴰ 456 (1973).

QUESTIONS

1. What is the specific holding in this case?
2. Does this case overrule *Terry* v. *Ohio?* Discuss.

3. Does this case permit full-custody searches based on legal arrests for minor traffic misdemeanors? Discuss. (Justice Marshall and the dissenters are of this persuasion.)

CORRECTIVE MEASURES TO UNCONSTITUTIONALLY SEIZED EVIDENCE

Fahy v. Connecticut
375 U.S. 85, 84 S.Ct. 229, 11 L.Ed. 2ᴰ 171 (1963)

SETTING: In Norwalk, Connecticut, on February 1, 1960, two swastikas were painted with black paint on the steps and walls of a synagogue. This occurred between 4 and 5 A.M. At about 4:40 A.M., Officer Lindwall of the Norwalk Police Department observed an automobile being operated without lights about a block from the synagogue. Lindwall stopped the car and found Fahy driving and Arnold as a passenger. Responding to questioning, Fahy said he and Arnold were going home after having been to a diner for some coffee. Lindwall checked the car and found a can of black paint and paint brush under the front seat. Having no reason to do otherwise, the officer released them. He followed the car to Fahy's home.

Later the same morning Lindwall heard about the painting incident and went to Fahy's home, entered the garage under his home, and removed the paint and brush from Fahy's car—all without having applied for or obtaining a warrant. About two hours later, Lindwall returned to the Fahy home with two other Norwalk officers. They then arrested Fahy and Arnold pursuant to a valid arrest warrant.

PROCEDURAL PROBLEM: Fahy was tried and convicted of wilfully injuring a building in violation of Connecticut law. The trial itself took place prior to *Mapp* v. *Ohio*, 367 U.S. 643 (1961), *supra*. At the trial the can of black paint and brush were admitted into evidence over Fahy's objection that it had been obtained by means of an illegal search and seizure. The Connecticut Supreme Court agreed with the lower court on the admissibility of the evidence. It also held that the *Mapp* decision applied to cases pending on appeal in Connecticut courts at the time the decision was rendered and the trial court erred in admitting the evidence. But the state supreme court affirmed Fahy's conviction because admission of the unconstitutionally seized evidence was a harmless error. The United States Supreme Court disagreed and reversed and remanded.

THE ISSUE: Was the admission of the unconstitutionally obtained evidence prejudicial error and therefore not harmless necessitation a reversal of the defendant's conviction?

THE ANSWER: Yes.

DISCUSSION: In regard to the issue in this case we must ask if there was a reasonable possiblity that the evidence complained of might have contributed to the conviction. Obviously the tangible evidence of the paint and brush was incriminating and was used to corroborate the testimony of Officer Lindwall to place Fahy near the crime scene and to the presence of the articles in Fahy's car. The admission of the articles made Lindwall's testimony much more damaging than it would have been without it.

Chief Justice Warren, writing for a five-man majority (another 5–4 decision), rejected the harmless error grounds upon which the state courts relied for upholding the conviction. He stated, ". . . nor can we ignore the cumulative prejudicial effect of this evidence upon the conduct of the defense at trial. It was only after admission of the paint and brush and only after their subsequent use to corroborate other state's evidence and only after the introduction of the confession that the defendants took the stand, admitted their acts, and tried to establish that the nature of those acts was not within the scope of the felony statute under which the defendants had been charged. . . . We merely note this course of events as another indication of the prejudicial effect of the erroneously admitted evidence. From the foregoing it clearly appears that the erroneous admission of this illegally obtained evidence was prejudicial to [Fahy] and hence it cannot be called harmless error. Therefore, the conviction is reversed. . . ."

The four dissenters, Justices Harlan, Clark, Stewart, and White, maintained that the issue in this case was whether the Fourteenth Amendment prevents a state from applying its harmless error rule in a criminal trial with respect to the erroneous admission of evidence obtained through an unconstitutional search and seizure. Harlan, writing for the dissenters, would have held that it would not. "It is obvious that there is no necessary connection between the fact that evidence was unconstitutionally seized and the degree of harm caused by its admission. The question of harmless error turns not on the reasons for admissibility but on the effect of the evidence in the context of a particular case. . . . It may well be that a confession is never to be considered nonprejudicial. In any event the standard applied here required a determination that exclusion of the unconstitutional evidence could not have changed the outcome of the trial. That is a much stricter standard than that of independently sufficient evidence which leaves open the possibility that the trier of fact did rely on the unconstitutional evidence, and, therefore, would have reached a different conclusion if the evidence had been excluded."

QUESTIONS

1. What remedy did the Court say is available to defendant in this case? Is the remedy too strict? What is your opinion?
2. What is the main contention of the dissenters? Are they in disagreement with the remedy of the majority or the fact-finding process by which it is to be applied?
3. Did the officer have probable cause to arrest Fahy initially? Discuss.

Mapp v. *Ohio*
367 U.S. 643, 81 S.Ct. 1684, 6 L.Ed. 2ᴰ 1081 (1961)

SETTING: Several Cleveland, Ohio police officers received information that a person wanted for questioning in connection with a bombing was hiding in Miss Mapp's home. The information also alleged that a large amount of policy paraphernalia was hidden in that house. With this information, the police went to Mapp's home. She lived on the top floor of a two-family dwelling with her daughter. Upon their arrival, the officers knocked on the door and demanded entrance. After telephoning her attorney, Mapp refused. The officers then advised their headquarters of the situation and placed the house under surveillance.

About three hours later, the same three officers were joined by four additional officers and once again demanded entrance. When Mapp did not come to the door immediately, at least one of the several doors to the house was forcibly opened and the police entered. In the meantime, Mapp's attorney arrived but the officers who were illegally in the home would not permit him to see Mapp or enter the house. It appeared from the evidence that the officers broke into her home just as she was coming down the stairs from the upper floor to answer the front door. She demanded to see the search warrant, and a paper, claimed to be a warrant, was waved in front of her by one of the officers. She grabbed it and placed it in her bosom. The officers struggled with her to retrieve the paper and as a result she was handcuffed because of her "belligerent" acts resulting from their attempts to get back the "warrant." A policeman then grabbed her, "twisted [her] hand" and she "yelled [and] pleaded with him" because it was hurting.

PROCEDURAL PROBLEM: Mapp was then forcibly taken upstairs to her bedroom, where the officers searched a chest of drawers, dresser, closet, and some suitcases. They looked at a photograph album and personal papers belonging to Mapp. The remainder of the second floor, including the child's bedroom, was searched. The officers then searched the basement and a trunk found therein. During this search, obscene materials were seized which were subsequently used in her conviction of possession of "lewd and lascivious books, pictures and photographs" in violation of Ohio law.

At the trial no search warrant was produced, nor was evidence showing the reason for this failure. The defendant was convicted and the Ohio Supreme Court affirmed, although it noted that a reasonable argument could be made that the conviction would be reversed because of the methods used to obtain the evidence. However, the Ohio court found determinative the fact that the evidence had not been taken "by the use of brutal or offensive physical force against the defendant." The United States Supreme Court reversed.

THE ISSUE: In a prosecution in a state court for a state crime, does the Fourteenth Amendment forbid the admission of evidence obtained by an unreasonable search and seizure?

THE ANSWER: Yes.

DISCUSSION: The factual validity of *Wolf* v. *Colorado*, 338 U.S. 25 (1949), *supra*, was directly challenged and found wanting by the Supreme Court. Justice Clark, writing for the majority, stated that the

> *contrariety of views of the States on the adoption of the exclusionary rule of Weeks was "particularly impressive"; and, in this connection, that it could not "brush aside the experience of states which deem the incidence of such conduct by the police too slight to call for a deterrent remedy . . . by overriding the [states'] relevant rules of evidence". . . . While in 1949, prior to the Wolf case, almost two-thirds of the States were opposed to the use of the exclusionary rule, now despite the Wolf case, more than half of those since passing upon it, by their own legislative or judicial decisions, have wholly or partly adopted or adhered to the Weeks rule. . . . Significantly, among those now following the rule is California, which according to its highest court, was "compelled to reach that conclusion because other remedies have completely failed to secure compliance with the constitutional provisions. . . ." People v. Cahan 44 Cal. 2D 434, 445, 282 P 2D 905, 911 (1955). In connection with this California case,*

we note that the second basis elaborated in Wolf *in support of its failure to enforce the exclusionary doctrine against the states was that "other means of protection" have been afforded "the right to privacy." . . . The experience of California that such other remedies have been worthless and futile is buttressed by the experience of other states. The obvious futility of relegating the Fourth Amendment to the protection of other remedies has, moreover been recognized by this court since* Wolf. . . .

It, therefore, plainly appears that the factual considerations supporting the failure of the Wolf *Court to include the* Weeks *exclusionary rule when it recognized the enforceability of the right of privacy against the States in 1949, while not basically relevant to the constitutional consideration, could not in any analysis, now be deemed controlling.*

Justice Clark addressed the argument that the adoption of the exclusionary rule as a legal remedy fetters law enforcement. He stated that the argument could not be taken lightly and that there was in fact evidence to this effect that carries some weight. However, the argument was rejected, and Black noted, citing *Elkins* v. *United States,* 364 U.S. 206 (1960):

The federal courts themselves have operated under the exclusionary rule of Weeks *for almost half a century; yet it has not been suggested either that the Federal Bureau of Investigation has thereby been rendered ineffective, or that the administration of criminal justice in the federal courts has been disrupted. Moreover the experience of the states is impressive. . . . The movement towards the rule of exclusion has been halting but seemingly inexorable.*

"The ignoble shortcut to conviction," Clark continued, "left open to the State tends to destroy the entire system of constitutional restraints on which the liberties of the people rest." Once the Court has recognized the right of privacy embodied in the Fourth Amendment as being enforceable against the states by virtue of the Fourteenth, Clark emphasized that the right can no longer be permitted to be an empty promise. "Because it is enforceable in the same manner and to like effect as other basic rights secured by the Due Process Clause, we can no longer permit it to be revocable at the whim of any police officer who, in the name of law enforcement itself, chooses to suspend its enjoyment."

Justice Black, in a separate concurring opinion, was unpersuaded that the Fourth Amendment standing alone would be sufficient to bar introduction into evidence against an accused of papers and effects seized from him in violation of its dictates. In Black's opinion, the Fourth Amendment contains no specific provision precluding the use of such evidence. He did, however, say, "Reflection on the problem . . . in light of the cases coming before the Court since *Wolf,* has led me to conclude that when the Fourth Amendment ban against unreasonable searches and seizures is considered together with the Fifth Amendment's ban against compelled self-incrimination, a constitutional basis emerges which not only justifies but actually requires the exclusionary rule."

Three dissenters, Justices Harlan, Frankfurter, and Whittaker, were of the opinion that the majority had lost sight of the doctrine of judicial restraint and proper regard for the doctrine of *stare decisis*. Accordingly, the majority should have considered them before deciding whether a past decision of the Court should be overruled. They were of the opinion that the *Wolf* rule was much sounder constitutional doctrine than that announced by the majority.

QUESTIONS

1. What remedy did the court adopt in this case in relation to evidence secured in violation of the constitutional right of privacy under the Fourth Amendment? For what purpose was this remedy adopted?
2. What is the holding of this case regarding the applicability of the Fourth Amendment in state criminal trials?
3. What is meant by the doctrine of judicial restraint and *stare decisis*, considered so important to the dissenting justices?

Bivens v. Six Unknown Named Agents of the Federal Bureau of Narcotics
403 U.S. 388, 91 S.Ct. 1999, 29 L.Ed. 2ᴰ 619 (1971)

SETTING: On November 26, 1965, Bivens was arrested and his home searched by agents of the Federal Bureau of Narcotics, who, acting under a claim of federal authority, entered his apartment and arrested him for alleged narcotics violations. The agents manhandled Bivens in front of his wife and children and threatened to arrest the entire family. They also searched the apartment "from stem to stern." Thereafter, Bivens was taken to a federal courthouse, where he was interrogated, booked, and subjected to a visual strip search. The arrest and search violated the defendant's constitutional rights of privacy.

PROCEDURAL PROBLEM: Bivens brought suit in the federal district court claiming that the arrest and search were effected without a warrant, that unreasonable force was employed in making the arrest, and that the arrest was made without probable cause. He sought $15,000 damages because of the "great humiliation, embarrassment, and mental suffering" he experienced as a result of the agents' unlawful conduct. The district court dismissed the defendant's complaint on the ground he failed to state a cause of action. The federal Court of Appeals affirmed, and the United States Supreme Court reversed.

THE ISSUE: May a defendant have a cause of action for damages against the federal government for a Fourth Amendment violation by a federal agent acting under color of his authority?

THE ANSWER: Yes.

DISCUSSION: Twenty-five years before this case, the United States Supreme Court reversed the question brought up in this case—whether or not violation of the command of the Fourth Amendment by a federal agent acting under color of his authority gives rise to a cause of action for damages consequent upon his unconstitutional conduct. Justice Brennan, writing for the majority in 1971, held that it does. In so doing, he rejected the argument that the right asserted, the right of privacy, was a creation of state and not federal law. Therefore, if the defendant wished to obtain money damages to redress the invasion of this right, he could only do so by suing in tort under state law in state courts. Consequently, the tort action would be against the federal agents as private individuals if it was found that they violated the Fourth Amendment. According to Justice Brennan:

> We think that [the government's] thesis rests upon an unduly re-strictive view of the Fourth Amendment's protection against unreasonable searches and seizures by federal agents, a view that has consistently been rejected by this court.

Brennan made clear that the Fourth Amendment operates as a limitation upon the exercise of federal power regardless of whether the state in whose jurisdiction that power is exercised would prohibit or penalize the identical act if engaged in by a private citizen. He further noted that "the interests protected by state laws regulating trespass and invasions of privacy and those protected by the Fourth Amendment's guarantee . . . may be inconsistent or even hostile." But he emphasized that one who demands admission under a claim of federal authority stands in a position in which the invocation of federal power will "normally render futile any attempt to resist an unlawful entry or arrest by resort to the local police."

In regard to the awarding damages for injuries suffered at the hands of the unconstitutional acts of federal officials, Brennan stated that "the Fourth Amendment does not in so many words provide for its enforcement by an award of monetary damages. . . ." But it is likewise well settled that federal courts may make use of "any available remedy to make good the wrong done." As Justice Brennan maintained, there is "no explicit congressional declaration that persons injured by a federal officer's violation of the Fourth Amendment may not recover money damages from the agents, but must instead be remitted to another remedy, equally effective in the view of Congress. The question is merely whether [Bivens], if he can demonstrate an injury consequent upon the violation by federal agents of his Fourth Amendment rights, is entitled to redress his injury through a particular remedial mechanism normally available in the federal courts."

Justice Harlan's concurring opinion agreed that Bivens' interest was one that should be protected even though Congress had enacted no legislation specifically authorizing damages. He concluded, "Damages as a traditional form of compensation for invasion of a legally protected interest may be entirely appropriate even if no substantial deterrant effects on future official lawlessness might be thought to result. . . . I do not think a court of law—vested with the power to accord a remedy— should deny him his relief simply because he cannot show that future lawless conduct will thereby be deterred."

Chief Justice Burger, in a strong dissent, argued that the majority decision created a damage remedy not provided in the Constitution and not enacted by Congress. He stated, "We would more surely preserve the important values of the doctrine of the separation of powers . . . by recommending a solution to the Congress as the branch of government in which the Constitution has vested the legislative power." The Chief Justice also strongly criticized the Fourth Amendment exclusionary rule, but made it very clear that he was not recommending that it be abandoned until a viable alternative could be developed. He recommended against abandoning the rule because of the new problems that would likely arise, such as the damage done to the public interest "if law enforcement officials were suddenly to gain the impression, however erroneous, that all constitutional restraints on police had somehow been removed—that an open season on 'criminals' had been declared."

The Chief Justice favored an entirely different remedy, "but it is one that in my view is as much beyond judicial power as the step the Court takes today. Congress should develop an administrative or quasi-judicial remedy against the government itself to afford compensation and restitution for persons whose Fourth Amendment rights have been violated."

QUESTIONS

1. What are compensatory monetary damages? How is the amount established? In your opinion, will they even begin to deter police invasion of privacy? Discuss.
2. What kind of "administrative or quasi-judicial agency" is the Chief Justice talking about in his dissent? What is your opinion as to what enforcement sanctions it might have?
3. Describe the main argument of the government as to why the injured person should not be permitted to file a complaint against the federal government, but must go through the state tort law process. Why do you believe the government made this argument?

Wong Sun v. *United States*
371 U.S. 471, 83 S.Ct. 407, 9 L.Ed. 2ᴰ 441 (1963)

SETTING: The setting in this case can best be divided into three separate situations.

1. Hom Way had been under surveillance by federal narcotics agents for six weeks. He was arrested on June 4, 1959 at 2 A.M., and heroin was found in his possession. Hom Way, who was not an informant, stated after his arrest that he purchased an ounce of heroin from one "Blackie Toy," a laundry proprietor on Leavenworth Street.

2. At 6 A.M. on June 4, 1959, several federal agents went to 1733 Leavenworth Street to the laundry operated by James Toy (the record did not make clear that James Toy and "Blackie Toy" were the same person). Agent Wong knocked on the door, said he wanted his laundry, and was told by James Toy it was not ready. Wong then announced he was a federal agent, whereupon Toy slammed the door and ran down the hallway of the "Oye Laundry" to his living quarters in the rear. Wong and other federal agents broke open the door and followed Toy into a bedroom; Toy then reached into a drawer. Wong drew his weapon, pulled Toy's hand from the drawer, and arrested and handcuffed him. A search of the premises revealed no narcotics and nothing incriminating in the drawer.

One of the federal agents said to Toy that Hom Way had gotten his narcotics from Toy, to which Toy responded, "No, I haven't been selling any narcotics at all. However I do know somebody who has." In response to a question as to who that person was, Toy stated, "I know him only as Johnny. I don't know his last name." Toy then described "Johnny's" house, the street where he lived, and a bedroom where "Johnny kept about a piece" of heroin and where Toy and Johnny used some heroin the preceding night.

The agents then located "Johnny's" house, entered, and found Johnny Yee in the bedroom. After a discussion, Yee took some tubes of heroin from a bureau drawer and surrendered them to the police. Later, at the Bureau of Narcotics office, Yee said the heroin had been brought to him four days earlier by Toy and another Chinese known as "Sea Dog." Upon further questioning, "Sea Dog" was identified as Wong Sun, the defendant in this case.

3. Agent Wong and several other federal officers took Toy to Wong Sun's neighborhood, where Toy pointed out a multi-family dwelling as the place Wong Sun resided. Wong rang the doorbell and the defendant's wife answered the door. After Agent Wong had identified himself, she said that Wong Sun was sleeping. Then Wong and several agents climbed the stairs, entered Wong Sun's apartment, went to the bedroom, and brought Wong Sun out in handcuffs. A thorough search of the apartment was conducted, but no narcotics were found.

PROCEDURAL PROBLEM: Later in the day on June 4, 1959, Toy and Yee were arraigned before a United States Commissioner for violation of federal narcotics laws. Each was released on his own recognizance. On June 5, Wong Sun was arraigned on a similar complaint and released on his own recognizance. Subsequently, Agent Wong interrogated Toy, Yee, and Wong Sun separately. A statement by Toy was prepared on which Toy made some handwritten corrections. He then refused to sign it, wanting to know "if the other persons involved in the case had signed theirs." Wong Sun also refused to sign the statement, although he admitted its accuracy.

Hom Way refused to testify at Wong Sun's trial. Yee was offered as the chief government witness but was excused because he refused to testify by invoking the privilege against self-incrimination and he flatly repudiated the statement he had given to Agent Wong. That statement was not offered in evidence, nor was there any testimony elicited from Yee identifying Wong Sun as the source of heroin or otherwise tending to support the charges against Wong Sun.

Wong Sun was convicted of fraudulent and knowing transportation and concealment of illegally imported heroin. The United States Court of

Appeals affirmed, holding that as to Toy's arrest, there was "no showing . . . that the agent [Wong] knew Hom Way to be reliable," and further found that nothing in the circumstances occurring at Toy's premises provided sufficient justification for an arrest without a warrant. As to Wong Sun's arrest, the Court of Appeals said that there was no showing that Yee was a reliable informant. In short, both arrests were considered illegal because they were not based on probable cause. However, the Court of Appeals did hold that the four items of proof were not the "fruits" of the illegal arrests and were therefore properly admitted in evidence.

THE ISSUE: Is evidence that is inadmissible against a co-defendant, because it was unconstitutionally obtained, likewise inadmissible against another co-defendant where no right of privacy of the latter was invaded?

THE ANSWER: No.

DISCUSSION: Was there reasonable cause for Toy's arrest? The United States Supreme Court concluded that there was not, and also that the bedroom search which followed the uninvited entry was also unlawful. The Court was of the opinion that "The threshold question in this case, therefore, is whether the officers could, on the information which impelled them to act, have produced a warrant for Toy. We think no warrant would have been issued on the evidence then available."

Because of the holding that the initial search was illegal, Toy's declarations in his bedroom should have been excluded if they were the fruits of the agents' unlawful actions. The exclusionary rule prohibits the use of unconstitutional invasions of the victim's privacy. The exclusionary rule is used to bar physical evidence, papers and effects, and verbal statements illegally overheard. "Thus, verbal evidence which derives so immediately from an unlawful entry and an unauthorized arrest as the officers' action in the present case is no less the 'fruit' of official illegality than the more common tangible fruits of the unwarranted intrusion. . . . Either in terms of deterring lawless conduct by federal officers, . . . or of closing the doors of the federal courts to any use of evidence unconstitutionally obtained, . . . the danger in relaxing the exclusionary rules in the case of verbal evidence would seem too great to warrant introducing such a distinction."

In this case the government claimed that the statements of Toy to the officers in his bedroom were admissible because they resulted from "an intervening independent act of a free will," and although closely consequent upon the invasion of privacy, should not be excluded because of the unlawful activity of the agents. To this "free will" argument Justice Brennan stated, "This contention, however, takes insufficient account of the circumstances. Six or seven officers had broken the door and followed on Toy's heels into the bedroom where his wife and child were sleeping. He had been almost immediately handcuffed and arrested. Under such circumstances it is unreasonable to infer that Toy's response was sufficiently an act of free will to purge the primary taint of the unlawful invasion."

Brennan also rejected a government contention that Toy's statements were exculpatory rather than incriminating by noting that the statements soon after being made turned out to be incriminating to Toy. Secondly, "when circumstances are shown such as those which induced these declarations, it is immaterial whether the declarations be termed exculpatory."

The next issue the Court considered was whether or not the exclusion of Toy's declarations required the exclusion as evidence of the narcotics taken from Yee, to whom the statements of Toy had led. The government prosecutors admitted that the drugs would not have been found except for the statements of Toy. Justice Brennan, for the majority in holding that the narcotics were obtained as a result of the initial unconstitutional arrest, stated that "the more apt question in such a case is 'whether, granting establishment of the primary illegality, the evidence to which instant objection is made has been come at by exploitation of that illegality or instead by means sufficiently distinguishable to be purged of the primary taint.' . . . We think it clear that the narcotics were 'come at by the exploitation of that illegality' and hence that they may not be used against Toy."

However, the Court had another approach to the standing of Wong Sun to challenge the admission of the tainted evidence against him. The Court noted that the arrest of Wong Sun was without probable cause or reasonable grounds, but that the inadmissibility of the narcotics against Toy did not bar their admissibility against Wong Sun. The majority held that "The exclusion of the narcotics as to Toy was required solely by their tainted relationship to information unlawfully obtained from Toy, and not by any official impropriety connected with their surrender by Yee. The seizure of this heroin invaded no right of privacy of person or premises which would entitle Wong Sun to its use at his trial."

In a separate consideration the Court also held that Wong Sun's unsigned confession was not the fruit of his unlawful arrest and was therefore properly admissible at the trial. Wong Sun voluntarily returned after several days on release on his own recognizance, and made the unsigned statement. The Court held that the arrest and statement had "become so attenuated as to dissipate the taint."

(The Court set aside the conviction of Wong Sun on other grounds.)

QUESTIONS

1. What reason did the United States Supreme Court give for holding that the evidence illegally seized from Yee could nevertheless be admissible in evidence against Wong Sun?
2. Why did not the Court use the due process clause to exclude as evidence the illegally seized narcotics from Yee? Discuss the possible problems this approach might involve.
3. What did this case hold as it pertained to Wong Sun? Toy? Yee?

Frisbie v. Collins
342 U.S. 519, 72 S.Ct. 509, 96 L.Ed. 541 (1952)

SETTING: While the defendant was living in Chicago, Illinois, Michigan officers forcibly seized, handcuffed, and blackjacked him and took him back to Michigan where he stood trial, was convicted of murder, and sentenced to life in prison.

PROCEDURAL PROBLEM: Collins brought this habeas corpus case to the United States District Court to secure his release from a Michigan penitentiary where he was serving his sentence. His contention was that his trial and conviction were under such circumstances as to deprive him of his right to due process under the Fourteenth Amendment and the Federal Kidnapping Act, 47 Stat. 326, as amended, 18 U.S.C. 1201, 18 U.S.C.A. 1201.

The district court denied the writ without a hearing on the grounds that the court in Michigan had the power to try Collins regardless of how his presence was secured. The United States Court of Appeals remanded the case on the ground that the Federal Kidnapping Act changed prior law that a state could constitutionally try and convict a defendant after securing jurisdiction by force. The United States Supreme Court reversed the Court of Appeals and upheld the district court decision.

THE ISSUE: Is a court deprived of its power to try a person for a crime when the person has been brought within the court's jurisdiction by a forcible abduction?

THE ANSWER: No.

DISCUSSION: Justice Black for the majority stated that there are no persuasive reasons for departing from the *Ker* v. *Illinois*, 119 U.S. 436 (1880) rule that a court has the power to try a person for a crime notwithstanding that the person had been brought within the jurisdiction of the court by force. The reason for the rule is that due process of law is satisfied when he is given a fair trial in accordance with constitutional procedural due process and when he is present and has been fairly apprised of the charges against him. Black emphasized that "There is nothing in the Constitution that requires a court to permit a guilty person rightfully convicted to escape justice because he was brought to trial against his will."

Addressing the issue of whether or not the Federal Kidnapping Act prohibited the defendant's conviction, the Court stated that it assumed that the Michigan officers violated the Act based on the facts alleged. However, the Act itself provides seven penalties for kidnapping which include among others imprisonment for a term of years or for life. In specific circumstances death could have been imposed. As Justice Black concluded, "We think the Act cannot be fairly construed so as to add to the list of sanctions, a sanction barring a state from prosecuting persons wrongfully brought to it by its officers." The remedy for the illegal acts by the Michigan officers was prosection under the Act. In summary, the rationale of the Court of Appeals that permitting the state officers to violate the Act to bring Collins to trial "would in practical effect lend encouragement to the commission of criminal acts by those sworn to enforce the law," was rejected.

QUESTIONS

1. What remedy was available to the defendant in this case? Was there one?
2. What rationale did the United States Supreme Court give for upholding Collins' conviction? What, if any, action could be taken against the Michigan officers?
3. What is the *Ker* v. *Illinois* cited by the Court about? Research this case and discuss it in class.

United States v. Calandra
414 U.S. 338, 94 S.Ct. 613, 38 L.Ed. 2ᴰ 561 (1974)

SETTING: Federal agents obtained a warrant authorizing a search of Calandra's business. The warrant was issued in connection with an illegal gambling operation. Calandra's business, a machine and tool company, occupied a two-story building; the tool shop was on the first floor and general offices were on the second. The agents executed the search warrant and a four-hour search was conducted of Calandra's business premises. More than three hours were spent searching the defendant's offices and files.

The agents found no gambling paraphernalia, but one did discover a card indicating that a Dr. Loveland had been making periodic payments to Calandra. The agent remembered that Loveland had been the victim of a "loan-sharking" enterprise under investigation by the United States Attorney's office for Northern Ohio. The agent concluded that the card bearing Loveland's name was a record of loan-sharking payments and therefore had it seized along with other evidentiary items.

PROCEDURAL PROBLEM: A few months later a special grand jury was convened for the Northern District of Ohio to investigate possible loan-sharking activities in violation of federal law. Calandra was subpoenaed in order to answer questions based on the evidence seized during the search of his place of business. He appeared but refused to testify before the grand jury, invoking his Fifth Amendment privilege against self-incrimination. The government then requested that he be given transactional immunity pursuant to 18 U.S.C. 2514. Calandra then requested and was granted a hearing postponement so a motion could be prepared to suppress the evidence seized in the search.

The United States District Court granted Calandra's motion to suppress and ordered the evidence returned. The court also ordered that Calandra need not answer any of the grand jury's questions based on the suppressed evidence. The court held that due process "allows a witness to litigate the question of whether the evidence which constitutes the basis for the questions asked of him before the grand jury has been obtained in a way which violates the constitutional protection against unlawful search and seizure." The court found that the search warrant had been issued without probable cause and that the search exceeded the scope of the warrant.

The Court of Appeals affirmed. The United States Supreme Court reversed in a 6–3 decision.

THE ISSUE: May a witness who is summoned to appear and testify before a grand jury refuse to answer questions on the ground that they are based on evidence obtained from an illegal search and seizure?

THE ANSWER: No.

DISCUSSION: Justice Powell for the majority noted that the Court of Appeals held that the exclusionary rule of the Fourth Amendment limits the grand jury's power to compel a witness to answer questions based on evidence obtained from a prior unlawful search and seizure. As Powell noted, the rule is a judicially designed remedy "to safeguard Fourth Amendment rights generally through its deterrent effect, rather than a personal constitutional right of the party aggrieved." However, as the majority pointed out, its broad deterrent purpose has never been interpreted to *prevent the use of illegally seized evidence in all proceedings against all persons.* The majority emphasized that, as with any remedial device, "the application of the rule has been restricted to those areas where its remedial objectives are thought to be most efficaciously served." This balancing process, according to Powell, has been confined to invoking the exclusionary rule in situations in which the government seeks to use the evidence to incriminate the victim of the unlawful search.

In deciding whether or not to extend the exclusionary rule to grand jury proceedings, the Court weighed the potential injury to the historic role of the grand jury against the potential benefits of the rule as applied in this context. Based on this balancing of interests, the Court decided that the extension of the exclusionary rule to grand jury hearings would seriously impede its operations. As Justice Powell stated,

> *Because the grand jury does not finally adjudicate guilt or innocence, it has traditionally been allowed to pursue its investigative and accusatorial functions unimpeded by the evidentiary and procedural restrictions applicable to a criminal trial. Permitting witnesses to invoke the exclusionary rule before a grand jury would precipitate adjudication of issues hitherto reserved for the trial on the merits and would delay and disrupt grand jury proceedings. Suppression hearings would halt the orderly progress of an investigation and might necessitate extended litigation of issues only tangentially related to the grand jury's primary objective. The probable result would be "protracted interruption of grand jury proceedings," effectively transforming them into preliminary trials on the merits. In some cases the delay might be fatal to the enforcement of the criminal law.*
> *In sum, we believe that allowing a grand jury witness to invoke*

the exclusionary rule would unduly interfere with the effective and expeditious discharge of the grand jury's duties.

The defendant argued in the case that each and every question based on evidence obtained from an illegal search and seizure constituted a fresh and independent violation of his constitutional rights because the grand jury's questions invaded his privacy and somehow violated his Fourth Amendment right. The Court completely disagreed with this position and commented that ordinarily a witness has no right of privacy before the grand jury. "He may invoke his Fifth Amendment privilege against compulsory self-incrimination, but he may not decline to answer on the grounds that his responses might prove embarrassing or result in an unwelcome disclosure of his personal affairs." Powell went on and noted that the purpose of the Fourth Amendment is to prevent unreasonable governmental intrusion into a person's privacy of his home, papers, or effects. In this case the original search and seizure was wrong according to the majority, but

> *Grand jury questions based on evidence obtained thereby involve no independent governmental invasion of one's person, house, papers, or effects, but rather the usual abridgement of personal privacy common to all grand jury questioning. Questions based on illegally obtained evidence by a grand jury should be proscribed presents not a question of rights but of remedies.*

Justices Brennan, Douglas, and Marshall, the dissenters, were of the opinion that the majority completely downgraded the exclusionary rule to a simple determination of whether its application in a particular type of proceeding furthers deterrence of future police conduct. The dissenters contended that the exclusionary rule was an enforcement tool to give content and meaning to the guarantees of the Fourth Amendment, not the rule's possible deterrent effect.

QUESTIONS

1. What is the specific holding in this case?
2. Based on this holding, could you argue that the exclusionary rule is not applicable in other kinds of civil proceedings? Why?
3. What is the position of the dissenters? Do you believe that they have a strong argument to support their position? Discuss.

Chapter 3

Due Process:
The Fourteenth Amendment

Constitution of the United States, Fourteenth Amendment

. . . [N]or shall any State deprive any person of life, liberty, or property, without due process of law. . . .

Adamson v. *California*
332 U.S. 46, 67 S.Ct. 1672, 91 L.Ed. 1093 (1947)

SETTING: Adamson was convicted of first degree murder in California and sentenced to death. The procedural issues in the case arose under the California constitution and a state statute.

PROCEDURAL PROBLEM: The California constitution provides that "no person shall be twice put in jeopardy for the same offense; nor be compelled, in any criminal case, to be a witness against himself; . . . but in any criminal case, whether the defendant testifies or not, his failure to explain or to deny by his testimony any evidence or facts in the case against him may be commented upon by the court and by counsel, and may be considered by the court or the jury." The California penal code provides substantially the same. The defendant did not testify and the district attorney argued his case according to the California constitutional provision.

Also, according to another section of the California penal code, where the defendant pleads not guilty and answers that he has suffered a previous conviction, the charge of the previous conviction may not be read to the jury, nor alluded to in the trial. The defendant admitted that he had suffered prior convictions of burglary, robbery, and larceny. A problem arises when the defendant admits the prior conviction and then takes the witness stand in his own behalf to deny or explain away other evidence against him. The California law permits the introduction of prior felony convictions to impeach the credibility of the testifying witness. This forces an accused person who has a prior felony record to choose between the risk of having his prior offenses revealed to the jury or of having it draw harmful inferences from uncontradicted evidence that can only be denied or explained by the defendant.

THE ISSUE: Was the defendant deprived of due process by the California procedure?

THE ANSWER: No.

DISCUSSION: The defendant in this case urged upon the United States Supreme Court that the Fifth Amendment privilege against self-incrimination is a fundamental national privilege or immunity protected against state abridgment by the Fourteenth Amendment due process clause. Justice Reed, who wrote the majority opinion, assumed that the California procedure would infringe a defendant's privilege against self-incrimination under the Fifth Amendment if the trial were in a federal court under a similar law. However, Reed pointed out that such an assumption does not determine Adamson's rights under the Fourteenth Amendment. "It is settled law that the clause of the Fifth Amendment, protecting a person from being compelled to be a witness against himself, is not made effective by the Fourteenth Amendment as a protection against state action on the ground that freedom from testimonial compulsion is a right of national citizenship or because it is a personal privilege or immunity secured by the Federal Constitution as one of the rights of man that are listed in the Bill of Rights."

Reed reasoned that the Bill of Rights was adopted to protect the individual against the federal government, and its provisions are not applicable in the states. In citing authority for this position he quoted *Twining* v. *New Jersey*, 211 U.S. 78 (1908): "The privilege against self-incrimination may be withdrawn and the accused put upon the stand as a witness for the state." Also as interpreted by the Court in the *Slaughter-house Cases*, 16 Wall 36 (1873), the privileges and immunities of national citizenship only are protected from state intrusion. The privilege against self-incrimination in the Bill of Rights is not a federal privilege or immunity secured to citizens by the Constitution against state action, according to the *Twining* decision. This then leaves the state free to abridge, within the limits of the due process clause, the privileges and immunities flowing from state citizenship. This idea accords with the constitutional doctrine of federalism by leaving to the states the responsibility of dealing with the privileges and immunities of their citizens except those inherent in national citizenship. According to Justice Reed, this constitutional construction has become embedded in our federal system as preserving the balance between state and federal power.

The majority affirmed the conclusion of the *Twining* and *Palko* v. *Connecticut*, 302 U.S. 319 (1937) cases that protection against self-incrimination is not a privilege or immunity of national citizenship.

Adamson advanced a second argument that if the privilege against self-incrimination is not protected by the privileges and immunities of the Fourteenth Amendment, the privilege under the Fifth Amendment is inherent in the right to a fair trial, which is protected by the due process clause of the Fourteenth Amendment. In short, Adamson argued that the due process clause of the Fourteenth Amendment protects the Fifth Amendment guarantee in the states.

Justice Reed noted that the specific contention of Adamson was rejected by *Palko*. "Nothing has been called to our attention that either the framers of the Fourteenth Amendment or the states that adopted intended its due process clause to draw within its scope the earlier amendments to the Constitution. *Palko* held that such provisions of the Bill of Rights are 'implicit in the concept of ordered liberty' and nothing more." The Court stated that the Fourteenth Amendment's due process does not protect the defendant's freedom from giving compulsory testimony in a state proceeding according to the same standards applied in federal proceedings under the Fifth Amendment. Therefore the Court had to determine whether the California procedure violated the protection against state action that due process does grant to a defendant. According to the rule of due process, the state is forbidden to compel a person to testify with threats of torture, injury, or exhaustion. Also forbidden are any types of coercion to force a person to testify. Anglo-American legal tradition excuses defendants from compulsory testimony. This is a matter of policy and not a mandate of due process under the Fourteenth Amendment, according to the majority. Therefore, the Court concluded that it was not concerned with the constitutionality of compulsory testimony but rather the constitutionality of comment upon a failure to testify.

Generally, comment on the failure to testify, at the time of *Adamson*, was forbidden. California was one of the few states that sanctioned the practice. The California practice was limited in that it permitted comment on the failure of the defendant to explain or deny by his testimony evidence or facts against him. It did not require any presumption either of guilt or truth of any fact. It allowed only inferences by directing the jury's attention to specific evidence that the defendant could explain or deny. Reed held regarding the California practice that, "However sound may be the legislative conclusion that an accused should not be compelled in any criminal case to be a witness against himself, we see no reason why comment should not be made on such silence." As reasons for this conclusion, the opinion of the majority went on to state that it would only be natural for the prosecution to point out the strength of the evidence because it was not denied or explained. If the facts were beyond the knowledge of the defendant he could explain this and little, if any weight would be given to the failure to testify.

Adamson argued that there was unfairness and coercion in the California procedure because if he took the stand, his prior convictions could be used to impeach him as a witness and if he did not take the stand, he suffered by having adverse comment on his failure to do so. Therefore, he contended, the California statute permitting comment denied his due process. In answer to this claim the Court said:

> We are of the view, however, that a state may control such a situation in accordance with its own ideas of the most efficient administration of criminal justice. The purpose of due process is not to protect an accused against a proper conviction but against an unfair conviction. When evidence is before a jury that threatens conviction, it does not seem unfair to require him to choose between leaving the adverse evidence unexplained and subjecting himself to impeachment through disclosure of former crimes. Indeed, this is a dilemma with which any defendant may be faced. If facts, adverse to the defendant, are proven by the prosecution, there may be no way to explain them favorably to the accused except by a witness who may be vulnerable to impeachment on cross-examination. The defendant must then decide whether or not to use such a witness. The fact that the witness may also be the defendant makes the choice more difficult but a denial of due process does not emerge from the circumstances.
>
> There is no basis in the California law for appellant's objection on due process or other grounds that the statutory authorization to comment on the failure to explain or deny adverse testimony shifts the burden of proof or the duty to go forward with the evidence. Failure of the accused to testify is not an admission of the truth of the adverse evidence. Instructions told the jury that the burden of proof remained upon the state and the presumption of innocence with the accused. Comment on failure to deny proven facts does not in California tend to supply any missing element of proof of guilt. It only directs attention to the strength of the evidence for the prosecution or to the weakness of that for the defense. The Supreme Court of California called attention to the fact that the prose-

cutor's argument approached the borderline in a statement that might have been construed as asserting "that the jury should infer guilt solely from defendant's silence." That court felt that it was improbable the jury was misled into such an understanding of their power. We shall not interfere with such a conclusion.

Justice Frankfurter, in emphasizing the idea that the due process clause of the Fourteenth Amendment does not incorporate the entire Bill of Rights, stated:

> *A construction which gives to due process no independent function but turns it into a summary of the specific provision of the Bill of Rights would, as has been noted, tear up by the roots much of the fabric of the law in the several States, and would deprive the States of the opportunity for reforms in legal process designed for extending the area of freedom. It would assume that no other abuses would reveal themselves in the course of time than those which had become manifest in 1791. Such a view not only disregards the historic meaning of "due process." It leads inevitably to a warped construction of specific provisions of the Bill of Rights to bring within their scope conduct clearly condemned by due process but not easily fitting into the pigeonholes of the specific provisions. It seems pretty late in the day to suggest that a phrase so laden with historic meaning should be given an improvised content consisting of some but not all of the provisions of the first eight Amendments, selected on an undefined basis, improvisation of content for the provisions selected. . . .*
>
> *The relevant question is whether the criminal proceedings which resulted in conviction deprived the accused of due process of law to which the United States Constitution entitled him. Judicial review of that guaranty of the Fourteenth Amendment inescapably imposes upon this Court an exercise of judgment upon the whole course of the proceedings in order to ascertain whether they offend those canons of decency and fairness which express the notions of justice of English-speaking peoples even toward those charged with the most heinous offenses. These standards of justice are not authoritatively formulated anywhere as though they were prescriptions in a pharmacopoeia. But neither does the application of the Due Process Clause imply that judges are wholly at large. The judicial judgment in applying the Due Process Clause must move within the limit of accepted notions of justice and is not to be based on the idiosyncracies of a merely personal judgment. The fact that judges themselves may differ whether in a particular case a trial offends accepted notions of justice is not disproof that general rather than idiosyncratic standards are applied. An important safeguard against such merely individual judgment is an alert deference to the judgment of the State court under review.*

NOTE: *Adamson* was overruled in *Mallory* v. *Hogan*, 378 U.S. 1 (1964), *infra.* Its specific holding was overruled in *Griffin* v. *California*, 380 U.S. 609 (1965), *infra.*

QUESTIONS

1. Frankfurter states that the *Adamson* test for due process is not based upon the "idiosyncracies of a merely personal judgment." Is this correct? Whose moral judgments furnish the answer to issues in cases?

2. How specific are the various Amendments in the Bill of Rights? Do they provide specific guidelines in direct, legally understandable language? Does the wording of the various protections invite "judicial moralizing"?

3. Write a dissenting opinion for the *Adamson* case. What points should be emphasized?

Rochin v. California
342 U.S. 165, 72 S.Ct. 205, 96 L.Ed 183 (1952)

SETTING: The Los Angeles Sheriff's Department had information that Rochin was selling narcotics. Three deputy sheriffs went to Rochin's home, entered an open outside door, and then forced their way through the bedroom door where they found Rochin sitting on the side of the bed upon which his wife was lying. The deputies saw two capsules on a nightstand beside the bed. When Rochin was asked what they were, he grabbed the capsules and put them in his mouth. The deputies "jumped upon him" and attempted to extract the capsules but were unsuccessful. He was handcuffed and taken to a hospital where one of the officers directed a doctor to force an emetic solution into Rochin's stomach through a tube. Vomiting resulted and in the matter were two capsules found to contain morphine.

PROCEDURAL PROBLEM: Rochin was tried and convicted of possessing morphine and sentenced to sixty days' confinement. The chief evidence against him was the two capsules. The defendant objected to their introduction because of the means used to secure them. The California District Court of Appeals affirmed despite the finding that the officers were guilty of breaking into and entering Rochin's room "and were guilty of unlawfully assaulting, battering, torturing, and falsely imprisoning the defendant at the alleged hospital." The California Supreme Court denied defendant's petition for a rehearing.

The United States Supreme Court granted certiorari because of the question raised as to the limitations which the due process clause of the Fourteenth Amendment imposes on the conduct of state criminal proceedings.

THE ISSUE: Was the shocking manner in which the evidence was extracted from Rochin in violation of the due process clause of the Fourteenth Amendment?

THE ANSWER: Yes.

DISCUSSION: Justice Frankfurter, for the majority, noted that "The vague contours of the Due Process Clause do not leave judges at large. We may not draw on our merely personal and private notions and disregard the limits that bind judges in their judicial function. Even though the concept of due process of law is not final or fixed, these limits are derived from considerations that are fused in the whole nature of our judicial process. These are considerations deeply rooted in reason and in the compelling traditions of the legal profession. The Due Process Clause places upon this Court the duty of exercising a judgment within the narrow confines of judicial power in reviewing State convictions upon interest of society pushing in opposite directions."

According to Frankfurter's conception of due process, it is not a revival of natural law. He also rejected the idea that due process of law is stagnant or that judges apply a mechanicalistic formula to solve problems. If this were the case, then there would be no need for judges as independent agents established by Article III of the Constitution. Frankfurter stated:

> *To practice the requisite detachment and to achieve sufficient objectivity no doubt demands of judges the habit of self-discipline and self-criticism, incertitude that one's own views are incontestible and alert tolerance toward views not shared. But these are precisely the presuppositions of our judicial process. They are precisely the qualities society has a right to expect from those entrusted with ultimate judicial power.*

Due process is not capriciously applied but must be viewed with reason and judicial restraint. Due process, in Frankfurter's estimation, is based on "disinterested inquiry pursued in the spirit of science, on a balanced order of facts exactly and fairly stated, on the detached consideration of conflicting claims, on a judgment not ad hoc and episodic but duly mindful of reconciling the needs both of continuity and of change in a progressive society."

How do these due process considerations, then, apply to the facts in *Rochin?* "We are compelled to conclude that the proceedings by which this conviction was obtained do more than offend some fastidious squeamishness or private sentimentalism about combatting crime too energetically. This is conduct that shocks the conscience. . . . They are methods too close to the rack and screw to permit the constitutional differentiation."

The majority in *Rochin* did not define due process more precisely than to say that convictions cannot be brought about by methods that offend "a sense of justice." It would be an abdication of the Court's responsibility to hold that in order to convict a person the police cannot extract by force what is in his mind but can extract what is in his stomach.

Frankfurter rejected the dichotomy between "real evidence" and verbal evidence, saying to do so is to ignore the reasons for excluding coerced confessions.

> *Use of involuntary verbal confessions is constitutionally obnoxious not only because of their unreliability. They are inadmissible under the Due Process Clause even though statements in them may be independently established as true. Coerced confessions offend the communities' sense of fair play and decency. So here, to sanction the brutal conduct which naturally enough was condemned by the court whose judgment is before us, would be to afford brutality the cloak of law. Nothing would be more calculated to discredit law and thereby brutalize the temper of society.*

Justice Black, in a concurring opinion, would have based the decision on the Fifth Amendment privilege because a person is compelled to be a witness against himself not only when he is compelled to testify "but also when as here, incriminating evidence is forcibly taken from him by a contrivance of modern science." Black emphasized that he thought a specific guarantee of the Bill of Rights offered more protection of individual liberty than that which can be accorded under such a nebulous term as due process.

According to Black, due process affords no guidelines for choice between competing considerations. He asks how one may find the avenues of investigating which will help discover the canons of conduct as universally favored that this Court should write them into the Constitution. "All we are told is that the discovery must be made by an 'evaluation based on a disinterested inquiry pursued in the spirit of science, on a balanced order of facts.'"

Black also challenged the majority on the elusive character of the due process standard. He noted that other constitutional provisions do provide some guidance, such as the Fourth Amendment, which prohibits "unreasonable searches and seizures." "There is, however, no express constitutional language granting power to invalidate *every* state law of *every* kind deemed 'unreasonable' or contrary to the court's notion of civilized decencies. . . . I long ago concluded that the accordianlike qualities of this philosophy must inevitably imperil all the individual liberty safeguards specifically innumerated in the Bill of Rights."

Justice Douglas, in dissenting, was of the opinion that Rochin's conviction had to be reversed, because taking evidence from him in the manner involved in this case violated the Fifth Amendment privilege against self-incrimination.

QUESTIONS

1. What test of due process as a constitutional rule did *Rochin* develop?
2. What was Black's fear when he stated that the due process concept can lead to the invalidation of *every* state law of every kind deemed unreasonable by the Court?
3. Would you say that compelling a person to give a blood sample violates due process? fingerprinting? handwriting exemplars? trying on clothing for identification? speaking for voice identification? See *Schmerber* v. *California*, 384 U.S. 757 (1966), *infra*.

Griswold v. *Connecticut*
381 U.S. 479, 85 S.Ct. 1678, 14 L.Ed. 2ᴰ 510 (1965)

SETTING: Griswold was the director of the Planned Parenthood League of Connecticut, which furnished information, instructions, and medical advice to married couples as a means to prevent conception. Fees were charged but sometimes the services were gratis. The defendant was convicted as an accessory under the *General Statutes of Connecticut:*

Section 53-32
> *Any person who uses any drug, medicinal article or instrument for the purpose of preventing conception shall be fined not less than fifty dollars or imprisoned not less than sixty days nor more than one year or be both fined and imprisoned.*

Section 54-196
> *Any person who assists, abets, counsels, causes, hires, or commands another to commit any offense may be prosecuted and punished as if he were the principal offender.*

PROCEDURAL PROBLEM: The conviction of Griswold was affirmed by the Connecticut Appellate Court against the contention that the accessory statute as applied violated the Fourteenth Amendment.

THE ISSUE: Did the Connecticut anti–birth control statute violate the Fourteenth Amendment?

THE ANSWER: Yes.

DISCUSSION: The issue is broad and not very precise in this case because seven members of the Court agreed that the statute violated the Fourteenth Amendment but could not agree on why it did.

Justice Douglas argued that the right of privacy was violated by the Connecticut statute under various guarantees provided in the Constitution. The right of association contained in the First Amendment is one. The Third Amendment in its prohibition against quartering of soldiers "in any house" in time of peace without the owner's consent is another aspect of privacy. The Fourth Amendment explicitly recognizes the right of the people to be secure in their homes, papers and effects against unreasonable searches. The Fifth Amendment protects an individual from being compelled to give testimony against himself. And the Ninth Amendment provides that the rights provided in the Constitution "shall not be construed to deny or disparage others retained by the people."

According to Douglas, the case concerned a relationship lying within the zones of privacy created by several constitutional safeguards. It concerned a law that seeks to achieve goals by means of having the maximum impact on a relationship—it forbade the use of contraceptives rather than regulation of their manufacture or sale. "Such a law cannot stand in the light of the familiar principle, so often applied by this Court, that a 'governmental purpose to control or prevent activities constitutionally subject to state regulation may not be achieved by means which sweep unnecessarily broadly and thereby invade the area of protected freedoms.' Would we allow the police to search the sacred precincts of marital bedrooms for telltale signs of the use of contraceptives? The very idea is repulsive to the notions of privacy surrounding the marriage relationship."

Justice Harlan was unable to perceive the emanations of privacy from the various amendments ennumerated by Justice Douglas. In Harlan's view, the proper constitutional inquiry is whether or not the Connecticut statute infringes the due process clause of the Fourteenth Amendment because the enactment violates the basic values "implicit in the concept of ordered liberty. . . . While the relevant inquiry may be aided by resort to one or more of the provisions of the Bill of Rights, it is not dependent on them or any of its radiations. The Due Process Clause of the Fourteenth Amendment stands, in my opinion, on its own bottom."

Justices Goldberg, Brennan, and Chief Justice Warren agreed that the Connecticut birth control statute violated the Fourteenth Amendment but stressed the Ninth Amendment. According to them, the Ninth Amendment may be regarded by some as a recent discovery but it is a part of the Constitution which the justices are sworn to uphold. "To hold that a right so basic and fundamental and so deep-rooted in our society as the right of privacy in marriage may be infringed because that right is not guaranteed in so many words by the first eight amendments to the Constitution is to ignore the Ninth Amendment and give it no effect whatsoever." The same trio of justices discussed their philosophy of due process and its relationship to safeguarding personal liberties. In Justice Goldberg's words,

> In a long series of cases this court has held where fundamental personal liberties are involved they may not be abridged by the states simply on a showing that a regulatory statute has some rational relationship to the effectuation of a proper state purpose. "Where there is a significant encroachment upon a personal liberty, the State may prevail only upon showing a subordinating interest which is compelling." The law must be shown "necessary, and not merely rationally related to the accomplishment of a permissible state policy."
>
> Although the Connecticut birth control law obviously encroaches upon a fundamental personal liberty, the State does not show that the law serves any "subordinating [state] interest which is compelling" or that it is "necessary . . . to the accomplishment of a permissible state policy."
>
> In sum, I believe that the right of privacy in the marital relation is fundamental and basic—a personal right "retained by the people" within the meaning of the Ninth Amendment.

Justice White was of the opinion that the Connecticut statute violated the Fourteenth Amendment, but for a somewhat different reason. He pointed out that Connecticut showed no justification for attempting to interfere with the marital relationship. "There is no serious contention that Connecticut thinks the use of artificial or external methods of contraception immoral or untrue in itself, or that the anti-use statute is founded upon any policy of promoting population expansion. Rather, the statute is said to serve the State's policy against all forms of promiscuous or illicit sexual relationships, be they premarital or extramarital, concededly a permissible and legitimate legislative goal." He concluded, however, that the statute in no way strengthened a policy of preventing illicit relationships.

The dissent of Justices Black and Stewart saw the decision as returning the Supreme Court to the period in the 1920s and 1930s in which they allegedly sat as a super-legislature that determined the wisdom, need, and propriety of laws that touched the economic problems, business affairs, and social conditions. Also the "recent discovery" by Justice Goldberg that the Ninth Amendment as well as the Fourteenth Amendment could be used to strike down "all state legislation which this Court thinks violates the 'fundamental principles of justice,' or is contrary to the 'traditions and [collective] conscience of our people,'" did not impress Black or Stewart as a valid constitutional policy.

QUESTIONS

1. What is the specific holding of this case?
2. Justice Douglas' idea of what due process means is clear. What is it? What are the problems in applying it to specific factual situations?
3. The amendments Justice Douglas cites as authority for his holding have one concept in common. What is it? What does each of the following Amendments concern as it pertains to this case: First, Third, Fourth, Fifth, Ninth?

NOTE: The concept of due process is also discussed in two important jury cases *infra*, *Duncan* v. *Louisiana*, 391 U.S. 145 (1968), and *Williams* v. *Florida*, 399 U.S. 78 (1970). Before reading these cases, write answers to the following questions, then compare them with the holdings of the United States Supreme Court.

1. Why is a jury trial a fundamental right?
2. Discuss the checks against the government it provides.
3. How does the jury trial reflect community standards?

Chapter 4

Electronic Eavesdropping

Olmstead v. United States
277 U.S. 438, 48 S.Ct. 564, 72 L.Ed. 944 (1928)

SETTING: Olmstead was one of several defendants who were convicted in the Washington Federal District Court of conspiracy to violate
the National Prohibition Act by unlawfully possessing, transporting, im-
porting, and selling intoxicating liquors. The conspiracy involved large
numbers of people employed in the total operation, various seagoing
vessels, secret underground storage areas, a central office, and a staff to
carry out the marketing part of the illegal activity. In a poor month sales
amounted to over $175,000. Olmstead was the leading conspirator and
general manager of the business. Much of the business was transacted by
telephone.

PROCEDURAL PROBLEMS: Information that led to the discovery of
the conspiracy, its nature, and extent was largely obtained by four federal
prohibition agents who intercepted telephone messages of the various
conspirators. The method used to secure the messages was to install wire
on the telephone lines in the basement of the building where the headquarters were located and on lines leading to the residences of several
of the defendants. The taps were made without any physical trespass to
the property of any of the defendants. The conspiracy was revealed *in
toto* through the use of the wiretaps. The taps showed the extent of the

conspiracy, the *modus operandi*, participants, and the dealings of Olmstead, the chief conspirator, with members of the Seattle Police Department. Messages to the police showed how they found reasons to release various conspirators. They were additionally made direct promises of payments as soon as an opportunity was available.

THE ISSUE: Were the messages passed over the telephone wires within the protection of the Fourth Amendment's prohibition of unreasonable searches and seizures?

THE ANSWER: No.

DISCUSSION: In addressing the question, Chief Justice Taft dismissed the argument that the Fifth Amendment's privilege against self-incrimination applied. There was no compulsion to induce the defendants to talk over their many telephone lines. They were continually and voluntarily transacting business without knowledge of the interception.

Addressing himself to the Fourth Amendment prohibition against unreasonable searches and seizures, Taft said, "The Amendment itself shows that the search is to be of material things—the person, the house, his papers or his effects. The description of the warrant necessary to make the proceeding lawful is that it must specify the place to be searched and the person or *things* to be seized."

Taft also noted that the Amendment did not forbid what was done by the police in this case. There was no seizure of anything because the sense of hearing only secured the evidence.

Was there an illegal entry by the police? Taft, in discussing this point, stated: "There was no entry of the houses or offices of the defendants. The language of the Amendment cannot be extended and expanded to include telephone wires reaching to the whole world from the defendant's house or office. The intervening wires are not part of his house or office any more than the highways along which they are stretched."

The common-law rule is that the admissibility of evidence is not affected by the illegality of methods used to obtain it. The evidence secured by the federal agents violated a Washington statute which made it a misdemeanor to intercept telegraphic or telephonic messages. Taft pointed out "that his own general experience shows that much evidence has always been receivable although not obtained in conformity to the highest ethics. Evidence secured by such means has always been received." He also noted that a state statute cannot affect the rules of evidence applicable to United States Courts.

In concluding, the Chief Justice emphasized that "A standard which would forbid the reception of evidence if obtained by other than nice ethical conduct by government officials would make society suffer and give criminals greater immunity than has been known heretofore. In the absence of controlling legislation by Congress, those who realize the difficulties in bringing offenders to justice may well deem it wise that the exclusion should be confined to cases where rights under the Constitution would be violated by admitting it."

Justice Brandeis dissented. In his exhaustive opinion he made several significant points, which we will see found a more favorable reception in later years. He noted that the progress of science in furnishing governments with means of espionage is not likely to stop with wiretapping. "Ways may some day be developed by which the government, without removing papers from secret drawers, can reproduce them in court, and by which it will be enabled to expose to a jury the most intimate occurrences of the home. Advances in the psychic and related sciences may bring means of exploring unexpressed beliefs, thoughts and emotions. 'That places the liberty of every man in the hands of every petty officer' was said by James Otis of much lesser intrusions than these. To Lord Camden a far slighter intrusion seemed 'subversive of all the comforts of society.' Can it be that the Constitution affords no protection against such invasions of individual security?"

Brandeis saw no difference between protection of a sealed letter and a private telephone message (*Ex Parte Jackson*, 96 U.S. 727 [1877]). He thought that tampering with the privacy of the telephone was more of an evil than tampering with the mails because when a telephone line is tapped, the persons at both ends of the line are subjected to invasion even though the conversations between them are proper and confidential. "As a means of espionage, writs of assistance and general warrants are but puny instruments of tyranny and oppression when compared with wire tapping."

Brandeis emphasized that in his opinion the Constitution conferred as against the government, the right to be let alone. "To protect that right, every justifiable intrusion by the government upon the privacy of the individual, whatever the means employed, must be deemed a violation of the Fourth Amendment. And the use, as evidence in a criminal proceeding, of facts ascertained by such intrusion must be deemed a violation of the Fifth."

According to Justice Brandeis, the fact that the government agents violated the Washington law to tap Olmstead's phones was sufficient grounds to reverse the conviction. He noted:

> *Decency, security, and liberty alike demand that government officials shall be subjected to the same rules of conduct that are commands*

of the citizen. In a government of laws, existence of the government will be imperiled if it fails to observe the laws scrupulously. Our government is the potent, the omnipresent teacher. For good or for ill it teaches the whole people by its example. Crime is contagious. If the government becomes a law breaker, it breeds contempt for the law; it invites anarchy. To declare that in the administration of the criminal law the end justifies the means—to declare that the government may commit crimes in order to secure the conviction of the private criminal—would bring terrible retribution. Against that pernicious doctrine this court should resolutely set its face.

Justice Holmes agreed in substantially all of the Brandeis dissent but also added he was not fully prepared to "say that the penumbra of the Fourth and Fifth Amendments covers the defendants, although I fully agree that the courts are apt to err by sticking too closely to the words of the law where these words import a policy that goes beyond them." Holmes also agreed that a government should not be permitted to use evidence that it obtained by committing a criminal act, as was done in this case. "It is desirable that criminals should be detected, and to that end that all available evidence should be used. It is also desirable that the government itself should not foster and pay for other crimes, when they are the means by which the evidence is obtained. We have to choose, and for my part I think it is less an evil that some criminals should escape than that the government should play an ignoble part."

Holmes in his dissent emphasized that the judge should not be permitted to have a hand in encouraging the government to commit illegal acts by admitting evidence secured as a result of the illegality.

If the existing code does not permit district attorneys to have a hand in such dirty business, it does not permit the judge to allow such inequities to succeed. . . . [T]he reason for excluding evidence obtained by violation of the Constitution seems to me logically to lead to including evidence obtained by a crime of the officers of the law.

QUESTIONS

1. What reasons were given by the majority for holding that conversations were not within the scope of the Fourth Amendment's prohibition against unreasonable searches and seizures? Do you agree or disagree with the reasons? Explain.
2. The majority suggested a solution to protect the use of intercepted telephone conversations. What was it?
3. Justice Brandeis fears for the future in his dissent. Have his fears become a reality?

NOTE: After *Olmstead,* Congress enacted the Federal Communications Act of 1934. Section 605 read in part:

> *[N]o person not being authorized by the sender shall intercept any communication and divulge or publish the existence, contents, substance, purport, effect, or meaning of such intercepted communication to any person. . . .*

The question of whether or not this section covered wiretapping by federal, state, or private persons was answered in the affirmative by *Naradone* v. *United States,* 302 U.S. 379 (1937); 308 U.S. 338 (1939); and *Benanti* v. *United States,* 355 U.S. 96 (1957). It was also held in *Weiss* v. *United States,* 308 U.S. 321 (1939) that the statute covered intra- as well as interstate communications.

In 1968, Section 605 was amended by Title III of the Crime Control Act of 1968, which permitted court-approved wiretapping and electronic eavesdropping by federal and state officers for a number of enumerated crimes. Pertinent parts of Title III are set out at the end of this chapter.

Goldman v. *United States*
316 U.S. 129, 62 S.Ct. 993, 86 L.Ed. 1322 (1942)

SETTING: Goldman and others were convicted of violating the federal Bankruptcy Act. In order to discover evidence of illegal negotiations, two federal agents entered one of the defendant's offices and one adjoining it and installed in a small aperture in the partition wall a listening apparatus with a wire to be attached to earphones extending into the adjoining office. This was accomplished for the purpose of overhearing a meeting between the defendants and an innocent informant. The next afternoon, when the meeting was to take place, one of the agents, two other persons, and a stenographer entered the adjoining room. They connected the earphones to the apparatus and found it did not work.

PROCEDURAL PROBLEM: They had placed another device against the partition wall that picked up the sounds in the adjoining office. With this the agents overheard the conversations and the stenographer recorded them.

Goldman was indicted and before trial, after learning about the eavesdropping, his attorney made a motion to suppress the evidence obtained. At the trial the evidence was admitted over the defendant's objection that its receipt in evidence violated the Fourth Amendment.

THE ISSUE: Was the use of the detectaphone without a physical intrusion to overhear the conversation a violation of the Fourth Amendment?

THE ANSWER: No.

DISCUSSION: The defendant claimed that the discovery of the trespass committed in his office, as well as the facts learned as a result of that trespass, aided in the subsequent discovery of the detectaphone in the adjoining office; and that these discoveries were a violation of the Fourth Amendment. The United States Supreme Court noted that

> *Whatever trespass was committed was connected with the installation of the listening apparatus. As respects it, the trespass might be said to be continuing and, if the apparatus had been used it might, with reason be claimed that the continuing trespass was the concomitant of its use. On the other hand, the relation between the trespass and the use of the detectaphone was that of antecedent and consequent. Both courts below have found that the trespass did not aid materially in the use of the detectaphone. Since we accept these concurrent findings, we need not consider a contention based on a denial of their merits.*
> *We hold that the use of the detectaphone by Government agents was not a violation of the Fourth Amendment.*

The defendant argued that there was an invasion of his privacy when he walked in his own office and fully intended that his conversation be confined within the room. He contended that he should not assume a risk of someone using a delicate sound detector and amplifier to overhear and record his conversations.

In rejecting this position, Justice Roberts for the majority said, "We think, however, the distinction is too nice for practical application of the constitutional guarantee and no reasonable or logical distinction can be drawn between what federal agents did in the present case and the state officers did in the *Olmstead* case."

The fact that the detectaphone also picked up telephone conversations led the defendant to argue that a communication falls within the protection of Section 605 of the Federal Communications Act once a speaker has uttered words with the intent that they constitute a transmission of a telephone conversation. The Court in rejecting this claim concluded that "What is protected is the message itself throughout the course of its transmission by the instrumentality or agency of transmission.

Words spoken in a room in the presence of another into a telephone receiver do not constitute a communication by wire within the meaning of the section. . . . The listening in the next room to the words . . . as he talked into the telephone receiver was no more the interception of a wire communication, within the meaning of the act, than would have been the overhearing of the conversation by one sitting in the same room."

QUESTIONS

1. Formulate and present a dissent to this majority opinion.
2. What is the specific holding of this opinion?
3. Distinguish the facts in this case as they pertain to overhearing telephone conversations by the use of the detectaphone from the interception and revealing of telephone conversations in Section 605.

Silverman v. United States
365 U.S. 505, 81 S.Ct. 679, 5 L.Ed. 2ᴰ 734 (1961)

SETTING: Silverman was convicted in a federal court of three counts of gambling. The Washington, D.C. police secured permission of the owner of an adjoining rowhouse in Washington to use the house as an observation post. From this house for a period of three consecutive days, the officers employed a so-called "spike mike" to listen to what was going on inside the house next door as related to the suspected gambling operations.

The "spike mike" was a microphone with a spike about a foot long attached to it, together with an amplifier, power pack, and earphones. The officers inserted the spike under a baseboard in a second-floor room in the vacant house and into a crevice extending several inches into the party wall until it hit something solid which then acted as a good sounding board. The hard object was a heating duct serving the defendant's home. Conversations on both floors could be easily heard through the earphones.

PROCEDURAL PROBLEM: At the trial the officers who overheard the conversations offered testimony regarding their content. Over the defendant's objection, the evidence was admitted and played a substantial part in Silverman's conviction. The federal Court of Appeals upheld the admission of the testimony, holding that the use of the "spike mike" did not violate the defendant's Fourth Amendment rights. The Court of Appeals relied largely on *Goldman* v. *United States,* 316 U.S. 129 (1942), *supra,* and *On Lee* v. *United States,* 343 U.S. 747 (1952), *infra.* The United States Supreme Court reversed.

THE ISSUE: Does the physical intrusion of a "spike mike" into a suspect's party wall from an adjoining home, making use of a sound-conducting heating duct, for the purpose of securing incriminating evidence, violate the suspect's Fourth Amendment rights?

THE ANSWER: Yes.

DISCUSSION: Speaking for the Court, Justice Stewart distinguished this case from *Goldman* v. *United States* because in *Goldman* there was no physical invasion of the premises:

> *Here, by contrast, the officers overheard the petitioner's conversa-*
> *tions only by usurping part of the petitioner's home or office—a heating*
> *system which was an integral part of the premises occupied by the peti-*
> *tioners, a usurpation that was effected without their knowledge and with-*
> *out their consent. In these circumstances we need not pause to consider*
> *whether or not there was a technical trespass under the local property*
> *law relating to party walls. Inherent Fourth Amendment rights are not*
> *inevitably measurable in terms of ancient niceties of tort or real property*
> *law.*

The Court concluded that its decision does not turn on the technicality of a trespass reflected in local law. "This Court," wrote Justice Stewart, "has never held that a federal officer may without a warrant and without consent physically enter into a man's office or home, there secretly observe or listen, and relate at the man's subsequent criminal trial what was seen or heard."

The claim was made that the use of the "spike mike" violated Section 605 of the Federal Communications Act because of the antenna used to overhear the conversations. Stewart, in rejecting the contention, stated that "While it is true that much of what the officers heard consisted of the [defendant's] share of telephone conversations, we cannot say that the officers intercepted these conversations within the meaning of the statute."

Justice Douglas, concurring, indicated that the decision should not be based on the kind of electronic equipment that was used. He indicated that the Court should be concerned about whether the person's privacy was violated, not about "nice distinctions" about the methods used to violate it.

QUESTIONS

1. Did *Silverman* overrule *Goldman?*
2. Note the distinctions between *Silverman* and *Goldman.*
3. Prepare an opinion upholding the use of the "spike mike" used in the *Silverman* case.

On Lee v. United States
343 U.S. 747, 72 S.Ct. 967, 96 L.Ed. 1270 (1952)

SETTING: On Lee operated a laundry in Hoboken, New Jersey. There were three major parts in the laundry: a customers' room opening to the street, a rear adjoining room for ironing, and living quarters behind the ironing room. On Lee was suspected of selling opium. Chin Poy, a friend and former employee of On Lee, and also "an undercover agent," entered the laundry and engaged On Lee in a conversation during which On Lee made some incriminating statements. On Lee did not know that Chin Poy was wired for sound with a small microphone in his pocket and an antenna running down his arm. Agent Lee, from the Bureau of Narcotics, was stationed outside the laundry with a receiving set. Through the front window Chin Poy could be seen and through the receiving set his conversation in Chinese with On Lee could be heard by Agent Lee. A few days later on a New York sidewalk, another conversation took place between Chin Poy and On Lee and Agent Lee again awaited the damaging admissions.

On Lee was convicted subsequently on a two-count federal indictment of selling and conspiring to sell opium. The Court of Appeals affirmed. On certiorari, the United States Supreme Court also affirmed.

PROCEDURAL PROBLEM: Chin Poy did not testify regarding On Lee's incriminating statements. However, Agent Lee, over the defendant's objection, was permitted to relate the conversations as heard with the aid of his receiving set. The defendant argued that the overheard evidence should have been excluded because the manner in which it was obtained violated Section 605 of the Federal Communications Act and the search and seizure provision of the Fourth Amendment.

THE ISSUES: (1) Did the seizure of the overheard conversation violate the search and seizure provision of the Fourth Amendment? (2) Did the seizure of the evidence violate Section 605?

THE ANSWERS: (1) No. (2) No.

DISCUSSION: Justice Jackson for the majority held that the conduct of Chin Poy did not amount to an unreasonable search and seizure as set forth by the Fourth Amendment. In referring to *Goldman* v. *United States* 316 U.S. 129 (1942), the Court noted that there was no physical trespass. Chin Poy entered the place of business with consent, by the implied invitation of On Lee. Jackson dismissed the argument that Chin Poy became a trespasser by his subsequent "unlawful conduct" by noting that previous Court decisions prevented the Court from resorting to "a fiction whose origin, history, and purpose do not justify its application where the right of the government to make use of evidence is involved."

Justice Jackson and the majority had a difficult time in ascertaining the Fourth Amendment issue.

> *[Defendant] was talking confidentially and discreetly with one he trusted, and he was overheard. This was due to aid from a transmitter and receiver, to be sure, but with the same effect as if Agent Lee had been eavesdropping outside an open window. The use of bifocals, fieldglasses, or the telescope to magnify the object of a witness's vision is a forbidden search or seizure, even if they focus without his knowledge or consent upon what one supposes to be private indiscretions. It would be dubious service to the genuine liberties protected by the Fourth Amendment to make them bedfellows with spurious liberties improvised by far-fetched analogies which would liken eavesdropping on a conversation, with the connivance of one of the parties, to an unreasonable search and seizure. We find no violation of the Fourth Amendment here.*

The majority additionally found there was no violation of Section 605 because "There was no interference with any communications facility which he possessed or was entitled to use. He was not sending messages to anybody or using a system of communications within the Act."

A final argument that the evidence should be excluded as a means of disciplining law enforcement officers was rejected. "The trend of the law in recent years," according to Jackson, "has been to turn away from rigid rules of incompetence in favor of admitting testimony and allowing the trier of fact to judge the weight to be given to it."

In concluding, Jackson emphasized that "the use of informers, accessories, accomplices, false friends, or any of the other betrayals which are dirty business may raise serious questions of credibility. To the extent they do, a defendant is entitled to broad latitude to probe credibility by cross-examination and to have the issues submitted to the jury with careful instructions. But to the extent that the argument for exclusion departs from such orthodox evidentiary canons as relevancy and credibility, it rests solely on the proposition that the government shall be arbitrarily penalized for the low morals of its informers. However unwilling we as individuals may be to approve conduct such as that of Chin Poy, such disapproval must not be thought to justify a social policy of the magnitude necessary to arbitrarily exclude otherwise relevant evidence. We think the administration of justice is better served if strategems such as we have here are regarded as raising, not questions of law, but issues of credibility. We cannot say that testimony such as this shall, as a matter of law, be refused all hearing."

QUESTIONS

1. If conversations are protected from unreasonable searches and seizures by the Fourth Amendment, why does it make any difference that they may have been seized by overhearing on a person-to-person basis or by the assistance of an electronic device?

2. What is the importance of the fact that Chin Poy and On Lee were friends? Is it the *sub rosa* police practices that police use that the court is concerned about rather than the surreptitious recording device used?

3. Discuss the distinctions between *On Lee* and *Goldman* v. *United States*, and *On Lee* and *Silverman* v. *United States*.

Lopez v. *United States*
373 U.S. 427, 83 S.Ct. 1381, 10 L.Ed. 2ᴰ 462 (1963)

SETTING: Davis was investigating possible evasion of excise taxes. On the afternoon of August 31, he went to Clauson's Inn in North Falmouth, Massachusetts, where he for the first time engaged Lopez in a conversation and asked if there was dancing in the inn. Lopez denied that there was and denied responsibility for placing an advertisement indicating that there was dancing. Davis left and noted in a report to his office that the inn was a "potential delinquent."

Davis returned to the inn October 21, observed dancing, and told Lopez that he thought that the inn might be liable for a cabaret tax. Lopez asked Davis to drop the matter and said, "You can drop the matter. Here's $200. Buy your wife a present. And I'll have more money for you at Christmas time. This is all I have now."

Davis reported the meeting to fellow agents and turned over to the regional inspector $420 which Lopez had given him. On October 24, Davis met with four other Internal Revenue Service inspectors who instructed him to keep an appointment with Lopez and to draw the conversation back to the October 21 meeting. Davis was equipped with two electronic devices, a pocket battery-operated transmitter, which did not work, and a pocket wire recorder which he used to record a conversation with Lopez later in the day in the private office of Lopez. The recorded conversation involved a repeat of the bribery attempts on October 21. Davis also testified at the trial.

PROCEDURAL PROBLEM: At a subsequent trial of Lopez on a bribery charge, the secret electronic recording of the conversation was admitted into evidence over defendant's objection that it had been obtained in violation of his rights under the Fourth Amendment.

THE ISSUE: Was the wire recording of the conversation between Davis and Lopez secured as a result of an unreasonable search and seizure under the Fourth Amendment and therefore inadmissible against the defendant?

THE ANSWER: No.

DISCUSSION: In a 6–3 decision the United States Supreme Court failed to take the opportunity to overrule *On Lee* v. *United States,* 343 U.S. 747 (1952). The Court held specifically that the recording of the conversation in the private office of the defendant by an Internal Revenue agent was admissible in a bribery trial at which the agent also testified.

Justice Harland for the majority concluded that "this case involves no 'eavesdropping' whatever in any proper sense of that term." He emphasized that the government did not use an electronic device to listen to conversations that it could not have heard in the first place. "Instead the device was used only to obtain the most reliable evidence possible of a conversation in which the Government's own agent was a participant and which that agent was fully entitled to disclose. And the device was not planted by means of an unlawful physical invasion of [defendant's] premises under circumstances that would violate the Fourth Amendment. It was carried out by an agent who was there with [defendant's] assent, and it neither saw nor heard more than the agent himself."

The Court additionally held that because Davis was in the defendant's private office with the consent of Lopez, he did not violate the privacy of the office by seizing something surreptitiously without defendant's knowledge. The only evidence Davis obtained consisted of statements made by Lopez to Davis, statements which Lopez well knew could be used against him by Davis. Harlan then stated, "We decline to hold that whenever an offer of a bribe is made in private, and the offeree does not intend to accept, that offer is a constitutionally protected communication."

Chief Justice Warren concurred with the result of the majority but was of the belief that *On Lee* was incorrectly decided and should not be given new life and authority by the Court.

The three dissenters, Justices Brennan, Douglas, and Goldberg, shared Warren's view. They were, however, especially concerned that permitting one party to a conversation to record it and then turn it over to law enforcement officers to be used as competent evidence in court would severely restrain all private, free, and spontaneous communications. As they noted, "In a free society, people ought not to have to watch their every word so carefully."

QUESTIONS

1. Distinguish *On Lee* from *Lopez*. Are they in fact readily distinguishable?
2. Are the fears of the three dissenters real or imaginary? Is their fear more of police recording conversations of a private nature rather than private citizens recording such conversations for use in court?
3. Explain the majority comment that this case involves no "eavesdropping." Was the practice used in *On Lee* more offensive than that used in *Lopez*? Could this be a reason for not overruling *On Lee*?

Berger v. New York
388 U.S. 41, 87 S.Ct. 1873, 18 L.Ed. 2ᴰ 1040 (1967)

SETTING: Under New York state law, state supreme court justices were permitted to order installation of recording devices upon "oath or affirmation of a district attorney or of the attorney general or of an officer above the rank of sergeant of any police department of the state or any political subdivision thereof." The oath must furnish a reasonable basis that evidence of a crime could be obtained by the recording device.

The statute also indicated that the court order must specify the duration of the eavesdrop, which could not exceed two months unless otherwise extended by the judge or justice who signed and issued the original order after satisfying himself that such an extention or renewal was in the public interest.

In a bribery investigation, an order from a justice of the New York Supreme Court permitted the installation of a recorder device in one Neyer's office for a period of sixty days. Based on a lead developed from the first installation of the eavesdrop, a second order was secured permitting an installation of a similar device in the office of Steinman. After about two weeks of eavesdropping, a conspiracy was uncovered involving the issuance of liquor licenses.

Berger was indicted as a "go-between" for the principal conspirators, although he was not named in the indictment.

PROCEDURAL PROBLEM: At Berger's trial, relevant parts of the recordings were received in evidence and played to the jury, all over defendant's objection. The parties stipulated that the district attorney had no information except the eavesdrop evidence upon which to present the case to the grand jury or to prosecute the defendant. The evidence was admitted and the New York statute upheld in the trial court. On certiorari the United States Supreme Court reversed.

THE ISSUE: Was the New York eavesdropping statute authorizing wiretaps and bugs fatally defective by Fourth Amendment standards?

THE ANSWER: Yes.

DISCUSSION: In a 5–4 decision, the Supreme Court held that the statute violated the Fourth and Fourteenth Amendments by its blanket grant of permission to eavesdrop and tap without adequate judicial supervision or protective procedures. Justice Clark, who wrote the majority opinion, emphasized that under the statute a belief that a particular offense was being or had been committed was not a prerequisite to the issuance of an eavesdropping order. Clark stated, "We have concluded that the language of the New York statute is too broad in its sweep resulting in a trespassory intrusion into a constitutionally protected area and is therefore violative of the Fourth and Fourteenth Amendments."

According to the majority, the first defect in the statute was that the New York statute lacked particularity:

> *The Fourth Amendment commands that a warrant issue not only upon probable cause supported by oath or affirmation, but also "particu-*

*larly describing the place to be searched and the things to be seized."
New York's statute lacks this particularization. It merely says that a
warrant may issue on reasonable grounds to believe that evidence of
crime may be obtained by the eavesdrop. It lays down no requirement
for particularity. . . . Indeed it authorizes the "indiscriminate use" of
electronic devices. . . .*

The second defect, according to Clark, was that the statute, in
permitting eavesdropping for a two-month period, was the equivalent of
a series of intrusions, searches, and seizures pursuant to a single showing
of probable cause. As Clark noted, "Prompt execution is also avoided.
During such a long and continuous (24 hours a day) period the conversations of any and all persons coming into the area covered by the device
will be seized indiscriminantly and without regard to their connection
to the crime under investigation. Moreover, this permits, as was done
here, extensions of the original two-month period—presumably for two
months each—on a mere showing that such an extension is 'in the public
interest.' Apparently the original grounds on which the eavesdrop order
was initially issued also form the basis for the renewal. This we believe
insufficient without a showing of present probable cause for the continuance of the eavesdrop."

The third defect to which Clark and the majority addressed themselves was that the statute did not call for automatic termination of the
eavesdrop once the conversation was seized. "This was left entirely to
the discretion of the officer."

And finally, the fourth reason for condemning the statute was that
it did not require some showing of special facts to justify an entry without consent. "[T]he statute's procedure, necessarily because its success
depends on secrecy, has no requirement for notice as do conventional
warrants, nor does it overcome this defect by showing some special facts.
On the contrary, it permits uncontested entry without any showing of
exigent circumstances. Such a showing of exigency, in order to avoid
notice would appear more important in eavesdropping, with its inherent
dangers, than that required when conventional procedures of search and
seizure are utilized."

Clark also pointed out that the statute provided for no return on
the warrant, thereby giving the officer full discretion as to the full use of
seized conversations of innocent as well as guilty parties. "In short, the
statute's blanket grant of permission to eavesdrop is without adequate
judicial supervision or protective procedures."

Clark also addressed the argument often made by law enforcement
officials that outlawing electronic eavesdropping will severely cripple
crime detection, especially in detecting organized crime activities. However, he commented that the majority "have found no empirical statistics

on the use of electronic devices (bugging) in the fight against organized crime. Indeed, there are even figures available in the wiretap category which indicate to the contrary." "In any event," Clark went on, "we cannot forgive the requirements of the Fourth Amendment in the name of law enforcement. This is no formality that we require today but a fundamental rule that has long been recognized as basic to the privacy of every home in America."

The government put forth the argument that neither a warrant nor a statute can be drawn so as to meet the requirements of the Fourth Amendment. To this, Clark went on to say that "If that be true, then the 'fruits' of eavesdropping devices are barred under the Amendment." Clark noted that in the past the Court has sustained the use of eavesdropping devices under specific circumstances and conditions. See *Osborn* v. *United States*, 385 U.S. 323 (1966).

Justice Douglas, in a concurring opinion, joined the majority "because at long last it overrules sub silentio *Olmstead* v. *United States*, 277 U.S. 438 (1928)." *Berger*, according to Douglas, brings wiretapping and other electronic surveillance directly within the provision of the Fourth Amendment. Douglas, however, would have gone much further than the majority did. "I do not see how any electronic surveillance that collects evidence or provides leads to evidence is or can be constitutional under the Fourth and Fifth Amendments. We can amend the Constitution and so provide—a step that would take us closer to the ideological group we profess to despise. Until the amending process ushers us into that kind of totalitarian regime, I would adhere to the protection of the privacy which the Fourth Amendment fashioned in Congress and submitted to the people, was designed to afford the individual. . . . I would adhere to . . . the exclusionary rule in state as well as federal trials—a rule fashioned out of the Fourth Amendment and constituting a high constitutional barricade against the intrusion of Big Brother into the lives of all of us."

The dissenters each filed a separate opinion. Justice White took the view that this case was not a proper vehicle for resolving the broad legislative and constitutional issues raised by the official use of wiretapping and eavesdropping. Justice Harlan believed that electronic eavesdropping, as permitted under the New York statute, was not an unreasonable search and seizure. He also was concerned over the increasing Court involvement in setting the pattern of criminal law enforcement throughout the country. The third dissenter, Justice Black, concluded that the Fourth Amendment does not bar the use of eavesdropping evidence in court. In Black's opinion, *Olmstead* v. *United States* was still good law. He also disagreed with the majority assumption that the Fourth Amendment bars invasions of privacy rather than merely

forbidding unreasonable searches and seizures. He observed that the
word *privacy* "simply gives this court a useful new tool . . . both to
usurp the policy-making power of the Congress and to hold more state
and federal laws unconstitutional when the court entertains a sufficient
hostility to them."

QUESTIONS

1. According to the opinion of the majority, what specific points must be
   in an eavesdropping statute to allow it to pass the test of constitutionality?
2. What five defects did Justice Clark find with the New York statute?
3. How did Clark handle the traditional law enforcement claim that it
   cannot operate against organized crime without an eavesdropping
   capability?

Katz v. *United States*
389 U.S. 347, 88 S.Ct. 507, 19 L.Ed. 2ᴰ 576 (1967)

SETTING: Katz was convicted under a federal statute for transmit-
ting wagering information from Los Angeles to Boston and Miami.

PROCEDURAL PROBLEM: At the trial the government introduced the
following evidence over the objection of Katz. FBI agents recorded the
defendant's end of conversations while he was placing calls from a
public telephone booth. The FBI overheard the conversations by attach-
ing an electronic listening and recording device to the outside of the
booth from which Katz made the calls. The federal Court of Appeals
affirmed the conviction rejecting Katz's argument that the recordings
had been secured in violation of his Fourth Amendment rights. The
Court of Appeals stated that because there was no physical intrusion
into the area occupied by Katz, the seizure was permissible on the
authority of *Goldman* v. *United States,* 316 U.S. 129 (1942).

THE ISSUE: Does the Fourth Amendment protect the privacy which
a person seeks to preserve even if the area is accessible to the public?

THE ANSWER: Yes.

DISCUSSION: A seven-man majority held that the Fourth Amendment is breached by the FBI's use of a nonpenetrating bugging device to record a gambler's end of a conversation made from a public telephone booth. Justice Stewart, in overruling both *Olmstead* v. *United States,* 277 U.S. 438 (1928), *supra* and *Goldman* v. *United States,* 316 U.S. 129 (1942), *supra,* emphasized that the Fourth Amendment "protects people not places." What a person exposes to the public, even in his home or office, is not a subject of Fourth Amendment protection. However, if he attempts to preserve something as secret, even in an area that is generally accessible to the public, it may be constitutionally protected.

The government stressed the fact that the telephone booth was partly constructed of glass so that Katz was as visible after entering the booth as before. The Court, however, noted that it was his conversation that he sought to keep confidential, not his presence. Stewart concluded that "One who occupies it, shuts the door behind him, and pays the toll that permits him to place a call, is surely entitled to assume that the words he utters into the mouthpiece will not be broadcast to the world. To read the Constitution more narrowly is to ignore the vital role that the public telephone has come to play in private communication."

The majority, in accepting the premise that the Fourth Amendment protection protects people and not simply areas, reasoned that the protection cannot turn on the presence or absence of a trespass into an enclosure. Stewart concluded that "the underpinnings of *Olmstead* and *Goldman* have been so eroded by our subsequent decisions that the 'trespass' doctrine there enumerated can no longer be regarded as controlling."

The Court also addressed the argument of the government that the FBI agents acted with great restraint in the bugging of the booth. It appeared that it was only bugged for brief periods during which Katz used it, and the agents took great care to overhear only the conversations of Katz. To this argument the majority noted that

> [I]t is clear that this surveillance was so narrowly circumscribed that a duly authorized magistrate, properly notified of the need for such investigation, specifically informed of the basis on which it was to proceed, and clearly appraised of the precise intrusion it would entail, could constitutionally have authorized, with appropriate safeguards, the very limited search and seizure that the Government asserts in fact took place.

Because the FBI did no more than it properly could have done, the government argued that the Court should retroactively validate the FBI's conduct. Stewart answered by stating that in the absence of a prior judicial determination by a magistrate, the evidence secured through the use of the bugging device is inadmissible.

Justices Douglas and Brennan, in concurring, addressed themselves to the issue of whether safeguards other than prior judicial authorization may be available in matters of "national security." In answering the question negatively, Douglas said that "Neither the President nor the Attorney General is a magistrate. . . . There is, so far as I understand constitutional history, no distinction under the Fourth Amendment between types of crimes." Justice White, also concurring, took exception with Douglas and Brennan by stating, "We should not require the warrant procedure and the magistrate's judgment if the President of the United States or his chief legal officer, the Attorney General, has considered the requirements of national security and authorized electronic surveillance as reasonable." Justice Harlan preferred to wait to provide such an answer "when an appropriate occasion presents itself, and I agree with the Court that this is not one."

Justice Black could not agree with the majority that electronic eavesdropping constitutes a search or a seizure:

> Since I see no way in which the words of the Fourth Amendment can be construed to apply to eavesdropping, that closes the matter for me. In interpreting the Bill of Rights, I willingly go as far as a liberal construction of the language takes me, but I simply cannot in good conscience give a meaning to words which they have never before been thought to have and which they certainly do not have in common ordinary usage. I will not distort the words of the Amendment in order to "keep the Constitution up to date" or "to bring it into harmony with the times." It was never meant for this Court to have such power, which in effect would make us a continuously functioning constitutional convention.

QUESTIONS

1. The Fourth Amendment does protect places as well as people. What are they? What point was Justice Stewart trying to make when he stated that the Fourth Amendment "protects people not places"?
2. Compare *Berger* with *Katz*. To what extent does *Katz* cut down on the *Berger* holding?
3. What are some of the various kinds of electronic surveillance that fall within the Katz holding?

Lee v. Florida
392 U.S. 378, 88 S.Ct. 2096, 20 L.Ed. 2ᴰ 1166 (1968)

SETTING: Lee ordered a private telephone installed in his home. No private lines were available and he was given a four-party line instead. On police orders, the telephone company installed a line on the same party line in the house next door to Lee's. The police then attached an automatic actuator, tape recorder, and earphones to the line. The equipment was so connected that the police could hear and record all conversations on the party line without lifting the receiver on the telephone. The police therefore had complete access to all of Lee's incoming and outgoing calls without the telltale "click" that would otherwise have warned conversing parties that someone on the line had picked up a receiver.

The police used the monitoring equipment to overhear and record calls, some of which were incriminating and were later introduced into evidence over Lee's objections. In affirming Lee's conviction, the state appellate court noted that there were no state or federal statutes applicable in Florida that would make wiretapping illegal and inadmissible in evidence.

PROCEDURAL PROBLEM: The finding of the state courts that there was no applicable statute making wiretapping illegal and evidence inadmissible in Florida was disputed by the United States Supreme Court.

THE ISSUE: Are the prohibitions in Section 605 of the Federal Communications Act against intercepting and divulging a communication, applicable in state prosecutions?

THE ANSWER: Yes.

DISCUSSION: In an earlier Supreme Court case, *Schwartz* v. *Texas*, 344 U.S. 199 (1952), the Court held that wiretapping evidence secured in violation of Section 605 was admissible in a state trial. This precedent met its demise in *Lee* v. *Florida* when by a 6–3 decision, the Court held that evidence obtained by police officers in violation of Section 605 of the Federal Communications Act cannot be used in state prosecutions.

According to Justice Stewart for the majority, the plain words of

Section 605 forbid anyone unless authorized by the sender to intercept a telephone message, and direct in equally clear language that *"no person"* shall divulge or publish the message or its substance to *"any person."* Stewart noted that "to recite the contents of the message in testimony before a court is to divulge the message."

The majority also noted that *Mapp* v. *Ohio* 367 U.S. 643 (1961) imposed the exclusionary rule upon the states and therefore the federal doctrine of excluding such evidence is applicable.

Stewart emphasized that doctrinal symmetry alone is not the basis for the *Lee* holding. "It is buttressed as well by the 'imperative of judicial integrity.' Under our Constitution no court, state or federal, may serve as an accomplice in the wilful transgression of the 'laws of the United States,' laws by which 'the Judges in every State [are] bound.' "

In *Schwartz* the Supreme Court expressed the hope that the penal provisions of the Communications Act would achieve the statutory prohibition of Section 605. Stewart stated, "That has been a vain hope" because experience had shown there was not a single reported prosecution of law enforcement officers for violation of Section 605 since it was enacted.

Justice Black dissented on the ground that Congress should amend the Communications Act if it wished to explicitly forbid state use of evidence secured in violation of Section 605. "I think it would be more for the Court to leave this job of rewriting Section 605 to the Congress." Justice Harlan, joined by Justice White, also dissenting, noted that the doctrine of *stare decisis* is of extreme importance in a case like this one because "Congress has considered the wiretapping problem many times, each time against what it naturally assumed to be a stable background of statute law. To vary that background with the inclinations of members of this Court is to frustrate orderly congressional consideration of statutory problems. I would therefore adhere to *Schwartz*."

QUESTIONS

1. What was the specific holding in this case?
2. What was Justice Stewart talking about when he used the phrase "doctrinal symmetry"?
3. What case did *Lee* overrule? What was the holding of the overruled case? Does not *Lee* merely carry out the plain meaning of the words of Section 605?

Alderman v. United States
394 U.S. 165, 89 S.Ct. 961, 22 L.Ed. 2ᴰ 176 (1969)

SETTING: Alderman and two others were convicted of conspiring to transmit murderous threats in interstate commerce. Evidence indicating that the place of business of one of the defendants was subjected to electronic surveillance by the government was discovered after the conviction. The government, responding to a petition for rehearing, stated that it had reviewed the overheard conversations and "no overheard conversation in which any of the [defendants] participated is arguably relevant to this prosecution." The United States Supreme Court in a *per curiam* opinion rejected this finding and remanded the case for further hearing. A second case was argued with *Alderman* concerning the same issue of disclosure. It is not further discussed here because the issue is identical to *Alderman*.

PROCEDURAL PROBLEM: The United States then sought to modify the Court's order that there must be a judicial determination of whether any of the prosecution's evidence was the product of the illegal surveillance. The government urged that because of the sensitive nature of the overheard conversations and in order to protect innocent persons mentioned in irrelevant parts of the overheard conversations, the surveillance records should be examined *in camera* by the trial judge, who would turn over to the defendants' counsel only those materials arguably relevant to their prosecution. The defendants opposed this motion and the United States Supreme Court agreed to hear the argument relating to the disclosure issue.

THE ISSUE: If evidence is secured by electronic surveillance, does the defendant have the right to examine the records of the overheard conversations without first having the material screened *in camera* by the trial judge?

THE ANSWER: Yes.

DISCUSSION: The defendants in this case won a greatly expanded right to discover when the Court held that persons who have standing are entitled to object to illegally secured evidence and to inspect records of the recorded conversations without first submitting the materials to be screened *in camera* by the trial judge. Justice White, writing for the majority, stressed that the task of extracting irrelevant information is one that should not be left to the trial courts. He stated, "Unavoidably, this is a matter of judgment, but in our view the task is too complex, and the margin of error too great, to rely wholly on the *in camera* judgment of the trial court to identify those records which might have contributed to the Government's case."

According to the majority, the facts in a hearing might have little or no importance to a judge. However, the defendant and his attorney must have the power to discover evidence that may bring out the unforeseen meaning of other evidence. "As the need for adversary inquiry is increased by the complexity of the issues presented for adjudication, and by the consequent inadequacy of *ex parte* procedures as a means for their accurate resolution, the displacement of well-informed advocacy necessarily becomes less justifiable."

The Court, however, limited its decision regarding electronic surveillance by stating that a defendant or a co-conspirator whose rights are not violated by illegal eavesdropping but who might be "aggrieved solely by the introduction of damaging evidence" in such eavesdropping, has no standing to object to the use of such evidence against him. White emphasized, "We adhere to these cases and to the general rule that Fourth Amendment rights which, like some other constitutional rights, may not be vicariously asserted. . . . There is no necessity to exclude evidence against one defendant in order to protect the rights of another. No rights of the victim of an illegal search are at stake when the evidence is offered against some other party. The victim can and very probably will object for himself when and if it becomes important for him to do so."

The majority carved out an exception to the "no standing" rule by holding that a homeowner has standing to object to unlawfully heard conversations that occurred in his property regardless of whether or not he was present or participated in them. "We adhere to the established view," Justice White went on, "that the right to be secure in one's house against unauthorized intrusion is not limited to protection against a policeman viewing or seizing tangible property—'papers' and 'effects.' The rights of the owner of the premises are as clearly invaded when the police enter and install a listening device in his home as they are when the entry is made to undertake a warrantless search for tangible property; and the prosecution as surely employs the fruits of an illegal search of the home when it offers overheard third-party conversations as it does when it introduces tangible evidence belonging not to the home owner, but to others."

Justice Harlan was in substantial agreement with the Court in refusing to expand the traditional standing doctrine to permit a Fourth Amendment challenge to be raised by either a co-defendant or a co-conspirator. However, he did dissent to the homeowner having standing to object to conversations in his home to which he was not a party. "Consequently, I would hold that, in the circumstances before us, standing should be granted only to those who actually participated in the conversation that has been illegally overheard." Harlan did suggest that although he would not permit homeowners to challenge conversations in which they were nonparticipants, he would adopt the government's position that the trial judge hold an *in camera* screening procedure concerning third-party conversations.

QUESTIONS

1. What is meant by "standing to object"?
2. What is the specific holding of this case in regard to:
   a. *In camera* hearings to discover the records of electronic surveillance?
   b. Standing to object by the defendants, co-defendants, co-conspirators?
   c. Standing to object by nonparticipant homeowners whose homes are invaded in violation of the Fourth Amendment?
3. What are the reasons behind Harlan's approach that a homeowner who did not participate in an overheard conversation secured illegally by intrusion into his home should not be permitted to object to the evidence?

United States v. *United States District Court for the Eastern District of Michigan, Southern Division*
407 U.S. 297, 92 S.Ct. 2125, 32 L.Ed. 2ᴰ 752 (1972)

SETTING: Three defendants, one a "White Panther," Plamondon, were charged by the United States with conspiring to destroy government property by bombing a CIA office.

PROCEDURAL PROBLEM: During pretrial proceedings the defendants moved to compel the United States to disclose certain electronic surveillance information and to determine whether or not evidence upon which the indictment was based was tainted.

The government then filed an affidavit of the attorney general, acknowledging that its agents overheard conversations in which defendant Plamondon participated. The affidavit also stated that the attorney general approved the wiretaps to gather intelligence information deemed necessary to "protect the nation from attempts of domestic organizations to attack and subvert the existing structures of the government." The logs of the wiretap were sealed for exhibit for *in camera* inspection by the United States District Court. On the basis of the affidavit and sealed exhibit, the government claimed that the surveillance was lawful as a reasonable exercise of the presidential power acting through the attorney general to protect the national security.

The United States District Court held that the surveillance violated the Fourth Amendment and ordered the government to disclose to Plamondon his overheard conversations. The Court of Appeals and the United States Supreme Court affirmed.

THE ISSUE: Does the presidential practice of authorizing warrantless electronic surveillance in internal matters constitutionally extend to activities of domestic "subversives"?

THE ANSWER: No.

DISCUSSION: In an 8–0 decision with Justice Rehnquist not participating, Justice Powell wrote that the "Fourth Amendment freedoms cannot properly be guaranteed if domestic security surveillances may be conducted solely within the discretion of the executive branch."

Powell recognized the presidential practice for over a quarter-century of ordering electronic surveillances. However, he also noted that there was no guidance from Congress or a definitive decision from the Supreme Court on the matter. The preservation and security of the nation is the most basic function of government, but even when used for this purpose, electronic surveillance is a dangerous tool. Powell additionally was of the opinion that not only the Fourth Amendment was involved but also the First. He noted, "History abundantly documents the tendency of government—however benevolent and benign its motives—to view with suspicion those who fervently dispute its policies. Fourth Amendment protections become more necessary when the targets of official surveillance may be those suspected of unorthodoxy in their political beliefs. The danger to political dissent is acute where the Government attempts to act under so vague a concept as the power to protect 'domestic security.'"

The decision emphasized that the Fourth Amendment's safeguards, with only a few exceptions, are based on the requirement for a warrant.

Government attorneys claimed that the power of the president to order electronic surveillance in cases of national security is contained in Title III, Omnibus Crime Control and Safe Streets Act, 18 U.S.C. 2511 (3):

> *Nor shall anything contained in this chapter be deemed to limit the constitutional power of the President to take such measures as he deems necessary to protect the United States against the overthrow of the Government by force or other unlawful means, or against any other clear and present danger to the structure or existence of the Government.*

Justice Powell wrote that Title III, in citing specific standards for judicial authority for electronic surveillance did not purport to authorize the wiretaps involved in this case.

> *At most, this is an implicit recognition that the President does have certain powers in specified areas. . . . But as far as the use of the President's electronic surveillance power is concerned, the language is neutral. Section 2511 (3) certainly confers no power. . . . It merely provides that the Act shall not be interpreted to limit or disturb such power as the President may have under the Constitution. In short, Congress left the presidential powers where it found them.*

The Fourth Amendment is not absolute in its terms of requiring a warrant. It must be borne in mind, however, that the fundamental power of the government to protect domestic security does not demand that the government be given virtually unchecked power to employ electronic surveillance against its citizens. Powell noted that Fourth Amendment "freedoms cannot properly be guaranteed if domestic security surveillance may be conducted solely within the discretion of the Executive Branch." Because this branch has an interest and is not a neutral party, the decision regarding the constitutionality of pursuing the investigation is not left to the decision of an impartial magistrate.

The government claimed that it should be exempted from the warrant required because disclosure to a magistrate of all or a significant part of the information involved in domestic security cases "would create serious potential dangers to the national security and to the lives of informants and agents. . . . Secrecy is the essential ingredient in intelligence gathering. . . . It noted that it did not reject this contention lightly "especially at a time of world-wide ferment and when civil disorders in this country are more prevalent than in the less turbulent periods of our history." But these claims, according to Justice Powell, do not permit a departure from traditional Fourth Amendment standards. "We recognize . . . the constitutional basis of the President's domestic security role, but we think it must be exercised in a manner compatible with the Fourth Amendment. In this case we hold that this requires an appropriate prior warrant procedure."

The Court expressed no opinion on issues involved when agents of a foreign country are involved. The Court also emphasized that the standards and procedures contained in Title III are not necessarily applicable in this case because a much different kind of investigation and surveillance may be involved in domestic intelligence-gathering than the investigation and surveillance of more conventional types of crime. Powell then invited the Congress "to consider protective standards" for domestic security which differ from those already set out in Title III.

Powell also refused the government's motion to overrule *Alderman* v. *United States,* 394 U.S. 165 (1969), *supra.*

QUESTIONS

1. Compare with and distinguish this case from *Alderman.* What is the specific holding in this case?
2. What is your interpretation of Section 2511 (3) as discussed by Justice Powell? Do you agree or disagree with the Court's interpretation? Discuss.
3. What was Justice Powell's main concern—upholding the safeguards of the Fourth Amendment or the survival of the United States? Is this question an accurate reflection of his concern? Discuss fully.

Gelbard v. *United States*
408 U.S. 41, 92 S.Ct. 2357, 33 L.Ed. 2ᴰ 179 (1972)

SETTING: The defendant and several others were cited for civil contempt for refusing to comply with a court order to testify before a federal grand jury. Federal agents during the course of a wiretap approved by a federal district judge overheard conversations between Gelbard and other individuals, who were the subjects of the taps.

PROCEDURAL PROBLEM: Gelbard was then called before the federal grand jury, but he declined to answer any questions based upon the intercepted conversations until afforded the opportunity to challenge the legality of the interceptions. Upon this refusal Gelbard was found in civil contempt and committed to custody for the life of the grand jury or until he answered the questions. The United States Supreme Court reversed the contempt citation.

THE ISSUE: Are grand jury witnesses entitled to invoke the statutory prohibition against use before a grand jury of evidence derived from the interception of oral or wire communications as a defense to contempt charges brought against them for refusing to testify?

THE ANSWER: Yes.

DISCUSSION: Federal law limits the adjudication of civil contempt to the case of a grand jury witness who refuses without just cause to comply with an order of the court to testify. 28 U.S.C. 2515 provides:

> *Whenever any wire or oral communication has been intercepted, no part of the contents of such communication and no evidence derived therefrom may be received in evidence in any trial, hearing, or other proceeding in or before any court, grand jury, department, officer, agency, regulatory body, legislative committee, or other authority of the United States, a State, or a political subdivision thereof if the disclosure of that information would be in violation of this chapter.*

Based on these two provisions, the issue is whether a showing that an interrogation would be based upon the illegal interception of Gelbard's communications constitutes a showing of "just cause" that precludes a finding of contempt. Justice Brennan concluded that section 2515 is an available defense to the contempt charge. It was intended by Congress that grand jury witnesses, in reliance upon the prohibition of section 2515, might refuse to answer questions based upon the illegal interception of their communications. Once the defense has alleged that the information sought from it is inadmissible in the grand jury hearings, the government is required to affirm or deny the occurrence of the alleged illegal interception. If it is not established that the overheard testimony was secured from legal sources, the contempt citation cannot stand.

QUESTIONS

1. What is contempt? What legal punishments usually are applied to a finding of civil contempt?
2. What is the holding of *Gelbard* v. *United States?*
3. Do you think that this decision will hinder the fact-finding efforts of a grand jury? Why?

United States v. White
401 U.S. 745, 91 S.Ct. 1122, 28 L.Ed. 2ᴰ 453 (1971)

SETTING: In 1966 White was tried and convicted of various illegal narcotics transactions. He was fined and sentenced as a second offender to twenty-five-year concurrent sentences. The evidence against him consisted of testimony of governmental agents who related conversations that occurred between White and a government informant, Harvey Jackson. The conversations were overheard by monitoring the frequency of a radio transmitter concealed on Jackson.

PROCEDURAL PROBLEM: All four of the conversations took place in Jackson's home; each of these conversations was overheard by an agent concealed in a kitchen closet with Jackson's consent and by a second agent outside the house using a radio receiver. Four other conversations—one in respondent's home, one in a restaurant, and two in Jackson's car—were overheard by the use of radio equipment. The prosecution was unable to locate and produce Jackson at the trial and the trial court overruled objections to the testimony of the agents who conducted the electronic surveillance. The jury returned a guilty verdict and defendant appealed.

The United States Court of Appeals, Seventh Circuit, reversed the conviction based on *Katz v. United States*, 389 U.S. 347 (1967), interpreting *Katz* to hold that the Fourth Amendment forbids the introduction of the agent's testimony in the circumstances of this case. The United States Supreme Court reversed the Court of Appeals, saying that *Katz* and the Fourth Amendment were being misinterpreted "and in any event erred in applying the *Katz* case to events that took place before that decision was rendered by this court."

THE ISSUE: Does the Fourth Amendment bar from evidence the testimony of governmental agents who related certain conversations that occurred between White and informant Jackson, and that the agents overheard by monitoring the frequency of a clandestine radio transmitter carried by Jackson?

THE ANSWER: No.

DISCUSSION: In announcing the plurality opinion of the Court, Justice White noted that the Fourth Amendment affords no protection to "a wrongdoer's misplaced belief that a person to whom he voluntarily confides his wrongdoing will not reveal it." (See *Hoffa* v. *United States*, 385 U.S. 293 (1966), Chapter 5.) White concluded that

> *If the conduct and revelations of an agent operating without electronic equipment do not invade the defendant's constitutionally justifiable expectations of privacy, neither does a simultaneous recording of the same conversations made by the agent or by others from transmissions received from the agent to whom the defendant is talking and whose trustworthiness the defendant necessarily risks.*

Is there a problem of the invasion of privacy in this case? In addressing this issue, White was of the opinion that

> *Our problem is not what the privacy expectations of particular defendants in particular situations may be or the extent to which they may in fact have relied on the discretion of their companions. Very probably, individual defendants neither know nor suspect that their colleagues have gone or will go to the police or are carrying recorders or transmitters. Otherwise, conversations would cease and our problem with these encounters would be nonexistent or far different from those now before us. Our problem, in terms of the principles announced in* Katz, *is what expectations of privacy are constitutionally "justifiable"—what expectations the Fourth Amendment will protect in the absence of a warrant. So far, the law permits the frustration of actual expectations of privacy by permitting authorities to use the testimony of these associates who for one reason or another have determined to turn to the police, as well as by authorizing the use of informants in the manner exemplified by* Hoffa *and* Lewis. *If the law gives no protection to the wrongdoer whose trusted accomplice is or becomes a police agent, neither should it protect him when that same agent has recorded or transmitted the conversations which are later offered in evidence to prove the State's case. . . .*
>
> *It is thus untenable to consider the activities and reports of the police agent himself, though acting without a warrant, to be a "reasonable" investigative effort and lawful under the Fourth Amendment but to view the same agent with a recorder or transmitter as conducting an "unreasonable" and unconstitutional search and seizure. . . .*
>
> *No different result should obtain where, as in* On Lee *and the instant case, the informer disappears and is unavailable at trial; for the issue of whether specified events on a certain day violate the Fourth Amendment should not be determined by what later happens to the informer. His unavailability at trial and proffering the testimony of other agents may raise evidentiary problems or pose issues of prosecutorial misconduct with respect to the informer's disappearance, but they do not appear critical to deciding whether prior events invaded the defendant's Fourth Amendment rights.*

Justice Brennan concurred in the result only because the electronic surveillance occurred before *Katz* was announced. Brennan was of the opinion that there should be no retrospective application of *Katz*. Brennan was also of the view that *Lopez* v. *United States*, 373 U.S. 427 (1963) and *On Lee* v. *United States*, 343 U.S. 747 (1952) were no longer the law and that current Fourth Amendment jurisprudence interposes a warrant requirement not only in cases of third-party electronic monitoring (the situation in *On Lee* and this case) but also in cases of electronic recording by a government agent of a face-to-face conversation with a criminal suspect, which was the situation in *Lopez*.

Justices Douglas, Harlan, and Marshall dissented.

QUESTIONS

1. What is Justice Brennan's main argument regarding the necessity for a search warrant in electronic surveillance cases?
2. Compare the holding in *White* with *On Lee* and *Lopez*. In your opinion, can they be distinguished other than based on the factual situation?
3. Write a dissenting opinion to the *White* case.

Chapter 5

Informants

Rugendorf v. United States
376 U.S. 528, 84 S.Ct. 825, 11 L.Ed. 2ᴰ 887 (1964)

SETTING: Rugendorf was convicted by a jury of knowingly receiving and concealing furs having a value of over $5,000 and having transported them in interstate commerce. The conviction was affirmed by the Court of Appeals despite the claims that the affidavit in support of the warrant, the authority upon which the furs were seized, and the names of certain confidential informants referred to in the affidavit should have been disclosed. The United States Supreme Court affirmed the conviction.

PROCEDURAL PROBLEM: A United States Commissioner issued the warrant under attack by Rugendorf on the strength of an affidavit signed on March 22, 1962 by FBI Agent Moore. The affidavit stated that Moore had reason to believe that about $40,000 in furs stolen from a Mountain Brook, Alabama home were concealed in a single-family residence at 3117 West Jarvis Avenue, Chicago. Moore supported his affidavit with statements that a special agent in Birmingham, Alabama had informed him that a large number of furs were stolen in Mountain Brook. It was further stated that a confidential informant who had furnished reliable information in the past told Agent Moore that he had recently seen about eighty fur jackets (but no full-length coats) in the basement of Rugendorf's home at 3117 West Jarvis Avenue in Chicago. The labels had been removed and the informant was told that the furs had been stolen.

Moore further supported the allegation, saying that FBI Special Agent McCormick had advised him that a confidential informant whom the FBI had found to be reliable told McCormick that Frank Schweihs of Chicago, and others, had committed the Alabama robbery. McCormick told Moore that on or about March 1, 1962, James Kelleher, a Chicago police officer, told McCormick that he saw Frank Schweihs at Rugendorf Brothers Meat Market, managed by Samuel Rugendorf; further, Agent McCormick advised Moore that another confidential informant who had furnished reliable information to the Federal Bureau of Investigation in the past had told McCormick that Leo Rugendorf was a fence for Frank Schweihs; that Samuel Rugendorf was Leo Rugendorf's brother and was associated in the meat business with his brother.

The affidavit also stated that another FBI Special Agent, J. J. Oitzinger, had told Moore that another confidential informant who had supplied the FBI with reliable information in the past had advised Oitzinger that Frank Schweihs, Tony Panzica, and Mike Condic were accomplished burglars who disposed of the proceeds of their burglaries through Leo Rugendorf.

Finally, the affidavit alleged that, upon checking the informant's description of the furs seen at 3117 West Jarvis Avenue, Moore found that the only reported burglary in the United States in the previous six months involving furs of that description and value was the one occurring in Mountain Brook, Alabama.

THE ISSUE: Does an affidavit in support of a search warrant based merely on the statements of unidentified reliable informants provide a sufficient basis for probable cause to issue the warrant?

THE ANSWER: Yes.

DISCUSSION: In attacking the validity of the warrant Rugendorf brought up an issue which the Court had never previously directly passed on. He claimed that probable cause did not exist because the only relevant citations in the affidavit were the one informant's statements that he had seen the furs in Rugendorf's basement. The majority commented, "We believe that there was substantial basis for the Commissioner to conclude that stolen furs were probably in [Rugendorf's] basement. No more is required." Citing *Jones v. United States,* 362 U.S. 257 (1960), the majority noted in conclusion "that hearsay may be the basis for a warrant. We cannot say that there was so little basis for accepting the hearsay . . . that the Commissioner acted improperly."

In a second argument, the defendant claimed that withholding the identities of the informants was a sufficient ground to require suppression of the evidence. However, the Court, once again citing *Jones*, stated that hearsay alone does not render an affidavit insufficient and therefore the commissioner need not have required the informants to be produced as long as there was a substantial basis for crediting the hearsay. Two minor irregularities in the affidavit failed to show any bad faith on the part of Agent Moore or any intentional misrepresentation on his part.

Rugendorf also asserted that at the minimum he was entitled to the names of the informants who reported seeing the furs in his basement in order to defend himself. The claim, however, was not raised in the trial court nor passed upon there. At the trial he relied entirely on seeking to suppress the evidence that was denied. Failing this, he sought for the first time on appeal to secure the name of the informant. Apparently by his argument he sought to bring the informant in as a participant in the crime—contending that this would obtain under *Roviaro* v. *United States*, 353 U.S. 53 (1957). The Court noted that after reviewing the facts in the case the "whole record shows that he requested the informers' name only in his attack on the affidavit supporting the search warrant. Having failed to develop the criteria of *Roviaro* necessitating disclosure on the merits, we cannot say on this record that the name of the informant was necessary to his defense."

QUESTIONS

1. As a Justice who does not agree with the majority in the case, write a dissenting opinion to the point that the identity of an informant if reliable is not necessary in order to establish probable cause to issue a warrant.
2. Why is an affidavit necessary to support issuance of a search warrant?
3. What is the specific holding in this case?

Hoffa v. *United States*
385 U.S. 293, 87 S.Ct. 408, 17 L.Ed. 2ᴰ 374 (1966)

SETTING: James Hoffa was convicted for endeavoring to bribe members of a jury during the so-called "Test Fleet" trial. Hoffa was president of the International Brotherhood of Teamsters. During the course of the trial (October 22 to December 23, 1962) he occupied a three-room suite in the Andrew Jackson Hotel in Nashville, Tennessee. Partain, a Baton Rouge, Louisiana teamster official, visited frequently with Hoffa and was seen with him in the hotel lobby, suite, courthouse, and elsewhere in Nashville. Partain made frequent reports to federal agent Sheridan concerning his conversations with Hoffa and others, disclosing endeavors to bribe members of the "Test Fleet" jury. Partain's report and subsequent testimony at Hoffa's trial unquestionably contributed to his conviction and that of several others.

PROCEDURAL PROBLEM: Prior to the Nashville trial of Hoffa, Partain was indicted for embezzling union funds and various state offenses were pending against him. He was released on bail and made several contacts with Hoffa. In his consultations with federal agents, Partain was admonished to be alert to the possibility of jury tampering by Hoffa. Partain agreed to this. After the "Test Fleet" trial was completed, the federal charges against Partain were dropped or not actively pursued and his wife received four monthly installments of $300.

THE ISSUE: Does evidence obtained by the government by means of deceptively placing a secret informer in the quarters and councils of a defendant violate the defendant's Fourth, Fifth, and Sixth Amendment rights so that the evidence may be suppressed in a subsequent trial on a different charge?

THE ANSWER: No.

DISCUSSION: In response to Hoffa's Fourth Amendment argument that the failure of Partain to disclose his role as a government informer vitiated the consent that Hoffa gave to Partain's repeated entries into Hoffa's suite and that by listening to Hoffa's statements, Partain conducted an illegal search for evidence, Justice Stewart for the majority stated:

> *Where the argument fails is in its misapprehension of the fundamental nature and scope of Fourth Amendment protection. What the Fourth Amendment protects is the security a man relies upon when he places himself or his property within a constitutionally protected area, be it his home or his office, his hotel room or his automobile. There he is protected from unwarranted governmental intrusion.*

In the present case it is evident that there is no Fourth Amendment interest involved. Hoffa was not relying upon the security of the hotel suite when he made incriminating statements to Partain or in his presence.

Partain did not enter the suite by force or stealth. He was not a surreptitious eavesdropper. Hoffa was relying upon the misplaced confidence that Partain would not reveal his wrongdoing. As Stewart concluded, "Neither this Court nor any member of it has ever expressed the view that the Fourth Amendment protects a wrongdoer's misplaced belief that a person to whom he voluntarily confides his wrongdoing will not reveal it. . . . Adhering to these views, we hold that no right protected by the Fourth Amendment was violated. . . ."

Hoffa's Fifth Amendment claim was also without merit. His incriminating conversations with Partain were entirely voluntary and for that reason, no right protected by the Fifth Amendment privilege against compulsory self-incrimination was violated.

Hoffa made two arguments that his Sixth Amendment right to counsel was violated. First, he claimed that Partain's presence in and around Hoffa's suite violated Hoffa's right to counsel because an essential ingredient thereof is the right of a defendant and his attorney to prepare for trial without intrusion on their confidential relationship by a governmental agent, Hoffa's trial adversary. Therefore, because Partain's presence in the suite violated the Sixth Amendment, the argument goes, any evidence acquired by reason of Partain's presence was constitutionally tainted and therefore inadmissible against Hoffa.

The Court rejected the argument because it was "far from clear to what extent Partain was present at conversations or conferences of the petitioner's counsel." Stewart also noted that previous decisions supported the proposition that a surreptitious invasion by a government agent into the defense's legal camp may violate the Sixth Amendment protection; these cases dealt with gross government intrusion. However, in the cited cases the government intrusion occurred in the relationship of the lawyer and his client and invalidated the trial at which the intrusion occurred. In this case, Stewart emphasized, the intrusion occurred at a prior trial, not the trial resulting in the conviction under review.

Hoffa's second Sixth Amendment argument was that once the government had adequate ground for taking him into custody and charging him, he could no longer be questioned without counsel. He cited *Massiah* v. *United States,* 377 U.S. 301 (1964) and *Escobedo* v. *Illinois,* 378 U.S. 478 (1964), *infra,* as authority. In rejecting the argument, the majority held that "Nothing in *Massiah* or *Escobedo,* or in any other case that has come to our attention, even remotely suggests this novel and paradoxical constitutional doctrine, and we decline to adopt it now. There is no constitutional right to be arrested. The police are not required to guess at their peril the precise moment at which they have probable cause to arrest a suspect, risking a violation of the Fourth Amendment if they act too soon, and a violation of the Sixth Amendment if they wait too long. Law enforcement officers are under no constitutional duty to call a halt to a criminal investigation the moment they have the minimum evidence to establish probable cause, a quantum of evidence which may fall short of the amount necessary to support a criminal conviction."

Finally, the defendant's argument was presented that the totality of the government's conduct was so shabby as to "offend those canons of decency and fairness which express the notions of justice of English-speaking peoples even toward those charged with the most heinous offenses" and therefore deny him due process under the Fifth Amendment. The argument boiled down to a general attack on the use of informers by the government. Stewart noted that insofar as the general attack on the use of informers is based on historic "notions" of "English-speaking peoples," it is without historical foundation. "Courts have countenanced the use of informers from time immemorial; in cases of conspiracies, or in other cases when the crime consists of preparing for another crime, it is usually necessary to rely upon them or accomplices because the criminals will almost certainly proceed covertly."

Chief Justice Warren in dissent found the "affront to the quality and fairness of federal law enforcement which this case presents, is sufficient to require an exercise of our supervisory powers." According to Warren, the government reached into the jailhouse to find a man under federal and state indictment for embezzlement, manslaughter, and kidnapping to use as an informer. Partain's indictments were much worse than Hoffa's. By its degrading actions, Warren said that the government paid a high price for the evidence it secured. He therefore could not agree that "what happened in this case is in keeping with the standards of justice of our federal system."

QUESTIONS

1. In your estimation, was Hoffa relying on the misplaced confidence that Partain would not reveal the conversation or that he was in the privacy of his hotel room and therefore protected from government spying?
2. What reasons did Justice Stewart give for rejecting the two Sixth Amendment arguments that Hoffa put forth? Was the first of the two reasons the stronger case for Hoffa?
3. Do you believe that people must take a risk in a free society that their friends or associates may be government agents planted to secure incriminating evidence and dutifully report it? Discuss.

Lewis v. United States
385 U.S. 206, 87 S.Ct. 424, 17 L.Ed. 2ᴰ 312 (1966)

SETTING: Cass, an undercover federal narcotics agent, telephoned defendant's home to inquire about purchasing some marijuana. Cass, who had not previously met Lewis, falsely identified himself and stated that a mutual friend had told him that Lewis might supply him with some marijuana. Lewis said he could and invited Cass to his home, where a sale occurred. Two weeks later a similar transaction occurred. Based on these transactions, Lewis was arrested and charged by a two-count indictment with narcotics law violations. He was convicted on both counts in the federal district court, and the Court of Appeals, First Circuit, affirmed. The United States Supreme Court on certiorari also affirmed.

PROCEDURAL PROBLEM: A pretrial motion to suppress the marijuana evidence and the conversations between Cass and defendant was denied and they were introduced at the trial. The defendant argued that in the absence of a warrant, any official intrusion upon the privacy of a home constitutes a Fourth Amendment violation and even though Cass was invited, the invitation was induced by fraud or deception.

THE ISSUE: Was the Fourth Amendment violated when a federal narcotics agent who misrepresented his identity and stated his willingness to purchase narcotics was invited into the defendant's home, where a narcotics transaction was consummated and the narcotics were thereafter introduced in evidence against the defendant in a criminal trial?

THE ANSWER: No.

DISCUSSION: Mr. Chief Justice Warren basically held that if the deception practiced by the federal agents were not permitted by the Constitution, then such a rule would be very near to saying that the use of undercover informants is unconstitutional *per se*. This far the majority was unwilling to go. Warren recognized the need for using informants by stating, "It has long been acknowledged by the decisions of this court . . . that, in the detection of many types of crimes, the government is entitled to use decoys and conceal the identity of its agents. The various protections of the Bill of Rights, of course, provide checks upon such official deception for the protection of the individual."

If there were a rule that it is unconstitutional *per se* to use informants, Warren went on, "such a rule would, for example, severely hamper the government in ferreting out those organized criminal activities that are characterized by covert dealings with victims who either cannot or do not protest. A prime example is provided by the narcotics traffic."

Did the fact that the agent entered the Lewis home to carry out the transactions compel a different conclusion? Warren emphasized that where the home is converted into a "commercial center to which outsiders are invited for purposes of transacting unlawful business, that business is entitled to no greater sanctity than if it were carried on in a store, a car, or on the street."

In his summarizing comments the Chief Justice stated:

> *In short, this case involves the exercise of no governmental power to intrude upon protected premises; the visitor was invited and willingly admitted by the suspect. It concerns no design on the part of government to observe or hear what was happening in the privacy of a home; the suspect chose the location where the transaction took place. It presents no question of the invasion of the privacy of a dwelling; the only statements repeated were those that were willingly made to the agent and the only things taken were the packets of marijuana voluntarily transferred to him. The pretense resulted in no breach of privacy; it merely encouraged the suspect to say things he was willing and anxious to say to anyone who would be interested in purchasing marijuana.*

Justice Douglas, in dissent, viewed the case as involving a breach of the privacy of a home by governmental agents who used duplicity to gain entrance into a home in order to secure evidence to convict the person of a crime. In condemning the practice he noted that "entering another's home in disguise to obtain evidence is a 'search' that would bring into play all the protective features of the Fourth Amendment." When the agent had reason to believe that Lewis possessed narcotics, "a search warrant should have been obtained."

QUESTIONS

1. Discuss the *modus operandi,* training, and general usage of undercover informants (agents) in narcotics cases. Because the work is often dangerous, would it not be a prudent step to have secured a warrant in this case?

2. Why did Chief Justice Warren state that if there was a holding in this case that the evidence was inadmissible in defendant's trial, it

would be tantamount to deciding that the use of undercover informants is unconstitutional *per se?* Would this result stem from following the dissenting rationale of Justice Douglas?
3. If a warrant were to be required in this case, where is the probable cause to secure it?

Roviaro v. United States
353 U.S. 53, 77 S.Ct. 623, 1 L.Ed. 2ᴰ 639 (1957)

SETTING: In 1955, Roviaro was convicted of violating federal narcotics laws. The indictment charging him with the crime alleged he sold heroin to one "John Doe." Before the trial, Roviaro moved to be furnished the name, address, and occupation of "John Doe." The government objected on the ground that he was an informant and that his identity was privileged. The motion was denied and defendant was convicted. The Court of Appeals upheld the conviction. The United States Supreme Court reversed.

PROCEDURAL PROBLEM: Roviaro, represented by counsel in the trial court, sought on several occasions to learn "John Doe's" identity on cross-examination. Such examination was not allowed.

At the trial, the government relied on the testimony of two federal narcotics agents, Durham and Fields, and two Chicago police officers, Bryson and Sims, each of whom knew the defendant by sight. On the night of August 12, 1954, these four officers met at 75th Steet and Prairie Avenue in Chicago with an informer described only as John Doe. Doe and his Cadillac car were searched and no narcotics were found. Bryson secreted himself in the trunk of Doe's Cadillac, taking with him a device with which to raise the trunk from the inside. Doe then drove the Cadillac to 70th Place and St. Lawrence Avenue, followed by Durham in one government car and Fields and Sims in another. After an hour's wait, at about 11 o'clock, Roviaro arrived in a Pontiac accompanied by an unidentified man. Roviaro immediately entered Doe's Cadillac, taking a front seat beside Doe. They then proceeded by a circuitous route to 74th Street near Champlain Avenue. Both government cars trailed the Cadillac, but only the one driven by Durham managed to follow it to 74th Street. When the Cadillac came to a stop on 74th Street, Durham stepped out of his car onto the sidewalk and saw defendant alight from the Cadillac about 100 feet away. Durham saw Roviaro walk a few feet to a nearby tree, pick up a small package, return to the open right front door of the Cadillac, make a motion as if depositing the package in the car, and then wave to Doe and walk away. Durham went immediately to the Cadillac and recovered a package from the floor. He signaled to Bryson to come out of the trunk and then walked down the street in time to see defendant reenter the Pontiac, parked nearby, and ride away.

Meanwhile, Bryson, concealed in the trunk of the Cadillac, had heard a conversation between John Doe and defendant after the latter had entered the car. He heard defendant greet John Doe and direct him where to drive. At one point, Roviaro admonished him to pull over to the curb, cut the motor, and turn out the lights so as to lose a "tail." He then told him to continue "further down." Roviaro asked about money Doe owed him. He advised Doe that he had brought him "three pieces this time." When Bryson heard Doe being ordered to stop the car, he raised the lid of the trunk slightly. After the car stopped, he saw Roviaro walk to a tree, pick up a package, and return toward the car. He heard defendant say, "Here it is," and "I'll call you in a couple of days." Shortly thereafter he heard Durham's signal to come out and emerged from the trunk to find Durham holding a small package found to contain three glassine envelopes containing a white powder.

A field test of the powder indicated that it contained an opium derivative; subsequent chemical analysis revealed that the powder contained heroin. The officers, at about 12:30 A.M. arrested Roviaro at his home and took him, along with Doe, to Chicago police headquarters. There he was confronted with Doe, who denied that he knew or had ever seen Roviaro.

THE ISSUE: Is it reversible error for the trial court to allow the government to refuse to disclose the identity of an undercover informant who has (1) taken a material part in proving the possession of certain drugs by the accused, (2) has been present with the accused at the occurrence of the alleged crime, and (3) might be a material witness as to whether the accused knowingly transported the drugs as charged?

THE ANSWER: Yes.

DISCUSSION: The majority upheld the defendant's claim that because Doe was an active participant in the crime, the government was not permitted to withhold his identity, whereabouts, and whether he was alive or dead at the time of the trial. Justice Burton for the majority emphasized that what is often known as an informer's privilege is in reality the government's privilege to withhold the identity of persons who furnish information of law violations to officers charged with enforcement of those laws.

The purpose of the governmental privilege is the furtherance and protection of the public interest in effective law enforcement. Justice Burton also noted that the scope of the privilege is limited by its underlying purpose. For example, where revelation of the contents of a communication do not tend to reveal the identity of an informant, the contents are not privileged. In the same light, once the informant's identity is revealed, the privilege is no longer applicable.

Burton also addressed an additional limitation on the applicability of the privilege stemming from the fundamental requirements of fairness. "Where the disclosure of an informant's identity, or of the contents of his communication, is relevant and helpful to the accused, or is essential to a fair determination of a cause, the privilege must give way. In these situations the trial court may require disclosure and, if the Government withholds the information, dismiss the action."

Burton emphasized that there can be no fixed rule with respect to disclosures. The issue is one of balancing the public interest in protecting the flow of information against a defendant's right to prepare his defense. "Whether a proper balance renders nondisclosure erroneous must depend on the particular circumstances of each case, taking into consideration the crime charged, the possible defenses, the possible significance of the informer's testimony, and other relevant factors."

According to Justice Burton, the circumstances of this case demonstrate that John Doe's possible testimony was highly relevant and might have been helpful to the defense. The defendant and Doe were alone and unobserved during crucial times. John Doe was the only witness the defendant had unless Roviaro took the stand in his own defense. Because Doe helped set up the criminal activities and played a prominent part in the transaction, his testimony might have disclosed that Roviaro was entrapped. Doe might have also thrown doubt on the identity of the package entered into evidence. He was also the only witness who could have testified concerning Roviaro's possible lack of knowledge of the contents of the package. Based on these and additional considerations the Court concluded, "This is a case where the Government's informer was the sole participant, other than the accused in the transaction charged. The informer was the only witness in a position to amplify or contradict the testimony of government witnesses. Moreover a government witness testified that Doe denied knowing [Roviaro] or even having seen him before. We conclude that, under these circumstances, the trial court committed prejudicial error in permitting the Government to withhold the identity of its undercover employee in the face of repeated demands by the accused for his disclosure."

In dissent, Justice Clark reasoned that the majority decision was totally unsound based on the facts presented in this case. "The short of it is that the conviction of a self-confessed dope peddler is reversed because the Government refused to furnish the name of its informant whose identity the undisputed evidence indicates was well known to the peddler. Yet the Court reverses on the ground of unfairness because of the Government's failure to perform this fruitless gesture. In my view this does violence to the common understanding of what is fair and unjust."

QUESTIONS

1. What is a privilege? List several important in the overall field of criminal law.
2. What factors did Justice Burton emphasize must be considered before ordering disclosure of the identity of an informant? Discuss each point.
3. What is a material witness? What is the specific holding in this case regarding disclosure of an informer's identity?

McCray v. Illinois
386 U.S. 300, 87 S.Ct. 1056, 18 L.Ed. 2ᴰ 62 (1967)

SETTING: McCray's arrest in Chicago took place at about seven in the morning on January 16, 1964. Officer Jackson and two fellow officers had a conversation with an informant early in the morning of January 16, who told them that McCray "was selling narcotics and had narcotics on his person and that he could be found in the vicinity of 47th and Calumet at this particular time." The officers drove to the location and when they spotted McCray, the informer pointed him out and then left on foot. Officer Jackson observed McCray talking to a couple of people and after seeing the police car, walk hurriedly between two buildings. "At this point," Jackson testified, "my partner and myself got out of the car and informed him we had information he had narcotics on his person, placed him in the police vehicle at this point." A search of the defendant followed, during which heroin was found in a cigarette package.

PROCEDURAL PROBLEM: Jackson testified that he had been acquainted with the informer for about a year and during that time he had supplied Jackson with accurate information about narcotics activities which resulted in numerous arrests and convictions. Jackson also testified that the names given to him by the informer often resulted in convictions.

When asked for the name of the informant by defense counsel, the state objected and the trial court sustained the objection. A second officer gave substantially the same testimony and was likewise asked the identity of the informant. The state's objection to this question was also sustained.

THE ISSUE: Did the Illinois court violate the defendant's constitutional right by not requiring the informant's identity to be revealed?

THE ANSWER: No.

DISCUSSION: According to the majority, a tip from an informant of known reliability that an accused had narcotics on his person was adequate to give the Illinois police probable cause for a warrantless arrest and search. Justice Stewart referred to *Roviaro* v. *United States*, 353 U.S. 53 (1957), *supra*, which involved the informer's privilege, not at a preliminary to determine probable cause for an arrest or search, but at the trial itself, where the issue was the fundamental one of guilt or innocence. The Court in *Roviaro* noted that the disclosure of the informant's identity was essential to a fair determination of the case. When this is so, the privilege must give way. However, *Roviaro* did not set forth a fixed rule regarding disclosure of the identity of an informant.

In response to the defendant's claim that his rights were violated when the state's objection was sustained, Justice Stewart emphasized, "We are now asked to hold that the Constitution somehow compels Illinois to abolish the informer's privilege from its law of evidence, and to require disclosure of the informer's identity in every such preliminary hearing where it appears that officers made the arrest or search in reliance upon facts supplied by an informer they had reason to trust." Justice Stewart noted that the argument was based on the due process clause of the Fourteenth Amendment and the Sixth Amendment.

In addressing the due process argument, Stewart said, "Nothing in the Due Process Clause of the Fourteenth Amendment requires a state court judge in every such hearing to assume the arresting officers are committing perjury." Citing *Spencer* v. *Texas*, 385 U.S. 554 (1967), Stewart wrote that to take such a step would be beyond the proper function of the Court. "It would be a wholly unjustifiable encroachment by this court upon the constitutional power of States to promulgate their own rules of evidence."

The Court was unclear as to why McCray thought his Sixth Amendment right to confrontation and cross-examination was violated by the Illinois informer's privilege. If it was because the refusal to reveal the informer's identity deprived him of the right to cross-examine a witness, the claim was invalid. If the argument were followed, no witness on cross-examination could ever assert a testimonial privilege "including the privilege against compulsory self-incrimination guaranteed by the Constitution itself. We have never given the Sixth Amendment such a construction, and we decline to do so now."

QUESTIONS

1. What is the specific holding of this case in regard to the due process clause of the Fourteenth Amendment and the confrontation clause of the Sixth Amendment?
2. Distinguish the factual situation and the holdings in *Roviaro* and *McCray*.
3. Write a dissenting opinion for this case based on the argument that the defendant is denied his right to confront a witness against him because the identity of the informant was not revealed.

Chapter 6

Right to Counsel

The first dramatic decision announcing the application of the due process clause of the Fourteenth Amendment to mandate the guarantee of the right of counsel in a state proceeding was in *Powell* v. *Alabama* in 1932. The peculiar facts in the case could have led to only one rational decision—that which the United States Supreme Court announced. The guarantee of the right of counsel in felony and misdemeanor cases in state courts, however, was still a long way off.

The cases in this chapter trace the history of the right to counsel from 1932 to 1973. The student can follow the changing philosophy of the Supreme Court justices from a period of judicial restraint through the years of the so-called "Warren Court." One can sense the development of the procedural protections guaranteed to a criminal defendant. There was an initial reluctance by the United States Supreme Court to become involved in the criminal procedures of the states; once the gate was breached, however, the Court did not hesitate to move rapidly toward insuring the availability of counsel at all stages of the criminal process.

Constitution of the United States, Sixth Amendment

In all criminal prosecutions, the accused shall enjoy the right . . . to have the Assistance of Counsel for his defense.

Constitution of California, Article 1, Section 13

In criminal prosecutions, in any court whatever, the party shall have the right . . . to appear and defend, in person and with counsel.

California Penal Code, Section 686

Rights of defendant in criminal action. In a criminal action the defendant is entitled . . . : (2) To be allowed counsel as in civil actions, or to appear and defend in person and with counsel.

Constitution of the State of Illinois, Article 2, Section 9

In all criminal prosecutions the accused shall have the right to appear and defend in person and by counsel.

Constitution of Alabama, Article 1, Section 6

That in all criminal prosecutions the accused has a right to be heard by himself and counsel, or either. . . .

Federal Rules of Criminal Procedure, Rule 44

(a) Right to Assigned Counsel. Every defendant who is unable to obtain counsel shall be entitled to have counsel assigned to represent him at every stage of the proceedings from his initial appearance . . . through the appeal, unless he waives such appointment.

Powell v. *Alabama*
287 U.S. 45, 53 S.Ct. 55, 77 L.Ed. 158 (1932)

SETTING: The defendants were several Negroes, tried in separate groups; all were charged with the crime of rape of two white girls. The record of the case shows that the two defendants in this specific case, along with a number of other Negroes, were on a freight train passing through Alabama. On the same freight train were seven white boys and two white girls. A fight developed and all of the white boys, with the exception of one Gilley, were thrown off the train. All the participants in the fight, including the two females, were in an open gondola car. A message was sent ahead reporting the fight and asking that every Negro be taken off the train.

Before the train reached Scottsboro, Alabama, a sheriff's posse seized the defendants and two other Blacks, along with both the girls. All were taken to Scottsboro, the county seat. Word of their coming and of the alleged assault preceded them, and a large crowd met the group in Scottsboro. The attitude of the crowd was one of great hostility, although it did not appear that the defendants were seriously threatened with harm or were in danger. The sheriff, however, called out the militia to help safeguard the prisoners. In fact, every step in the criminal process from arraignment to sentencing was accompanied by the militia. It was perfectly apparent that from beginning to end, the proceedings took place in an atmosphere of tense, hostile, and excited public sentiment. During the entire time, the military closely confined and guarded the defendants.

The record of the trial gives the age of only one defendant, age nineteen; but it does clearly indicate that most, if not all of them were young and were constantly referred to as "the boys." All were not Alabama residents; all were illiterate.

PROCEDURAL PROBLEM: During the trial both girls testified that they had been assaulted by six different Negroes in turn. With the exception of Gilley, who testified in rebuttal, none of the white boys was called to testify.

The defendants were arraigned immediately upon return of the indictment and pleaded not guilty. Apparently they were not asked whether they had or were able to employ counsel, wished to have appointed counsel, or had friends or relatives with whom they wished to communicate. The importance of affording the defendants the opportunity to consult with friends or relatives is demonstrated by the fact that very soon *after* conviction, counsel appeared on their behalf.

Six days after the indictment, the trials began. The trial judge stated that he had appointed "members of this bar [Alabama] to represent them, I expect that is right." Thus until the very morning of the trial, no lawyer had been named or definitely designated to represent the defendants. Prior to that time the trial judge had appointed "all members of the bar" for the limited purpose of arraigning the defendants. During the trial it appeared that the participation of one member of the Alabama bar was willing to offer whatever services he could, but the record of the trial indicated that the appearance of counsel was more *pro forma* than active and zealous.

THE ISSUE: In light of the above circumstances discussed, could it be said that the defendants were accorded the right to counsel in a substantial sense in a state capital case?

THE ANSWER: No.

DISCUSSION: In reaching this result, a defendant charged with a serious crime cannot be stripped of his right to have sufficient time to have the advice of counsel and prepare his defense. Under these circumstances, justice cannot proceed calmly and deliberately but depends on the rule of the mob.

In deciding as it did, the United States Supreme Court also had to decide whether the denial of assistance of counsel, as provided for in all criminal prosecutions by the Alabama Constitution, countervened the due process clause of the Fourteenth Amendment to the federal Constitution. In light of the facts outlined in the above discussion—the ignorance and illiteracy of the defendants, their youth, the public hostility, the imprisonment and surveillance by the militia, the lack of communication with friends and relatives, and the fact that they stood to be sentenced to death—the U.S. Supreme Court held that it was a denial of due process to fail to afford to the defendants reasonable time and opportunity to secure counsel.

Even if the trial could and did provide the opportunity to secure counsel, and even if the defendants did not have the ability to employ their own counsel, the court stated that the necessity of counsel was so vital and imperative that the failure of the trial court to make an effective appointment of counsel was also a denial of due process under the Fourteenth Amendment.

In summary, the United States Supreme Court held that at least in a capital case, where the defendant is unable to employ counsel and is incapable of adequately making his own defense because of ignorance, feeble-mindedness, illiteracy, or the like, it is the duty of the court, whether requested or not, to assign counsel as a requisite of the due process of law. This duty is not discharged by an assignment at such a time or under such circumstances as to preclude the giving of effective aid in the preparation and trial of the case.

The judgments of the state courts against the defendants were reversed and the cases were remanded for new proceedings consistent with the holding of the U.S. Supreme Court decision.

QUESTIONS

1. In your opinion, at what step in the proceeding should an accused be afforded the right to counsel of his own choosing?
2. How do you feel this decision was accepted by the states in the 1930s? What are the reasons for your answer?

3. The *Powell* v. *Alabama* case was restricted to a very narrow holding as it pertains to the right of counsel. What is it?

Betts v. Brady
316 U.S. 455, 62 S.Ct. 1252, 86 L.Ed. 1595 (1942)

SETTING: The defendant was indicted for robbery by the state of Maryland. At his arraignment, he advised the judge that because of a lack of funds, he was unable to employ counsel. The judge refused to appoint an attorney for him, explaining that the practice in the Circuit Court of Carroll County was to appoint counsel for indigent only in rape and murder prosecutions.

The defendant, without waiving his asserted right to counsel, entered a not guilty plea, elected to be tried without a jury, and had witnesses summoned at his request. He examined his own witnesses and cross-examined those of the state. His own witnesses tended to establish an alibi. The defendant was afforded the opportunity to testify but preferred not to take the witness stand. Upon finding him guilty, the judge imposed a sentence of eight years.

PROCEDURAL PROBLEM: While serving his sentence, the defendant filed a petition for a writ of habeas corpus with the state court in which he alleged he was deprived of the right of the assistance of counsel guaranteed by the Fourteenth Amendment of the federal Constitution. The petition was rejected. Another petition filed some six months later by the defendant was heard by the Maryland Court of Appeals (the highest court in Maryland). Based on an agreed set of facts which were incorporated into the record, the Chief Judge of the Maryland Court of Appeals granted the writ but denied the requested relief and returned the defendant to custody. The defendant then filed a writ of certiorari with the United States Supreme Court.

THE ISSUE: Does due process of law demand that in every criminal case, whatever the circumstances, a state must furnish counsel to an indigent defendant?

THE ANSWER: No.

DISCUSSION: In his argument for relief, the defendant stated that the rule that could be deduced from previous United States Supreme Court decisions was that in every case, whatever the circumstances, a person charged with a crime who is unable to obtain counsel must be furnished counsel by the state. However, the Supreme Court pointed out that although the defendant was correct, none of the decisions squarely adjudicated the question presented in this case.

The Court noted that the issue was whether the furnishing of counsel in all cases to an indigent is dictated by notions of inherent, natural, and fundamental fairness. The Sixth Amendment of the federal Constitution pertains to the national courts. Does the rule express so fundamental and essential a principal that it is made obligatory upon the states by the Fourteenth Amendment? Referring to the legislative, con-stitutional, and judicial history of the states, the Court deduced that the appointment of counsel was not a fundamental right essential to a fair trial. The Supreme Court noted that in light of the judicial, legislative, and historical evidence, it would not hold that the concept of due process incorporated into the Fourteenth Amendment obligates the states, what-ever their own views, to furnish counsel in every case.

The Supreme Court in effect said that the states were required to provide a lawyer for a crime only where special circumstances indicated that the lack of counsel would result in a trial lacking "fundamental fairness."

The state conviction in *Betts* v. *Brady* was affirmed.

Following the *Betts* v. *Brady* decision, the Supreme Court held re-peatedly that the failure of the state to appoint counsel to aid an indigent in his defense *did* violate the due process clause of the Fourteenth Amendment because of the special circumstances of each case. The fol-lowing case decisions serve as examples:

Williams v. *Kaiser,* 323 U.S 471 (1954), technical defenses

Tompkins v. *Missouri,* 323, U.S. 485 (1954), capital offense

Rice v. *Olson,* 324 U.S. 786 (1945), question of federal jurisdiction

Moore v. *Michigan,* 355 U.S. 155 (1957), life imprisonment for murder, technical defenses to murder

Hudson v. *North Carolina,* 363 U.S. 697 (1960), complicated trial procedure

Chewing v. *Cunningham,* 368 U.S. 443 (1962), technical interpreta-tion of a statute

In summary, *Betts* v. *Brady* was gradually eroded by many cases that extended the special circumstances test. It was difficult to distinguish the necessity of counsel in a capital case in Alabama *(Hamilton* v. *Alabama* 368 U.S. 52 [1961]) from a murder charge in Michigan where the penalty was life imprisonment *(Moore* v. *Michigan, supra).*

The stage was set for *Gideon* v. *Wainwright* in 1963.

QUESTIONS

1. How did the opinion in *Betts* v. *Brady* answer the argument that due process does not require appointment of counsel in all criminal cases in a state?
2. Discuss the kinds of special circumstances that necessitate appointment of counsel. How can one rationalize the dictates of the due process clause with the special circumstances rule?
3. Note the distinctions between the holdings in *Powell* v. *Alabama* and *Betts* v. *Brady*. Do you agree with each holding?
4. What points would you emphasize if you had to prepare a dissenting opinion to *Betts* v. *Brady*?
5. If the Supreme Court had held that an attorney must be provided in all felony criminal cases, what practical problems would likely have been encountered by the states?

Gideon v. *Wainwright*
372 U.S. 335, 83 S.Ct. 792, 9 L.Ed. 2ᴰ 799 (1963)

SETTING: Mr. Gideon was charged in a Florida state court with having broken into and entered a poolroom with the intent to commit a misdemeanor. The offense is a felony under Florida law and is frequently a form of burglary in the law of most states. The defendant appeared in court as indigent and requested appointment of a lawyer. The judge denied the request, stating that under the Florida law, counsel could only be appointed when a person is charged with a capital offense.

Gideon then went to trial before a jury, and he conducted his defense about as well as a layman could be expected to. He made an opening statement to the jury, cross-examined prosecution witnesses, presented his own defense witnesses, declined to testify in his own defense, and made a short final argument emphasizing his innocence. The jury convicted him and a five-year sentence was imposed.

He filed a writ of habeas corpus in the Florida Supreme Court attacking his conviction and sentence on the ground that the trial court's refusal to appoint an attorney for him denied him rights guaranteed to him by the Constitution. The Florida Supreme Court denied relief.

PROCEDURAL PROBLEM: Since the *Betts* v. *Brady* decision, the problem of a defendant's constitutional right to an attorney in a state court had been a continuing source of controversy and litigation in both state and federal courts. The facts upon which Betts claimed he was denied his right to have an attorney appointed for him are very similar to those in *Gideon*. The problem was clear: Should *Betts* v. *Brady* be overruled?

THE ISSUES: The issues faced by the court were simple but of gigantic importance: (1) Is an indigent defendant charged in a state court with a noncapital felony entitled to the assistance of a lawyer as a matter of right under the due process clause of the Fourteenth Amendment? (2) Should *Betts* v. *Brady* be overruled?

THE ANSWERS: (1) Yes. (2) Yes.

DISCUSSION: The Sixth Amendment provides a stricture on prosecution in the federal courts by stating that "In all criminal prosecutions, the accused shall enjoy the right . . . to have the Assistance of Counsel for his defense." Betts argued that this right extended to indigent defendants in state courts by virtue of the due process clause of the Fourteenth Amendment. The United States Supreme Court in 1932 rejected this on the basis of historical data by concluding that the appointment of counsel was not a fundamental right, essential to a fair trial.

The Court in *Gideon* v. *Wainright,* however, accepted the Betts argument that a fundamental right essential to a fair trial is made obligatory upon the states by the Fourteenth Amendment. The Court said that *Betts* was wrong, however, in concluding that the Sixth Amendment's guarantee of counsel is not one of the fundamental rights. The *Gideon* Court pointed out numerous decisions decided before *Betts* v. *Brady* holding that the right to counsel was indeed fundamental and *Betts* made a departure from the law at the time it was decided.

Unless counsel is provided under our adversary system, a poor defendant who cannot hire a lawyer cannot be assured a fair trial. Governments set up massive legal machinery and hire the best lawyers available to prepare and present cases. Those who can afford attorneys hire the best within their means. The fact that the government *hires* the best lawyers to prosecute cases and affluent defendants *hire* the best counsel they can to defend constitutes the strongest indications of the belief that lawyers are a necessity, not a luxury, in a criminal case.

By the time of *Gideon* v. *Wainwright* in 1963, the law in almost all states provided that the indigent had a right under state law to appointed counsel in all felony cases. When the Supreme Court by unanimous decision overruled *Betts* v. *Brady* by *Gideon* v. *Wainwright,* there was very little problem in most states, but if the decision had occurred in 1942 when *Betts* was decided, the criminal procedure of requiring counsel in all criminal cases would have caused great dislocation in most of the country.

Who is an indigent? There is no universal or even widely accepted definition of this. Is the fact that a defendant is unable to make bail proof of indigency? Some judges take this position, and if a defendant goes before this kind of judge it would seem to be important to forego bail in order to preserve the right to have court-appointed counsel. One may ask whether a person who is accused of a crime, even falsely, should be required to use his life savings and mortgage his home in order to be represented by counsel. If he is not indigent when the allegation is made, quite often he will be after he defends himself (even if he is successful in securing an acquittal).

The rule followed by many judges in determining indigency is to evaluate the total financial picture of the person. One case held that a person who had $1,000 and no obligations is not indigent. In still other situations a person having much more but also having many family and business obligations may be indigent. It has been stated that in essence the test to be applied to ascertain indigency is whether or not a private attorney would be interested in representing the defendant in his present economic circumstances recognizing that the cost of legal representation will vary according to the standards in the community, the complexity of the case, and the expenses necessary to defend it.

As noted above, the question of indigency is a question of fact which the judge determines based on a completely flexible standard. Depending upon the case, a fairly well-off person will be declared indigent if the costs of the defense will financially ruin him and his family. In summary, the assignment of counsel to indigent defendants has proven to be quite a problem. The following materials offer an insight into its complexity:

76 *Harvard Law Review*, 579 (1962–63)

56 *Journal of Criminal Law, Criminology and Police Science*, 503 (1965)

13 *Stanford Law Review*, 522 (1961)

People v. *Ferry*, 237 Cal. App. 2ᴰ 880, 47 Cal. Rptr. 324 (1965)

27 *Michigan State Bar Journal*, 13, 19 (April 1948)

Hill v. *Superior Court*, 46 Cal. 2ᴰ 169, 293 P.2ᴰ 10 (1956)

In *Griffin* v. *Illinois*, 351 U.S. 12 (1956), full direct appellate review could only be had in Illinois when the appellate court was furnished with a copy of the trial proceedings certified by the trial judge. The transcript was sometimes costly and was furnished free only to indigent defendants sentenced to death. The United States Supreme Court held that an indigent convicted of a felony was entitled to a free transcript of a trial for the purposes of appeal if transcripts were usable by nonindigents. Mr. Justice Black noted that "in criminal trials a state can no more discriminate on account of poverty than on account of race, religion, or color. Plainly the ability to pay costs in advance bears no rational relationship to a defendant's guilt or innocence and could not be used as an excuse to deprive a defendant of a fair trial. . . . It is true that a state is not required by the federal constitution to provide appellate courts or a right to appellate review at all. . . . But that is not to say that a State that does grant appellate review can do so in such a way that discriminates against some convicted defendants on account of their poverty." This very holding subsequently was held to be applicable to an indigent convicted of a misdemeanor who desired a transcript for aid in appeal. The opinion noted that a defendant need not always be given a complete verbatim transcript. Suitable alternatives in individual cases may be a partial transcript or a stipulation of facts. However, when an indigent misdemeanant's grounds for appeal make out a "colorable need for a complete transcript," the state bears the burden that an alternative will suffice. The Court emphasized that the line between a felony and a misdemeanor is an unreasonable distinction forbidden by the Fourteenth Amendment. *Mayer* v. *City of Chicago*, 404 U.S. 189 (1971).

QUESTIONS

1. In your particular jurisdiction, what effect did *Gideon* v. *Wainwright* have on providing counsel to indigents in felony cases?
2. The specific holding of *Gideon* did not extend to all criminal cases. What is meant by this statement, and why do you think some jurisdictions restricted were reluctant to extend the right to counsel to *all* criminal offenses?
3. Do you believe that a rich felony defendant represented by counsel of his choosing has a better chance of acquittal than an indigent who is represented by appointed counsel? Explain your response.
4. In a concurring opinion to *Gideon*, Justice Douglas reiterated his belief that the Fourteenth Amendment protects from infringement by the states the privileges, protections, and safeguards granted by the Bill of Rights. What is the thrust of this argument? Discuss fully.

Hamilton v. Alabama
368 U.S. 52, 82 S.Ct. 157, 7 L.Ed. 2ᴰ 114 (1961)

SETTING: The defendant was convicted of the crime of breaking and entering a dwelling at night with the intent to ravish, and was sentenced to death. On his appeal, Hamilton claimed that he had been denied the assistance of counsel at the arraignment. The Alabama Supreme Court noted that the right to counsel under both federal and state constitutions included the right to counsel at the arraignment. The Court did not reach the merits of this because it did not wish to impeach the trial court minutes, which indicated that the defendant did have counsel at the arraignment. Alabama procedure did not permit this kind of impeachment on an appeal. Apparently the defendant was represented by appointed counsel on a first indictment charging him with burglary. Later the present indictment, relating to the same incident, was returned. His previously appointed counsel was notified that the defendant would be rearraigned, but *no* lawyer appeared at the second arraignment. The early appointment of the attorney did not carry over to the second arraignment.

The defendant then sought certiorari with the United States Supreme Court and Alabama responded to the petition that Hamilton could attack the Alabama judgment by introducing extrinsic evidence by use of *coram nobis*. He then proceeded the suggested way in the Alabama courts. This time the Alabama Supreme Court again recognized that the defendant had a right to be represented by counsel under Alabama law, but nevertheless denied the defendant's bid for relief by stating that there was no showing that the defendant was disadvantaged in any way by the absence of an attorney when he entered his not guilty plea. The United States Supreme Court next granted the defendant's application for certiorari.

PROCEDURAL PROBLEM: Under Alabama criminal procedure, the insanity defense had to be pleaded at the arraignment or the opportunity was lost. Thereafter the plea could not be made except at the discretion of the trial court judge, and his refusal to accept the late plea was not reversible on appeal. At the arraignment pleas in abatement, motions to quash based on systematic racial exclusion had to be made, or motions that the grand jury was improperly drawn had to be made. It should also be noted that in Alabama indigents are seldom furnished counsel until arraignment. Hurried or perfunctory conferences with newly appointed counsel, usually in the courtroom, followed by a quick plea of guilty or settlement of the case with the prosecutor, left the door open to ineffective assistance of counsel and involuntary or improperly inducing a plea because the defendant was often not fully aware of all of the consequences of the plea. In short, the defendant's right to a speedy trial might indeed result in too speedy a trial.

It is clear that because of the myriad, complex legal issues that might arise at the Alabama arraignment, the defendant would be at a great disadvantage without the advice of an attorney.

THE ISSUE: Is the arraignment a "critical stage" in criminal prosecution, so that denial of the right of counsel is a violation of due process?

THE ANSWER: Yes.

DISCUSSION: What happens at the arraignment may affect the whole trial. Available defenses may be irretrievably lost if not then and there asserted. As stated in *Powell* v. *Alabama, supra,* the accused in a capital case requires the guiding hand of counsel at every stage in the proceedings against him. Without it, even if he is not guilty, he faces the danger of conviction because he does not know how to establish his innocence.

The Supreme Court emphasized that when one pleads to a capital charge without benefit of counsel, the court *will not stop to determine whether or not prejudice actually results.* The degree of prejudice may never be known. It is only the presence of counsel that enables the defendant to have an opportunity to plead intelligently. In other words, a "critical stage" is any part of a criminal proceeding in which certain rights may be sacrificed.

The arraignment has differing consequences in the various jurisdictions. Under federal procedure, the arraignment is the preliminary stage where an accused is informed of the indictment and pleads to it, thereby establishing the issue to be tried at the trial. Rules 10 and 11, Federal Rules of Criminal Procedure, 18 U.S.C.A.

What is the usual arraignment procedure? It is normally nothing more than calling the accused to the bar of the court, asking if he is represented by counsel, appointing an attorney if he is indigent, reading and explaining the indictment, and demanding a plea. Its primary purpose is to obtain from the accused his answer, or plea, to the indictment. Depending on the statutes in various states, several additional matters are covered at the arraignment:

1. The defendant must be advised of his right to a speedy trial. If the state has a statutory time set within which the accused must be tried, he should be advised of the limit.

2. He must be advised of his right to confront and cross-examine witnesses who testify against him in court.

3. He must be advised of his right to produce his own witnesses and that he has the power of the court behind him to compel witnesses to testify.

4. He must be advised of his right to a jury trial and will receive one unless the right is waived.

5. He must be advised of his right to refuse to testify.

6. He must be advised that he has a right to be admitted to bail unless the offense is capital. He must be advised that he may be released on his own recognizance if evidence is presented to the court that there is good cause for this procedure.

7. Where applicable, he must be advised of his right to a preliminary hearing within the mandatory time period.

8. If there are co-defendants, each one is advised of his right to a separate counsel if there is a conflict of interest and of his right to a separate trial.

For a good discussion of the provision of defense services, see *Standards Relating to Providing Defense Services*, American Bar Association Project on Standards for Criminal Justice, Advisory Committee on the Prosecution and Defense Functions (Chicago: American Bar Association, 1967).

QUESTIONS

1. Give the distinction between the arraignment and the preliminary hearing. Discuss why some legal scholars have stated that there is definitely a need for counsel at the preliminary hearing but seldom is counsel necessary at the arraignment.
2. In your jurisdiction, is there an arraignment provided for misdemeanors? Should counsel be provided in misdemeanor arraignments? Discuss the various arguments that may be put forth for and against this.
3. Discuss the statement that when one pleads to a capital charge, the court will not stop to determine whether or not prejudice actually resulted from the lack of counsel. What was the United States Supreme Court saying with this statement?

Douglas v. California
372 U.S. 353, 83 S.Ct. 814, 9 L.Ed. 2ᴅ 811 (1963)

SETTING: The two defendants, Douglas and Meyes, were jointly tried and convicted on an information charging them with thirteen felony counts. A single public defender was appointed to represent them. At the beginning of the trial, the public defender moved for a continuance, giving as reasons that the case was very complex, that he was not as well prepared as he should have been, and that there was a conflict of interest between the prisoners requiring the appointment of separate counsel for each of them. The motion was denied. Thereafter, the defendants dismissed the public defender, claiming the lawyer was unprepared and renewed the motion for a continuance. They also made a new motion for separate counsel to be appointed. Both motions were again denied. Douglas and Meyes were subsequently convicted by a jury of all thirteen counts and were both given prison terms. Both appealed to the California District Court of Appeal under a statute giving them that right. The District Court of Appeal affirmed the conviction. The California Supreme Court subsequently denied a writ of discretion review.

PROCEDURAL PROBLEMS: The Court record showed that under the California rule of criminal procedure, if a defendant requested the aid of counsel in an appeal, the appellate court was directed to make an independent investigation of the record and determine whether it would be of advantage to the defendant or helpful to the court to have counsel appointed. Counsel was appointed if the answer was "yes" but not if the answer was "no." The record also indicated that the defendants were indigent.

THE ISSUE: Where a defendant is granted a *first appeal* from a criminal conviction as a matter of right, does the due process clause of the Fourteenth Amendment mandate that an indigent be afforded the right to be represented by court-appointed counsel?

THE ANSWER: Yes.

DISCUSSION: The United States Supreme Court by a 6–3 vote held invalid under the Fourteenth Amendment the California requirement conditioning an indigent defendant's right to court-appointed counsel on an appellate court's determination that assistance of counsel would be helpful.

Mr. Justice Douglas, who wrote the majority opinion, stated that it was clear that "there is lacking that equality demanded by the Fourteenth Amendment where the rich man who appeals of right, enjoys the benefits of counsel's examination into the record, research of the law, and marshalling of arguments on his behalf, while the indigent, already burdened by a preliminary determination that his case is without merit is forced to shift for himself. The indigent, where the record is unclear or the errors are hidden has only the right to a meaningless ritual, while the rich man has a meaningful appeal."

The Court was not concerned in this case with problems that could arise from the denial of counsel for the preparation of a petition for discretionary review beyond the stage in the appellate process at which the claims have been presented by a lawyer and passed upon by the appellate court. It was careful, however, to point out that under the Fourteenth Amendment a state can provide for differences in procedures as long as the result does not amount to a denial of due process nor result in invidious discrimination. In Justice Clark's dissent, he noted that in the previous term of the Court over 1,200 in forma pauperis applications were received, and in none of them had an attorney been appointed. Had the Court been required to read these briefs and listen to oral arguments in all of the cases, the work of the Court would have been greatly hindered. Was this the practical reason that the Court took the pains it did to limit the Douglas application to the first appeal only?

Should the Douglas holding result in the requirement of counsel at all appellate stages? One prominent attorney insists that it will. 52 A.B.A.J. 135 (1966).

The Supreme Court decided in two per curiam decisions that the Douglas case was retroactive in its application—Smith v. Crouse, 378 U.S. 584 (1963); Ruark v. Colorado, 378 U.S. 585 (1963).

What kind of defense and argument should an attorney make when he is appointed to represent a defendant on appeal? It appears that the constitutional requirement of substantial equality and fair process would be attained only if the lawyer acts in the role of an active advocate in the client's behalf rather than as a friend of the court. He should raise possible points and present arguments in favor of his client. Anders v. California, 386 U.S. 738 (1967).

What is effective aid of counsel? The rationale of the right of counsel is simply stated. Not even the most well-informed intelligent layman can adequately preserve his rights without the assistance of trained legal counsel. As has been seen, the Sixth Amendment provides the right for assistance of counsel. If this is not an illusory right, it must apply equally to the rich and poor and is available at the very early stages of the criminal processes. The simple right to counsel itself is insufficient. The right to counsel implies the right to assistance of effective counsel. In order to be effective, the lawyer must be available early in the proceedings—from the arrest on. Generally speaking, the claim by a defendant that a particular defense counsel was incompetent or ineffective has not been greeted in a favorable light. The rule followed in most courts is generally expressed in *People* v. *Washington,* 41 Illinois 2ᴰ 16, 241 N.E. 2ᴰ 425 (1968), in which the Court stated that "the conduct of counsel [defense] . . . is that of only one of the officers of the court whose duty it is to see that the defendant receives a fair trial," and counsel's mistakes, "although indicative of a lack of skill or even incompetency, will not vitiate the trial unless on the whole the representation is of such a low caliber as to amount to no representation and to reduce the trial to a farce."

The reasons for this reluctance to find that a counsel was ineffective is in part self-defense on the part of the court; to grant the claim of inefficiency is to implicitly censure the trial court. The appellate court is in effect saying that the trial court permitted an injustice to occur in its presence because it did not know or would not do its job. What judge wants to say this about one of his colleagues! Also, because there are many appointed attorneys used in the country, many of whom by their own admission know little about criminal law and procedure, few would accept assignment if they were likely to be called ineffective in their defense of their client. Another very practical reason for not readily declaring that counsel is ineffective is that it is entirely feasible that an attorney with a desperate case will insure that his client will receive a new trial by deliberately committing errors.

The mere claim by a layman that his counsel is ineffective is totally unrealistic. How equipped is he to appraise the lawyer's professional skills? This point permeates the atmosphere when such a claim is made.

The *Douglas* v. *California* judgment was vacated and the case remanded to the California District Court of Appeal for further proceedings not inconsistent with the United States Supreme Court opinion.

QUESTIONS

1. In many states, mental commitment proceedings are civil in nature. If this is the situation in your state, what is the law regarding appointment of counsel for a person during the commitment proceedings? Discuss the pros and cons of your state's procedure.

2. Why do you think the Supreme Court gave retrospective application to *Douglas* v. *California?*
3. Is it sound policy for a Supreme Court decision to be based partly on the idea that if an attorney had to be appointed in all appeal petitions, the work of the court would bog down? What becomes of the idea that a defendant is guaranteed a fair trial from the beginning to the end of the criminal process if this concept is adopted? Discuss.

Coleman v. *Alabama*
399 U.S. 1, 90 S.Ct. 1999, 26 L.Ed. 2ᴰ 387 (1970)

SETTING: The defendants were convicted in an Alabama Circuit Court of assault with an intent to commit murder by shooting a man and wife who had parked on an Alabama highway to change a flat tire. In Alabama the preliminary hearing is not a required step in criminal procedure; the prosecutor may seek an indictment directly from the grand jury without a preliminary hearing. At the preliminary hearing the accused is not required to advance any defenses, and failure to do so does not preclude him from using every defense he may have at the trial. In Alabama, the admission of testimony at a preliminary hearing is barred at the trial in cases in which the accused does not have the benefit of cross-examination by and through counsel. Thus, nothing occurring at an Alabama preliminary hearing in the absence of counsel can substantially prejudice the rights of an accused who is on trial.

The defendants were denied the benefit of court-appointed counsel at a preliminary hearing prior to their indictment. They claim that the preliminary hearing is a "critical stage" of the prosecution and that Alabama's failure to provide them with the appointed counsel at the hearing unconstitutionally denied them the assistance of counsel.

PROCEDURAL PROBLEM: The problem here involves determination of whether or not a particular hearing in the criminal process is a "critical stage" requiring the provision of counsel. The phrase "critical stage" is used to describe any aspect of a preliminary phase of the total criminal process that is part of the "criminal prosecution" as this phrase is used in the Sixth Amendment.

THE ISSUE: Is the preliminary hearing a "critical stage" in a criminal prosecution requiring the appointment of counsel for an indigent defendant?

THE ANSWER: Yes.

DISCUSSION: Woven into the seven separate opinions among the eight Justices who participated in the case is the rule that an Alabama preliminary hearing is a "critical stage" of a criminal proceeding at which a lawyer is required. Five of the Justices (three of whom also wrote separate opinions) held that the Sixth Amendment makes counsel a requirement at the Alabama preliminary hearing even though the Alabama procedure allows the prosecutor to skip the preliminary hearing by taking his case directly to the grand jury. The defendant also does not waive his defenses by not presenting them, and in those cases in which the defendant has no counsel at the preliminary hearing, no evidence brought out can be used against him at the subsequent trial. Even with these factors, Justice Brennan emphasized that the Alabama preliminary hearing was a "critical stage." The Court noted that the guiding hand of counsel at the preliminary hearing is essential to protect the indigent accused against an erroneous or improper prosecution. The lawyer's skilled examination and cross-examination of witnesses may expose fatal weaknesses in the prosecutor's case, which may lead the magistrate to refuse to bind the accused over. Also, the interrogation of witnesses by an experienced lawyer can fashion a vital impeachment tool for use in cross-examination of the state's witnesses at the trial. In addition, the attorney can preserve testimony favorable to the accused of a witness who does not appear at the trial.

Trained criminal counsel can effectively discover the case that the state has against his client and thereby prepare a proper defense to meet the expected case at the trial. As another reason for the necessity of counsel, one might make effective arguments that alternative approaches to criminal action might be ordered—such as mental commitment or further psychiatric examination. Arguments regarding bail may be largely overlooked without the guidance of counsel. Because the purpose of the preliminary hearing is to determine whether or not there is probable cause for charging the defendant with a criminal offense, adequate representation of an accused will insure that this mandate is met.

The dissenting Justices found no precedent for the holding of the majority. The dissenters saw no reason to reverse a conviction following a trial that was not shown to have been tainted in any way by the happenings at the preliminary hearing.

The majority remanded the case to the Alabama courts to ascertain whether the denial of counsel at the preliminary hearing was harmless error. Mr. Justice Stewart, in dissent, stated, "All I can say is that if the Alabama courts can figure out what they are supposed to do with the case now that it has been remanded to them, their perspectives will far exceed mine." The other dissenter, Chief Justice Burger, agreed that as a sound policy matter, counsel should be available to all persons at a preliminary hearing. This should be by statute or court rule. He disagreed with the notion that the Constitution commands appointment of counsel because the preliminary hearing is a "criminal prosecution."

In *Adams* v. *Illinois*, 405 U.S. 278 (1972) the Supreme Court held that *Coleman* had no retroactive application to preliminary hearings conducted prior to the *Coleman* decision because the lack of counsel at a preliminary hearing involves less danger to the integrity of the truth-determining process at trial than the omission of counsel at the trial itself or on appeal.

The Supreme Court vacated the defendants' convictions and remanded the case to the Alabama courts for proceedings not inconsistent with the opinion and to determine whether denial of counsel was harmless error.

QUESTIONS

1. What is the harmless error doctrine? With this doctrine in mind, and with the holding that the preliminary hearing is a "critical stage" in a criminal prosecution, what steps or reconsideration of the case could the Alabama courts take?
2. Does the following procedure satisfy the *Coleman* holding? There is no counsel appointed at the preliminary hearing, but at arraignment on a grand jury indictment, state procedure permits the appointment of counsel who can insist upon a reexamination of all evidence presented at the preliminary examination and the attorney does so insist.
3. In your state, what steps occur at a preliminary hearing? In your estimation, do these amount to a "critical stage" in a criminal prosecution?

Mempa v. *Rhay*
389 U.S. 128, 88 S.Ct. 254, 19 L.Ed 2^D 336 (1967)

SETTING: This case was a consolidation of two cases, each of which raised the issue of counsel at a probation revocation hearing. Mempa pleaded guilty to "joyriding" and was placed on probation for two years on the condition that he spend thirty days in the county jail. The imposition of the sentence was deferred. About four months later, the Spokane County prosecuting attorney moved to have Mempa's probation revoked because he had been involved in a burglary. A hearing was held in the Spokane County Superior Court which the defendant, then seventeen years of age, and his step-father attended. He was not represented by counsel nor was he asked whether he wished to have counsel appointed for him. There was no inquiry made regarding the appointed counsel who had represented him previously.

PROCEDURAL PROBLEM: At the hearing Mempa was asked if it was true that he was involved in the alleged burglary; he answered that it was. A probation officer testified without cross-examination that according to his information, Mempa had been involved in the burglary and had previously denied participation in it. The court did not ask Mempa if he had anything to say or any evidence to offer, but immediately ordered Mempa's probation revoked and sentenced him to ten years in prison. The judge also stated that he would recommend to the parole board that Mempa be required to serve only a year.

Subsequently, Mempa filed for a writ of habeas corpus with the Washington Supreme Court, claiming that he had been deprived of his right to counsel at the proceeding at which his probation was revoked and his deferred sentence imposed. The writ was denied by the Washington Supreme Court and the United States Supreme Court later granted a writ of certiorari.

THE ISSUE: Does a defendant have a right to the assistance of counsel at a probation revocation hearing at which a deferred sentence may be imposed?

THE ANSWER: Yes.

DISCUSSION: Citing *Hamilton* v. *Alabama* and *Gideon* v. *Wainwright, supra,* the Supreme Court noted that there has been no occasion to enumerate the various stages in a criminal proceeding at which counsel was required; but clearly both of these cases stand for the proposition that appointment of counsel for an indigent is necessary at every stage of a criminal proceeding where substantial rights of a criminal accused may be affected. In particular, the sentencing in a criminal case is indeed a "critical stage" in the criminal prosecution.

The prosecution argued that the probation revocation hearing was not a sentence hearing because Mempa had been previously sentenced and then placed on probation. The revocation hearing was, in effect, a mere formality which constituted a part of the probation revocation proceeding because Washington law gave the judge little discretion in sentencing. He was required to sentence for the maximum term provided by law, with the state Board of Prison Terms and Parole actually determining the length of time to be served.

The sentencing judge and prosecutor are required by statute to make recommendations regarding the time to be served, the character of the defendant, and the circumstances of the crime. Because the Board places weight on the recommendations, the assistance of counsel to marshal facts, introduce mitigating evidence, and generally assist the defendant in presenting his case is obviously necessary. In addition, in Washington other legal rights may be lost if not exercised at this stage. For example, the state law provides that an appeal in a case in which a guilty plea is followed by probation can only be taken after sentence is imposed following probation revocation. An unaided defendant might very well be totally unaware of the important legal rights he has at the probation revocation hearing.

In summary, the Supreme Court did not question the Washington deferred-sentencing procedure. It did, however, decide that an attorney must be afforded at the Washington proceeding whether it be labeled a probation revocation hearing or a deferred-sentence proceeding.

The state court judgments were reversed and the two cases remanded for new hearings.

As to a *parolee's* right to assigned counsel at a parole revocation hearing, see *Rose* v. *Haskins,* 388 F. 2ᴰ 91 (6th Cir., 1968). Also providing relevant reading is "Sentencing, Probation and the Rehabilitative Ideal: The View from *Mempa* v. *Rhay*," 47, *Texas Law Review* 1 (1968).

Does the Constitution require a hearing before probation may be revoked? Justice Cardozo rejected this idea in *Escoe* v. *Zerbst,* 295 U.S. 490 (1935); "[W]e do not accept the petitioner's contention that the privilege [probation] has a basis in the Constitution, apart from any statute. Probation or suspension of sentence comes as an act of grace to one convicted of crime, and may be coupled with such conditions in respect of its duration as Congress may impose."

An indigent person is entitled to appointment of counsel to represent him at a revocation of probation hearing where sentence had been pronounced, but execution thereof had been suspended during good behavior, even though the proceeding to review performance on probation is not a criminal trial. See *Perry* v. *Willard,* 247 Oregon 145, 427 P. 2ᴰ 1020 (1967).

QUESTIONS

1. What is the purpose of probation? Is this purpose served by treating the revocation of probation hearing as an adversary-type proceeding? Discuss.

2. Is the rationale behind *Mempa* v. *Rhay* the concern that the probation officers and judges have almost absolute discretionary power at probation revocation hearings that is too often abused?

3. Suppose a probationer had his probation revoked because he was involved in a burglary and he is later acquitted of the burglary. Should the acquittal bar revocation of probation based on the alleged commission of that offense?

Argersinger v. *Hamlin*
407 U.S. 25, 92 S.Ct. 2006, 32 L.Ed. 2ᴰ 530 (1972)

SETTING: The defendant, an indigent, was charged in Florida with carrying a concealed weapon. The potential punishment for the offense was up to six months' imprisonment, a $1,000 fine, or both. Upon a court trial at which the defendant was not represented by counsel, he was convicted and sentenced by the judge to ninety days in jail. In a habeas corpus petition to the Florida Supreme Court, the defendant argued that because he was indigent and not provided with an attorney, he could not present his defenses to the charges against him. The Florida Supreme Court rejected the defendant's claim regarding counsel by a 4–3 vote. The majority decided to follow precedent and held that the right to court-appointed counsel extended only to trials "for non-petty offenses punishable by more than six months' imprisonment." From the state holding, the defendant was granted his petition for certiorari, which was filed with the United States Supreme Court.

PROCEDURAL PROBLEM: Since the *Gideon* v. *Wainwright* decision, *supra,* there had been a question as to whether or not a defendant had the constitutional right to be represented by counsel in cases that were felonies, the specific holding based on the *Gideon* facts. The provisions of the Sixth Amendment selectively have been made applicable to the states by virtue of the Fourteenth Amendment. One is the constitutional requirement of a public trial in state proceedings. Another is the right to be informed of the nature and cause of the accusation. Still another is the right of confrontation. The right to compulsory process for obtaining witnesses in one's favor is also constitutionally required in the states. These rights were never limited to felonies or to lesser but serious offenses.

The right to a jury trial, also guaranteed by the Sixth Amendment by virtue of the Fourteenth, was limited to trials in which the potential punishment was six months' imprisonment or more. Although there was some historical basis for limiting a jury trial to serious criminal cases, the Sixth Amendment extended the right to counsel beyond its common-law scope.

THE ISSUE: Does the Sixth Amendment, through application of the Fourteenth Amendment, extend the right of appointment of counsel to misdemeanors?

THE ANSWER: Yes.

DISCUSSION: The Supreme Court in this decision extended the right to counsel to include not only felonies but any crime for which the accused could be jailed. The Court rejected the premise that because prosecutions for crimes punishable by imprisonment of less than six months may be tried without a jury, they may be tried without a lawyer. The assistance of counsel is often a requisite to the very existence of a fair trial. In a misdemeanor situation, the Court emphasized that legal questions which can lead to actual imprisonment even for a brief period can be as complex as when a person may be sentenced for a felony. For example, the simple vagrancy cases often involve thorny constitutional questions even though very short sentences may be imposed.

Guilty pleas loom as a large problem in great numbers of misdemeanor and felony cases. Certainly, counsel is needed so that a defendant can know exactly what he is doing, that he is being fairly treated by the prosecution, and that he is completely aware that he faces the prospect of going to prison. Another reason for the importance of counsel in misdemeanor cases is that the sheer number of cases may create an obsession for speedy disposition of cases at the expense of fair trials. Misdemeanor prosecutions too often result in assembly-line justice. One study concluded that misdemeanants who face trial without a lawyer are five times more likely to go to trial than those who have an attorney. The latter are five times more likely to have their charges dismissed.

One can see then that the misdemeanor involves problems that require the assistance of counsel to secure a fair trial just like the felony. The United States Supreme Court held that in the absence and knowing waiver by a defendant, no person may be imprisoned for any offense whether classified as petty, misdemeanor, or felony, unless he is represented by counsel at his trial. In short, the label that a state places on a particular crime has no significance.

Three of the concurring justices—Brennan, Douglas, and Stewart—noted that law students may provide an important source of legal representation to the indigent. Chief Justice Burger acknowledged that this decision would place a burden on the states but this should hardly be a surprise because the same recommendation was made by the American Bar Association five years earlier.

While concurring in the result, Justices Rehnquist and Powell thought that the due process considerations of fundamental fairness rather than an inflexible rule based on possible imprisonment should determine an indigent's right to counsel. Mr. Justice Powell believed that the majority's assessment of the country's legal resources to handle the new caseload was unrealistic because in many instances there are simply not enough lawyers available to handle misdemeanor cases. Small communities are likely to be seriously affected and may wind up with no credible means of enforcing misdemeanors against indigents.

The recognition of the right to counsel in prosecutions for minor traffic offenses which may have possible jail sentences poses some serious legal and practical difficulties. New York, California, and several other states have solved this problem by holding that such incidents are designated to be "traffic infractions" and not crimes. In California, in particular, a category of offenses known as infractions are not punishable by imprisonment. The trial of an infraction is by the court without a jury or assigned counsel. Most traffic violations have been made infractions.

If an indigent has a right to have an assigned counsel, why should he not be assigned an investigator, psychiatrist, criminalist, etc., if any or all of these are important in the case? Someday an enterprising lawyer is going to claim that these kinds of expert services are essential to the preparation of an adequate defense, and insist that to go to trial without benefit of the services would be so fundamentally unfair that his client will be denied due process of the law. Certainly a rich person will avail himself of these services, and to permit a trial to depend on the amount of money a defendant has is a denial of the equal protection clause of the Fourteenth Amendment. Already a few cases have held that an indigent defendant in a criminal case has a right to the assistance of the state by appointment of an investigator or expert in preparation of his defense. See 55 *Cornell Law Review*, 632 (1970) and Annotation, 34 A.L.R. 3^D 1256 (1970).

QUESTIONS

1. Does your state utilize the public defender or appointed-counsel system? If you were in trouble, which would you rather have as your counsel? Do you believe that an attorney who is not paid for his services will adequately defend a person who has violated a misdemeanor-type traffic ordinance carrying a potential jail sentence?
2. What is the experience in your area regarding the number of misdemeanants who request counsel? Did Justice Powell correctly anticipate the situation in your area?
3. Remember that the appointment of counsel is subject to the judge's discretion. How do judges in your area pick assigned counsel? What are the prominent arguments, pro and con, regarding counsel assignment in your area?

Chapter 7

Lineups

United States v. *Wade*
388 U.S. 218, 87 S.Ct. 1926, 18 L.Ed. 2ᴰ 1149 (1967)

SETTING: A man with a small strip of tape on each side of his face entered a federally insured bank in Texas, and forced the cashier and vice-president at gunpoint to fill a pillowcase with the bank's money. The man then drove away with an accomplice who was waiting in a stolen car outside the bank. The bank robbery occurred on September 21, 1964.

On March 23, 1965, Wade and two others were indicted for conspiracy to rob the bank. A second indictment was returned charging Wade and the accomplice with the actual robbery of the bank. Wade was arrested on April 6, 1965, and counsel was appointed to represent him on April 26, 1965.

Fifteen days later, without notice to Wade's attorney, an FBI agent arranged to have the two bank employees observe a lineup using Wade and five or six other prisoners. The lineup was conducted in a courtroom in the county courthouse. Each person in the lineup wore strips of tape on his face as the robber had. Also upon direction, each person in the lineup was directed to speak the words allegedly uttered by the bank robber. The two bank employees identified Wade in the lineup as the bank robber.

PROCEDURAL PROBLEM: On direct examination at the trial, the two bank employees were asked if the bank robber were in the room. They answered in the affirmative. On cross-examination, the prior lineup identification was elicited from both of the employees. At the close of the testimony, Wade's counsel moved for a judgment of acquittal, or in the alternative, to strike the employees' court identifications on the ground that conduct of the lineup without notice to and in the absence of his appointed counsel violated the defendant's Fifth Amendment privilege against self-incrimination and the Sixth Amendment's provision for the assistance of counsel. After the motion was denied, the defendant was convicted.

The Fifth Circuit Court of Appeals reversed the conviction and ordered a new trial at which the in-court identification was to be excluded, holding that the lineup did not violate the Fifth Amendment rights of the defendant, but that it did violate the Sixth Amendment right of counsel because of the absence of the lawyer who had already chosen to represent the defendant. On certiorari to the United States Supreme Court, the judgment of the Court of Appeals was reversed and remanded to that court with directions to enter new judgment vacating the conviction and remanding the case to the federal district court for proceedings consistent with the United States Supreme Court's opinion. In its opinion, the Supreme Court addressed itself to whether or not the Fifth and Sixth Amendments prohibit the use of the police lineup in the absence of counsel.

THE ISSUES: (1) Did appearing in an out-of-court police lineup without the assistance of counsel deprive the defendant of his privilege against self-incrimination? (2) Does the presence of a defendant at a post-indictment police lineup without the assistance of counsel deprive him of his right to an attorney at a "critical stage" of the criminal process?

THE ANSWERS: (1) No. (2) Yes.

DISCUSSION: According to the majority of the Justices, because post-indictment police lineups constitute a critical stage in the prosecutional process, the right to counsel obtains at that time.

The majority rejected the claim that the lineup in question violated the defendant's privilege against self-incrimination. Citing as authority for this position *Schmerber* v. *California*, 384 U.S. 757, the majority had no doubt that compelling the accused merely to exhibit his person for observation by a prosecution witness prior to trial invoked no compulsion of the accused to give evidence having testimonial significance. Similarly, compelling Wade to speak within hearing distance of the witnesses, even to utter words purportedly said by the robber, was not compulsion to utter statements of a testimonial nature. Wade was required to use his voice as an identifying physical characteristic, not as testimonial evidence of guilt. It is important to note that the government offered no evidence of anything Wade did or said at the lineup that implicated the Fifth Amendment privilege.

The majority, in an opinion by Justice Brennan, did not find the *Schmerber* case controlling on the right to counsel issue. The claim pressed by the defendant, however, was that the aid of an attorney at the lineup was indispensible to protect the basic right of a criminal defendant —his right to a fair trial at which the witnesses against him might be cross-examined meaningfully.

The reality of contemporary prosecution and police practices was noticed by the Court: "[T]oday's law enforcement machinery involves critical confrontations of the accused by the prosecution at pretrial proceedings where the results might well settle the accused's fate and reduce the trial itself to a mere formality. In recognition of these realities of modern criminal prosecution our cases have construed the Sixth Amendment guarantee to apply to 'critical' stages of the proceedings." Consequently, in addition to the aid of a lawyer at the trial, the accused must be given the guarantee that he need not stand alone against the state at any stage in the criminal prosecution, formal or informal, in or out of court, where the presence of counsel would assist or reduce the right of the accused to a fair trial.

The majority opinion noted that the procedure in which the accused is compelled by the State to be confronted by witnesses for identification is especially susceptible to dangers and various factors that might seriously impede a fair trial. As stated, "There is a grave potential for prejudice, intentional or not, in the pretrial lineup, which may not be capable of reconstruction at trial, and since the presence of counsel itself can often avert prejudice and assure a meaningful confrontation at trial, there can be little doubt that for Wade the post-indictment lineup was a critical stage of the prosecution at which he was as much entitled to the aid [of counsel] . . . as at the trial itself."

Is a new trial to be granted where an accused is denied a motion to strike courtroom identification? The majority answered this issue by quoting *Wong Sun v. United States*, 371 U.S. 471: "[W]hether granting establishment of the primary illegality, the evidence to which instant objection is made has been come at by exploitation of that illegality or instead by means sufficiently distinguishable to be purged of the primary taint."

The Chief Justice and Justice Douglas agreed with the majority on the Sixth Amendment issue, but believed that compulsory lineup violates the privilege against self-incrimination contained in the Fifth Amendment. Justice Fortas did not believe that a person placed in a lineup could be compelled to utter words used in the commission of the crime.

Former Justice Black would have followed the approach of the Chief Justice and Justice Douglas, but would have reached a different disposition of the case. "[T]he Court remands the case to the District Court to consider whether the courtroom identification of [accused] was the fruit of the illegal lineup, and, if it were, to grant him a new trial unless the Court concludes that the courtroom identification was harmless error. I would reverse the Court of Appeals' reversal of . . . [the] conviction but I would not remand for further proceeding since the prosecution not having used the out-of-court lineup identification against [the defendant] at his trial, I believe the conviction should be affirmed."

Two other lineup cases also tie in with *Wade* v. *United States*. In *Stovall* v. *Denno* the Supreme Court held that the requirements of *Wade* could only be applied to lineup cases held after June 12, 1967, the date of the *Wade* decision. In *Gilbert* v. *California*, 388 U.S. 263, the *Wade* principle was reaffirmed and the point reemphasized regarding testimony that is the direct result of the illegal lineup. Regarding such identifications, only a *per se* exclusionary rule can be an effective weapon to insure that police authorities will respect the constitutional right of the accused to have counsel at the lineup. The state, therefore, is not permitted to show that the testimony was from an independent source. The Court also noted that taking of handwriting exemplars does not violate the Fifth Amendment privilege against self-incrimination.

See *United States* v. *Simmons*, 390 U.S. 377 (1968), for use of photographs for identification purposes during the investigation stage. No question of the right to counsel is raised if no charges were lodged nor arrests made. For a contra holding, see *United States* v. *Zeiler*, 427 F. 2ᴰ 1305 (3ᴰ Cir., 1970).

QUESTIONS

1. What is the role of counsel at a police lineup? Discuss.
2. Are police lineup identifications always made accurately by witnesses? What are some ways that a lineup can be unduly suggestive as to the identity of a particular accused?
3. If a lawyer notices unfair practices in the conduct of a lineup, how does he make this known in your jurisdiction?

Kirby v. Illinois
406 U.S. 682, 92 S.Ct. 1877, 32 L.Ed. 2ᴰ 411 (1972)

SETTING: On February 21, 1968, Shard reported to the Chicago police that on February 20, two men robbed him on a Chicago street of a wallet containing, among other things, a Social Security card and some traveler's checks. On February 22, two police officers stopped Kirby and his companion, Bean, on West Madison Avenue in Chicago. When asked for identification, Kirby produced a wallet containing Shard's traveler's checks and Social Security card. Additional papers bearing Shard's name were also found on the defendants. Upon inquiry about Shard's property, the officers were told that the traveler's checks were play money and then later that the things had been won in a crap game. Both Kirby and Bean were arrested and taken to a police station. At the time of the stop and then the arrest, the officers did not know about the Shard robbery; they learned this after arriving at the police station and checking the records.

A police car then picked up Shard and brought him to the police station. Shard positively identified the defendant and Bean as soon as he entered the room where they were seated at a table. There was no lawyer present—neither suspect asked for one, nor were they advised of their right to have counsel present. Some six weeks later, both were indicted for the robbery of Shard. Counsel was appointed at the arraignment, at which they pleaded not guilty. A pretrial motion to suppress Shard's identification was filed and was denied. Shard then testified at the trial and described his February 22 identification at the police station. He then identified both men in court as the men who had robbed him. Shard was cross-examined in detail regarding the circumstances of his identification of the two defendants.

The jury found them guilty and the conviction was subsequently upheld in appeal in the Illinois courts. The United States Supreme Court granted certiorari.

PROCEDURAL PROBLEM: The right to counsel at police-conducted lineups announced by *United States* v. *Wade* is not as broad as most lower courts assumed it to be. *Wade* involved post-indictment police lineup and most state and federal courts extended the right to counsel to pre-indictment lineups. The only exception was in the instance in which there was an on-the-scene showup conducted very soon after the commission of the offense. See *Stovall* v. *Denno*, 388 U.S. 293 (1967) for an example of the exception.

THE ISSUE: Does the *Wade-Gilbert per se* exclusionary doctrine regarding identification testimony based on a post-indictment police lineup apply to those lineups that occur prior to indictment or other formal charge?

THE ANSWER: No.

DISCUSSION: The Supreme Court, by a 5–4 vote, held that the right to counsel did not apply to a police-arranged investigatory confrontation between the victim and the suspects held at the police headquarters two days after the crime was committed and a very short time after the suspects had been arrested, but prior to bringing any kind of formal charges.

The main opinion in the case had the unequivocal support of three Justices that *Wade* does not mandate defense counsel at identification proceedings prior to formally charging the defendant. As the majority opinion noted;

> *In this case we are asked to import into a routine police investigation an absolute constitutional guarantee historically and rationally applicable only after the onset of formal prosecutorial proceedings. We decline to do this. . . . The rationale of those cases was that an accused is entitled to counsel at any "critical stage" of the prosecution and that a post-indictment lineup is such a "critical stage."*

Mr. Justice Stewart did not specify what was meant by "formal charges," but he had previously emphasized in *Massiah* v. *United States*, 377 U.S. 201, and in his dissent in *Escobedo* v. *Illinois*, 378 U.S. 478, that the indictment is the beginning of the "critical stage" of a criminal case. Justice Stewart also emphasized that abuse of the identification procedure during the investigation stage of a case can still be remedied under the due process clause of the Fifth or Fourteenth Amendments.

Mr. Justice Powell concurred in the result only and stated his belief that the *Wade* and *Gilbert* "per se exclusionary rule should not be extended." The Chief Justice concurred and simply held "that the right to counsel attaches as soon as criminal charges are formally made against an accused and he becomes the subject of a criminal prosecution."

A strong dissent by Justice Brennan, the author of the majority opinion in *Wade*, noted that the *Wade-Gilbert* rule was to protect the "most basic right" of a defendant—the right to have a fair trial at which witnesses against him can be meaningfully cross-examined. Joined by Douglas and Marshall, the three dissenters stated that

*Counsel is required at those confrontations because "the dangers in-
herent in eye-witness identification and the suggestibility inherent in the
context of the pretrial identification," . . . mean that the protection must
be afforded to the [accused].*

Several interesting articles regarding lineups are:

Williams and Hammelmann, "Identification Parades," Part 1, *Criminal Law Review* (1963), p. 479.

Read, "Lawyers at Line-ups: Constitutional Necessity or Avoidable
Extravagance?" 17 *UCLA Law Review*, 339 (1969).

McGowan, "Constitutional Interpretation and Criminal Investigation," 12, *William and Mary Law Review*, 235 (1970).

Note, 55, *Minnesota Law Review*, 779 (1971) Annotation, 39 A.L.R.
3ᴰ 487, 791 (1971).

QUESTIONS

1. Discuss the idea that the *Wade-Kirby* holdings tend to exist in books
   rather than in actual practice.
2. Do you consider in-court identification suggestive? If so, should the
   inability of a witness to identify a defendant at a pretrial lineup or
   photograph be excluded as later in-court identification? (See *United
   States* v. *Toney,* 440 F. 2ᴰ 590 [6th Cir., 1971].)
3. What are the arguments for restricting the right of counsel at a police
   lineup to those held only after formal charges are brought? Discuss
   each.

Simmons v. *United States*
390 U.S. 377, 88 S.Ct. 967, 19 L.Ed. 2ᴰ 1247 (1968)

SETTING: A robbery of a federally insured savings and loan association occurred on February 27, 1964, at about 1:45 P.M. On February 28,
FBI agents obtained from the sister of Andrews, one of the suspects,
some six snapshots of Andrews and Simmons. The photographs consisted
largely of group photographs of Andrews, Simmons, and others. Later on
February 28, five bank employees who witnessed the robbery at the
savings and loan association were separately shown the photographs.
Each one identified Simmons. At a later time, the same five witnesses

were again interviewed by the FBI and shown an indeterminate number of pictures. Again, all identified Simmons. At the trial the government did not introduce any of the photographs but relied upon in-court identification of the five eyewitnesses, each of whom swore that Simmons was one of the robbers.

PROCEDURAL PROBLEM: Simmons did not claim that he was entitled to counsel at the time the pictures were shown to the witnesses. Rather, he asserted that in the circumstances the identification procedure was so unduly prejudicial as to fatally taint his conviction. The Court noted that despite the hazards of photograpic identification, the procedure has been widely used by law enforcement agencies from the standpoint both of apprehending offenders and sparing suspects the embarrassment of arrest by allowing eyewitnesses to exonerate them through scrutiny of photographs. The Court further stated: "The danger that use of the technique may result in convictions based on misidentification may be substantially lessened by a course of cross-examination at trial which exposes the jury to the method's potential for error."

THE ISSUE: Does the use of photographs for pretrial identification involve a constitutional problem?

THE ANSWER: No.

DISCUSSION: The Court, speaking through Justice Harlan, ruled: "We are unwilling to prohibit its employment, either in the exercise of our supervisory power, or still less, as a matter of constitutional requirement. Instead, we hold that each case must be considered on its own facts, and that convictions based on eyewitness identification at trial following a pretrial identification by photograph will be set aside on that ground only if the photographic identification procedure is impermissibly suggestive as to give rise to a very substantial likelihood of irreparable misidentification."

In applying this standard to this case, Simmons' claim must fail for the following reasons:

1.   There was no claim that the FBI resort to the photographic identification procedure was unnecessary because a serious felony had been committed. The culprits were still at large. The clues led to Simmons. It was crucial for the FBI to ascertain whether or not they were on the right track. The justification in this case was hardly less compelling than that found by the Court to permit the "one-man lineup" in *Stovall* v. *Denno,* 388 U.S. 293.

2. There was little chance that the procedure used in this case led to misidentification of Simmons. The robbery took place on an afternoon in a well-lighted bank. No masks were worn. The five bank employees observed Simmons for a full five minutes. The same witnesses were shown photographs only a day later while their memories were still fresh. At least six photographs were shown to each witness separately. Simmons and Andrews appeared several times in each series. There was no evidence to indicate that the witnesses were told anything about the progress of the investigation, or that the FBI agents suggested which persons in the photographs were under suspicion.

3. Under the conditions in this case, all five witnesses identified Simmons as one of the robbers, while none identified Andrews, who was as prominent in the photographs as Simmons. Subsequently the initial identifications were affirmed by the witnesses. On cross-examination at trial none of the witnesses displayed any doubt about their identification of Simmons.

Taken together, all these circumstances leave little room for doubt that the identification of Simmons was correct. The Court held that the factual surroundings of the identification process in this case did not deny Simmons due process of law or call for a reversal under the Supreme Court's supervisory authority over the federal court system.

Police Use of Photographs. The "Rogue's Gallery" is an old and accepted police practice. It is often used because (1) a lineup may be impractical, (2) there are no suspects and the police want witnesses to view persons with criminal records for similar crimes, and (3) the police may not want to alert a possible suspect that he is under investigation at that time. If a photograph is used, then it should be current. Remember that it only shows how a person appeared at the time the photograph was taken. Generally followed procedures in police departments are that:

1. Each witness views the photographs separately.

2. Several photographs of persons of the same general description and appearance are shown at the same time. There is no requirement that the photographs be exclusively of persons having criminal records for similar offenses. Witnesses should be shown all photographs on file of persons who have been arrested for that crime and who fit the general description. Photographs of suspects of other offenses should be used only if there are no similar pictures of persons arrested for the offense currently charged.

3. Mug shots should not be mixed with ordinary photographs.

4. If identification is made, all photographs viewed by the witness are collected and recorded. If in a book, the officer must note the page the witness viewed and be prepared to bring it to court.

Does the Sixth Amendment require the presence of a lawyer at a post-indictment photographic identification? The Supreme Court held in the negative in *United States* v. *Ash,* 93 S.Ct. 2568 (1973).

QUESTIONS

1. What is meant by the supervisory power that the Supreme Court has over the federal court system.
2. Give the distinctions between the constitutional problems in *Kirby* v. *Illinois* and *Simmons* v. *United States.*
3. Rather than having all five eyewitnesses view photographs, can you think of an identification procedure that would possibly have been more reliable in this case?

Foster v. *California*
394 U.S. 440, 89 S.Ct. 1127, 22 L.Ed. 2ᴰ 402 (1969)

SETTING: Three persons robbed a Western Union office. The day after the crime, one of the robbers, Clay, surrendered to the police and implicated Foster and Grice. Allegedly, Grice waited in a car and Foster and Clay entered the office. Grice and Foster were tried together; Foster was convicted and Grice was acquitted. The California District Court of Appeals affirmed the conviction and the state supreme court denied review. The United States Supreme Court granted centiorari, limited to the question of whether or not the conduct of the police lineup resulted in a violation of Foster's constitutional rights.

PROCEDURAL PROBLEM: The only witness to the crime was the night manager of the office. After Foster was arrested, the manager was called to the police station to view a three-man lineup. Foster was in the lineup. He was tall—about six feet; the other two men in the lineup were about five feet or five feet six inches in height. Foster wore a leather jacket which the night manager said he saw underneath the coveralls worn by the robber.

After viewing the lineup, the night manager could not positively identify Foster as the robber. He thought that he was, but was not sure. The night manager then asked to speak with Foster, who was brought into an office and placed across from the manager at a table. No one else was in the room except prosecuting officials. The manager still could not positively identify Foster. He subsequently testified at the trial that he was unsure about the identification of Foster even after the one-to-one confrontation across the table.

About ten days after the first lineup, the night manager viewed a second lineup, which consisted of five men. Foster was the only person in the second lineup who had also been in the first. The night manager was now convinced that Foster was the robber.

THE ISSUE: Were the lineup procedures used in this case so unfair as to violate due process?

THE ANSWER: Yes.

DISCUSSION: This case provided one kind of police lineup that predated *United States* v. *Wade,* 388 U.S. 218. The procedure was unduly suggestive. Justice Fortas, writing for the majority, noted that the suggestive elements in the identification procedure made it all but inevitable that Foster would be identified whether or not he was in fact the robber. "In effect, the police said to the witness, '*This* is the man.' . . . This procedure so undermined the reliability of the eyewitness identification as to violate due process."

The majority used the "totality of circumstances" test to which Justice Black took exception. He argued that the majority used the test to "justify its invading the constitutional right of jury trial." He stated that the test was used to strike down what the Court deemed to be unfair rather than on the ground of a constitutional violation. Black stated that the Constitution "does not generally prohibit conduct deemed unfair by the courts." Justice Black stressed his fear of adopting the "totality of circumstances" test as a constitutional standard.

Lineup Composition.   The Supreme Court is concerned about suggestive lineups. The following procedures are followed in most police departments:

1.   Five or six persons including the suspect, should participate in a lineup.

2. Unless an attorney is present, *all* prisoners and suspects should sign a lineup waiver form.

3. All persons in a lineup should be of the same sex, race, and about the same age. They should have about the same height, weight, skin coloring, hair, and physical build of the accused.

4. Participants should wear the same kind of clothing; i.e., all should be in prison garb, suits, rumpled clothing, as the case may be.

5. The accused should be randomly placed in the lineup in order to avoid any suggestibility.

6. Persons known to the witness should not be included in the lineup with the suspect.

7. If private citizens are recruited for the lineup, they should execute a consent form that there are no charges against them, that they have not been arrested, are under no compulsion to participate, and are free to leave; minors should receive permission from their parent or guardians to participate in the lineup.

QUESTIONS

1. Why do you believe that Justice Black did not favor the "totality of circumstances" test as a constitutional rule? Discuss.
2. Would the second lineup have been unduly suggestive had all the participants in the first lineup been included in the second? Was the fact that two were missing in reality the basis for the objection of the majority opinion?
3. What are the procedures used in conducting a police lineup in your jurisdiction? Are they fair?

Neil v. *Biggers*
409 U.S. 188, 93 S.Ct. 375, 34 L.Ed. 2ᴰ 401 (1972)

SETTING: At a habeas corpus hearing, a federal district court held in an unexpected opinion that a stationhouse identification procedure in which the victim of a rape identified the defendant as her attacker was so unduly suggestive that it violated due process. The Court of Appeals affirmed and certiorari was granted by the United States Supreme Court.

The victim testified that on the evening of January 22, 1965, a youth with a butcher knife grabbed her in the doorway to her kitchen. The testimony of the victim included the following

A. [H]e grabbed me from behind, and grappled—twisted me on the floor. Threw me down on the floor.

Q. And there was no light in the kitchen?

A. Not in the kitchen.

Q. So you couldn't have seen him then?

A. Yes, I could see him, when I looked up in his face.

Q. In the dark?

A. He was right in the doorway—it was enough light from the bedroom shining through. Yes, I could see who he was.

Q. You could see? No light? And you could see him and know him then?

A. Yes.

When the victim screamed, her 12-year-old daughter came to her bedroom and also began to scream. The assailant threatened to kill both of them if the child did not keep quiet. The child stopped screaming. The victim was then forced to walk at knifepoint a few blocks and was taken into a woods and raped. The victim testified that there was a bright full moon. After the incident, the victim returned home. In reaching its decision, the district court characterized her testimony as a very general description of the accused. Not mentioned by the district court was the fact that at a habeas corpus hearing she also described her assailant as being between 16 and 18 years old, between five feet ten inches and six feet tall, having a dark brown complexion, and weighing between 180 and 200 pounds. This testimony was subsequently corroborated by an officer.

PROCEDURAL PROBLEM: Over the next seven months, the victim viewed suspects in her home or at the stationhouse, some in lineups and some in showups. She was also shown between thirty and forty photographs. She identified no one. On August 17, she went to the police station to view the defendant, who had been detained on another charge. The police tried to conduct a suitable lineup but could find no one in the city jail or juvenile home fitting the defendant's unusual description. Consequently a showup was conducted which consisted of the defendant walking past the victim in the presence of two detectives. At the request of the victim, the police directed the defendant to utter, "Shut up or I'll kill you." The victim identified the defendant and testified she had no doubt about the identification.

At the habeas corpus hearing she firmly reiterated her positive identification.

THE ISSUE: Was the pretrial identification (showup) conducted in such an unduly suggestive manner as to deprive the defendant of due process?

THE ANSWER: No.

DISCUSSION: The primary evil to be avoided in an identification process is a very substantial likelihood of irreparable misidentification. It is this likelihood that violates a defendant's right to due process. Suggestive confrontations are disapproved because they increase the probability of misidentification.

Justice Powell, writing for the majority, rejected a strict rule that unnecessary suggestiveness alone requires the exclusion of evidence because the confrontation and trial preceded *Stovall* v. *Denno,* 388 U.S. 293 (1967), when the court first gave notice that the suggestiveness of confrontation procedures was anything other than a matter to be argued to the jury.

Under the "totality of circumstances" test, was the identification reliable even though the confrontation procedure was suggestive? The Court stated that it disagreed with the district court:

> *As indicated by our cases, the factors to be considered in evaluating the likelihood of misidentification include the opportunity of the witness to view the criminal at the time of the crime, the witness' degree of attention, the accuracy of the witness' prior description of the criminal, the level of certainty demonstrated by the witness at the confrontation, and the length of time between the crime and the confrontation.*

The facts satisfy the general considerations posed by the Court. There was, however, a seven-month lapse between the rape and the confrontation. This would seriously weaken an identification under normal circumstances. In this case, however, the testimony is undisputed that the victim made no previous identification at any of the showups, lineups, or photographic viewings. She thus had a good record for reliability and resisted whatever suggestiveness was inherent in a showup. Weighing all these factors, the Court found no substantial likelihood of misidentification and the evidence of identification was properly allowed to go to the jury, which apparently found the identification reliable.

QUESTIONS

1. In your opinion, was the showup of the defendant and two detectives unduly suggestive? What precautions should be taken at a showup of the kind found in this case to reduce the possibility of suggestiveness?

2. How are showups conducted in your jurisdiction? Do you believe that they violate a defendant's right to due process? Discuss.

3. In your estimation, is the aid of counsel of more importance at a lineup or showup? What are your reasons?

Chapter 8

Privilege
against Self-Incrimination

Constitution of the United States, Fifth Amendment

. . . [N]or shall be compelled in any criminal case to be a witness against himself.

Constitution of the State of California, Article 1, Section 13

. . . [N]or be compelled, in a criminal case, to be a witness against himself.

Constitution of Arkansas, Article 2, Section 8

. . . [N]or shall any person be compelled, in a criminal case, to be a witness against himself.

Constitution of the State of Illinois, Article 1, Section 10

No person shall be compelled in a criminal case to give evidence against himself. . . .

Constitution of the State of Minnesota, Article 1, Section 7

No person . . . shall be compelled in any criminal case to be a witness against himself.

Brown v. *Mississippi*
297 U.S. 278, 56 S.Ct. 461, 80 L.Ed. 682 (1936)

SETTING: Stewart was murdered on March 30, 1934. Subsequently,
Brown and two others were indicted for the slaying. They were arraigned,
assigned counsel, and pleaded not guilty. When the trial started, it was
found that there was no evidence sufficient to submit the case to the jury
besides the confessions of each defendant. The confessions as alleged by
the defendants were secured as the result of physical torture and were
false. To show the absolute brutal way the confessions were extorted,
the following quote is extracted in its entirety from the majority opinion
by Chief Justice Hughes:

> *The crime with which these defendants, all ignorant Negroes, are*
> *charged, was discovered about one o'clock* P.M. *on Friday, March 30,*
> *1934. On that night one Dial, a deputy sheriff, accompanied by others,*
> *came to the home of Ellington, one of the defendants, and requested him*
> *to accompany them to the house of the deceased, and there a number of*
> *white men were gathered, who began to accuse the defendant of the*
> *crime. Upon his denial they seized him, and with the participation of the*
> *deputy they hanged him by a rope to the limb of a tree, and having let*
> *him down, they hung him again and when he was let down the second*
> *time, and he still protested his innocence, he was tied to a tree and*
> *whipped, and still declining to accede to the demands that he confess,*
> *he was finally released and he returned with some difficulty to his home,*
> *suffering intense pain and agony. The record of the testimony shows that*
> *the signs of the rope on his neck were plainly visible during the so-called*
> *trial. A day or two thereafter the said deputy, accompanied by another,*
> *returned to the home of the said defendant and arrested him, and de-*
> *parted with the prisoner towards the jail in an adjoining county, but*
> *went by a route which led into the State of Alabama; and while on the*
> *way, in that State, the deputy stopped and again severely whipped the*
> *defendant, declaring that he would continue the whipping until he con-*
> *fessed, and the defendant then agreed to confess to such a statement as*
> *the deputy would dictate, and he did so, after which he was delivered*
> *to jail.*
>
> *The other two defendants, Ed Brown and Henry Shields, were also*
> *arrested and taken to the same jail. On Sunday night, April 1, 1934, the*
> *same deputy, accompanied by a number of white men, one of whom was*
> *also an officer, and by the jailer, came to the jail and the two last named*
> *defendants were made to strip and they were laid over chairs and their*
> *backs were cut to pieces with a leather strap with buckles on it and they*
> *were likewise made by the said deputy definitely to understand that the*
> *whipping would be continued unless and until they confessed and not*
> *only confessed but confessed in every matter of detail as demanded by*
> *those present; and in this manner the defendants confessed the crime,*

and as the whippings progressed and were repeated, they changed or adjusted their confession in all particulars of detail so as to conform to the demands of their torturers. When the confessions had been obtained in the exact form and contents as desired by the mob, they left with the parting admonition and warning that, if the defendants changed their story at any time in any respect from that last stated, the perpetrators of the outrage would administer the same or equally effective treatment.

Further details of the brutal treatment to which these helpless prisoners were subjected need not be pursued. It is sufficient to say that in pertinent respects the transcript reads more like pages torn from some medieval account, than a record made within the confines of a modern civilization which aspires to an enlightened constitutional government.

All this having been accomplished, on the next day, that is, on Monday April 2, when the defendants had been given time to recuperate somewhat from the tortures to which they had been subjected, the two sheriffs, one of the county where the crime was committed, and the other of the county of the jail in which the prisoners were confined, came to the jail, accompanied by eight other persons, some of them deputies, there to hear the free and voluntary confession of these miserable and abject defendants. The sheriff of the county of the crime admitted that he had heard of the whipping, but averred that he had no personal knowledge of it. He admitted that one of the defendants, when brought before him to confess, was limping and did not sit down, and that this particular defendant then and there stated that he had been strapped so severely that he could not sit down, and as already stated, the signs of the rope on the neck of another of the defendants were plainly visible to all. Nevertheless the solemn farce of hearing the free and voluntary confessions was gone through with, and these two sheriffs and one other person then present were the three witnesses used in court to establish the so-called confessions, which were received by the court and admitted in evidence over the objections of the defendants duly entered of record as each of the said three witnesses delivered their alleged testimony. There was thus enough before the court when these confessions were first offered to make known to the court that they were not, beyond all reasonable doubt, free and voluntary; and the failure of the court then to exclude the confessions is sufficient to reverse the judgment, under every rule of procedure that has theretofore been prescribed, and hence it was not necessary subsequently to renew the objections by motion or otherwise.

The spurious confessions having been obtained—and the farce last mentioned having been gone through with on Monday, April 2d—the court, then in session, on the following day, Tuesday, April 3, 1934, ordered the grand jury to reassemble on the succeeding day, April 4, 1934, at nine o'clock, and on the morning of that day last mentioned the grand jury returned an indictment against the defendants for murder. Late that afternoon the defendants were brought from the jail in the adjoining county and arraigned, when one or more of them offered to plead guilty, which the court declined to accept, and, upon inquiry whether they had or desired counsel, they stated that they had none, and did not suppose that counsel could be of any assistance to them. The court thereupon appointed counsel, and set the case for trial for the following morning at nine o'clock, and the defendents were returned to the jail in the adjoining county about thirty miles away.

The defendants were brought to the courthouse of the county on the following morning, April 5th, and the so-called trial was opened, and was concluded on the next day, April 6, 1934, and resulted in a pretended conviction with death sentences. The evidence upon which the conviction was obtained was the so-called confessions. Without this evidence a peremptory instruction to find for the defendants would have been inescapable. The defendants were put on the stand, and by their testimony the facts and the details thereof as to the manner by which the confessions were extorted from them were fully developed, and it is further disclosed by the record that the same deputy, Dial, under whose guiding hand and active participation the tortures to coerce the confessions were administered, was actively in the performance of the supposed duties of a court deputy in the courthouse and in the presence of the prisoners during what is denominated, in complimentary terms, the trial of these defendants. This deputy was put on the stand by the state in rebuttal, and admitted the whippings. It is interesting to note that in his testimony with reference to the whipping of the defendant Ellington, and in response to the inquiry as to how severely he was whipped, the deputy stated, "Not too much for a Negro; not as much as I would have done if it were left to me." Two others who had participated in these whippings were introduced and admitted it—not a single witness was introduced who denied it. The facts are not only undisputed, they are admitted, and admitted to have been done by officers of the state, in conjunction with other participants, and all this was definitely well known to everybody connected with the trial, and during the trial, including the state's prosecuting attorney and the trial judge presiding.

PROCEDURAL PROBLEM: The jury convicted the defendants and the Mississippi Supreme Court affirmed the convictions. Then the defendants moved in the Mississippi Supreme Court to arrest the judgment and for a new trial because all the evidence against them was secured by coercion and brutality known to the court and district attorney. The state court considered and rejected defendants' contentions. The United States Supreme Court granted certiorari to consider whether the due process requirement of the Fourteenth Amendment was violated by the convictions in this case.

THE ISSUE: Do the convictions, which rest solely upon confessions shown to have been extorted by state officers by brutality and violence, violate the due process of the law required by the Fourteenth Amendment of the United States Constitution?

THE ANSWER: Yes.

DISCUSSION: The state stressed that under *Twining* v. *New Jersey*, 211 U.S. 78 (1908), the exemption from self-incrimination in state courts is not secured by the federal Constitution. The Court, however, noted that that requirement is not involved in this case. That clause is concerned with an accused being "called as a witness and required to testify. Compulsion by torture to extort a confession is a different matter." While the state is free to establish its own procedure, it must do so limited by the requirement of due process of the law. A state may not contrive a conviction to deprive a defendant of liberty by deliberate deception of the court and jury by presenting "perjured testimony." And a trial is just as much of a pretense where the authorities contrive convictions based on confessions secured by violence. Hughes noted, "It would be difficult to conceive of methods more revolting to the sense of justice than those taken to procure the confessions of these petitioners, and the use of the confessions thus obtained as the basis for conviction and sentence was a clear denial of due process."

On one technical matter claimed by the state that because the counsel objected to the admissibility of the confessions but did not move for their exclusion, the Supreme Court noted, "We are not concerned with a mere question of state practice, or whether counsel for petitioners was competent or mistakenly assumed that their first objects were sufficient. . . . The duty of maintaining constitutional rights of a person on trial for his life rises above mere rules of procedure and wherever the court is clearly satisfied that such violations exist, it will refuse to sanction such violations and apply the corrective.'" (Citing *Fisher* v. *State*, 145 Miss. 116, 110 So. 361 [1926].)

In his concluding remarks condemning the Mississippi case, Chief Justice Hughes declared:

> *In the instant case, the trial court was fully advised by the undisputed evidence of the way in which the confessions had been procured. The trial court knew that there was no other evidence upon which conviction and sentence could be based. Yet it proceeded to permit conviction and to pronounce sentence. The conviction and sentence were void for want of the essential elements of due process, and the proceeding thus vitiated could be challenged in any appropriate manner. Mooney v. Holohan, supra. It was challenged before the Supreme Court of the State by the express invocation of the Fourteenth Amendment. That court entertained the challenge, considered the federal question thus presented, but declined to enforce petitioners' constitutional right. The court thus denied a federal right fully established and specially set up and claimed and the judgment must be*
> *Reversed.*

QUESTIONS

1. On what authority that you already have read were the defendants afforded the assistance of counsel? Was the aid, in your estimation, competent?

2. What reason did Hughes give for not invoking the Fifth Amendment's privilege against self-incrimination in this case?

3. Under what authority did the state argue that the Fifth Amendment privilege against self-incrimination did not apply in the state? Why do you think that incorporation of the various constitutional procedural safeguards were so slow in coming in criminal cases?

Spano v. *New York*
360 U.S. 315, 79 S.Ct. 1202, 3 L.Ed. 2^D 1265 (1959)

SETTING: Spano, 25 years of age, a derivative citizen of the United States, and with a junior high school education, was drinking in a bar. The decedent, a former professional boxer, took some of Spano's money and beat him severely. After some assistance by the bartender, Spano walked to his apartment, secured a gun, and walked another eight or nine blocks to where the deceased was frequently found. He fired five shots, two of which struck and killed the deceased. Spano disappeared for the next week or so. A week later the Bronx grand jury returned an indictment charging Spano with murder in the first degree and a warrant was issued. Two days after the indictment Spano called Bruno, a close friend of about ten years. Bruno was a police recruit who was still in the police academy. Spano described the beating and told Bruno he intended to secure a lawyer and give himself over to the authorities. Bruno relayed the information to his superiors. The next day Spano, accompanied by his attorney, surrendered to the authorities.

PROCEDURAL PROBLEM: The surrender took place at 7:10 P.M. on February 4. At 7:15 P.M. the questioning in the assistant district attorney's office began. Spano's attorney had told him previously to answer no questions. The record revealed that the questioning was persistent and continuous by teams of police officers. Spano repeatedly asked for his attorney but the requests were denied. At 11:00 P.M. Spano was given two sandwiches and some coffee.

At 12:15 A.M. on February 5, after five hours of questioning, and still no confession, Spano was transferred to another police station. The questioning resumed at 12:40 A.M., once again by numerous police officers and to some extent by the assistant district attorney. Spano's requests for his attorney were denied.

Those in charge of the investigation then decided that Bruno could be of use. He was briefed and told to play on the sympathies of Spano and emphasize their deep friendship. Bruno was told to say he was "in a lot of trouble" because of his contacts with Spano. This was not true. He was told to extract sympathy from Spano for Bruno's pregnant wife and three children. Spano would not confess during three sessions under this kind of pressure. However, in the fourth session directed by a police lieutenant and lasting a full hour, Spano succumbed to Bruno's prevarications and agreed to make a statement. This took place at 3:25 A.M. and the statement was completed at 4:05 A.M.

This was not the end, however. In an effort to find the bridge from which he had dropped the gun, Spano was driven around until well after 6:00 A.M. During this time the bridge was located and he also made some damaging statements to the officer.

At 10:15 A.M. the same morning, Spano was arraigned.

At the trial, the confession was introduced and the jury was instructed to rely on it if it was found to be voluntary. Apparently they did, because the defendant was convicted and sentenced to death. The New York courts affirmed and the United States Supreme Court granted certiorari to resolve the serious due process problems presented under the Fourteenth Amendment. The Supreme Court reversed the conviction.

THE ISSUE: Was the defendant denied due process under the Fourteenth Amendment by introduction of the Spano confession for jury consideration at the trial?

THE ANSWER: Yes.

DISCUSSION: The Court found it unnecessary to answer the defendant's claim that after indictment no confession obtained in the absence of counsel can be used without violating the Fourteenth Amendment. Chief Justice Warren stated, "We find use of the confession obtained here inconsistent with the Fourteenth Amendment under traditional principles."

Warren emphasized that the use of involuntary confessions does not turn alone on their untrustworthiness. "It also turns on the deep rooted feeling that the police must obey the law; that in the end life and liberty can be as much endangered from illegal methods used to convict those thought to be criminals as from the actual criminals themselves." In explaining the abhorrence that this country has for coercing confessions, the majority opinion held that on all the facts Spano's conviction could not stand.

The Court emphasized the past history of Spano, which included emotional instability, the length of the interrogation by teams of skilled interrogators, the leading of Spano to include in his confession exactly

what the authorities wanted, and the devious tactic of playing on his
sympathy by using an old friendship finally to elicit the confession. The
totality of the situation led to the defeat of Spano's will to resist. There
was a tremendous amount of official pressure, fatigue, and sympathy
falsely aroused. The police were not merely investigating a crime; the
grand jury had already returned an indictment charging Spano. The
police were primarily intent in extracting a confession. The Court stated,
"When such intent is shown, this Court has held that the confession
obtained must be examined with the most careful scrutiny. . . . Accordingly, we hold that petitioner's conviction cannot stand under the
Fourteenth Amendment."

The opinions of the concurring justices emphasized the lack of
counsel and secret nature of the post-indictment interrogation, and the
decision was reached that the confession of Spano was not admissible as
evidence.

QUESTIONS

1. What test did Warren use to determine whether a confession is admissible—trustworthiness or due process? Explain the difference. Does
   the test used in this case signal a change in the Court's thinking regarding the admissibility of confessions?
2. Why did the Court not base its decision on the denial of counsel as
   the concurring justices did?
3. Did the concurring opinions reach the central issue in the case which
   the majority apparently could not agree upon?

Massiah v. United States
377 U.S. 201, 84 S.Ct. 1199, 12 L.Ed. 2ᴰ 246 (1964)

SETTING: Massiah, a merchant seaman, was arrested, arraigned, and
later indicted by a federal grand jury for possession of narcotics on a
United States vessel. Subsequently, another indictment was found charging Massiah and another person with the same substantive offense. The
indictment included a count of conspiracy to possess, conceal, and facilitate the sale of narcotics. Massiah retained a lawyer, pleaded not guilty,
and was released on bail.

Colson, the other person, without Massiah's knowledge, decided to
cooperate with the government agents in their continuing investigation

of the narcotics activities of Massiah, Colson, and others. Colson agreed to have a radio transmitter installed in his automobile, by means of which a federal agent, Murphy, could overhear conversations with Colson from some distance away.

PROCEDURAL PROBLEM: As a result of his agreement and installation of the device, Colson and Massiah held a lengthy conversation in the automobile during which Massiah made several incriminating statements. Murphy, by prearrangement with Colson, overheard the conversation. At Massiah's trial these incriminating statements were brought before the jury through Murphy's testimony over the objection of Massiah's counsel. The defendant was convicted of several related narcotics offenses and the Court of Appeals affirmed. The United States Supreme Court granted certiorari.

THE ISSUE: Is a defendant denied his constitutional rights under the Fifth and Sixth Amendments in a federal trial when evidence of his own incriminating words is used against him—this evidence having been secured after his indictment by federal agents who surreptitiously recorded the conversations with the assistance of a co-defendant, and in the absence of his counsel, while he was out on bail?

THE ANSWER: Yes.

DISCUSSION: Justice Stewart for the majority held that incriminating post-indictment statements made by a defendant to a co-defendant, while defendant was out on bail, and in the absence of counsel—the evidence having been surreptitiously recorded by the police with the co-defendant's assistance—could not be used at the defendant's trial. Stewart emphasized that the Court was dealing with a federal case in which the Sixth Amendment guarantees are directly applicable. The majority did not question that in many cases including this one, it is entirely proper to continue an investigation of the suspected criminal activities of the defendant and his co-defendants, even though the defendant has already been indicted. "All we hold is that the defendant's own incriminating statements, obtained by federal agents under the circumstances here disclosed, could not constitutionally be used by the prosecution as evidence against *him* at his trial."

The dissenters, Justices White, Clark, and Harlan, expressed great dissatisfaction with the majority decision. White, writing for the three, stated that "A civilized society must maintain its capacity to discover transgressions of the law and identify those who flout it. . . . It will just not do to sweep these disagreeable matters under the rug or pretend that they are not there at all." The dissenters found it a rather ominous occasion when a constitutional rule is developed which bars the use of highly probative, relevant, and reliable evidence regarding the issues before the trial court—the issue here being whether the defendant did or did not commit the acts charged.

Justice White also appeared to anticipate what the future would hold by stating that admissions given at any time after the right of counsel attaches would likely come within the *Massiah* holding. He only had to wait a short time.

QUESTIONS

1. Do you think that the real concern of the Court was the right to counsel or the deceit used by the government in carrying out their undercover work?

2. Although this decision appears to be based on the Sixth Amendment right to counsel, does not the decision greatly expand the privilege against self-incrimination? Explain.

3. Suppose a particular state uses the information to initiate criminal prosecution—would *Massiah* apply after filing of the information? Suppose the defendant did not hire a counsel—may he still invoke *Massiah?*

Malloy v. Hogan
378 U.S. 1, 84 S.Ct. 1489, 12 L.Ed. 2ᴰ 653 (1964)

SETTING: The defendant was arrested in Connecticut during a gambling raid, pleaded guilty to the Connecticut misdemeanor of pool selling, and was sentenced to one year in jail and fined $500. After serving ninety days, the defendant's sentence was suspended and he was placed on probation for two years. Some sixteen months after his guilty plea, the defendant was ordered to testify before a court-appointed referee who was conducting an inquiry into gambling and other criminal activities in Hartford County. The defendant refused to answer a number of questions on the grounds that he might incriminate himself. The questions could have led to the gathering of evidence from persons about whom he was asked which in turn might have proved incriminating to him. For his refusal to answer, he was held in contempt and the state appellate courts affirmed the contempt citation. The Supreme Court of the United States granted certiorari and reversed the conviction.

PROCEDURAL PROBLEM: In this case the Court was asked to reconsider prior decisions holding that the privilege against self-incrimination is not safeguarded against state action by the Fourteenth Amendment. The Court was faced with the issue of overruling a prior decision, *Twining* v. *New Jersey*, 211 U.S. 78 (1908), which it had declined to do on a previous occasion in *Adamson* v. *California*, 332 U.S. 46 (1947). The Fifth Amendment's privilege against self-incrimination was not available in a state proceeding.

THE ISSUE: Does the Fourteenth Amendment incorporate the Fifth Amendment's privilege against self-incrimination so as to be applicable in the states under the same standard as applicable in federal trials?

THE ANSWER: Yes.

DISCUSSION: The Court's majority opinion, written by Justice Clark, noted that "The marked shift to the federal standard in state cases began with *Lisenba* v. *California*, 314 U.S. 219 (1942), where the Court spoke of the accused's 'free choice to admit, to deny, or refuse to answer.' The shift reflects recognition that the American system of criminal prosecution is accusatorial, not inquisitorial, and that the Fifth Amendment privilege is its essential mainstay. Governments, state and federal, are thus constitutionally compelled to establish guilt by evidence independently and freely secured, and may not by coercion prove a charge against an accused out of his own mouth."

Brennan announced the specific holding overruling *Twining* to be that the Fourteenth Amendment secures "against state invasion the same privilege that the Fifth Amendment guarantees against federal infringement—the right of a person to remain silent unless he chooses to speak in the unfettered exercise of his own will and to suffer no penalty . . . for such silence."

What is the "federal standard" mentioned by the Court? "The privilege afforded not only extends to answers that would in themselves support a conviction . . . but likewise embraces those that would furnish a link in this chain of evidence needed to prosecute." The judge, in applying this standard, "must be *perfectly clear,* from a careful consideration of all the circumstances in the case, that the witness is mistaken, and that the answer(s) *cannot possibly* have such tendency to incriminate." The judge must therefore make his decision on the nature of the question, which is often extremely difficult. The nature of the kind of hearing is not the test to be applied to determine whether or not questions are incriminating.

The majority concluded that as to each of the questions put to defendant it was "evident from the implications of the question in the setting in which it [was] asked, that a responsive answer to the question or an explanation of why it [could not] be answered might be dangerous because injurious disclosure would result."

The law of most, if not all, states restricts the invocation of the privilege against incrimination to criminal cases. The privilege, however, as noted by Malloy extends to all hearings. If limited to its precise and literal meaning the privilege would be all but meaningless. For example, with the great number of investigative hearings that we find in our government, simply assuring a person that he does need to testify against himself when he has been brought to trial on criminal charges is not very reassuring. The purpose of the privilege in protecting against the oppressive nature of government would be hollow if it could not be invoked in any situation in which the answer to a question would tend to incriminate. The privilege simply means that a person need not take any chance of supplying information that would remotely lead to a criminal charge against him. In *Malloy* the questions asked by the referee had the potentiality of doing just this.

QUESTIONS

1. What privilege did this case incorporate into the Fourteenth Amendment?
2. How is the privilege against self-incrimination worded in the constitution of your state? Does the provision limit invocation of the privilege to only criminal cases? How has the privilege been expanded under your state laws?
3. What is the "federal standard" for determining whether or not a question is incriminatory? Discuss the "link in the chain" issue. What does it mean?

Murphy v. Waterfront Commission of New York Harbor
378 U.S. 52, 84 S.Ct. 1594, 12 L.Ed. 2ᴰ 678 (1964)

SETTING: Murphy and others were subpoenaed by the Waterfront Commission of New York Harbor to testify at a hearing concerning a work stoppage. Murphy refused to respond to certain questions about the stoppage on the ground that the answers might tend to incriminate him. The Commission then granted him immunity under New Jersey and New York statutes. He still refused to respond to the questions because the answers might also tend to incriminate him under federal law, to which the grants of immunity did not apply. He was therefore held in civil and criminal contempt. The New Jersey Supreme Court reversed the criminal contempt conviction on procedural grounds but affirmed the civil contempt judgments. The state courts held that a state may constitutionally compel a witness to give testimony that might be used against him in a federal prosecution.

PROCEDURAL PROBLEM: The Commission argued that the United States Supreme Court should adhere to the established rule in *United States* v. *Murdock,* 284 U.S. 141 (1931), that the constitutional privilege against self-incrimination does not protect a witness in one jurisdiction against being compelled to give testimony which could be used to convict him in another jurisdiction. The *Malloy* v. *Hogan,* 378 U.S. 1 (1964) decision and this decision were handed down on the same day. The Supreme Court indicated that because of the *Malloy* holding, it was necessary to reconsider the *Murdock* rule.

THE ISSUE: Is it constitutionally permissible for one jurisdiction within our federal system to compel a witness, who has been granted immunity from prosecution under its laws, to give testimony which might then be used to convict him of a crime against another such jurisdiction?

THE ANSWER: No.

DISCUSSION: The Court, in overruling *Murdock,* held that the constitutional privilege against self-incrimination protects a state witness against incrimination under federal as well as state law, and a federal witness against incrimination under state as well as federal law. The majority noted that its review of pertinent Supreme Court cases and their English antecedents revealed that "*Murdock* did not adequately consider the relevant authorities and has been significantly weakened by subsequent decisions."

Mr. Justice Goldberg for the majority stated that the English rule was exactly opposite from that which *Murdock* relied on—thus *Feldman* v. *United States,* 322 U.S. 487 (1944), which held that evidence compelled by a state grant of immunity could be used by the federal government, was also overruled.

The majority concluded that in light of the history, policies, and purposes of the privilege against self-incrimination, the "privilege protects a state witness against self-incrimination under federal as well as state law and a federal witness against incrimination under state as well as federal law."

Justices Harlan and Clark concurred in the majority conclusion but based their conclusion on the "ground that such a rule is protective of the values which the federal privilege against self-incrimination expresses, without in any way interfering with the independent action of the States and the Federal Government in their respective spheres. Increasing interaction between the State and Federal Governments speaks strongly against permitting federal officials to make prosecutorial use of testimony, which a State has compelled when that same testimony could not constitutionally have been compelled by the Federal Government and then used against the witness."

QUESTIONS

1. What is meant by a statutory grant of immunity from prosecution? Does your jurisdiction have such an immunity statute? What are its provisions?
2. Give several situations in which a state may grant immunity from prosecution. Why is it frequently granted?
3. Compare the reasons which the Harlan concurrence gave for concurring in the holding of the majority with the reasons given by Justice Goldberg. Which are more persuasive?

Escobedo v. *Illinois*
378 U.S. 478, 84 S.Ct. 1758, 12 L.Ed. 2ᴰ 977 (1964)

SETTING: Escobedo was arrested without a warrant for the murder of his brother-in-law at about 2:30 A.M. on January 19, 1960. He made no statements to the police and was released at 5:00 P.M. on the same afternoon pursuant to a writ of habeas corpus obtained by a lawyer who had been retained by Escobedo. On January 30 one DiGerlando, who was in police custody and had been indicted along with Escobedo for the murder, told the police that Escobedo fired the fatal shots. Escobedo was rearrested and urged to confess but all he did was ask to see his attorney. For hours, Escobedo asked to speak with his attorney during the time he was being interrogated. On each occasion his request was denied, even though once the attorney and Escobedo waved to each other from adjoining rooms.

Ultimately DiGerlando was brought to the interrogation room to confront Escobedo. During one exchange, Escobedo said, "I didn't shoot Manuel, you did it." Here Escobedo admitted some knowledge of the crime. Subsequently, he further implicated himself and then gave a written statement. During this entire procedure no one advised Escobedo of his constitutional rights.

PROCEDURAL PROBLEM: The questioning here was conducted before Escobedo was indicted. He requested and was denied the opportunity to consult with his own attorney. There was a formal arrest and the defendant was in police custody as a result of a police investigation that had focused on Escobedo as a prime suspect. In the face of serious accusations, the police saying that they had evidence that Escobedo had fired the fatal shots, he was not advised of his rights to remain silent. He was urged to make incriminating statements.

THE ISSUE: Under the circumstances of this case, was the refusal by the police to honor Escobedo's request to consult with his attorney during the course of interrogation a denial of the assistance of counsel in violation of the Sixth Amendment made obligatory upon the states by virtue of the Fourteenth Amendment, thereby rendering inadmissible in a state criminal prosecution the information elicited by the police during the interrogation?

THE ANSWER: Yes.

DISCUSSION: The Court held that even before indictment, when the process shifts from investigatory to accusatory, and the focus is on the accused and its purpose is to elicit a confession, the accused's request to consult his lawyer and the lawyer's request to see him must be granted. Confessions obtained while this consultation is being prevented by the police cannot be admitted into evidence against him.

The conduct of the police in this case was totally unreasonable and outrageous. The Court might well have stated that obtaining the confession in such a manner was so totally unfair as to deny the defendant due process. It chose, however, to broaden the constitutional rights of a person accused of a crime.

It must be noted that the Court was progressing step by step in making counsel available to an accused in the criminal process. Here the Court held that the right to counsel is not postponed until after an indictment is returned as in *Massiah* v. *United States,* 377 U.S. 201 (1964), *supra.* The Court was quite concerned here with the process of police investigations and the abuses that may stem therefrom.

Escobedo took the step from *Gideon* v. *Wainwright,* 372 U.S. 335 (1963), which made the right to counsel in a noncapital felony case binding on the states, and *Miranda* v. *Arizona,* 384 U.S. 436 (1966), which brought the right out of the courtroom into the situation in which a defendant is in police custody and the process of interrogation is initiated.

Justice Goldberg severely questioned the use of confessions as a means of securing criminal convictions by stating, "This Court also has recognized that 'history amply shows that confessions have often been extorted to save law enforcement officials the trouble and effort of obtaining valid and independent evidence.' We have also learned the companion lesson of history that no system of criminal justice can or should survive if it comes to depend for its continued effectiveness on the citizens' abdication through unawareness of their constitutional rights. No system worth preserving should have to *fear* that if an accused is permitted to consult with a lawyer, he will become aware of, and exercise these rights. If the exercise of constitutional rights will thwart the effectiveness of a system of law enforcement, then there is something very wrong with that system."

Justice Harlan, one of the four dissenters, announced that he thought "the rule announced today is most ill-conceived in that it seriously and unjustifiably fetters perfectly legitimate methods of criminal law enforcement." Justice Stewart was of the opinion that the majority had converted by its "own rhetoric" a routine police investigation of an unsolved homicide into distorted "analogue of a judicial trial."

Justice White, another dissenter, forecast the trend of the Court decisions by stating, "The decision is thus another major step in the direction of the goal which this Court seemingly has in mind—to bar from evidence all admissions obtained from an individual suspected of crime, whether involuntarily made or not. It does of course put us one step 'ahead' of the English judges who have had the good sense to leave the matter of a discretionary one with the trial court. I reject this step and the invitation to go farther which the Court has now issued."

White also rang the alarm that *Escobedo* would cripple law enforcement "and its task made a great deal more difficult, all in my opinion, for unsound, unstated reasons, which can find no home in any of the provisions of the Constitution."

Escobedo was to be applied retroactively only in trials begun after the decision was announced. *Johnson* v. *New Jersey,* 384, U.S. 719 (1966).

For several interesting discussions of *Escobedo* and *Massiah,* see

56 *Journal of Criminal Law, Criminology, and Police Science* 412 (1965), 49 *Minnesota Law Review* 47 (1964), 78 *Harvard Law Review* 217 (1964–1965).

QUESTIONS

1. Once the investigation has ceased to be a general inquiry of an unsolved crime but has begun to focus on a particular suspect, what right comes into play according to this case? What does the word "focus" mean as used in this case?
2. If a suspect is not in police custody and the investigation has not yet begun to focus on him, does he have any rights to protect? Should he even be advised of his right to remain silent?
3. Why did the Court in this case limit its holding to the specific facts in the case after using broad sweeping language throughout the opinion? Discuss the possible reasons.

Miranda v. *Arizona*
384 U.S. 436, 86 S.Ct. 1602, 16 L.Ed. 2ᴰ 694 (1966)

SETTING: Ernesto Miranda was found guilty by an Arizona court of kidnapping and attacking a young woman. Subsequently, his conviction was upheld by the Arizona Supreme Court. In the appellate action by the United States Supreme Court, he asked the Court to reverse the conviction, which it did. Miranda, through his attorney, argued that he was denied his rights under the Fifth and Fourteenth Amendments to the advice of an attorney during the time he was interrogated by the police. The specific facts established that on March 3, 1963, an 18-year-old girl was kidnapped and attacked near Phoenix, Arizona. On the morning of March 13, Miranda was arrested and taken to the police station. At the time of the arrest, Miranda was 23 years old, poor, had a ninth-grade education, and, according to a medical examination, had an emotional illness. At the police station, the victim picked Miranda out of the lineup. His questioning started at about 11:30 A.M. At the beginning, Miranda denied his guilt, but after about two hours of questioning, he confessed orally in great detail. He then wrote a brief statement describing the crime and admitting to it. At the top of the statement was a paragraph stating that the confession was made voluntarily without any threats or promises of immunity and with "full knowledge of my legal rights, understanding any statement I make may be used against me."

PROCEDURAL PROBLEM: At his jury trial, the written confession was admitted into evidence over the objection of his attorney. The officer testified to the prior oral confession made by Miranda during the questioning. He was convicted and sentenced to from 20 to 30 years' imprisonment. The Arizona Supreme Court determined that Miranda's constitutional rights had not been violated. The state affirmance stressed the fact that Miranda did not specifically request counsel.

THE ISSUE: Does the Fifth Amendment bar the use of exculpating or inculpating statements that stem from custodial interrogation where such statements are secured without first advising a suspect of his constitutional right to remain silent and assurance of a continuous opportunity to exercise this right?

THE ANSWER: Yes.

DISCUSSION: The Court here addressed itself to setting up rules to prevent police abuse in stationhouse interrogations. It declared that the Fifth Amendment's protection against self-incrimination must be protected religiously in the situations in which an accused is in custody and a process of interrogation has begun which has the goal of securing a confession. The Court held that the prosecution may not use statements obtained from custodial interrogation of the defendant unless it shows that there were procedural safeguards in effect to secure the privilege against self-incrimination.

The first issue the majority, in a 5–4 decision, dealt with was the meaning of "custodial interrogation." Chief Justice Warren, writing for the majority, defined it as "questioning initiated by law enforcement officers after a person has been taken into custody or otherwise deprived of his freedom of action in any significant way."

The next major issue was how to protect the right against self-incrimination. The Court set out certain procedural safeguards which must be employed:

> *Prior to any questioning, the person must be warned that he has a right to remain silent, that any statement he does make may be used as evidence against him, and that he has a right to the presence of an attorney, either retained or appointed. The defendant may waive effectuation of these rights, provided the waiver is made voluntarily, knowingly, and intelligently. If, however, he indicates in any manner and at any stage of the process that he wishes to consult an attorney before speaking, there*

can be no questioning. Likewise, if the individual is alone and indicates in any manner that he does not wish to be interrogated, the police may not question him. The mere fact that he may have answered some questions or volunteered some statements on his own does not deprive him of the right to refrain from answering any further inquiries until he has consulted with an attorney and thereafter consents to be questioned.

The Court noted the modern practice of in-custody interrogation is psychologically rather than physically oriented. The primary technique is the isolation of the accused. Citing the numerous books and manuals devoted to extracting confessions, the Court noted that the theme running through them is that privacy between the accused and the interrogator is the principal psychological factor contributing to a successful interrogation. The various other techniques have the aim of putting the accused "in a psychological state where his story is but an elaboration of what the police purport to know already—that he is guilty."

In summing up the overall condemnation of the interrogation techniques used by the police, Warren concluded:

It is obvious that such an interrogation environment is created for no purpose other than to subjugate the individual to the will of his examiner. This atmosphere carries its own badge of intimidation. To be sure, this is not physical intimidation, but it is equally destructive of human dignity. The current practice of incommunicado interrogation is at odds with one of our Nation's most cherished principles—that the individual may not be compelled to incriminate himself. Unless adequate protective devices are employed to dispel the compulsion inherent in custodial surroundings, no statement obtained from the defendant can truly be the product of his free choice.

The Court also recognized the claim "that each police station must have a 'stationhouse lawyer' present at all times to advise prisoners." The Court pointed out that this is not the case. But if the police propose to interrogate a person they must make known to him that he is entitled to a lawyer. If they do not interrogate, the need for the advice is not present.

In answer to another argument that the needs of society for interrogation outweigh the privilege, the Court stated that "The whole thrust of our foregoing discussion demonstrates that the Constitution has prescribed the rights of the individual when confronted with the power of government when it is provided in the Fifth Amendment that an individual cannot be compelled to be a witness against himself. That right cannot be abridged. . . ."

The majority likewise did not find any weight in the claim that there is a waiver of the privilege if the individual answers some questions or gives some information on his own prior to invoking his right to remain silent. Rather the fact that there has been lengthy interrogation or incommunicado incarceration before a statement is made is strong evidence that the accused did not validly waive his rights.

Justice Clark, in a dissenting opinion, was unable to join the majority "because its opinion goes too far on too little while my dissenting brethren do not go quite far enough." Clark would have preferred to look at the totality of circumstances to determine whether or not a confession was voluntary.

The other three dissenters—Harlan, Stewart, and White—claimed that the majority opinion established poor constitutional law and questioned the impact it would have on effective law enforcement. The three dissenters stated they could not predict with any accuracy the effect on law enforcement but did note that some crimes cannot be solved without confessions, that ample expert testimony attests to their importance in crime control, and that the Court is taking a real risk with the welfare of society by imposing these new rules on the country. They noted that the social costs of crime are too great to call the new rules anything but a hazardous experimentation.

Prior to *Miranda*, state courts addressed themselves to the problems involving police investigating and the right to counsel. For example, see *People* v. *Dorado*, 62 California 2ᴰ 338 (1965).

Many police agencies have printed warning cards which every officer must read to suspects who are in custody or detained and who are about to be questioned. A "Miranda Card" is pictured below.

WARNING OF CONSTITUTIONAL RIGHTS

1. You have the right to talk to a lawyer and have him with you while you are being questioned.
2. If you want a lawyer but cannot afford one, the court will appoint one for you.
3. You have the right to remain silent.
4. Anything you say can and will be used against you in court.

WAIVER

After the warning, ask the following questions and secure an affirmative answer to each to obtain a waiver:

1. Do you understand each of these rights I have explained to you?
2. With these rights in mind, do you wish to talk to us now?

QUESTIONS

1. What is the essential difference between *Miranda* and *Escobedo?*
2. What does the majority opinion mean when it states that force can be mental as well as physical?
3. What constitutional warning must be given to an accused who is in custody and is about to be interrogated?
4. What does Justice Clark think the rule should be in determining whether or not a confession is voluntary?
5. Do you think that this opinion will cripple effective law enforcement?
6. What did the majority members mean when they stated that a waiver must be voluntary, knowing, and without promises of immunity given?

Jackson v. *Denno*
378 U.S. 368, 84 S.Ct. 1774, 12 L.Ed. 2ᴰ 908 (1964)

SETTING: Jackson robbed the desk clerk of a hotel. Later Jackson killed an officer and was himself wounded in the exchange of gunfire. Jackson was taken to a hospital, where he gave an oral confession. About two hours later he executed a more damaging written confession. Both confessions were subsequently introduced at his trial. He was convicted of murder. A writ of habeas corpus was denied and the United States Supreme Court granted certiorari. The conviction was reversed.

PROCEDURAL PROBLEM: At the trial there was some dispute in the evidence over whether or not the written confession was voluntary or involuntary. According to New York procedure then, where a question was raised about the voluntariness of a confession, the trial court submitted the issue to the jury along with the other issues in case. The jury was instructed to disregard the confession entirely if it was found to be involuntary. If it found that the confession was voluntary, the jury was to determine the truth and reliability of it and afford it weight accordingly. According to the established practice in New York, the judge only excluded a confession when it was without a doubt involuntary. The New York procedure was formerly upheld by the United States Supreme Court in *Stein* v. *New York*, 346 U.S. 156 (1953).

THE ISSUE: Did the New York procedure permitting the jury to
determine as a factual matter whether a confession is voluntary or involuntary contravene a defendant's Fourteenth Amendment due process
rights?

THE ANSWER: Yes.

DISCUSSION: The Supreme Court indicated that the New York
procedure could not square with the dictates of due process. In its view
the procedure "employed in this case did not afford a reliable determination of the voluntariness of the confession offered in evidence of the trial."
It did not adequately protect the defendant's right to be free of a conviction based upon a coerced confession and therefore cannot withstand
constitutional attack under the due process clause of the Fourteenth
Amendment. As the Court noted:

> . . . [T]he evidence given the jury invariably injects irrelevant and
> impermissible considerations of truthfulness of the confession into the
> assessment of voluntariness. Indeed the jury is told to determine the
> truthfulness of the confession in assessing its probative value.

Noting that the *Stein* Court assumed that the jury reliably found the facts
against the accused, the *Jackson* Court was not willing to make this
assumption. Justice White, writing for the majority, also emphasized that
it cannot be assumed that a jury which finds a confession to be involuntary
will then disregard it. "If it finds the confession involuntary, does the
jury—indeed, can it—then disregard the confession in accordance with its
instructions?"

The majority emphasized that in the New York procedure the jury
returns only a general verdict of guilt or innocence. "It is impossible to
determine whether the jury found the confession voluntary and relied
upon it, or involuntary and supposedly ignored it." According to White,
the procedure poses serious threats to the constitutional rights of a defendant.

There are usually three procedures used to determine whether or
not a confession is voluntary. They are: (1) the rule in which the judge
alone determines the issue—this is the usual or orthodox rule; (2) the rule
used in Massachusetts, under which the jury does not hear a confession
unless the judge ascertains that it is voluntary. Then the jury hears the
evidence on which the judge made his decision of voluntariness and may
decide based on its consideration that the confession was involuntary and
disregard it; (3) the New York rule, under which the confession is admitted unless it is unquestionably involuntary. The Court apparently finds
nothing objectionable in the first two but rejects the latter.

Three of the four *Jackson* dissenters—Harlan, Clark, and Stewart—never "thought it open to doubt that the States were free to allocate the trial of issues, whether in criminal or civil cases, between the judge and jury as they deemed best." Justice Black thought in dissent that *Stein* had been properly decided and should not be overruled.

QUESTIONS

1. What was the specific holding in this case? What was wrong with the New York procedure?
2. What are the three usual methods of determining the voluntariness of a confession? Discuss the strengths and weaknesses of each.
3. What is the major problem of returning a general verdict under the New York procedure? Is it a substantial concern?

Harris v. *New York*
401 U.S. 222, 91 S.Ct. 643, 28 L.Ed. 2ᴰ 1 (1971)

SETTING: New York police charged Harris with selling heroin to an undercover police officer. At the trial one police officer testified regarding the sales, another to corroborative matters, and another to the chemical analysis of the heroin. Harris then took the stand and denied the sales of heroin but did acknowledge that he knew the undercover officer. He also admitted to selling a glassine bag containing baking powder to the officer.

PROCEDURAL PROBLEM: On cross-examination the defendant was asked whether he had made specified statements to the police immediately after his arrest on January 7. The statements partially contradicted his statements at the trial. In response to the cross-examination by the prosecutor, Harris testified that he could not remember virtually any of the questions or answers recited by the prosecutor. Harris' counsel then asked that the written statement, from which the questions and answers were read, be entered into the record for appeal purposes. The statement was not shown to the jury.

The trial judge then instructed the jury that the statements attributed to the defendant could only be used in passing on the credibility of Harris as a witness and not on the issue of guilt or innocence. In the closing summation, counsel for both sides argued the substance of the impeaching statement.

During the trial the prosecutor explicitly conceded that the statements were inadmissible under *Miranda* v. *Arizona,* 384 U.S. 436 (1966), because Harris had not been advised of his right to an attorney when taken into custody and asked the questions. There was also no claim that the confession was coerced or involuntary. The defendant was convicted and the New York appellate court affirmed. The United States Supreme Court did likewise.

THE ISSUE: May in-custody statements that satisfy legal standards of trustworthiness, even though excluded by the *Miranda* decision from the prosecution's case in chief, nevertheless be used to impeach the credibility of a testifying defendant?

THE ANSWER: Yes.

DISCUSSION: For the first time since the *Miranda* decision, the Supreme Court appeared to reduce rather than expand the scope of the *Miranda* exclusionary rule. The statements made by Harris, although inadmissible under *Miranda,* were allowed, however, to be used for the narrower purpose of impeaching his credibility as a witness.

Chief Justice Burger acknowledged *Miranda* comments that confessions or admissions obtained in violation of its requirement may not be admissible for any purpose. Burger indicated that the language was not necessary for the Court's holding and "cannot be regarded as controlling." Because *Miranda* barred the prosecution from making its case with statements from an accused in custody without having or effectively waiving counsel, "It does not follow . . . that evidence is inadmissible against an accused . . . [or] is barred for all purposes. . . ."

In face of the claim that this decision might encourage impermissible police conduct, the majority rejected the argument, stating:

> *The impeachment process here undoubtedly provided valuable aid to the jury in assessing petitioner's credibility and the benefits of this process should not be lost, in our view, because of the speculative possibility that impermissible police conduct will be encouraged thereby. Assuming that the exclusionary rule has a deterrent effect on proscribed police conduct, sufficient deterrence flows when the evidence in question is made unavailable to the prosecution in its case in chief.*

The Supreme Court reaffirmed and even extended *Walder* v. *United States,* 347 U.S. 62 (1954), which many had thought was no longer valid under *Miranda.* In *Walder* the Court permitted impeachment of a defendant regarding collateral matters although the evidence might be inadmissible in the case in chief. *Harris* broadened the *Walder* decision by permitting impeachment as to testimony having a direct bearing on the crime charged.

Justice Brennan, writing for Douglas and Marshall in dissent, read *Miranda* as completely barring any statements obtained in violation of the guidelines. Brennan contended that

> *All these policies point to one overriding thought: the constitutional foundation underlying the privilege is the respect a government must accord to the dignity and integrity of its citizens. These values are plainly jeopardized if an exception against admission of tainted statements is made for those used for impeachment purposes. Moreover it is monstrous that courts should aid or abet the law-breaking police officer.*

Brennan also acknowledged that even though deterrence was only a part of the objective of *Miranda:* "I fear that today's holding will seriously undermine the achievement of that objective. The Court today tells the police that they may freely interrogate an accused incommunicado and without counsel and know that although any statement they obtain in violation of *Miranda* cannot be used on the State's direct case, it may be introduced if the defendant has the temerity to testify in his own defense. This goes far toward undoing much of the progress made in conforming police methods to the constitution."

QUESTIONS

1. Compare the holding in this case with the holding in *Miranda.* Does it seriously weaken the *Miranda* rule?
2. Do you believe that the *Harris* decision will encourage police misconduct in securing inadmissible confessions which can be used for impeachment only?
3. In what way did this decision modify and expand *Walder* v. *United States?* What is meant by collateral matters as compared with evidence bearing directly on the guilt or innocence of the crime charged?

Orozco v. *Texas*
394 U.S. 324, 89 S.Ct. 1095, 22 L.Ed. 2ᴰ 311 (1969)

SETTING: The defendant shot and killed a man for making remarks to his female companion. After the shooting at a cafe, Orozco left the scene and went to his boarding house to sleep. At about 4:00 A.M. four

police officers went to the boarding house, and were admitted by an
unidentified female who told them that Orozco was asleep in his room.
The officers went into the room and began to question Orozco.

PROCEDURAL PROBLEM: In the questioning of Orozco he was asked
if he had been to the cafe at which the shooting occurred. When he
answered in the affirmative, he was asked if he owned a gun, to which
he answered "Yes." He was also asked on two occasions where the gun
was located and admitted that it was in the washing machine in the
back room of the boarding house. During this questioning he was not
advised of his right to remain silent, to have the advice of a lawyer, or
to have one appointed for him if he could not afford to hire one. According to testimony of the officers, Orozco was under arrest when questioned
in the bedroom and not free to leave.

Ballistics tests indicated that the gun found in the washing machine
had fired the fatal shot. The defendant objected to the officers' relating
his statements. Orozco was convicted and the Texas Court of Criminal
Appeals held that *Miranda* did not preclude introduction of the statements. The United States Supreme Court reversed.

THE ISSUE: Was the questioning of the defendant while at home in
bed custodial in nature, thereby necessitating the fourfold Miranda
warning to be given?

THE ANSWER: Yes.

DISCUSSION: This case resolved two questions concerning the scope
and application of the *Miranda* case. Justice Black first held for the majority that the questioning of Orozco was indeed custodial. In response
to the state argument that because the defendant was interrogated in
his home and in familiar surroundings *Miranda* should not apply, the
Court stated that the "*Miranda* opinion declared that the warnings were
required when the person being interrogated was 'in custody at the station *or otherwise deprived of his freedom af action in any significant
way.'*" Black emphasized the statements of the officers that Orozco was
"under arrest" and that this is the kind of deprivation of freedom that
Miranda describes.

Justice White, one of the dissenters, argued that the *Orozco* decision carries the *Miranda* rule to "new and unwarranted extremes. . . .
Even accepting *Miranda*, the Court extends the rule here and draws the
straitjacket even tighter." White also still questioned the importance of
Miranda by noting that if it is justified at all "it rests on the likelihood
that in a sufficient number of cases exposure to stationhouse practices

will result in compelled confessions and that additional safeguards should be imposed in all cases to prevent possible erosion of Fifth Amendment values." He argued that the very purpose of *Miranda* was ignored in this decision: "The Court wholly ignores the question whether similar hazards exist or are even possible when police arrest and interrogate on the spot, whether it be on the street corner, or in the home, as in this case."

QUESTIONS

1. What is meant by "stationhouse" interrogation? How does it differ in Justice White's opinion from the interrogation in this case?
2. In what areas did *Orozco* extend *Miranda*?
3. In your opinion, does the holding in this case deter offensive police conduct more than the holding in *Miranda*? more than in *Harris*?

Schmerber v. *California*
384 U.S. 757, 86 S.Ct. 1826, 16n L.Ed. 2ᴰ 908 (1966)

SETTING: The defendant was arrested at a hospital while receiving treatment for injuries which he had apparently received in an accident involving the automobile which he was driving.

At the direction of one of the police officers, a blood sample was withdrawn from Schmerber's body by a trained physician. A chemical analysis revealed that the percent of weight of alcohol in his blood at the time of the offense indicated that he was intoxicated.

PROCEDURAL PROBLEM: At the defendant's trial the report of the analysis was admitted into evidence over the objections of the defendant's attorney, who contended that the withdrawal of the blood and admission of the analysis in evidence denied the defendant due process under the law under the Fourteenth Amendment as well as, *inter alia*, his privilege against self-incrimination under the Fifth Amendment. He was convicted of driving an automobile under the influence of intoxicating liquor and the California Appellate Courts affirmed. The United States Supreme Court granted certiorari and also affirmed the conviction.

THE ISSUE: Does the scope of the Fifth Amendment's privilege against self-incrimination embrace taking blood samples involuntarily?

THE ANSWER: No.

DISCUSSION: The idea that many defendants had that a claim of self-incrimination, especially in view of the ever-enlarging protection of the defendant's constitutional rights, was an infallible key to the jailhouse door was given a jolt in *Schmerber*. In another 5–4 decision, Justice Brennan for the majority adhered to *Breithaupt* v. *Abrams*, 352 U.S. 432 (1957), which held that the prosecution can use evidence withdrawn from an unconscious person who could not object and that this did not offend the Court's sense of justice. However, the majority in *Schmerber* went *Breithaupt* one step better by holding that such evidence is admissible even though the accused objects, upon the advice of counsel, to the extraction of blood. As the Court stated, "We hold the privilege protects an accused only from being compelled to testify against himself; or otherwise provide the State with evidence of a testimonial or communicative nature, and that the withdrawal of blood and use of the analysis in question in this case did not involve compulsion to these ends." It is clear therefore that the privilege reaches only communications of an accused. It is fulfilled "only when the person is guaranteed the right 'to remain silent unless he chooses to speak in the unfettered exercise of his own will.'" It is also clear that the privilege also reaches written communications. Compulsion to make a suspect reveal real or physical evidence does not violate the privilege, however. "The distinction which has emerged, often expressed in different ways, is that the privilege is a bar against compelling 'communications' or 'testimony,' but that compulsion which makes a suspect or accused the source of 'real or physical evidence' does not violate it."

The defendant also pressed claims under the Fourth, Sixth, and Fourteenth Amendments, but the Court emphasized that they were of no help to Schmerber. Withdrawal of blood was, in short, a reasonable and appropriate method of determining intoxication in an arrest confrontation.

Justice Fortas thought that the state should not be permitted to use violence to secure evidence against a person. In the opinion of Fortas, forcible extraction of blood is act of violence.

Justices Black and Douglas favored a broad interpretation of the Fifth Amendment but did not agree with the distinction between testimonial and real evidence. According to them, no person should be compelled in any way to furnish evidence of any kind that may be used against him. As Black noted:

> I am happy that the Court itself refuses to follow Professor Wigmore's implication that the Fifth Amendment goes no further than to bar

the use of forced self-incriminating statements coming from a "person's own lips." It concedes . . . that the Fifth Amendment bars a state from compelling a person to produce papers he has that might tend to incriminate him. . . . Certainly there could be few papers that would have any more "testimonial" value to convict a man of drunken driving than would an analysis of the alcoholic content of a human being's blood introduced in evidence at a trial for driving while under the influence of alcohol. In such a situation blood, of course, is not oral testimony given by an accused but it can certainly "communicate" to a court and jury the fact of guilt.

QUESTIONS

1. Distinguish between physical and testimonial evidence.
2. Immediately after this decision, several states enacted "implied consent" laws. Why?
3. Does the dissent by Black and Douglas make sense to you when the police continually warn of the dangers of drunks on the highways? Discuss fully the implication of the Black-Douglas dissent. What is their main difference with the position of the majority?

Garrity v. New Jersey
385 U.S. 493, 87 S.Ct. 616, 17 L.Ed. 2ᴰ 562 (1967)

SETTING: Garrity and other defendants in this case were New Jersey police officers. The Supreme Court of New Jersey ordered that alleged irregularities in handling cases in various New Jersey borough municipal courts be investigated by the state attorney general, who was invested with broad inquiry and investigatory powers. The attorney general was to make a report to the New Jersey Supreme Court regarding the alleged fixing of traffic tickets.

PROCEDURAL PROBLEM: The defendant was called to testify and warned (1) that anything he said might be used against him in any state proceeding; (2) that he had the privilege to refuse to answer if disclosure would tend to incriminate him; but (3) if he refused to answer he would be subject to removal from office.

Because New Jersey had no immunity statute applicable in the circumstances of this case, none was granted to the defendant who answered the questions. Some of the answers were subsequently used in criminal prosecution of the defendant for conspiracy to obstruct the administration of traffic laws. The defendant was convicted and the conviction was affirmed in the various state courts over the defendant's argument that his statement was coerced by reason of the fact that if he refused to answer, he could lose his job with the police department. The choice, therefore, was to incriminate himself or forfeit his job. The United States Supreme Court reversed the convictions.

THE ISSUE: Does the Fifth Amendment preclude the admission of statements as being coerced when such statements are made by police officers who are being investigated by state authorities and who are given the choice of either incriminating themselves or of forfeiting their jobs for refusing to testify as provided by a state statute?

THE ANSWER: Yes.

DISCUSSION: In starting off, coercion that vitiates a confession can be mental or physical. The question here, therefore, is whether Garrity and the other defendants were deprived of their free choice to admit, to deny, or to refuse to answer. The choice, as Justice Douglas noted for the majority, was for the defendant to forfeit his job or to incriminate himself. The option given was, as the majority noted, the antithesis of free choice to speak out or to remain silent. The practice is likely to exert such pressure upon an individual "as to disable him from making a free and rational choice." Douglas stated, "We think the statements were infected by the coercion inherent in this scheme of questioning and cannot be sustained as voluntary under our prior decisions."

In answer to the claim that there was a waiver, the majority stated that where the choice is "between the rock and the whirlpool, duress is inherent in deciding to waive one or the other. . . . The cases are therefore quite different from the situation where one who is anxious to make a clean breast of the whole affair volunteers the information."

In his concluding remarks, Douglas said, "We now hold the protection of the individual under the Fourteenth Amendment against coerced statements prohibits use in subsequent criminal proceedings of statements obtained under threat of removal from office, and that it extends to all, whether they are policemen or other members of the body politic."

In this 5–4 decision, three of the dissenters—Harlan, Clark, and Stewart—feared that the majority rule would seriously and needlessly hinder the protection of other important public values. Because the sanctions are constitutionally permissible, the dissenters believed that the warning given of possible discharge for a refusal to answer questions was not constitutionally objectionable.

QUESTIONS

1. The holding in this case is much broader than the issue that faced the Court. What was the broad scope of the holding and why do you think the Court made it as broad as it did?

2. What considerations were the dissenters thinking about when they indicated that the state has a real interest in having employees give pertinent information about their employment?

3. Compare the facts and holding in *Garrity* with *Murphy* v. *Waterfront Commission of New York Harbor*. If there were an applicable immunity statute and Garrity had been granted immunity, could he have been compelled to testify? Would he then have been subject to criminal prosecution? loss of his job? Discuss.

Gardner v. *Broderick*
392 U.S. 273, 88 S.Ct. 1913, 20 L.Ed. 2ᴰ 1082 (1968)

SETTING: Gardner was a New York policeman who claimed that he was unlawfully dismissed because he refused to waive his privilege against self-incrimination. Pursuant to a subpoena, he appeared before a New York County grand jury which was investigating alleged bribery and corruption of police officers in connection with illegal gambling operations. He was advised that the grand jury proposed to examine him regarding performance of his official duties.

PROCEDURAL PROBLEM: When Gardner appeared before the grand jury, he was advised of his privilege against self-incrimination but was asked to sign a waiver of immunity after being told he would be dismissed if he did not sign. He refused, was given an administrative hearing, and fired solely because of his refusal to sign the waiver. Gardner sought reinstatement as a patrolman and back pay. The New York Appellate Courts affirmed the dismissal. The United States Supreme Court reversed.

THE ISSUE: Can a public official be discharged for refusing to surrender his privilege against self-incrimination?

THE ANSWER: No.

DISCUSSION: In *Garrity* v. *New Jersey*, 385 U.S. 493 (1967), the
Court held that a public official cannot be compelled to give incriminating
statements by the threat of losing his job; such statements cannot be used
against him. In *Gardner* v. *Broderick* it was ruled that they could not be
discharged for refusing to surrender that privilege. Justice Fortas, writing
the majority opinion, emphasized the narrow scope of this decision by
stating that had Gardner "refused to answer questions specifically, directly, and narrowly relating to the performance of his official duties,
without being required to waive his immunity with respect to the use
of his answers or the fruits thereof in a criminal prosecution of himself, . . . the privilege against self-incrimination would not have been
a bar to his dismissal."

The opinion emphasized that "He was dismissed solely for his
refusal to waive the immunity to which he is entitled if he is required
to testify despite his constitutional privilege." Fortas also noted that it
was clear that Gardner's testimony was demanded before the grand jury
in part so that it might be used to prosecute him, and "not solely for the
purpose of securing an accounting of his performance of his public trust.
If the latter had been the only purpose, there would have been no reason
to seek to compel [defendant] to waive his immunity."

QUESTIONS

1. Under this decision, may a public employee still be discharged for
poor performance of his duties without having the chance of being
reinstated because of a violation of his Fifth Amendment privilege?
Explain the kinds of situations in which this is permissible.
2. Contrast this opinion with *Garrity* v. *New Jersey*. What is the basic
difference between these two cases?
3. How would the *Gardner* rule be applied if used in conjunction with
the holding in *Murphy* v. *Waterfront Commission of New York Harbor*,
supra?

Uniformed Sanitation Men's Association v. *Commissioner of Sanitation*
392 U.S. 280, 88 S.Ct. 1917, 20 L.Ed. 2ᴰ 1089 (1968)

SETTING: In 1966, the New York Commissioner of Investigation
investigated alleged illegal activities of employees of the Uniformed

Sanitation Men's Association. During the investigation some fifteen employees were summoned before the Commissioner to give testimony regarding the alleged actions.

PROCEDURAL PROBLEM: Each employee was advised that if he refused to testify with respect to his official conduct or the conduct of any other city employee on the grounds of self-incrimination, his employment and eligibility for other city employment would terminate. Twelve of the members refused to testify, asserting the constitutional privilege against self-incrimination. A disciplinary hearing was held and they were dismissed on the explicit ground provided in the city charter that they refused to testify.

The remaining three answered the questions put to them, denying the charges, and were suspended "for irregularities arising out of their employment." They were then summoned to a grand jury hearing and asked to sign waivers of immunity. They refused and as a result they were subsequently dismissed on the sole ground that they had refused to sign the waivers in violation of the New York charter. The dismissals were upheld by the New York Courts, which based their decision on the New York State case of *Gardner* v. *Broderick*, 282 N.Y.S. 2^D 487 (1967). This decision was reversed by the United States Supreme Court on the day that the Uniformed Sanitation Men's Association case was decided. It must be emphasized that the members were not discharged merely for refusing to account for their conduct as city employees. They were dismissed for invoking and refusing to waive their constitutional right against self-incrimination.

THE ISSUE: Is the constitutional privilege against self-incrimination violated by the discharge of the employees for refusing to sign immunity waivers before a grand jury or for invoking their constitutional privilege against self-incrimination before the New York Investigation Commission?

THE ANSWER: Yes.

DISCUSSION: In *Garrity* v. *New York*, 87 S.Ct. 616 (1967), the Supreme Court held that testimony compelled by threat of dismissal from employment could not be used in a criminal prosecution of a witness. But *Garrity* had not been decided when these twelve employees were given the choice of being fired or incriminating themselves. They were entitled to remain silent because it was clear that New York was seeking not merely an accounting of their use or abuse of their public trust, but testimony from their own lips which, despite the constitutional prohibition, could be used to prosecute them criminally.

Justice Fortas, who wrote the majority opinion, emphasized that had the employees refused to answer questions specifically, narrowly, and directly relating to job performance on pain of dismissal without the requirement of relinquishment of the constitutional privilege, "this case would be entirely different." He held further that: "Here the precise and plain impact of the proceedings . . . was to present them [the employees] with a choice between surrendering their constitutional rights and their jobs." Public employees, like all other persons, are entitled to constitutional benefits, including the privilege against self-incrimination.

Justices Harlan and White concurred; Harlan wrote, "I can find no solidly acceptable course . . . other than to concur in these judgments." He did so because he found in the *Spevack* v. *Klein,* 385 U.S. 511 (1967) and *Garrity* v. *New Jersey,* 385 U.S. 493 (1967) opinions a "procedural formula whereby, for example, public officials may now be discharged and lawyers disciplined for refusing to divulge to appropriate authority information pertinent to the faithful performance of their offices." According to Justice Harlan this was "a welcome breakthrough in what *Spevack* and *Garrity* might otherwise have been thought to pretend."

QUESTIONS

1. Does the institution you are attending have a rule or regulation addressing testimony given to administrators, investigative agencies, and the like? What are its provisions? Does it have a provision regarding the privilege against self-incrimination or waiver of immunity? Discuss.
2. Distinguish this case from *Garrity* v. *New Jersey* and *Gardner* v. *Broderick.*
3. What do you think Justice Harlan was concerned about in his concurring opinion?

Spevack v. *Klein*
385 U.S. 511, 87 S.Ct. 625, 17 L.Ed. 2ᴰ 574 (1967)

SETTING: Spevack, a lawyer, was called before a proceeding for professional misconduct. He refused to honor a *subpoena duces tecum* served on him to produce certain financial records. He also refused to testify at the judicial inquiry. Both refusals were based on the claim that the records and his testimony would tend to incriminate him.

PROCEDURAL PROBLEM: The New York Supreme Court, Appellate Division, ordered Spevack disbarred, holding that the constitutional privilege against self-incrimination was not available to him. The decision was based on the holding in *Cohen* v. *Hurley,* 366 U.S. 117 (1961), which approved disbarment of an attorney who "obstructed" an investigation of his professional fitness by claiming the privilege against self-incrimination when asked to produce records and answer questions bearing on alleged "ambulance chasing." In a 5–4 majority the *Cohen* Court held that the disbarment "was predicated not upon any unfavorable inference which [the State] drew from petitioner's assertion of the privilege . . . nor upon any purpose to penalize him for its exercise, but solely upon his refusal to discharge obligations which, as a lawyer, he owed to the court. [A]ll that New York has in effect held is that petitioner by resort to a privilege against self-incrimination, can no more claim a right not to answer with respect to matters within the competence of the Court's supervisory powers over members of the bar, than could a trustee claim a right not to be removed from office for failure to render accounts which might incriminate him."

The Court majority, in short, held that New York could construe its own privilege against self-incrimination as not to make it available in judicial inquiry of this character. *Cohen* also held that the privilege against the self-incrimination clause was not binding on the state by virtue of the Fourteenth Amendment. Between the *Cohen* and *Spevack* cases, the Supreme Court decided in *Malloy* v. *Hogan,* 378 U.S. 1 (1964), that the Fourteenth Amendment makes the Fifth Amendment's privilege against self-incrimination fully applicable to the states and that federal standards are to be applied.

THE ISSUE: Because the Fifth Amendment privilege has been incorporated into the Fourteenth Amendment, is the protection extended to lawyers as well as to other individuals, thereby overruling *Cohen* v. *Hurley?*

THE ANSWER: Yes.

DISCUSSION: Justice Douglas, writing for the majority, noted that the threat of "disbarment and the loss of professional standing, professional reputation, and of livelihood are powerful forms of compulsion to make a lawyer relinquish the privilege." The Supreme Court did not approach this case as if disbarment were a consequence against which Spevack could have properly guarded by invoking the privilege against self-incrimination. Even if disbarment were not a criminal action, Spe-

vack could still have withheld his records from the professional misconduct proceeding on the grounds that he felt that producing the
records could lead to a criminal prosecution.

Justice White, in dissent, could see no reason for refusing to permit
the state to pursue a valid state interest in discharging employees who
refused to cooperate in the state's efforts to determine qualification to
continue to do a job (*Garrity* v. *New Jersey*). He adopted the same
reasoning in *Spevack* and saw little practical basis in terms of the Fifth
Amendment for preventing disbarment of a lawyer who refuses to talk
about the performance of his public duty.

QUESTIONS

1. There is obviously a need to cleanse the bar of lawyers who are guilty
   of misconduct or who are dishonest and lack integrity. What legal
   device could have been used by the state to have Spevack testify and
   reveal his records?
2. *Malloy* v. *Hogan* speaks of a defendant's right to remain silent without
   the fear of suffering a penalty. What possible penalty would Spevack
   have incurred had he testified or produced the records? Was the threat
   of the penalty real or imaginary?
3. Distinguish the holding in this case from *Garrity* v. *New Jersey, supra*.
   Is it important to distinguish the duties performed by the lawyer and
   the policeman? Discuss.

Kastigar v. *United States*
406 U.S. 441, 92 S.Ct. 1653, 32 L.Ed. 2ᴰ 212 (1972)

SETTING: The defendant was subpoenaed to appear before a federal
grand jury. The government believed he would assert his privilege against
self-incrimination and applied to the federal district court for an order
directing Kastigar to testify and produce evidence before the grand jury
under a grant of immunity under 18 U.S.C. sections 6002–6003.

PROCEDURAL PROBLEM: Kastigar opposed the order, claiming that
the scope of the federal immunity was not coextensive with the scope of
the privilege against self-incrimination. Therefore it was not sufficient to
supplant the privilege and compel his testimony. Kastigar appeared at

the grand jury hearing, but refused to answer questions, asserting his privilege against self-incrimination. He was cited for contempt and the federal Court of Appeals affirmed. The United States Supreme Court granted certiorari and affirmed.

THE ISSUE: Must a reluctant witness be granted full transactional immunity (immunity from prosecution for offenses to which the testimony relates) from future prosecution before he may be compelled to waive his privilege against self-incrimination?

THE ANSWER: No.

DISCUSSION: The defendant argued first of all that the provisions of the Fifth Amendment deprives Congress of the power to enact laws that compel self-incrimination, even if complete immunity from prosecution is granted prior to the compulsion of the incriminating testimony. In substance, the gist of the argument is that no immunity statute can afford a lawful basis for compelling incriminating testimony. The Court rejected this argument and reaffirmed *Ullmann v. United States*, 350 U.S. 422 (1956), which upheld the constitutionality of immunity statute.

Secondly, the defendant argued that the scope of the immunity granted was not coextensive with the scope of the Fifth Amendment privilege and therefore is not sufficient to supplant the privilege and compel testimony over a claim of the privilege. Section 6002 provides that when the district court orders the witness to testify over a claim of the privilege,

> *the witness may not refuse to comply with the order on the basis of his privilege against self-incrimination; but no testimony or other information compelled under the order (or any information directly or indirectly derived from such testimony or other information) may be used against the witness in any criminal case, except a prosecution for perjury, giving a false statement, or otherwise failing to comply with the order.*

The question of whether the immunity granted by this statute was coextensive with the Fifth Amendment was based on Kastigar's argument in drawing a distinction between transactional immunity and immunity from use and derivative use. The defendant argued that immunity must be full transactional immunity in order to be coextensive with the Fifth Amendment. The Court, speaking through Justice Powell, held that immunity from use and derivative use is coextensive with the scope of the privilege against self-incrimination and is therefore sufficient to compel testimony over a claim of the privilege. Transactional immunity affords a witness full immunity from prosecution for the offense to which the compelled testimony relates. It is a considerably broader protection than that provided by the Fifth Amendment. "The privilege has never been construed to mean that one who invokes it cannot subsequently be prosecuted. Its sole concern is to afford protection against being 'forced to give testimony leading to the infliction of penalties affixed to . . . criminal acts.'"

The defendant next argued that the use and derivative use immunity does not adequately protect a witness from the possible incriminating uses of the compelled testimony. According to the argument, "it will be difficult and perhaps impossible . . . to identify, by testimony or cross-examination, the subtle ways in which the compelled testimony may disadvantage a witness. . . ." The defendant's claim presupposed that the prohibition in the statute would be impossible to enforce. The Court emphasized that the government has a very heavy burden of proof by stating, "This burden of proof . . . is not limited to a negation of taint; rather, it imposes on the prosecution the affirmative duty to prove that the evidence it proposes to use is derived from a legitimate source wholly independent of the compelled testimony."

In dissent, Justices Marshall and Douglas thought that it is entirely futile to expect enforcement of the prohibition against the use and derivative use of testimony. Marshall could not agree that a total ban on use would be possible as long as the government could still convict on the basis of independent evidence. As he noted, the good faith of the prosecutor is not a sufficient safeguard. "The Court today sets out a loose net to trap tainted evidence and prevent its use against the witness, but it accepts an intolerably great risk that tainted evidence will in fact slip through that net."

Marshall also noted that there is a vast difference between an immunity statute and the immunity that is inadvertently granted "by an unconstitutional interrogation." An immunity statute operates in advance of the event and it authorizes—even encourages—interrogation that would violate the Fifth Amendment. The grant of immunity must remove the danger of incrimination completely, while the exclusionary rule comes into play *after* the interrogation or search has occurred. In other words, the grant of immunity enables the prosecuting attorney to make a calm, reassured decision regarding whether or not to forego a prosecution in order to obtain information that he would not be able to acquire otherwise.

QUESTIONS

1. What is meant by transactional immunity? use and derivative use immunity?

2. What were the major points in Justice Marshall's dissent? Do you agree with his analysis? Explain your answer fully.
3. Is the immunity statute in your jurisdiction a transactional immunity statute or a use and derivative use statute?

Zicarelli v.
New Jersey State Commission of Investigation
406 U.S. 472, 92 S.Ct. 1670, 32 L.Ed. 2ᴰ 234 (1972)

SETTING: The New Jersey State Commission of Investigation subpoenaed Zicarelli to testify concerning organized crime, racketeering, and political corruption in Long Branch, New Jersey. In the course of several appearances before the Commission, he invoked his privilege against self-incrimination and refused to answer a series of 100 questions. The Commission granted him immunity under a New Jersey statute and ordered him to answer the questions. Notwithstanding the grant of immunity, he persisted in his refusal to answer. The Commission then petitioned the Superior Court of Mercer County for an order directing Zicarelli to show cause why he should not be adjudged in contempt of the Commission and committed to jail until such time as he purged himself of contempt by testifying as ordered. At the hearing on the order to show cause, he challenged on several grounds, one of which was that the statutory immunity was insufficient in several respects to compel testimony over a claim of the privilege. The Superior Court rejected this connection, and ordered him incarcerated until such time as he testified as ordered. The Supreme Court of New Jersey affirmed the judgment of the Superior Court. The United States Supreme Court noted probable jurisdiction to consider Zicarelli's challenges to the sufficiency of the immunity authorized by the New Jersey statute.

PROCEDURAL PROBLEM: After a witness testifies under the grant of immunity, the statute further provides that

> He shall be immune from having such responsive answer given by him or such responsive evidence produced by him, or evidence derived therefrom used to expose him to criminal prosecution or penalty or to a forfeiture of his estate, except that such person may nevertheless be prosecuted for any perjury committed in such answer or in producing such evidence, or for contempt for failing to give an answer or produce evidence in accordance with the order of the commission . . .

This statute provided protection from the use and derivative use of testimony compelled under the grant of immunity. The same kind of federal statute was upheld under the Fifth Amendment attack in *Kastigar v. United States*, 406 U.S. 441 (1972), *supra.*

THE ISSUE: In order to be constitutionally acceptable, must a state immunity provide complete "transactional" immunity in addition to use and derivative use immunity?

THE ANSWER: No.

DISCUSSION: The United States Supreme Court found no constitutional flaw in the state immunity statute limiting the immunity to "responsive" answers and evidence secured from the witness. In response to the claim that there should be statutory guidelines to define what is meant by the word "responsive," Justice Powell for the majority stated that such guidelines are unnecessary. He noted that the New Jersey courts had already provided such guidance by holding that "fairly construed, the statute protects the witness against answers and evidence he in good faith believed were demanded." Responsiveness is therefore not used in a technical legal sense but rather "in a construction cast in terms of ordinary English usage and the good-faith understanding of the average man." The Court also pointed out that the accused under the New Jersey statute is hardly prejudiced by the lay usage of responsiveness because a witness before the Commission is entitled to have in advance of his testimony a statement of the subject matter on which the Commission intends to examine him. This advance knowledge of the subject matter of the inquiry provides a background and context that will aid a witness in determining what information the questions seek. Justice Powell emphasized that "The responsiveness limitation is not a trap for the unwary; rather it is a barrier to those who would intentionally tender information not sought in an effort to frustrate and prevent criminal prosecution."

Zicarelli also advanced the contention that the testimony sought by the investigating commission would expose him to prosecution by foreign governments. Because of his international reputation he insisted that he could not be compelled to testify because neither the New Jersey nor the Fifth Amendment privilege can prevent either use of his testimony or prosecution by a foreign jurisdiction. To support this argument, Zicarelli produced numerous newspaper and magazine articles to support his self-incrimination claim. The articles labeled Zicarelli the "foremost internationalist" in organized crime and detailed numerous illegal ventures. Powell reasoned there never was a real danger of being compelled to disclose information that might incriminate Zicarelli under foreign law. Therefore the evidence did not present a constitutional question.

QUESTIONS

1. Compare the factual situations of this case with *Kastigar* v. *United States*. What are the major differences?
2. Does your jurisdiction have an immunity statute similar to the one in this case? What is the construction given to it in regard to use and derivative use of compelled evidence under your state court decisions?
3. What reasons did Justice Powell give for stating that Zicarelli did not furnish information that incriminated himself under foreign law?

Chapter 9

Speedy Trial

Constitution of the United States, Sixth Amendment

In all criminal prosecutions, the accused shall enjoy the right to a speedy . . . trial. . . .

Constitution of California, Article I, Section 13

In criminal prosecutions in any court, whatsoever, the party shall have the right to a speedy and public trial.

Constitution of Alabama of 1901, Section 6

That in all criminal prosecutions the accused has a right to . . . a speedy, public trial. . . .

Constitution of Virginia, Section 8

That in criminal prosecutions a man hath a right to demand . . . a speedy trial. . . .

Klopfer v. North Carolina
386 U.S. 213, 87 S.Ct. 988, 18 L.Ed. 2ᴰ 1 (1967)

SETTING: On February 24, 1964, defendant was indicted by the grand jury of Orange County for the crime of criminal trespass, a misdemeanor punishable by fine and imprisonment in an amount and duration determined by the court in the exercise of its discretion. The indictment charged that he entered a restaurant on January 3, 1964, and, "after being ordered to leave the premises, wilfully and unlawfully refused to do so, knowing or having reason to know that he had no license to remain." Prosecution on the indictment began during the March 1964 Special Criminal Session of the Superior Court of Orange County; but, when the jury failed to reach a verdict, the trial judge declared a mistrial and ordered the case continued for the term.

Several weeks prior to the April 1965 Criminal Session of the Superior Court, the State's solicitor informed defendant of his intention to have a *nolle prosequi* with leave entered in the case. During the session, petitioner, through his attorney, opposed the entry of such an order in open court. In spite of defendant's opposition, the court indicated that it would approve entry of a *nolle prosequi* with leave if requested to do so by the solicitor. But the solicitor declined to make a motion for a *nolle prosequi* with leave. Instead, he filed a motion with the court to continue the case for yet another term, which motion was granted.

The calendar for the August 1965 Criminal Session of the court did not list Klopfer's case for trial. To ascertain the status of his case, Klopfer filed a motion expressing his desire to have the charge pending against him permanently concluded in accordance with the applicable laws of the State of North Carolina and of the United States as soon as was reasonably possible. Noting that some eighteen months had elapsed since the indictment, petitioner, a professor of zoology at Duke University, contended that the pendency of the indictment greatly interfered with his professional activities and with his travel here and abroad. "Wherefore," the motion concluded, "the defendant . . . petitions the Court that the Court in the exercise of its general supervisory jurisdiction inquire into the trial status of the charge pending against the defendant and . . . ascertain the intention of the State in regard to the trial of said charge and as to when the defendant will be brought to trial."

In response to the motion, the trial judge considered the status of petitioner's case in open court on Monday, August 9, 1965, at which time the solicitor moved the court that the State be permitted to take a *nolle prosequi* with leave. Even though no justification for the proposed entry was offered by the State, and, in spite of defendant's objection to the order, the court granted the State's motion.

On appeal to the Supreme Court of North Carolina, the defendant contended that the entry of the *nolle prosequi* with leave order deprived him of his right to a speedy trial as required by the Fourteenth Amendment to the United States Constitution. The state supreme court affirmed the lower-court decision, which rejected Klopfer's claim.

PROCEDURAL PROBLEM: Under North Carolina criminal procedure, when the prosecuting attorney of a county determines that he does not desire to proceed further with a prosecution, he may take a *nolle prosequi,* thereby declaring that he will not at that time prosecute the suit further. Its effect is to permit the defendant to come and go at his will without entering into a recognizance to appear at any other time. But the taking of the *nolle prosequi* does not permanently terminate proceedings on the indictment. On the contrary, when a *nolle prosequi* is entered, the case may be restored to the trial docket when ordered by the judge upon the solicitor's application. And if the solicitor petitions the court to *nolle prosequi* the case "with leave," the consent required to reinstate the prosecution at a future date is implied in the order and the solicitor, without further order, may have the case restored for trial. Because the indictment is not discharged by either a *nolle prosequi* or a *nolle prosequi* with leave, the statute of limitations remains tolled.

In this case, neither the state court below nor the state solicitor offered any reason why the case of the defendant should have been dismissed except for the suggestion of the state supreme court that the solicitor, having tried the defendant once and having obtained only a mistrial, may have concluded that another attempt would not be worth the time and expense.

THE ISSUES: (1) Is a state permitted to indefinitely postpone an indictment without stated justification over the objection of an accused who has been released from custody without violating the guarantee of the right to a speedy trial? (2) Is the Sixth Amendment standard governing the right to a speedy trial made obligatory on the states by the due process clause of the Fourteenth Amendment?

THE ANSWERS: (1) No. (2) Yes.

DISCUSSION: The constitutional guarantee of a right to a speedy trial bars the North Carolina *nolle prosequi* with leave procedure which can be entered over a defendant's objection and without justification and which permits reinstitution of a prosecution without any further order. As the Supreme Court emphasized,

> The [defendant] is not relieved of the limitations placed upon his liberty by this prosecution merely because its suspension permits him to go "whithersoever he will." The pendency of the indictment may subject him to public scorn and deprive him of employment, and almost certainly will force curtailment of his speech, associations and participation in unpopular causes. By indefinitely prolonging this oppression, as well as the "anxiety and concern accompanying public accusation," the criminal prosecution condoned in this case by the Supreme Court of North Carolina clearly denies the [defendant] the right to a speedy trial which we hold is guaranteed to him by the Sixth Amendment of the Constitution of the United States.

The Supreme Court recognized that there have been widely varying differences of opinion as to what provisions of the Sixth Amendment apply to the states through the Fourteenth Amendment. Citing incorporation of the Sixth Amendment provisions, the Supreme Court held that the right to a speedy trial is as fundamental as any of the rights secured by the Sixth Amendment. The Court also noted that each of the fifty states guarantees the right to a speedy trial today. The history of the right to a speedy trial and its reception in this country clearly establish that it is one of the most basic rights preserved by our Constitution.

Mr. Justice Harlan, in a concurring opinion, did not rest his decision on the "speedy trial" provision of the Sixth Amendment, but upon the ground that the North Carolina procedure which permitted state prosecuting officials to put a person under the cloud of an unliquidated criminal charge for an indefinite period violates the fundamental fairness assigned by the due process clause of the Fourteenth Amendment.

The following states by case decision have stated that the right to a speedy trial affords affirmative protection against an unjustified postponement of a trial for an accused discharged from custody:

California	Illinois
Indiana	New York
Kentucky	Maine
Maryland	Wyoming
Michigan	Colorado
Minnesota	Iowa
Idaho	Utah

By rule or legislation in eighteen states, any defendant, whether at large or in custody, whose trial has been unduly delayed is entitled to a dismissal.

Arizona	Louisiana	Oklahoma
California	Maine	Oregon
Florida	Montana	South Dakota
Georgia	Nevada	Utah
Idaho	New Jersey	Washington
Iowa	North Dakota	Virginia

QUESTIONS

1. What are the constitutional, legislative, court rules and court decisions pertaining to the speedy trial guarantee in your jurisdiction?
2. Is the *nolle prosequi* used in your jurisdiction? If it is, compare it to the North Carolina procedure. Does it have the same speedy trial objections as the North Carolina practice?
3. Do you believe that Justice Harlan's concurring opinion, that fairness under the due process clause should be used to test the North Carolina procedure, is workable when determining whether or not a person has been denied a speedy trial? Discuss.

Smith v. *Hooey*
393 U.S. 374, 89 S.Ct. 575, 21 L.Ed. 2ᴰ 607 (1969)

SETTING: In 1960, the defendant was indicted in Harris County, Texas, upon a charge of theft. He was then, and at the time of the court decision, a prisoner in the federal penitentiary at Leavenworth, Kansas. Shortly after the state charge was filed against him, the defendant mailed a letter to the Texas trial court requesting a speedy trial. In reply, he was notified that "he would be afforded a trial within two weeks of any date [he] might specify at which he could be present." Thereafter, for the next six years, the defendant, "by various letters, and more formal so-called 'motions,'" continued periodically to ask that he be brought to trial. Beyond the response already alluded to, the State took no steps to obtain the defendant's appearance in the Harris County trial court. Finally, in 1967, the defendant filed in that court a verified motion to dismiss the charge against him for want of prosecution. No action was taken on the motion.

The defendant then brought a mandamus proceeding in the Supreme Court of Texas, asking for an order to show cause why the pending charge should not be dismissed. Mandamus was refused in an informal and unreported order of the Texas Supreme Court. The defendant then sought certiorari in the United States Supreme Court, which was granted.

PROCEDURAL PROBLEM: In refusing to issue a writ of mandamus, the Supreme Court of Texas relied upon and reaffirmed its decision of a year earlier in *Cooper* v. *State,* 400 S.W. 2ᴰ 890. In that case, as in the present one, a state criminal charge was pending against a man who was an inmate of a federal prison. He filed a petition for a writ of habeas corpus *ad prosequendum* in the Texas trial court, praying that he be brought before the court for trial, or that the charge against him be dismissed. Upon denial of that motion, he applied to the Supreme Court of Texas for a writ of mandamus. In denying the application, the court acknowledged that an inmate of a Texas prison would have been clearly entitled to the relief, but held that "a different rule is applicable when two separate sovereignties are involved." The court viewed the difference as "one of power and authority." While acknowledging that if the state authorities were "ordered to proceed with the prosecution . . . and comply with certain conditions specified by the federal prison authorities, the relator would be produced for trial in the state court," it nonetheless denied relief because it thought "[t]he true test should be the power and authority of the State unaided by any waiver, permission or act of grace of any other authority." Four Justices dissented, expressing their belief that "where the State has the power to afford the accused a speedy trial it is under a duty to do so."

THE ISSUE: Is a federal prisoner who faces criminal charges in a state court, by virtue of his incarceration, precluded from asserting his right to a speedy trial?

THE ANSWER: No.

DISCUSSION: There can be no doubt that if the defendant in the present case had been at large for a six-year period following his indictment, and had repeatedly demanded that he be brought to trial, the State would have been under a constitutional duty to try him. *Klopfer* v. *North Carolina,* 386 U.S. at 213. And Texas conceded that if during that period he had been confined in a Texas prison for some other state offense, its obligation would have been no less. But the Texas Supreme Court held that because defendant was, in fact, confined in a federal prison, the State is totally absolved from any duty at all under the constitutional guarantee. The Supreme Court did not agree.

In view of the realities in the case, the Supreme Court thought that the Texas Supreme Court was mistaken by permitting doctrinaire concepts of power and authority to submerge the practical demands of the constitutional right to a speedy trial. The Sixth Amendment right to a speedy trial cannot be lightly dispensed with. As a rationale for its holding in this case, the following excerpt from *Barber* v. *Page*, 390 U.S. 719 (involving the right of confrontation) was given:

> We start with the fact that the State made absolutely no effort to obtain the presence of Woods at trial other than to ascertain that he was in a federal prison outside Oklahoma. It must be acknowledged that various courts and commentators have heretofore assumed that the mere absence of a witness from the jurisdiction was sufficient ground for dispensing with confrontation on the theory that "it is impossible to compel his attendance, because the process of the trial Court is of no force without the jurisdiction, and the party desiring his testimony is therefore helpless."
>
> Whatever may have been the accuracy of that theory at one time, it is clear that at the present time increased cooperation between the States themselves and between the States and the Federal Government has largely deprived it of any continuing validity in the criminal law. . . .
>
> . . . The Court of Appeals majority appears to have reasoned that because the State would have had to request an exercise of discretion on the part of federal authorities, it was under no obligation to make any such request. Yet as Judge Aldrich, sitting by designation, pointed out in dissent below, "the possibility of a refusal is not the equivalent of asking and receiving a rebuff." In short, a witness is not "unavailable" for purposes of the foregoing exception to the confrontation requirement unless the prosecutorial authorities have made a good-faith effort to obtain his presence at trial. The State made no such effort here, and, so far as this record reveals, the sole reason why Woods was not present to testify in person was because the State did not attempt to seek his presence. The right of confrontation may not be dispensed with so lightly.

Based upon this reasoning, the Court held that the Sixth Amendment right to a speedy trial may not be so lightly disregarded. Upon the defendant's demand, Texas had a constitutional duty to make a diligent, good-faith effort to bring the defendant to trial in Harris County.

QUESTIONS

1. What is meant by the statement that a constitutional right to a speedy trial is self-executing and does not implement legislation?
2. What does it mean when a person waives his right to a speedy trial?
3. In your jurisdiction, does the granting of an excessive number of continuances to the State give a basis for claiming that there is a denial of a speedy trial?

Dickey v. Florida
398 U.S. 30, 90 S.Ct. 1564, 26 L.Ed. 2ᴰ 26 (1970)

SETTING: The victim, Clark, was the only witness to an armed robbery which occurred in June 1960 in Gadsden County, Florida. Shortly
thereafter, the defendant, Dickey, was arrested on federal bank robbery
charges and placed in jail in Jackson County, Florida. He was there
identified by Clark. He was convicted on the federal charges and sent to
Leavenworth and subsequently Alcatraz. No effort was made to serve
defendant with a Florida warrant but a detainer was filed against him
as soon as he left the state.

In 1962, 1963, and 1966, defendant requested trial or withdrawal
of the detainer by the Gadsden County Circuit Court on the ground he
was unavailable for trial. This was denied by the Circuit Court and
ultimately the Florida Supreme Court in 1967. The Supreme Court, however, dismissed his petition without prejudice.

Dickey then filed a motion with the Gadsden Circuit Court to dismiss
the detainer because of denial of his rights to a speedy trial. The state
prosecutor then took steps to obtain Dickey's presence for trial. Before
the trial, the defendant moved for a dismissal because of the prejudicially
long delay during which his alibi witness, his sister, had died. He was
convicted of the Florida charge and sentenced to ten years in the state
prison, the sentence to run consecutively with the federal term he was
serving. Dickey's appeal in the Florida courts failed.

PROCEDURAL PROBLEM: The record in this case established that defendant was available to the state of Florida at all times during the
seven-year period before he was brought to trial. The defendant made
repeated efforts to be brought to trial. The state gave no tenable reason
for deferring the trial in the face of Dickey's diligent efforts. During the
seven-year delay, two witnesses died and other alleged potential witnesses
became unavailable. Police records had been destroyed.

THE ISSUE: Is a defendant who is available for trial for a period of
some seven years deprived of his right to a speedy trial by such an unjustified delay when it can be shown that he was prejudiced thereby?

THE ANSWER: Yes.

DISCUSSION: Here Florida brought the defendant back to the state and tried and convicted him after a lapse of seven years, during which he repeatedly demanded and was denied trial.

The majority opinion observed that the right to a speedy trial is not abstract or theoretical. It is rooted in the hard reality for the need to have charges against a person promptly tried. If the case for the State calls upon the accused to meet charges rather than rest on the weaknesses of the State's case, the time to meet them is when the case is fresh. Old claims have never been favored by the law, especially in criminal cases. Many accused persons seek to put off the trial as long as possible by all kinds of delaying tactics. Nevertheless, the right to a prompt inquiry into the criminal charges is fundamental and the duty of the charging authority is to provide a prompt trial. Justice Burger stated:

> This is brought sharply into focus when, as here, the accused presses for an early confrontation with his accusers and with the state. Crowded dockets, the lack of judges or lawyers, and many other factors make some delays inevitable. Here, however, no valid reason for the delay existed; it was exclusively for the convenience of the State. On this record the delay with its consequent prejudice is intolerable as a matter of fact and impermissible as a matter of law.

In a concurring opinion, Justice Brennan saw a possible retroactivity question: this prosecution began seven years before *Klopfer* v. *North Carolina*, 386 U.S. 213, was decided. Assuming that *Klopfer* was not retroactive, he viewed the question as whether the defendant's trial was unconstitutionally delayed under due process standards applicable to the states prior to *Klopfer*. Discussing the due process clause as it pertains to a speedy trial, Brennan noted:

> Deliberate governmental delay designed to harm the accused, however, constitutes abuse of due process. It lessens the deterrent value of any conviction obtained. And it very probably reduces the capacity of the accused to defend himself; unlike the prosecution, he may remain unaware that charges are pending and thus fail to take steps necessary to his defense. Accordingly, some of the interests protected by the Speedy Trial Clause can be threatened by delay prior to arrest or indictment. Thus it may be that for the purposes of the Clause to be fully realized, it must apply to any delay in the criminal process which occurs after the government decides to prosecute and has sufficient evidence for arrest or indictment.

This, however, does not necessarily mean that the government should be denied broad discretion to determine that its evidence is insufficient to make worthwhile an arrest or indictment, nor that it may not have legitimate reasons for delay other than insufficient evidence; moderate delay necessary for law enforcement operations, such as the completion of undercover work involving a number of suspects, may be compatible with the speedy trial clause.

The question of whether, after an accused has been arrested or indicted, he may challenge prior governmental delay, is distinct from the question of whether before arrest or indictment he may bring an action to compel the government to begin formal proceedings against him.

QUESTIONS

1. What reasons can you think of that caused a seven-year delay in beginning the prosecution of this case? Did the State want to try the case at a later time possibly because of heavy dockets where the defendant was not in custody or was in custody at state expense awaiting trial?

2. Should it make any difference that the delay objected to was between the arrest and indictment? Did the lack of objection amount to a waiver of a speedy trial? See *U.S. v. Colitto*, 319 F. Supp. 1077 (E.D.N.Y., 1970).

3. Does not the holding in this case encourage a defendant awaiting a second trial, whether currently in custody or not, to request the trial on the second charges without delay? Can his delay in requesting an immediate trial be interpreted to be a waiver of his right to a speedy trial?

United States v. *Marion*
404 U.S. 307, 92 S.Ct. 455, 30 L.Ed. 2ᴰ 468 (1971)

SETTING: On April 21, 1970, the defendants were federally indicted on nineteen counts of fraud in selling and installing home improvements, alterations of contracts, and deliberate nonperformance of contracts. The period covered by the indictment was March 15, 1965 to February 6, 1967; the earliest specific alleged act occurred on September 3, 1956; the latest on January 19, 1966.

PROCEDURAL PROBLEM: On May 5, 1970, the defendants filed a motion to dismiss the indictment because of the failure to commence prosecution of the alleged offenses in such time as to afford the defendants their rights under due process of law and to a speedy trial under the Fifth and Sixth Amendments. Marion was one of the employees of Allied Enterprises, Inc. which was the company through which the alleged fraudulent schemes had occurred.

On February 6, 1967, Allied Enterprises was the subject of a Federal Trade Commission cease and desist order. In October 1967, the fraudulent practices were reported in the *Washington Post* newspaper. The article also noted that the United States Attorney for the District of Columbia was investigating and indictments were forthcoming shortly. The statements attributed to the United States Attorney did not specifically mention the company but Allied was mentioned in the newspaper story. In the summer of 1968, Allied delivered some papers to the United States Attorney and conducted an interview with Marion as a company officer. The grand jury that indicted the defendants was not empaneled until September 1969. The defendants were not informed of the grand jury's concern until March 1970, when the indictments were returned.

Marion, in moving to dismiss the indictment as being returned an unreasonably and oppressively length of time after the alleged offenses, argued:

1. That the indictment required memory of many specific acts and conversations occurring several years before, and
2. That the delay was because of the indifference or negligence of the United States Attorney in investigating and presenting the case to the grand jury.

No specific prejudice was claimed or demonstrated, however.

The federal district court dismissed the indictment for lack of speedy prosecution, noting that the interval between 1967 and 1970, must have caused serious damage to the defense's case. According to the district court, the prosecution should have been brought in 1967 or early in 1968.

The United States Supreme Court on direct appeal by the government reversed the district court judgment.

THE ISSUE: Unless prejudice is shown, is a defendant denied the constitutional right to a speedy trial in a situation in which the indictment for the offense is found three years after the occurrence of the alleged criminal acts?

THE ANSWER: No.

DISCUSSION: The defendants did not claim that they were denied their Sixth Amendment rights to a speedy trial by the two-month delay between the return of the indictment and its dismissal. Marion claimed that the three-year delay, however, was so substantial and inherently prejudicial that the Sixth Amendment required dismissal of the indictment. The Supreme Court stated that the speedy trial provision has no application until the putative defendant in some way becomes an accused, an event that occurred on April 21, 1970, when the indictment was returned.

The speedy trial provision is effective only when a criminal prosecution has begun and extends only to those persons accused in the course of the prosecution. These provisions, as noted by the majority, "seem to afford no protection to those not yet accused, nor would they seem to require the Government to discover, investigate, and accuse any person within any particular period of time. The Amendment would appear to guarantee to a criminal defendant that the Government will move with dispatch which is appropriate to assure him an early and proper disposition of the charges against him. '[T]he essential ingredient is orderly expedition and not mere speed.'"

What are the major evils that the speedy trial provision protects against, apart from actual or possible prejudice? To legally arrest, the necessity of probable cause that a crime was committed must be established. The arrest is an act which seriously interferes with a defendant's liberty, whether on bail or not, and which may disrupt his employment, drain his financial resources, curtail associations, subject him to public disrepute, and create anxiety in him, his friends, and his family. So viewed, it is understandable that it is either a formal charge or else the actual restraints imposed by arrest and holding to answer a criminal charge that engage the particular protections of the Sixth Amendment's speedy trial provision. As the majority once again stated,

> *Invocation of the speedy trial provision thus need not await indictment, information, or other formal charge. But we decline to extend the reach of the amendment to the period prior to arrest. Until this event occurs, a citizen suffers no restraints on his liberty and is not the subject of public accusation: his situation does not compare with that of a defendant who has been arrested and held to answer. Passage of time, whether before or after arrest, may impair memories, cause evidence to be lost, deprive the defendant of witnesses, and otherwise interfere with his ability to defend himself. But this possibility of prejudice at trial is not itself sufficient reason to wrench the Sixth Amendment from its proper context. Possible prejudice is inherent in any delay, however short; it may also weaken the Government's case.*

The majority also noted that the government's concession that the Fifth Amendment due process clause would require a dismissal of an indictment if it were shown that a deliberately planned pre-indictment delay caused substantial prejudice and was so intended. But the question whether such violation occurred must be decided on a case-by-case basis. In this case there was no showing of prejudice or intentional delay to gain an advantage, despite the thirty-eight month delay between the end of the alleged fraudulent scheme and the indictment.

QUESTIONS

1. Distinguish this case from *Dickey* v. *Florida*.
2. What reasons did the Court give for stating that the speedy trial provision of the Sixth Amendment takes affect after the arrest or after formal charges are filed?
3. Is the case-by-case approach to determine if there has been a due process violation under the Fifth Amendment workable? Discuss.

Barker v. *Wingo*
407 U.S. 514, 92 S.Ct. 2182, 33 L.Ed. 2ᴰ 101 (1972)

SETTING: Barker and Manning were apprehended shortly after the slaying of two persons in Christian County, Kentucky, on July 20, 1958. They were indicted on September 15 and counsel was appointed on September 17. Barker's trial was scheduled for October 21, 1958. Kentucky had a stronger case against Manning and believed that Barker could not be convicted without Manning's testimony. Manning did not wish to incriminate himself. On October 23, Manning was brought to trial and the State sought and obtained the first of sixteen continuances. Barker made no objection. The State wished to convict Manning and thereby remove possible self-incrimination objections thereby assuring his testimony against Barker. The State of Kentucky had some difficulty convicting Manning, needing six separate trials to finally convict him of murdering the two victims. The final conviction was secured in December 1962.

PROCEDURAL PROBLEM: In February 1963, the first term of the Christian County Circuit Court after Manning's conviction, March 19 was set for Barker's trial date. On the day scheduled for the trial, the State again moved for a continuance until the June term. The reason was that the chief witness was ill. Barker's objection to the continuance was unsuccessful. The witness was still ill on June 19, the trial date, and the trial was continued until the September 1963 term over the defendant's objection. The court, when it granted the continuance, announced that if Barker were not tried during the September term, the prosecution would be dismissed. The trial was set for October 9, 1963, at which time Barker moved to dismiss the indictment because his right to a speedy trial had been violated. After denial of this claim, the trial began; Manning testified, and Barker was convicted of murder and sentenced to life imprisonment.

THE ISSUE: Was the defendant denied the right to a speedy trial?

THE ANSWER: No.

DISCUSSION: The importance of this case is not that the United States Supreme Court permitted the conviction of Barker to stand but rather that inflexible rules setting forth what is or is not a speedy trial will not do. For the first time, the Court squarely faced the question of just when a defendant has been denied his right to a speedy trial.

In addition to the protection of the accused, there are some societal rights which must be considered which are sometimes in opposition to the rights of the accused. The inability of the current court system to handle the large backlog of cases in urban areas permits a defendant to plead to reduced charges and otherwise negotiate pleas. Persons released on bond have the opportunity to commit other crimes. The longer a defendant is released, the more tempting becomes his opportunity to jump bail, commit other crimes, and/or escape. Long periods of incarceration are expensive from a monetary standpoint. It is also well established that lengthy exposure to overcrowded and delapidated jails has a destructive effect on human character and makes the rehabilitation of the individual offender much more difficult.

The deprivation of the right to a speedy trial may work to the advantage of a defendant, which is a much different situation. Delay is a common defense tactic. Unlike the right to counsel or privilege against self-incrimination, deprivation of the right to a speedy trial does not *per se* prejudice the ability of the defendant to defend himself.

Perhaps most important, the right to a speedy trial is more vague than are other procedural rights. For example, it is impossible to determine with any degree of precision exactly when the right is denied. One cannot definitely say how long is too long in a system in which justice is supposed to be swift but deliberate. As a consequence, the Court noted, there is no fixed point in the criminal process when the State can put to the defendant the choice of either exercising or waiving the right to a speedy trial.

The Court discussed two rigid approaches which are often used to eliminate some of the uncertainty courts experience in protecting the right to a speedy trial. The first argument, which was rejected by the Court, was to interpret the Constitution as meaning that a defendant is required to be offered a trial within a specified time limit. Although various jurisdictions have done this, the Supreme Court rejected the idea as a constitutional standard because it would require the Court to engage in legislative or rule-making activity rather than in the adjudicative process. The Court establishes rules only when mandated by the Constitution, and the Court stated that although states are free to prescribe reasonable time periods, there is no constitutional basis for the United States Supreme Court to hold that the speedy trial right can be guaranteed and quantified into a specific number of days, weeks, or months.

The Court also rejected the so-called "demand rule" by which a defendant waives any consideration of his right to a speedy trial for any period prior to which he has not demanded a trial. The objection to the rule is that it presumes a waiver of fundamental right by inaction and is totally inconsistent with the Court's pronouncement on waiver of constitutional rights.

The Court adopted a balancing test in which the conduct of both the defendant and prosecution is weighed. Four factors are to be isolated and considered to determine whether the speedy trial provision should be invoked:

1. *Length of delay.* Until there is some delay that is presumptively prejudicial, there is no need to inquire into the other factors. And the length of delay is of necessity dependent on other circumstances in the case. For example, the length of delay which can be tolerated for a simple street crime is considerably less than for a serious complex conspiracy charge.

2. *Reasons for the delay.* Different weights must be assigned to the different reasons why the government delayed prosecution. Deliberate delay weighs heavily against the prosecution. Negligence by the State will weigh less heavily but will be considered because the responsibility for prosecution rests with the State, not the defendant. For example, a valid reason for a delay might be a missing witness.

3. *Defendant's effort to assert right.* The strength of the defendant's efforts will be affected by the length of the delay, the reasons for the delay, and most particularly, by the personal prejudice he experiences. The more serious the deprivation, the more likely the defendant is to complain. The defendant's assertion of his speedy trial right is entitled

to strong weight in determining whether or not he has been deprived of the right. The Court noted that the defendant's demand for a prompt trial will always weigh heavily in his favor, while a failure to assert the right will make it difficult for him to prove that he was denied it.

4. *Prejudice to the defendant.* The defendant's prejudice will be considered in light of his pretrial incarceration; if any, the anxiety or concern that he suffers; and most seriously the impairment of his defense occasioned by the delay. The last is the most serious because the inability of the defendant to prepare his defense because a witness has died or disappeared during the delay skews the fairness of the trial. Prejudice can also occur where a defense witness is unable to recall events long in the past.

Applying the balancing test to the Barker situation, the Court concluded that a post-indictment delay of more than four years, although unjustified, did not prejudice a defendant who did not demand a speedy trial until approximately three years after he was indicted, and who probably did not want to be tried until final disposition of his separately tried co-defendant's case.

Statutory Guarantee of a Speedy Trial. The state of California has implemented the state constitutional guarantee to a speedy trial by legislative enactment, as noted by the majority in *Barker:*

California Penal Code, Section 1382

When prosecution may be dismissed. The court, unless good cause to the contrary is shown, must order the action to be dismissed in the following cases:

1. When a person has been held to answer for a public offense and an information is not filed against him within fifteen days thereafter.

2. When a defendant is not brought to trial in a superior court within sixty days after the finding of the indictment or filing of the information or, in case the cause is to be tried again following a mistrial, an order granting a new trial from which an appeal is not taken, or an appeal from the superior court, within sixty days after such mistrial has been declared, after entry of the order granting the new trial, or after the filing of the remittitur in the trial court; except that an action shall not be dismissed under this subdivision if it is set for trial on a date beyond the sixty-day period at the request of the defendant or with his consent, express or implied, or because of his neglect or failure to appear and

if the defendant is brought to trial on the date so set for trial or within ten days thereafter.

3. Regardless of when the complaint is filed, when a defendant in a misdemeanor case in an inferior court is not brought to trial within thirty days after he is arraigned if he is in custody at the time of arraignment, or in all other cases, within forty-five days after his arraignment, or in case the cause is to be tried again following a mistrial, an order granting a new trial from which an appeal is not taken, or an appeal from the inferior court, within thirty days after such mistrial has been declared, after entry of the order granting the new trial, or after the remittitur is filed in the trial court or, if the new trial is to be held in the superior court, within thirty days after the judgment on appeal becomes final; except that an action shall not be dismissed under this subdivision (1) if it is set for trial or within ten days thereafter or (2) if it is not tried on the date set for trial because of the defendant's neglect or failure to appear, in which case he shall be deemed to have been arraigned within the meaning of this subdivision on the date of his subsequent arraignment on a bench warrant or his submission to the court.

If the defendant is not represented by counsel, he shall not be deemed under this section to have consented to the date for his trial unless the court has explained to him his rights under this section and the effect of his consent. Amended, Stats. 1967, Chap. 263.

QUESTIONS

1. Discuss the balancing test adopted by *Barker* v. *Wingo*.
2. Does your jurisdiction have a statutory enactment similar to the California provision above? Compare them.
3. What is meant when the Supreme Court stated that the right to a speedy trial is "so slippery"?
4. What is the "demand rule" as used in *Barker* v. *Wingo?*
5. The Court stated that "delay is a common defense tactic." Explain this statement. Give some examples.

Strunk v. *United States*
412 U.S. 434, 93 S.Ct. 2260, 37 L.Ed. 2ᴰ 56 (1973)

SETTING: Strunk was convicted of interstate transportation of a stolen automobile and sentenced to five years in prison. This sentence was to run concurrently with a one- to three-year sentence he was serving pursuant to a state court conviction.

PROCEDURAL PROBLEM: Prior to the trial the federal district court denied a motion to dismiss the federal charge because the defendant had been denied the right to a speedy trial. The Court of Appeals reversed the holding and held that he had been denied a speedy trial but that the "extreme" remedy of outright dismissal of the charges was unwarranted. The case was remanded to the district court with instructions to reduce Strunk's sentence 259 days in order to compensate for the unnecessary delay that had occurred between the return of the indictment and Strunk's arraignment.

The defendant, in his petition for a writ of certiorari to the United States Supreme Court, claimed that once a judicial determination has been made that an accused has been denied a speedy trial, the only remedy available to the court is to reverse the conviction, vacate the sentence, and dismiss the indictment. The government did not file a cross-petition challenging the finding that there was a denial of a speedy trial. The Court of Appeals rejected the lack of staff personnel in the United States Attorney's Office as a justification for the delay. The Court also found that Strunk had given notice that he intended to preserve his right to a speedy trial.

THE ISSUE: Is the remedy of outright dismissal the only possible remedy for denial of the right to a speedy trial?

THE ANSWER: Yes.

DISCUSSION: Writing for the Court, Chief Justice Burger stated, "In light of the policies which underlie the right to a speedy trial, dismissal must remain, as *Barker* noted, the only possible remedy." Reduction of the sentence by the length of delay is not an adequate remedy.

The Chief Justice noted that the denial of the right to a speedy trial is unlike some of the other guarantees of the Sixth Amendment. He stated that the "failure to afford a public trial, an impartial jury, notice of charges, or compulsory service can ordinarily be cured by providing those guaranteed rights in a new trial. The speedy trial guarantee recognizes that a prolonged delay may subject the accused to an emotional stress that can be presumed to result in the ordinary person from uncertainties in the prospect of facing public trial or of receiving a sentence longer than, or consecutive to, the one he is presently serving—uncertainties that a prompt trial removes. We recognize, as the Court did in *Smith* v. *Hooey,* that the stress from a delayed trial may be less on a prisoner already confined, whose family ties and employment have been interrupted, but other factors such as the prospect of rehabilitation may also be affected adversely. The remedy chosen by the Court of Appeals does not deal with these difficulties."

QUESTIONS

1. Compare this decision with *Barker* v. *Wingo, supra.* What are the significant differences?
2. Write a dissenting opinion to this case, emphasizing that a flexible standard is necessary to determine whether or not outright dismissal is the proper remedy.
3. What interests can you give for a defendant demanding a speedy trial even though he is already in prison?

Chapter 10

Negotiated Plea

PLEA BARGAINING *

Conviction by a plea of guilty in contrast to conviction by trial occurs very frequently in the criminal justice system. For example, in California in 1969, of the 28 percent of the felony arrests that resulted in conviction, approximately 21 percent were on pleas of guilty and 7 percent by trial.[1] Persons accused of criminal conduct many times nego-

	Drug Arrests			Non-Drug Arrests		
	1967	1968	1969	1967	1968	1969
Yearly Total	29,039	41,957	62,849	97,947	107,538	117,728
Total cases disposed of in Superior Court	10,250	13,636	23,819	32,126	34,568	38,143
Total cases convicted in Superior Court	7,492	10,237	18,666	27,229	30,218	31,904
Total cases convicted by Plea ..	4,384	6,419	13,639	27,177	21,615	23,899
Total cases convicted by Trial .	3,108	3,818	5,027	7,052	8,603	8,005

---

* The material in this section is taken from George T. Felkenes, "A Sociological Study of the Prosecutor's Office" (Doctor of Criminology diss., University of California, Berkeley, 1970), pp. 75–88. Footnotes have been renumbered.

[1] California: Department of Justice, Bureau of Criminal Statistics, *Crime and Delinquency in California* (Sacramento: State Printer, 1969), pp. 17–22.

tiate a guilty plea with the prosecutor for reasons beneficial to both parties. The most common form of plea bargaining—pleading guilty to a reduced charge—first eliminates the need for an expensive, time-consuming trial; and, second, complex issues such as admissibility of evidence are largely avoided. Moreover, a guilty plea assures conviction, whereas a trial by jury may raise some doubts in the minds of the triers of fact.[2]

A defendant's incentives to participate in plea bargaining are generally (1) reduction in the charge, (2) promise of a lenient sentence, (3) dismissal of other charges, or (4) avoidance of any stigmatic label attached to conviction of certain crimes (e.g., sexual psychopath).[3]

Extensive materials have been compiled on the subject of plea bargaining, the most comprehensive report probably being done by Donald Newman for the American Bar Association. His published results in book form, entitled *Conviction: The Determination of Guilt or Innocence Without Trial*, comprehensively examine the plea negotiation process in the three states of Kansas, Michigan, and Wisconsin. It was his field study that prompted a series of questions concerning the negotiated guilty plea in this study.

From a practical viewpoint, the advantages of plea bargaining for the prosecutor are undeniable. This fact was recognized by 80 percent of the district attorneys who acknowledged that plea bargaining is justified.[4] Responses justifying the procedure included:

> *Yes, plea bargaining is justified. The machinery of the Administration of Justice would not work without plea bargaining. Plea bargaining is an integral part of the system. Presently, our system of justice does not have enough facilities, personnel, or money to function without plea bargaining.*
>
> *Plea bargaining is absolutely necessary from an administrative standpoint, for without it, the system could not survive. If all cases were brought to trial, the system would grind to a halt in one day. The aim of plea bargaining is to obtain substantial justice in the shortest possible time. All that are connected with the transaction are involved, but there are levels of involvement. Two aspects of plea bargaining; one is of the charges made, the second is of the sentence given. (The judge does not*

---

[2] Donald J. Newman, *Conviction: The Determination of Guilt or Innocence Without Trial* (Boston: Little Brown and Company, 1966), pp. 95–97.

[3] *Ibid.*, p. 97.

[4] Some of the district attorneys distinguished between plea bargaining for felonies and for misdemeanors, stating that the former occurs many times on the arraignment date and the latter on the date of trial. It is assumed that the majority of the attorneys who did not make this disinction were speaking of felonies and misdemeanors collectively.

take part, but he does expect a synopsis leaving the actual negotiation to the trial lawyers.) Any crime can be negotiated. The more serious the crime is, the harder it is to negotiate. Bargaining generally occurs at the earliest stages of the proceedings, and it least often occurs on the day of the trial because by then, a great amount of effort has already been expended. It is essentially conducted outside of the courtroom and it is the reasonableness of the participants that determines the success or failure.

Plea bargaining is justified, and it is found, in most cases, dependent on the strength of the case. Primarily, the defense attorney and the prosecutor handle the plea bargaining with the police being referred to for the little known facts. There is very little negotiation involved in sex crimes and in drug cases it often depends on the amount of narcotics involved. It is attempted to have negotiations completed as early as possible in order to minimize the cost and effort that goes into the trial. This bargaining is generally conducted between the attorneys with the judge approving the recommended actions of the lawyers. The success or failure of bargaining is determined by the crime itself.

It is often stated that plea bargaining is the most expeditious way of gaining convictions in a judicial process overburdened with cases and limited in resources according to most of the district attorneys. Only two of the forty-four attorneys justifying plea bargaining did so because it could provide the defendant with a "break," thus taking into consideration any mitigating facts surrounding the crime which the prosecution saw including whether or not the defendant was a "hard core" or a marginal offender.

The four prosecutors opposed to the negotiated guilty plea expressed in rather strong language that they would have no part of it. They admitted that their consciences predominate over the pragmatic arguments that they would not use it to clear court calendars, and that they only accept a plea when the defendant says he is actually guilty of that charge to which he is pleading. One district attorney put it this way:

If someone has committed a crime, he should receive the proper punishment for that crime. I don't think that a defendant should receive a lighter sentence or plead guilty to a lesser crime merely because the courts are congested.

Another opponent denounced it on different grounds:

It places the administration of justice in the same category as a couple of used-car salesmen buying and selling from one another. It is demeaning in that the accused never receives a fair negotiation. We are always in the power position. After all, who wants to spend his savings to go on trial and then lose and be put away?

Several of the individuals denounced and justified it at the same time:

> *I am opposed to any kind of plea bargaining but it is an absolutely necessary evil because of the overcrowded criminal calendars. I justify it to myself on this ground alone. No one would even receive a semblance of justice without it.*

TABLE 1
PLEA BARGAINING JUSTIFIED?

	Number	Percent
Yes	44	80.0
No	4	7.3
No Response	7	12.7
Total	55	100.0

The prevalence of plea bargaining was verified by nearly two-thirds of the district attorneys, who revealed that it occurred very frequently, or, as some said, "in almost every case." An additional 18.2 percent stated that its use was quite common. Only one prosecutor said that plea bargaining was very rare, and in the light of the contrary responses received especially from other district attorneys in his office, it is doubtful that his perception was accurate.[5]

TABLE 2
PREVALENCE OF PLEA BARGAINING

	Number	Percent
Very prevalent, almost every case	34	61.8
Quite common	10	18.2
Very rare	1	1.8
No response	10	18.2
Total	55	100.0

---

[5] Plea negotiation takes numerous forms and is hopefully used by both the prosecution and the defense for their advantage. The negotiation may be for the purpose of reducing the number of charges brought against the defendant or lessening the severity of a particular charge. Promises regarding the kinds of sentences are also common, especially when it must be remembered that in all probability the defense attorney has a fairly strong opinion as to the guilt of his client but is seeking the best "deal" in the form of sentencing. See Newman, *Conviction,* pp. 78–90.

Every respondent acknowledged that the normal participants in the plea-bargaining process are the district attorney and the defense attorney. However, there was less agreement concerning the other parties involved. Almost two-thirds (65.5 percent) included the judge, in that he usually intervenes only to approve or disapprove the agreement reached by the attorneys. Also included by 18.2 percent of the district attorneys were the police, who, while not actually physically present during many bargaining sessions, were occasionally contacted—not so much for their opinion on whether the crime should be reduced, but simply for background facts which would help the attorney make the actual plea decision.

Typical remarks included:

> *Negotiation takes place in approximately 75 to 90% of all cases with the opposing attorneys handling most of the actual negotiation. The police may be called upon to give the matter of the crime, and the judge enters into it only to approve or disapprove the final plea.*

> *The police, D.A., Defense Counsel, Probation Officer, the Judge, the Bailiff, and the clerk can all have some influence of plea bargaining. The judge who gets involved in the actual negotiations is beyond the scope of his function. He should approve or disapprove and let us seek the best negotiation with the defense attorney. It is not the judge's responsibility to insure that the best deal is achieved by anyone. They play Santa Claus to the defendant all of the time. Judge will promise more leniency for a guilty plea for disposition of the case than based on merit alone.*

TABLE 3
OFFICIALS INVOLVED IN PLEA BARGAINING

	Number	Percent
District attorney, defense attorney, and judge to some extent	26	47.3
District attorney, defense attorney, judge, and police	10	18.2
District attorney and defense attorney	4	7.3
Defendant and others	2	3.6
Everyone	3	5.4
All other	2	3.6
No response	8	14.5
Total	55	99.9

The types of crimes most often subject to plea bargaining generally consist of crimes that are most easily reduced or should be reduced under certain circumstances. Most easily reduced are crimes against property and minor violent offenses such as simple assault. These crimes, together with crimes that reflect the correctional needs of the defendant, specifically first offender crimes, were mentioned by 32.7 percent of the district attorneys. Slightly less, 27.3 percent, thought that narcotic, marijuana, and drug offenses were reduced most often.[6] Far from identifying specific crimes, one out of five prosecutors believes that all crimes are equally subjected to plea bargaining.

TABLE 4
CRIMES MOST OFTEN SUBJECTED TO PLEA BARGAINING

	Number	Percent
First offender crimes, minor felonies, nonviolent crimes, alternative felony-misdemeanors	18	32.7
Narcotics offenses, marijuana, dangerous drugs	15	27.3
All crimes, none more than any other	11	20.0
Homicide	5	9.1
All other	3	5.4
No responses	3	5.4
Total	55	99.9

When asked the converse question of the least subjected crimes, the district attorneys overwhelmingly (63.6 percent) selected crimes of violence, serious crimes, and capital offenses. Additionally, two individuals indicated that they were hesitant to engage in plea negotiation when the crimes involved a high degree of publicity. This may reflect a common attitude, but one which most attorneys are reluctant to admit.

If plea bargaining is to take place, it is beneficial to both parties in terms of costs and effort for the bargaining to occur at the earliest practical time in the proceedings. Practicality for the prosecution would entail sufficient time to assume that a good case can be developed and

---

[6] In regard to narcotics offenses, it appears that the legislatures in particular are upset over the prevalence of charge or sentence reduction by their attempts to set mandatory sentences and specific crime classifications to such a common narcotics offense as possession of marijuana. Newman, *Conviction*, pp. 99, 177–78; California: Health and Safety Code (1970), Sec. 11715.6. See also the case of *People* v. *Temorio*, 89 Cal. Rptr. 249, 473 P2d 993 (1970), in which the California Supreme Court declared unconstitutional section 11718 of the *Health and Safety Code*. This section provided that only the District Attorney had the power to dismiss specific narcotics charges under certain conditions. The California Supreme Court held that the act of the District Attorney was an infringement of judicial power and was therefore unconstitutional. In short, the statute breached the separation of powers doctrine.

TABLE 5
CRIMES LEAST OFTEN SUBJECTED TO PLEA BARGAINING

	Number	Percent
Crimes of violence, serious crimes, capital crimes	35	63.6
None in particular	4	7.4
Trivial crimes	2	3.6
Crimes with a high degree of publicity	2	3.6
All other	5	9.1
No response	7	12.7
Total	55	100.0

for the defense, enough time to study the case to assume that the bargaining is the best arrangement for the client. For this reason, it is apparent that plea bargaining occurs most often before the trial begins. The district attorneys' responses were not specific enough to establish at what particular stage of the proceedings it usually occurs. Almost half (49.1 percent) simply stated that it occurs prior to trial or at the earliest stage of proceedings. In contrast, nearly one-third placed it on the day of the trial or just before the trial,[7] with one district attorney stating that the most common time for plea bargaining was when the "counselors were approaching the counsel table prior to jury selection." Several prosecutors noted that

> Plea bargaining most often occurs in misdemeanor cases at the day set for trial and in felony cases, the time of arraignment to Superior Court. Bargaining occurs least often for misdemeanors at the time of arraignment, for felonies, at the preliminary hearing. It is very seldom conducted outside the courtroom. When it is outside the courtroom it is in an office or a hallway. There were many factors cited for the failure of success of a bargaining session. Some were the calendar, strength of the case, seriousness of the crime, the reliability of witnesses, relationship between the defendant and the victim and the attitude of the officers involved.

More specific responses were received when a question was asked regarding the stages where plea bargaining least occurs. Ten of the attorneys gave the expected response that plea bargaining occurred least

---

[7] It would appear that the practice of plea bargaining taking place on the day of the trial or just before it begins is largely a jurisdictional policy within specific counties. In an interview with the training officer in each county, the comment was made that Lasso, Opportunity, and Virtue Counties negotiate up to the time of trial, whereas most of the other county district attorney offices negotiate up to the time the formal charges are made or prior to the time specifically set for trial.

TABLE 6

**STAGES OF THE COURT PROCEEDING WHERE
PLEA BARGAINING MOST OFTEN OCCURS**

	Number	Percent
Prior to trial, earliest stage of proceedings	27	49.1
Day of trial	18	32.7
Any time	1	1.8
No response	9	16.4
Total	55	100.0

often after the start of the trial, owing to the fact that a major reason for plea bargaining is to prevent an expensive and lengthy trial when both the prosecutor and defense attorneys feel that a trial might not be in the best interests of the defendant. Other specific responses reflect the different procedures utilized in the three counties studied. Because of the fact that one county attempts to screen its cases before the preliminary hearing and thus allows only the most substantial and solid ones to advance to the arraignment stage, these district attorneys mentioned that plea bargaining occurred least before arraignment (by inference it occurs most before the preliminary hearing). The other counties do just the reverse; that is, they screen their cases after the preliminary hearing, thus these attorneys (30.9 percent) said it occurs least often before the preliminary hearing.

Plea bargaining takes place in various settings. In many cases it occurs in the courtroom in formal conversations between the prosecutors and the defense attorneys. Other times it occurs elsewhere. When the

TABLE 7

**STAGES OF THE COURT PROCEEDINGS WHERE
PLEA BARGAINING LEAST OFTEN OCCURS**

	Number	Percent
Before preliminary hearing	17	30.9
After trial begins	10	18.2
Any time	4	7.3
At time of filing	3	5.4
Before arraignment	3	5.4
All other	4	7.3
No response	14	25.4
Total	55	99.9

attorneys were queried as to how often plea bargaining occurs outside the courtroom, the responses were far from unanimous. Slightly less than one-quarter (23.6 percent) thought that it almost always takes place in the courtroom, mentioning that it usually transpires either before the trial convenes, during the lull periods, or recesses. On the other hand, slightly less (21.8 percent) said that extra-courtroom bargaining happens always or frequently. Part of this disparity may be due to the failure to define the phrase "outside the courtroom," for there was some confusion exhibited over its meaning. Another possibility is that some district attorney offices and/or individual district attorneys may by willful choice or habit prefer to conduct the bargaining at different locations. Furthermore, since it is usually the defense attorney who initiates the question of bargaining, he may be the one who determines where the session takes place. This possibility was mentioned by several attorneys:

> *The policy in our office is to permit the accused to initiate the negotiations. He might see me in the men's room, movie, home, court or any place. It is difficult to state with any precision where the negotiating sessions take place. I wish they were during office hours, however.*

TABLE 8
PLEA BARGAINING CONDUCTED OUTSIDE OF THE COURTROOM

	Number	Percent
Always	3	5.4
Frequently (50 percent or more of the cases)	9	16.4
Occasionally (20 percent of the cases)	7	12.7
Rarely (less than 20 percent of the cases)	13	23.6
Other	3	5.4
No response	20	36.4
Total	55	99.9

When plea bargaining is conducted outside the courtroom setting, the most frequently mentioned alternative was the district attorney's office. The next most frequent places, each representing 9.1 percent of the responses, were the judge's chambers, the hallway outside the courtroom, and telephonic communications between the attorneys' offices.

The final question asked concerning plea bargaining was: "What factors determine the success or failure of a bargaining session?" Unfortunately, over half of the district attorneys gave rather vague responses such as the "strengths and weaknesses of the case" and "how much each

TABLE 9

USUAL SETTING FOR EXTRA-COURTROOM PLEA BARGAINING

	Number	Percent
District attorney's office	16	29.1
Hallway outside courtroom	5	9.1
Judge's chambers	5	9.1
Telephone (public, office, and private)	5	9.1
Any private place (restaurants, bar meetings, social gatherings, etc.)	4	7.3
No response, unknown	20	36.4
Total	55	100.1

attorney wishes to give up." The nature of the offense controlled the success or failure of the sessions, according to 14.5 percent of the respondents, while another 10.9 percent thought the determining factor was the previous record of the defendant. Interestingly, two prosecutors gave as partial responses the perceived attitudes of the judge and the attorney's own supervisor.

> *There is one judge in our county who is highly suspicious of plea bargaining. As a consequence, I am reluctant to talk to defense attorneys in a negotiation session unless the judge is present. Ours is a relatively small county and I know what to expect before this judge if he is unaware of the particulars of how a plea of guilty to a reduced charge was arrived at. I just do not care to be embarrassed in court. In effect the judge to an extent determines the success of my negotiation attempts.*

A relatively new prosecutor stated:

> *My supervisor partially determines the failure or success of a bargaining session. He has peculiarities, especially in drug cases. He just will not permit me to negotiate a plea to a lesser offense if the accused is from his city. The setting plus my knowledge of Mr. X are two factors in a number of my cases.*

Brady v. United States
397 U.S. 742, 90 S.Ct. 1463, 25 L.Ed. 2ᴰ 747 (1970)

SETTING: In 1959, Brady was charged with kidnapping under the federal kidnapping statute (Lindbergh Law). The defendant faced the death penalty if the jury verdict so recommended because the indictment

TABLE 10
FACTORS DETERMINING THE SUCCESS OR FAILURE OF A
PLEA BARGAINING SESSION

	Number	Percent
Strength and weaknesses of the case, how much each attorney wishes to give up, the preponderance of evidence against the defendant	30	54.5
Nature of offense	8	14.5
Previous record of defendant	6	10.9
All other	6	10.9
No response	5	9.1
Total	55	99.9

charged that the kidnapping victim was not released unharmed. Represented by counsel, the defendant at first elected to plead not guilty. Apparently the trial judge was not willing to try the case without a jury; the defendant made no serious attempt to reduce the possibility of a death penalty by waiving a jury trial. The defendant then learned that a co-defendant who had confessed to the authorities would plead guilty and then become a witness against him. Brady then changed his plea to guilty, and this plea was accepted after the trial judge questioned him twice on the voluntariness of the plea. Brady was subsequently sentenced to fifty years in prison (later reduced to thirty).

PROCEDURAL PROBLEM: In 1967, Brady sought relief in the New Mexico District Court, claiming that his plea of guilty was not voluntary because the Lindbergh Law, 18 U.S.C., section 1201(a) operated to coerce his plea, because of impermissible pressure by his attorney upon him, and because his plea was induced by various representations with respect to reduction of sentence and clemency. The district court found that Brady's counsel did not use impermissible pressure upon him to plead guilty and no representations were made with respect to a reduced sentence or clemency. The district court also held that section 1201(a) was constitutional and determined that the defendant had decided to plead guilty when he learned that his co-defendant was going to plead guilty. In short, the defendant pleaded guilty by reason of other matters and not by reason of the statute or because of acts of the trial judge. The plea was voluntarily and knowingly made.

The Court of Appeal affirmed and the United States Supreme Court granted certiorari. The Supreme Court affirmed the district and Circuit Courts' decisions.

Brady claimed that the holding in *United States* v. *Jackson*, 390 U.S. 570 (1968), that 18 U.S.C. 1201(a) was constitutional except for the penalty provision which imposed an impermissible burden upon the exercise of a constitutional right. The question in *Jackson* was to determine whether or not the Constitution permits the establishment of a death penalty applicable only to those defendants who assert their rights to contest their guilt before a jury. The effect of such a provision is to discourage assertion of the Fifth Amendment right not to plead guilty and to deter exercise of the Sixth Amendment right to demand a jury trial. Because the legitimate goal of limiting the death penalty to cases in which a jury recommends it could be achieved without penalizing those defendants who pleaded not guilty and elect a jury trial, the death penalty provision needlessly penalized the assertion of a constitutional right.

Brady now claimed that since the Supreme Court had said that the inevitable effect of the death penalty provision of section 1201(a) was the needless encouragement of guilty pleas and jury trial waivers, *Jackson* required the invalidation of all guilty pleas entered under the section 1201(a), at least when the fear of death is shown to have been a factor in a plea. The Supreme Court rejected this claim.

THE ISSUE: Does the process of negotiating pleas of guilty amount to rendering any such plea involuntary and therefore unconstitutional?

THE ANSWER: No.

DISCUSSION: Central to any guilty plea and the foundation for entering judgment against a defendant is his admission in open court that he committed the acts charged. As a witness against himself he is protected by the Fifth Amendment from being forced to do so—hence the minimum requirement that the plea must be voluntary. The plea also gives consent to enter a judgment of conviction without a trial—a waiver of his right to a trial before a judge and jury. These waivers of constitutional rights must be voluntary, knowing, intelligent acts done with sufficient awareness of the relevant circumstances and likely consequences. The guilty plea of Brady was not invalid on either of these points.

What factors are to be considered in determining the voluntariness of a guilty plea? Voluntariness can be determined only by considering all the relevant circumstances surrounding it. One such circumstance is the possibility of a heavier sentence after conviction at a trial. It may be that Brady, recognizing that there was a strong case against him with only a slight chance of acquittal, preferred to plead guilty and thus limit the penalty to life rather than select a jury which could result in the death penalty being imposed.

In every case the state to some degree encourages guilty pleas at every important step in the criminal prosecution. For some defendants, the knowledge that they have committed a wrongful act is adequate reason for pleading guilty. For others, arrest and charging is sufficient to jar them into admitting their guilt. These pleas are all valid in spite of the state's responsibility for motivating the pleas.

Of course coercion may not be used to compel pleas of guilty. But there was absolutely nothing of this sort claimed by Brady, nor was there any evidence that he was so gripped by fear of the death penalty or hope of leniency that he did not or could not with the help of counsel weigh rationally the advantages of going to trial against the advantages of pleading guilty.

The Supreme Court also rejected the argument that it violates the Fifth Amendment to influence or encourage a guilty plea by opportunity or promise of leniency and that a guilty plea is coerced and invalid if influenced by the fear of a possibly higher penalty for the crime charged if a conviction is secured after the state is put to its proof. As the Court stated:

> We decline to hold, however, that a guilty plea is compelled and invalid under the Fifth Amendment whenever motivated by the defendant's desire to accept the certainty or probability of a lesser penalty rather than face a wider range of possibilities extending from acquittal to conviction and a higher penalty authorized by law for the crime charged.

The record supported the conclusion that Brady's plea was voluntarily made. He was advised by counsel, made aware of the charges against him, and there was nothing to indicate his lack of mental competence. Once his co-defendant had pleaded guilty and became available to testify, he pleaded guilty, perhaps to ensure that he would face no more than life imprisonment or a term in prison.

The fact that Brady did not anticipate *United States* v. *Jackson, supra,* does not impugn the reliability of the plea. There is no constitutional requirement that a defendant be permitted to disown his in-court admissions that he perpetrated an act with which he is charged simply because it later develops that the state would have had a weaker case than the defendant had thought or that the maximum penalty then assumed applicable was held inapplicable in subsequent judicial decisions.

In a companion case, *McCann* v. *Richardson,* 397 U.S. 759 (1970), the Court considered the extent to which an otherwise valid guilty plea may be impeached in collateral proceedings by proof that the plea was motivated by a prior coerced confession. The Court concluded:

> In our view a defendant's plea of guilty based on reasonably com-

petent advice is an intelligent plea not open to attack on the ground that counsel may have misjudged the admissibility of the defendant's confession. Whether a plea of guilty is unintelligent and therefore vulnerable when motivated by a confession erroneously thought admissible in evidence depends as an initial matter, not whether a court would consider counsel's advice to be right or wrong, but on whether the advice was within the range of competence of an attorney demanded in criminal cases. On the one hand, uncertainty is inherent in predicting court decisions; but on the other hand defendant's facing felony charges are entitled to the effective assistance of competent counsel. Beyond this we think the matter, for the most part, should be left to the good sense and discretion of the trial courts with the admonition that if the right to counsel guaranteed by the Constitution is to serve its purpose, defendants cannot be left to the mercies of incompetent counsel and that judges should strive to maintain proper standards of performance by attorneys who are representing defendants in criminal cases in their courts.

QUESTIONS

1. Research the question of how widespread plea negotiations are in your jurisdiction.
2. What are the arguments for and against plea bargaining?
3. What are some psychological pressures that may be used by the government to induce a plea of guilty?

Santobello v. New York
404 U.S. 257, 92 S.Ct. 495, 30 L.Ed. 2ᴰ 427 (1971)

SETTING: The facts are not in dispute. The state of New York indicted defendant in 1969 on two felony counts, promoting gambling in the first degree, and possession of gambling records in the first degree. He first entered a plea of not guilty to both counts. After negotiations, the assistant district attorney in charge of the case agreed to permit the defendant to plead guilty to a lesser-included offense, possession of gambling records in the second degree, conviction of which could carry a maximum prison sentence of one year. The prosecutor agreed to make no recommendation as to the sentence.

On June 16, 1969, Santobello accordingly withdrew his plea of not guilty and entered a plea of guilty to the lesser charge. He represented to the sentencing judge that the plea was voluntary and that the facts of the case, as described by the assistant district attorney, were true. The court accepted the plea and set a date for sentencing. A series of delays followed, owing primarily to the absence of a pre-sentence report, so that by September 23, 1969, defendant had still not been sentenced. By that date Santobello acquired new defense counsel.

Santobello's new counsel moved immediately to withdraw the guilty plea. In an accompanying affidavit, the defendant alleged that he did not know at the time of his plea that crucial evidence against him had been obtained as a result of an illegal search. The accuracy of this affidavit was subject to challenge because the defendant had filed and withdrawn a motion to suppress, before pleading guilty. In addition to his motion to withdraw his guilty plea, he renewed the motion to suppress and filed a motion to inspect the grand jury minutes.

These three motions in turn caused further delay until November 26, 1969, when the court denied all three and set January 9, 1970, as the date for sentencing. On January 9, Santobello appeared before a different judge, the judge who had presided over the case to this juncture having retired. Defendant renewed his motions, and the court again rejected them. The court then turned to consideration of the sentence.

PROCEDURAL PROBLEM: At this appearance, another prosecutor had replaced the prosecutor who had negotiated the plea. The new prosecutor recommended the maximum one-year sentence. In making this recommendation, he cited Santobello's criminal record and alleged links with organized crime. Defense counsel immediately objected on the ground that the State had promised defendant before the plea was entered that there would be no sentence recommendation by the prosecution. He sought to adjourn the sentence hearing in order to have time to prepare proof of the first prosecutor's promise. The second prosecutor, apparently ignorant of his colleague's commitment, argued that there was nothing in the record to support this claim of a promise, but the State, in subsequent proceedings, has not contested that such a promise was made.

The sentencing judge ended discussion with the following statement quoting extensively from the pre-sentence report:

> *Mr. Aronstein [Defense Counsel], I am not at all influenced by what the District Attorney says, so that there is no need to adjourn the sentence, and there is no need to have any testimony. It doesn't make a particle of difference what the District Attorney says he will do, or what he doesn't do.*
>
> *I have here, Mr. Aronstein, a probation report. I have here a history of a long, long serious criminal record. I have here a picture of the life history of this man. . . .*
>
> *"He is unamenable to supervision in the community. He is a professional criminal." This is in quotes. "And a recidivist. Institutionalization—"; that means, in plain language, just putting him away, is the only*

means of halting his anti-social activities, and protecting you, your family,
me, my family, protecting society. "Institutionalization." Plain language,
put him behind bars.

Under the plea, I can only send him to the New York City Correc-
tional Institution for men for one year, which I am hereby doing.

The judge then imposed the maximum sentence of one year.

THE ISSUE: Once a plea bargain has been arrived upon, can the
prosecution breach the agreement even where the breach arguably had
no effect on the sentence imposed by the judge?

THE ANSWER: No.

DISCUSSION: In the previous cases decided by the United States
Supreme Court, negotiated pleas of guilt were recognized as an integral
part of the criminal justice system. The cases emphasized that once a bargain has been agreed upon, it will not be overturned lightly. Chief Justice
Burger in *Santobello* now emphasized that a breach of the agreement by
a prosecutor by failure to carry out his part of the plea bargain cannot
go unrectified even if the breach arguably had no effect on the sentence
imposed. In stressing the prosecutor's obligation to uphold his part of the
agreement, Burger stated:

> *This phase of the process of criminal justice, and the adjudicative*
> *element inherent in accepting a plea of guilty, must be attended by safe-*
> *guards to insure the defendant what is reasonably due in the circum-*
> *stances. Those circumstances will vary, but a constant factor is that when*
> *a plea rests in any significant degree on a promise or agreement of the*
> *prosecutor, so that it can be said to be part of the inducement or consid-*
> *eration, such promise must be fulfilled.*
>
> *On this record [Santobello] "bargained" and negotiated for a par-*
> *ticular plea in order to secure dismissal of more serious charges, but also*
> *on condition that no sentence recommendation would be made by the*
> *prosecutor. It is now conceded that the promise to abstain from a recom-*
> *mendation was made, and at this stage the prosecution is not in a good*
> *position to argue that its inadvertent breach of agreement is immaterial.*
> *The staff lawyers in a prosecutor's office have the burden of "letting the*
> *left hand know what the right hand is doing" or has done. That the breach*
> *of agreement was inadvertent does not lessen its impact.*

The Chief Justice stated that this result is required even though the
sentencing judge was unaware of the earlier prosecution promise and
stated that the prosecution recommendation did not influence him. In conclusion, the majority noted:

> *Nevertheless, we conclude that the interest of justice and appropri-*

ate recognition of the duties of the prosecution in relation to promises made in the negotiation of pleas of guilty will be best served by remanding the case to the state courts for further consideration. The ultimate relief to which Santobello is entitled we leave to the discretion of the state court, which is in a better position to decide whether the circumstances of this case require only that there be specific performance of the agreement on the plea, in which case [Santobello] should be resentenced by a different judge, or whether, in the view of the state court, the circumstances require granting the relief sought by [Santobello], i.e., the opportunity to withdraw his plea of guilty. We emphasize that this is in no sense to question the fairness of the sentencing judge; the fault here rests on the prosecutor, not on the sentencing judge.

In dissent, Justices Marshall, Brennan, and Stewart believed that a defendant should be permitted to withdraw his plea in these circumstances and exercise his right to a trial if he desires. Justice Marshall stated, "When a prosecutor breaks the bargain, he undercuts the basis for the waiver of constitutional rights implicit in the plea. This it seems to me, provides the defendant ample justification for rescinding the plea. . . . I would remand the case with instructions that the plea be vacated and [Santobello] given the opportunity to replead to the original charges in the indictment."

QUESTIONS

1. What is the main point of difference between the majority and dissenting opinions?
2. Distinguish this case from the preceding one, *Brady* v. *United States*.
3. Should it make a difference that the prosecution acted in complete innocence, as in this case? Why do you suppose that the Court did not give much, if any, weight to this argument? Discuss.

McMann v. *Richardson*
397 U.S. 759, 90 S.Ct. 1441, 25 L.Ed. 2ᴰ 763 (1970)

SETTING: Richardson was indicted in April 1963 for murder in the first degree. Two attorneys were assigned to represent him. He initially pleaded not guilty, but in July withdrew his plea and pleaded guilty to murder in the second degree, specifically admitting at the time that he had struck the victim with a knife. He was convicted and sentenced to a term of thirty years to life. Following the denial without a hearing of his application for collateral relief in the state courts, Richardson filed his petition for habeas corpus in the United States District Court for the Northern District of New York, alleging in conclusory fashion that his plea of guilty was induced by a coerced confession and by ineffective court-appointed counsel. His petition was denied without a hearing, and he appealed to the Court of Appeals for the Second Circuit, including with his appellate brief a supplemental affidavit in which he alleged that he was beaten into confessing the crime, that his assigned attorney conferred with him only ten minutes prior to the day the plea of guilty was taken, that he advised his attorney that he did not want to plead guilty to something he did not do, and that his attorney advised him to plead guilty to avoid the electric chair, saying that "this was not the proper time to bring up the confession" and that Richardson "could later explain by a writ of habeas corpus how my confession had been beaten out of me."

PROCEDURAL PROBLEM: The United States Court of Appeals, Second Circuit, reversed the defendant's conviction and remanded it to the lower court for further hearing. The United States Supreme Court granted certiorari and vacated the Court of Appeals decision. The core of the Court of Appeals argument was the proposition that if in a collateral proceeding a guilty plea was shown to have been triggered by a coerced confession—if there would have been no plea had there been no confession—the plea is vulnerable, at least in cases coming from New York, where the guilty plea was taken prior to *Jackson* v. *Denno*, 378 U.S. 368 (1964). (See Chapter 8.) The United States Supreme Court, Justice White writing for the majority, was unable to agree with this proposition.

THE ISSUE: Is a defendant who, on the advice of counsel, enters a guilty plea entitled to a habeas corpus hearing based on petitions alleging that his confession was coerced and that the coerced confession induced the guilty plea?

THE ANSWER: No.

DISCUSSION: The majority noted that the validity of entering a guilty plea will depend on the opportunity to make a free choice. "The admission may not be compelled, and since the plea is also a waiver of trial and . . . it must be an intelligent act 'done with sufficient awareness of the relevant circumstances and likely consequences.'"

White further noted that after conviction on such a plea a counseled defendant is not entitled to relief if his factual claims are accepted when his petition for habeas corpus only alleges that his confession is coerced and that it motivated his plea. When a guilty plea is entered, competent counsel for the defendant must make a difficult choice, and it is not the duty of the courts to second-guess a defense attorney's advice that a guilty plea is best for the defendant, even if the advice is erroneous. White stated: "Waiving trials entails the inherent risk that the good-faith evaluations of a reasonably competent attorney will turn out to be mistaken either as to the facts or as to what a court's judgment might be on the facts." Such questions of facts cannot be answered with "certitude; yet a decision to plead guilty must necessarily rest upon counsel's answers, uncertain as they may be."

The majority, in discussing the reasons why a defendant needs to make more than merely allegations of an improperly induced confession after a negotiated guilty plea is made, stated:

> Since we are dealing with a defendant who deems his confession crucial to the State's case against him and who would go to trial if he thought his chances of acquittal were good, his decision to plead guilty or not turns on whether he thinks the law will allow his confession to be used against him. For the defendant who considers his confession involuntary and hence unusable against him at a trial, tendering a plea of guilty would seem a most improbable alternative. The sensible course would be to contest his guilt, prevail on his confession claim at trial, on appeal, or, if necessary, in a collateral proceeding, however guilty he might be. The books are full of cases in New York and elsewhere, where the defendant has made this choice and has prevailed. If he nevertheless pleads guilty the plea can hardly be blamed on the confession which in his view was inadmissible evidence and no proper part of the State's case. Since by hypothesis the evidence aside from the confession is weak and the defendant has no reasons of his own to plead, a guilty plea in such circumstances is nothing less than a refusal to present his federal claims to the state court in the first instance—a choice by the defendant to take the benefits, if any, of a plea of guilty and then to pursue his coerced-confession claim in collateral proceedings. Surely later allegations that the confession rendered his plea involuntary would appear incredible, and whether his plain bypass of state remedies was an intelligent act depends on whether he was so incompetently advised by counsel concerning the forum in which he should first present his federal claim that the Constitution will afford him another chance to plead.
>
> A more credible explanation for a plea of guilty by a defendant who would go to trial except for his prior confession is his prediction that the law will permit his admissions to be used against him by the trier of fact. At least the probability of the State's being permitted to use the confession as evidence is sufficient to convince him that the State's case is too strong to contest and that a plea of guilty is the most advantageous course. Nothing in this train of events suggests that the defendant's plea, as distinguished from his confession, is an involuntary act. His later petition for collateral relief asserting that a coerced confession induced his plea is at most a claim that the admissibility of his confession was mistakenly assessed and that since he was erroneously advised, either under the then

applicable law or under the law later announced, his plea was an unintelligent and voidable act. The Constitution, however, does not render pleas of guilty so vulnerable.

The Court also discussed in detail the crucial difference between a conviction following a plea of guilty that was induced by the threat of introducing an involuntary confession, and a conviction based on the admission of a coerced, involuntary confession.

> *A conviction after trial in which a coerced confession is introduced rests in part on the coerced confession, a constitutionally unacceptable basis for conviction. It is that conviction and the confession on which it rests that the defendant later attacks in collateral proceedings. The defendant who pleads guilty is in a different posture. He is convicted on his counseled admission in open court that he committed the crime charged against him. The prior confession is not the basis for the judgment, has never been offered in evidence at a trial, and may never be offered in evidence. Whether or not the advice the defendant received in the pre-Jackson era would have been different had Jackson then been the law has no bearing on the accuracy of the defendant's admission that he committed the crime.*

The dissenting opinion of Justices Brennan, Douglas, and Marshall noted that the majority is moving in the direction of insulating from attack all negotiated pleas of guilty "no matter what unconstitutional action of government may have induced a particular plea." The dissenters emphasized that any conviction following a trial based on a guilty plea which was extorted by violence or mental coercion violates the federal due process clause and is therefore invalid. The dissenters were also disturbed that the majority "abruptly forecloses any inquiry" into the interrelationship between a guilty plea and an antecedent confession, which the defendant has the responsibility of demonstrating. The dissenters also recognized that the existence of a coerced confession does not of itself invalidate a guilty plea.

QUESTIONS

1. What is the specific holding in this case?
2. Review *Jackson* v. *Denno* in Chapter 8. According to *McMann* v. *Richardson*, would it make any difference whether the guilty plea was negotiated before or after *Jackson?* Discuss the rationale for your answer.
3. Do you believe that a guilty plea induced by the threat of introducing

an involuntary confession is a violation of due process? Give reasons for your answer.

North Carolina v. Alford
400 U.S. 25, 91 S.Ct. 160, 27 L.Ed. 2^D 162 (1970)

SETTING: On December 2, 1968, Alford was indicted for first degree murder, a capital offense under North Carolina law. The court appointed an attorney to represent him, and this attorney questioned all but one of the various witnesses who Alford said would substantiate his claim of innocence. The witnesses, however, did not support Alford's story but gave statements that strongly indicated his guilt. Faced with strong evidence of guilt and no substantial evidentiary support for the claim of innocence, Alford's attorney recommended that he plead guilty, but left the ultimate decision to Alford himself. The prosecutor agreed to accept a plea of guilty to a charge of second degree murder, and on December 10, 1968, Alford entered a plea of guilty to the reduced charge.

Before the plea was finally accepted by the trial court, the court heard the sworn testimony of a police officer who summarized the State's case. Two other witnesses besides Alford were also heard. Although there was no eyewitness to the crime, the testimony indicated that shortly before the killing Alford took his gun from his house, stated his intention to kill the victim, and returned home with the declaration that he had carried out the killing. After the summary presentation of the State's case, Alford took the stand and testified that he had not committed the murder but that he was pleading guilty because he faced the threat of the death penalty if he did not do so. In response to the questions of his counsel, he acknowledged that his counsel had informed him of the difference between second and first degree murder and of his rights in case he chose to go to trial. The trial court then asked Alford if, in light of his denial of guilt, he still desired to plead guilty to second degree murder and he answered, "Yes, sir. I plead guilty on—from the circumstances that he [Alford's attorney] told me." After eliciting information about Alford's prior criminal record, which was a long one, the trial court sentenced him to thirty years' imprisonment, the maximum penalty for second degree murder.

PROCEDURAL PROBLEM: Alford sought post-conviction relief in the state courts and was denied. After failing in his first efforts to have his conviction overturned in the federal courts, the Federal Court of Appeals, Fourth Circuit reversed on the ground that Alford's guilty plea was made involuntarily, based on the ground that his plea was involuntary because its principal motivation was fear of the death penalty.

THE ISSUE: Is a plea of guilty, made voluntarily and upon the advice of competent counsel, still valid despite protestations of innocence by the defendant?

THE ANSWER: Yes.

DISCUSSION: Mr. Justice White for the majority noted that state and federal courts are divided on whether a guilty plea can be accepted when it is accompanied by protestations of innocence "and hence contains only a waiver of trial but no admission of guilt." White based much of his discussion on the holding in *Hudson* v. *United States,* 272 U.S. 451 (1926), in which it was held that a federal judge has the power to impose a prison sentence after accepting a plea of *nolo contendere,* a plea in which a defendant does not expressly admit his guilt but nonetheless waives his right to trial and authorizes the court for purposes of the case to treat him as if he were guilty. As the majority noted:

> Implicit in the nolo contendere *cases is a recognition that the Constitution does not bar imposition of a prison sentence upon an accused who is unwilling expressly to admit his guilt but who, faced with grim alternatives, is willing to waive his trial and accept the sentence. . . .*
> Nor can we perceive any material difference between a plea that refuses to admit commission of the criminal act and a plea containing a protestation of innocence when, as in the instant case, a defendant intelligently concludes that his interests require entry of a guilty plea and the record before the judge contains strong evidence of actual guilt. Here the State had a strong case of first degree murder against Alford. Whether he realized or disbelieved his guilt, he insisted on his plea because in his view he had absolutely nothing to gain by a trial and much to gain by pleading. Because of the overwhelming evidence against him, a trial was precisely what neither Alford nor his attorney desired. Confronted with the choice between a trial for first degree murder, on the one hand, and a plea of guilty to second degree murder, on the other, Alford quite reasonably chose the latter and thereby limited the maximum penalty to a 30-year term. When his plea is viewed in light of the evidence against him, which substantially negated his claim of innocence and which further provided a means by which the judge could test whether the plea was being intelligently entered, its validity cannot be seriously questioned. In view of the strong factual basis for the plea demonstrated by the State and Alford's clearly expressed desire to enter it despite his professed belief in his innocence, we hold that the trial judge did not commit constitutional error in accepting it.

Justice White concluded that there was no proof that supported Alford's contention that his plea was unconstitutionally obtained.

A strong dissent by Justices Brennan, Douglas, and Marshall pointed out that they believed *Brady* v. *United States*, 397 U.S. 742 (1970) was wrong that a guilty plea induced by an unconstitutional threat may be used to subject the defendant to a risk of death, "so long as the plea is entered in open court and the defendant is represented by competent counsel who is aware of the threat, albeit not of its unconstitutionality."

The dissenters concluded that *Alford's* majority decision made clear that "its previous holding was intended to apply even when the record demonstrated that the actual effect of the unconstitutional threat was to induce a guilty plea from a defendant who was unwilling to admit his guilt."

QUESTIONS

1. What, in your estimation, is the main philosophical difference between the majority and dissent on the issue of the validity of plea bargaining?
2. Distinguish the holding in this case from the holding in *Santobello*. Could this holding have been arrived at in any other way than on the specific factual situation?
3. Do the holdings of the cases in this chapter give a strong indication that the United States Supreme Court recognizes the reality of criminal prosecutions and accepts the value of plea negotiation? Discuss.

Chapter 11

Bail

Constitution of the United States, Eighth Amendment

Excessive bail shall not be required. . . .

Constitution of Virginia, Section 10

That excessive bail ought not to be required. . . .

Constitution of the State of Ohio, Article 1, Section 9

All persons shall be bailable by sufficient sureties, except for capital offenses. . . .
Excessive bail shall not be required. . . .

Stack v. Boyle
342 U.S. 1, 72 S.Ct. 1, 96 L.Ed. 3 (1951)

SETTING: Indictments were returned in the Southern District of California charging twelve defendants with conspiracy to violate the Smith Act. After arrest, bail was set at widely varying amounts—$2,500, $7,500, $75,000, and $100,000. Schneiderman, one of the defendants, had his bail reduced to $50,000 before his removal from New York to California. The government moved to increase bail for all defendants and the District Court for Southern California fixed a uniform bail of $50,000 for each defendant.

PROCEDURAL PROBLEM: The defendants moved to reduce bail as being excessive under the Eighth Amendment to the United States Constitution. They filed financial statements, family resources, health records, prior criminal records, and other data in support of their motion. The only evidence offered by the government was a record showing that four persons who had previously been convicted under the Smith Act had forfeited bail. No evidence was produced tying the four persons to the defendants. At a hearing on the bail issue, it was established that the defendants' records were correct. The district court denied the bail-reduction motion. The Court of Appeal, Ninth Circuit, affirmed. The Supreme Court remanded the case with instructions that hearings should be held in the district court for the purpose of setting reasonable bail.

THE ISSUE: Based upon the facts set forth, were the defendants denied their rights under the Eighth Amendment by having excessive bail set?

THE ANSWER: Yes.

DISCUSSION: The federal law provides that a person arrested for a noncapital offense must be admitted to bail. This right permits the unhampered freedom to prepare a defense and prevents punishment before conviction. Without bail, the presumption of innocence would be meaningless.

The right to be released before trial is conditioned on the accused giving assurance that he will be present for trial and submit to sentence if found guilty. Modern practice requires a bail bond or deposit of a sum of money subject to forfeiture as assurance that the defendant will be present. *Bail set at an amount higher than reasonably necessary to effect this purpose is excessive under the Eighth Amendment.* Bail for any individual defendant must be based upon standards relevant for its purpose of securing the defendant's presence at trial. In this case, if the defendants were convicted of the charged offense, they each faced up to five years' imprisonment and a fine of not more than $10,000. The bail was fixed at a much higher amount than was usually fixed in similar offenses with similar penalties. There was absolutely no factual showing to justify the amounts in this case.

The government asked the courts to depart from the norm by arguing that each defendant was a pawn in a conspiracy and would flee the country if set free. The Court answered that the fact of an indictment alone justifying a need for unusually high bonds is totally arbitrary and would interject into our system totalitarian principles Congress is constantly seeking to avoid.

There must be evidence upon which to justify setting bail at a higher amount than is usually set. In the absence of such a showing, fixing bail before trial in cases similar to this one cannot be squared with statutory and constitutional standards for bail. For these reasons, the Supreme Court remanded the case to the district court with instructions to apply the above guidelines in fixing reasonable bail.

The bail system has received considerable criticism in recent years. Most bail is obtained by paying a fee to a professional bondsman. The premium is forfeited regardless of whether or not the accused appears to stand trial. This fact argues against the use of bail to secure the presence of accused persons. The bail system also works an undeniable hardship on those who are unable to afford it—the poor. The bail works in favor of those who can afford it. Whether existing inequities in the bail system can be solved on a constitutional level is, however, open to question.

Is bail excessive merely because the accused cannot give it? Generally, no. See *Ex parte Duncan*, 53 *California* 410 (1879).

Offenses Not Bailable. A defendant charged with an offense punishable by death cannot be admitted to bail when the proof of his guilt is evident or the presumption thereof is great. The finding of an indictment or information does not add to the strength of the proof or the presumptions drawn therefrom.

Bail after Conviction. Generally, after conviction bail is a matter of discretion except for misdemeanors. After a conviction of an offense not punishable by death, a defendant who has appealed may be admitted to bail as a matter of right when the appeal is from a judgment imposing a fine only, or from a judgment imposing imprisonment in misdemeanors. In all other cases, the matter of bail rests with the sound discretion of the judge who has the duty to exercise it. Appellate courts may review the trial court bail decision when it is denied after conviction.

QUESTIONS

1. Is bail a matter of right in all criminal cases? Discuss the various instances in which bail may never be granted.

2. Discuss the statement, "Bail is most discriminatory to the poor."
3. What is the law in your jurisdiction governing admission to bail?

Schilb v. Kuebel
404 U.S. 357, 92 S.Ct. 479, 30 L.Ed. 2ᴰ 502 (1971)

SETTING: Illinois law provides three ways in which an accused can secure his pretrial release: (1) personal recognizance; (2) execution of a bail bond, with a deposit of 10 percent of the bail, all but 10 percent of which (amounting to 1 percent of the bail) is returned on performance of the bond conditions, and (3) execution of a bail bond, secured by a full-amount deposit in cash, authorized securities, or certain real estate, all of which is returned on performance of the bond conditions. Schilb, charged with two traffic offenses, secured pretrial release after depositing 10 percent of the bail fixed. He was convicted of one offense and acquitted of the other. After he paid his fine, all but 1 percent of the bail (amounting to $7.50) was refunded.

PROCEDURAL PROBLEM: In this class section, he thereafter challenged the Illinois system on due process and equal protection grounds, claiming that the 1 percent retention charge is imposed on only one segment of the class gaining pretrial release, on the poor but not on the rich; and that its imposition on an accused found innocent constitutes a court cost against the nonguilty.

Schilb, by this purported state class action against the court clerk, the county, and the county treasurer, attacked the statutory 1 percent charge on Fourteenth Amendment due process and equal protection grounds. The Circuit Court of St. Clair County upheld the statute and dismissed the complaint. The Supreme Court of Illinois affirmed, with two Justices dissenting. The United States Supreme Court affirmed.

DISCUSSION: In Illinois, prior to January 1, 1964, the professional bail bondsman system with all its abuses was in full bloom in Illinois. Under that system the bondsman collected the maximum fee (10 percent of the amount of the bond) permitted by statute and retained this entire amount even though the accused fully satisfied the conditions of the bond. Payment of this substantial premium was required of the good risk as well as of the bad. The results were that a heavy and irretrievable burden fell upon the accused, to the excellent profit of the bondsman, and that professional bondsmen, and not the courts, exercised significant control over the actual workings of the bail system.

One of the stated purposes of the new Illinois bail provisions was to rectify this offensive situation. The purpose appears to have been accomplished. It is said that the bail bondsman abruptly disappeared in Illinois owing primarily to the success of the 10 percent bail deposit provision.

The Illinois Code, as it read at the time Schilb was arrested and charged, provided the eligible accused could obtain pretrial release in three ways:

1. He could be released on his personal recognizance.

2. He could execute a bail bond and deposit with the clerk cash equal to only 10 percent of the bail or $25, whichever was the greater. When bail is made in this way and the conditions of the bond have been performed, the clerk returns to the accused 90 percent of the sum deposited. The remaining 10 percent (1 percent of the bail) is retained by the clerk "as bail bond costs."

3. He could execute a bail bond and secure it by a deposit with the clerk of the full amount of the bail in cash, or in stocks and bonds authorized for trust funds in Illinois, or by unencumbered nonexempt Illinois real estate worth double the amount of the bail. When bail is made in this way and the conditions of the bond have been performed, the clerk returns the deposit of cash or stocks or bonds, or releases the real estate, as the case may be, without charge or retention of any amount.

In each case bail is fixed by a judicial officer. The code prescribes factors to be considered in fixing the amount of bail, and either the State or the defendant may apply to the court for an increase or for a reduction in the amount of bail or for alteration of the bond's conditions.

The parties stipulated that when bail in a particular case is fixed, the judge's discretion in such a matter is not guided by statute, rule of court, or any definite, fixed standard; various and diverse judges in fact fix the amount of bail for the same types of offenses at various and diverse amounts, without relationship as to guilt or innocence of the particular defendant in a criminal charge, and without relationship of the particular offense charged and the bail fixed. They also stipulated that the actual cost of administering the provisions of said code bail sections are substantially the same, but there may probably be a slightly greater cost in the administration of the section in which the full amount is deposited with the court clerk to secure the bail bond (number 3 above).

THE ISSUE: Does the Illinois bail system violate the equal protection clause of the Fourteenth Amendment?

THE ANSWER: No.

DISCUSSION: The prohibition of the equal protection clause prevents invidious discrimination, and if any state of facts can be conceived to justify the statutory discrimination, the legislative act will not be disturbed. The Supreme Court has also refined the traditional test and stated that a statutory classification based upon suspect criteria or affecting fundamental rights will encounter difficulties unless justified by a compelling governmental interest.

Bail is basic in our system of law, and the Eighth Amendment's proscription of excessive bail has been assumed to have application to the states through the Fourteenth Amendment. The Court in this case was not concerned with any fundamental right to bail or with any Eighth or Fourteenth Amendment question. The concern was with the 1 percent cost-retention provision. The distinction which the Court had to make was whether or not the statute discriminated invidiously and without a rational basis.

Schilb made three points in his argument attacking the Illinois statute:

1.   The 1 percent retention charge is imposed upon only one segment of the class gaining pretrial release. It is true that there is no charge made upon an accused who is released on his own recognition. The former Illinois bail statute did not charge people when released on their own recognizance. The Court noted that the State incurred no paperwork costs and assumed no more of an obligation than under the former statute. All this provides a rational basis of distinction between deposit and personal recognition situations.

2.   The 1 percent retention charge is imposed on the poor and non-affluent and not on the rich and affluent. This argument centers on the idea that justice be applied equally to all persons. In discussing the economic realities of depositing full bail or paying a 10 percent deposit, of which the state retains 1 percent for administrative costs, the Court noted that by retaining the 90 percent and depositing it in a dividend-paying account, the interest will more than pay the 1 percent administrative cost. In other words, it is by no means clear that the route of depositing the full amount of bail as security is more attractive to the affluent than paying a 10 percent deposit and forfeiting 1 percent for various administrative costs. The situation then is not one in which it can be assumed that the

Illinois plan works to deny relief to the poor man merely because of his poverty.

3.   The statutory 1 percent imposition with respect to an accused found innocent amounts to a court cost assessed against a guilty person. This argument is basically that the person found innocent and already put to the expense, anguish, and disgrace of a trial is then assessed a cost for exercising his right to release pending trial. The Court had no trouble with this argument; the 1 percent cost is considered an administrative cost imposed on the guilty and innocent alike who seek the benefit of the 10 percent bail deposit provision.

The Supreme Court refrained from nullifying the Illinois bail statute which brought reform and needed relief to the state's bail system.

Usual Bail Procedure.   Although this outline may vary in each jurisdiction, a typical bail process takes the following form:

1.   Persons who may take bail:
   a.   Officer in charge of the jail where the defendant is held in custody.
   b.   Clerk of an inferior court in the district in which the offense is alleged to have been committed.
   c.   Clerk of a trial court in which the case against the defendant is pending.

2.   Kinds of acceptable bail:
   a.   Cash
   b.   Bond by a surety

3.   Amount of bail for a misdemeanor:
   a.   Fixed on the warrant of arrest if a complaint is filed.
   b.   As set by the judge if the defendant has been arraigned.
   c.   According to a schedule of bail fixed and approved by a judge or judges in the district in which the alleged offense has been committed.

4.   Amount of bail for a felony:
   a.   Fixed by the warrant of arrest if a complaint is filed.
   b.   As set by a judge if the defendant has been arraigned.
   c.   Where there has been no arrest warrant issued, nor complaint filed, nor arraignment, bail can usually be set upon application to the magistrate having jurisdiction of the offense or a commissioner of the court having jurisdiction over the offense.

QUESTIONS

1. Discuss the bail system used in your jurisdiction. What criticisms have been leveled at it over the past years?
2. Compare the bail statutes in your jurisdiction with those in the *Schilb* case. What are the similarities and distinctions? Would the statute in your jurisdiction probably be upheld under the equal protection clause as interpreted in this case?
3. Discuss the purpose of bail. Does it really accomplish its purpose? Are there alternatives to posting cash bail? What are they? Discuss.

Chapter 12

Jury Trial

Constitution of the United States, Sixth Amendment

In all criminal prosecutions, the accused shall enjoy the right to . . . trial . . . by an impartial jury. . . .

Constitution of Maine, Article 1, Section 6

To have a speedy, public and impartial trial, and, except in trials by martial law or impeachment, by a jury of the vicinity.

Constitution of Michigan of 1963, Article 1, Section 14

The right of a trial by jury shall remain. . . .

Constitution of Maryland, Article 21

That in all criminal prosecutions, every man hath a right to . . . trial by an impartial jury. . . .

Duncan v. Louisiana
391 U.S. 145, 88 S.Ct. 1444, 20 L.Ed. 2ᴰ 491 (1968)

SETTING: Duncan was nineteen years old when tried. While driving in Plaquemines Parish on October 13, 1966, he saw two of his younger cousins engaged in a conversation with four white boys by the side of the highway. His cousins recently had transferred to an all-white school and had reported racial incidents at the school. Duncan stopped the car, got out, and approached the six boys. Although the evidence was in dispute, the witnesses agreed that the defendant spoke to the white boys, encouraged his cousins to leave and enter his car, and that he was about to enter his car and drive away. The whites testified that before Duncan got into the car, Landry, a white boy, had been slapped on the elbow by the defendant. The Negroes testified that there was more of a touching rather than slapping.

The trial judge concluded that this was a simple battery and convicted Duncan of the same.

PROCEDURAL PROBLEM: The offense was a misdemeanor punishable by up to two years in prison and a $300 fine. Duncan sought a jury trial which the trial judge denied because Louisiana law grants jury trials only in cases in which imprisonment at hard labor or death may be imposed. Upon conviction, Duncan was fined $150 and sentenced to sixty days in jail. The Louisiana Supreme Court upheld the conviction by rejecting the defendant's argument that the denial of jury trial violated his rights guaranteed by the United States Constitution. On review, the United States Supreme Court reversed the conviction.

THE ISSUE: Is the fundamental right to a jury trial guaranteed by the federal Constitution applicable in state criminal cases by application of the Fourteenth Amendment where the crimes are classified as serious offenses?

THE ANSWER: Yes.

DISCUSSION: The test for determining whether a right is fundamental has been phrased in different ways:

1. Is the right among those fundamental principles of liberty and justice which lie at the base of all our civil and political institutions?

2. Is the right basic to our system of jurisprudence?

3. Is the right essential to a fair trial?

The defendant claimed that the right to a jury trial meets all of the requirements. The Louisiana position, however, was that the Constitution imposes no right to give a jury trial in a criminal case regardless of the seriousness of the crime or the size of the punishment that may be imposed.

The United States Supreme Court majority opinion, in rejecting the Louisiana claim, stated:

> *Because we believe that the trial by jury in criminal cases is fundamental to the American scheme of justice, we hold that the Fourteenth Amendment guarantees a right of jury trial in all criminal cases which—were they to be tried in a federal court—would come within the Sixth Amendment's guarantee.*

The majority noted that the Court has in recent cases been applying provisions of the first eight amendments to the states and in doing so had adopted a new approach to the "incorporation" doctrine. Earlier, the crucial question seemed to be whether a civilized system could be imagined that would not accord the particular protection. More recent cases, however, have proceeded upon the valid assumption that state criminal processes are not imaginary and theoretical schemes but real systems bearing almost every characteristic of the common-law system developing in the United States and England.

The question, then, is whether the procedure is fundamental to an Anglo-American regime of ordered liberty. Mr. Justice White, who wrote the majority opinion, stated that when the question is approached this way, the issue is quite different from older cases which indicated that states might abolish the jury trial. *Maxwell* v. *Dow,* 176 U.S. 581 (1900). He noted that it is easy to imagine a fair and equitable criminal process without a jury system; but there are none in the American states.

The Court determined that the jury trial receives strong support. The laws of every state guarantee a right to a jury trial in serious criminal cases; no state has dispensed with it; nor is there any significant movement underway to do so.

Justice White emphasized:

> *We would not assert, however, that every criminal trial—or any particular trial—held before a judge alone is unfair or that a defendant may never be as fairly treated by a judge as he would be by a jury. Thus we hold no constitutional doubts about the practices, common in both federal and state courts, of accepting waivers of jury trial and prosecuting*

petty crimes without extending a right to jury trial. However, the fact is that in most places more trials for serious crimes are to juries than to a court alone; a great many defendants prefer the judgment of a jury to that of a court. Even where defendants are satisfied with bench trials, the right to a jury trial very likely serves its intended purpose of making judicial or prosecutorial unfairness less likely.

In this case, the specific question was whether jury trial could be denied on a charge of simple battery which carried a penalty of two years imprisonment and a fine. The Court noted that it is true that there is a category of petty crimes which is not subject to the Sixth Amendment jury-trial mandate and should not be subject to the Fourteenth Amendment jury-trial requirement applied to the states.

The question of whether Louisiana could insist on trying this case without a jury was answered in the negative. It was noted that although the boundaries of the petty offense category, which were tried in England and the Colonies without juries, have always been held to be exempt from the otherwise comprehensive language of the Sixth Amendment; a crime punishable by two years is based, "on past and contemporary standards in this country, a serious crime and not a petty offense."

Where is the line to be drawn between petty and serious offenses? The court did not reach this issue, but did state:

> *In determining whether the length of the authorized prison term or the seriousness of other punishment is enough in itself to require a jury trial, we are counseled by* District of Columbia v. Clawans, 300 U.S. 617 (1937), *to refer to objective criteria, chiefly the existing laws and practices in the Nation. In the federal system, petty offenses are defined as those punishable by no more than six months in prison and a $500 fine. In 49 of the 50 States crimes subject to trial without a jury, which occasionally include simple battery, are punishable by no more than one year in jail. Moreover, in the late 18th century in America crimes triable without a jury were for the most part punishable by no more than a six-month prison term, although there appear to have been exceptions to this rule. We need not, however, settle in this case the exact location of the line between petty offenses and serious crimes. It is sufficient for our purposes to hold that a crime punishable by two years in prison is, based on past and contemporary standards in this country, a serious crime and not a petty offense. Consequently, the defendant was entitled to a jury trial and it was error to deny it.*

Should the length of the penalty actually imposed, not the length of the authorized sentence, be critical in determining whether a jury trial should be granted? The Court rejected the argument that the penalty actually imposed be the critical factor. The penalty authorized for a particular crime is of course relevant in determining whether it is serious or not and may in itself, if severe enough, subject the trial to the requirement of the Sixth Amendment. The authorized penalty at a minimum serves as a gauge of the community's social and ethical judgments. Louisiana apparently considers the offense quite serious, judging from the penalty affixed.

In the case of a punishment not prescribed by statute, the offense is deemed "serious" if the sentence actually imposed is two years or more. *Bloom* v. *Illinois*, 391 U.S. 194 (1968). But an offense is "petty" if the sentence imposed is six months or less. *Cheff* v. *Schnackenberg*, 384 U.S. 373 (1966).

QUESTIONS

1. If your state has a constitutional provision guaranteeing a jury trial, is such a provision necessary in light of the holding of this case?
2. What is the incorporation doctrine? Discuss.
3. What new assumption did the Court make in this case when it noted that fundamental protections should not be based on theoretical abstractions? Discuss.

Swain v. *Alabama*
380 U.S. 202, 85 S.Ct. 824, 13 L.Ed. 759 (1965)

SETTING: Swain, a Negro, was indicted and convicted of rape in the Circuit Court of Talladega County, Alabama, and sentenced to death. The defendant filed motions to quash the indictment, to strike the trial-jury venire, and to declare void the petit jury chosen in this case, all because of "invidious discrimination" in selection of the jurors. The Alabama Supreme Court denied the motions and affirmed the conviction. The Supreme Court granted certiorari and affirmed the conviction.

The Court, citing precedent, stated that there can be no state-sanctioned, systematic exclusion of an identifiable group in the community from participation in the criminal justice process. This violates the equal protection clause. And although a Negro defendant is not entitled to a jury containing members of his race, a state-sanctioned purposeful and deliberate denial of Negroes on account of race violates the equal protection clause.

However, purposeful discrimination must be proved, not merely assumed or asserted. The Court commented that while the selection of prospective jurors was somewhat haphazard and little effort was made to insure that all groups in the community were fully represented, it was of the opinion that the defendant's burden of proof was not carried. An imperfect system is not equivalent to purposeful discrimination based on race.

PROCEDURAL PROBLEM: The defendant claimed as one of his arguments the exercise of peremptory challenges to exclude Negroes from serving on trial juries. In Talladega County, the petit jury venire drawn in criminal cases is thirty-five, unless a capital offense is involved, in which case about a hundred names are drawn. After excuses and challenges for cause, the venire for a capital case is reduced to about seventy-five. The jury is then "struck," a peremptory challenge exercised alternately, two "struck" by the defense, one by the prosecution, until twelve jurors remain. This is essentially the Alabama struck jury system for both criminal and civil cases. In this case, the six Negroes were struck by the prosecution in the process of selecting the jury to try Swain. The main claim of Swain was the striking of the six Negroes from the petit jury. No evidence was taken. The Supreme Court agreed with the Alabama courts in denying Swain's motion seeking to invalidate the alleged purposeful striking of the Negroes' names from the jury that was to try Swain.

THE ISSUE: Is the use of peremptory challenges, which apparently has not been proven to have been used to consistently and systematically exclude Negroes from serving on petit jury, a violation of the Fourteenth Amendment?

THE ANSWER: No.

DISCUSSION: The peremptory challenge has very old credentials. Peremptories were used on both sides in the law in England after the separation of the Colonies; this common law provided the beginning for peremptories in America. Congress provided very early in our history for peremptory challenges in the federal courts. The history in the federal system was paralleled in the state system. The defendant's right to such challenges was conferred by statute and often corresponded closely to English practice. The twentieth century has experienced some attacks on the peremptory challenge on the grounds of expense, delays, and elimination of qualified jurors, but the system still survives.

The peremptory challenge has grown in usage in this country, while it has fallen from favor in England, because juries here are drawn from a greater cross-section of a heterogeneous society. The *voir dire* examination in America is extensive and probing and operates as a predicate to exercise peremptories. The Court noted that the right is one of the most important rights secured to an accused. Although the incidence of the peremptory challenge by the prosecutor has differed from that of the defendant, the view in the United States has been that the system should guarantee not only freedom from any bias against the accused but also from any prejudice against the State.

Although challenges for cause permit rejection of jurors for narrowly defined, provable, and legally recognizable reasons based on partiality, the peremptory permits rejection for a real or imagined partiality that is less easily designated or demonstrable. It is exercised frequently for reasons thought to be irrevelant to a trial: race, religious affiliations, occupation, or nationality. The question the defense or the prosecution must ask is not whether the juror of a particular race or nationality is in fact partial, but whether one from a different group is less likely to be partial.

With these considerations in mind, the Court stated that it could not hold that striking of Negroes as permitted by Alabama law in a particular case is a denial of equal protection of the laws. To subject the prosecutor's challenge in a particular case to the demands and traditional standards of the equal protection clause would entail a radical change in the nature and operation of the challenge. It would no longer be peremptory. The prosecutor's judgment underlying the challenge would be the subject of scrutiny for reasonableness and sincerity. A great many challenges would be banned.

In light of the purposes and functions the peremptory challenge serves in a pluralistic society, the Court felt it could not hold that the Constitution requires an examination of the prosecutor's reasons for its exercise in any given case.

The Court did not reach the issue of using peremptory challenge to systematically and deliberately exclude Negroes. If the proof would show a reasonable inference that Negroes are excluded from juries for reasons wholly unrelated to the outcome of the case and the peremptory challenge is used to deny the Negro the opportunity to participate in the criminal justice system the same as the white person, then the peremptory challenge is being improperly used. The record in this case did not demonstrate this improper usage.

QUESTIONS

1. In your jurisdiction, what are the number of peremptory challenges permitted in the various classifications of criminal offenses?

2. What is a challenge for cause? What are the grounds for challenging for cause in your jurisdiction?

3. What reason did the Court give for the increased use of the peremptory challenge in America? Do you think the reason is valid? Discuss.

Williams v. *Florida*
399 U.S. 78, 90 S.Ct. 1893, 26 L.Ed. 2ᴰ 446 (1970)

SETTING: The defendant filed a motion to impanel a twelve-man jury instead of a six-man jury provided by Florida law in all but capital cases. The motion made prior to his trial for robbery was denied, and he was subsequently convicted as charged and sentenced to life imprisonment. The various state appeals regarding violation of Williams' Sixth Amendment rights were unsuccessful and the United States Supreme Court granted certiorari. The judgment of the Florida District Court of Appeals was affirmed.

PROCEDURAL PROBLEM: In *Duncan* v. *Louisiana* the Supreme Court held that the Fourteenth Amendment guarantees the right to a jury trial in the states in all criminal cases where they are eligible to be tried by a jury in a federal court. The defendant's trial for robbery on July 3, 1968, clearly fell within the scope of that holding.

THE ISSUE: Is a twelve-man jury a constitutional requirement?

THE ANSWER: No.

DISCUSSION: In examining the debates that led to adoption of the Article III right to a jury trial, as well as the Sixth Amendment right, Mr. Justice White, who delivered the majority opinion, found that there was indication that the constitutional right to a jury trial was to be equated with the common-law right in all its details. In discussing the debates at the Constitutional Convention over the form of the Article III jury-trial right, three significant features emerged concerning the relationship between the common law and constitutional rights to a jury trial.

1. First, the framers of the Constitution refused to include in Article III the common-law right to be tried by a jury of the vicinage (jury of the neighborhood), even though the vicinage requirement was

as much a part of the common-law jury of the eighteenth century as was the twelve-man jury requirement.

2. Provisions which would have explicitly tied the jury concept to the accustomed requisites of the time were eliminated. Mr. Justice White acknowledged that it was arguable that the "accustomed requisites" were thought to be included in the jury concept; it was also equally plausible that the omission was meant to free the Constitution jury right from the common-law requisites.

3. Finally, contemporary legislative and constitutional provisions indicate "that where Congress wanted to leave no doubt that it was incorporating existing common law features of the jury system, it knew how to use express language to that effect." Thus, the Judiciary Bill signed by the President on the same day that the House and Senate finally agreed on the form of the amendment to be submitted to the states, provided in certain cases for the narrower "vicinage" requirements which the House had wanted to include in the amendment.

From this, the majority concluded that there was absolutely no indication that the founding fathers explicitly decided to equate the common law and constitutional characteristics of the jury. "Nothing in this history suggests, then, that we do violence to the letter of the Constitution by turning to other than purely historical considerations to determine which features of the jury system, as it existed at common law, were preserved in the Constitution."

The relevant inquiry must be the function that the particular feature performs in relation to the purposes of the jury trial. "Measured by this standard the twelve-man requirement cannot be regarded as an indispensible component of the Sixth Amendment."

What is the traditional purpose of the jury trial? Justice White stated that it was to give a criminally accused the right to be tried by his peers— to safeguard him against the overzealous prosecutor or biased or inadequate judge. On this point the opinion noted:

> *Given this purpose, the essential feature of a jury obviously lies in the interposition between the accused and his accuser of the common-sense judgment of a group of laymen, and the community participation and shared responsibility which results from that group's determination of guilt or innocence. The performance of this role is not a function of the particular number of the body which makes up the jury. To be sure, the number should probably be large enough to promote group deliberation, free from outside attempts at intimidation, and to provide a fair possibility for obtaining a representative cross-section of the community. But we find little reason to think that these goals are in any meaningful sense less likely to be achieved when the jury numbers six, than when it numbers twelve—particularly if the requirement of unanimity is retained.*

And certainly the reliability of the jury as a factfinder hardly seems likely to be a function of its size.

The majority rejected the argument that a twelve-man jury gives a defendant a greater advantage since he will have more chances of finding a juror who will insist on acquittal and thus prevent conviction. They noted that the advantage might just as easily belong to the state, which only needs one juror to insist on guilt to prevent acquittal.

The argument that a twelve-man jury will represent more of the community was likewise rejected. The Court stated: "Even the twelve-man jury cannot insure representation of every distinct voice in the community, particularly given the use of the peremptory challenge."

In closing, the Court emphasized that its holding does nothing more than to leave "these considerations to Congress and the States, unrestrained by an interpretation of the Sixth Amendment which would forever dictate the precise number which can constitute a jury."

QUESTIONS

1. Discuss the arguments for and against requiring twelve-man juries in criminal cases.
2. What reasons did Justice White give for his conclusion that the founding fathers did not intend to mandate a constitutional requirement of a twelve-man jury?
3. What is the law in your jurisdiction covering the numbers of jurors in both criminal and civil cases?

Johnson v. Louisiana
406 U.S. 356, 92 S.Ct. 1620, 32 L.Ed. 2ᴰ 152 (1972)

SETTING: Johnson was arrested without a warrant at his home on January 20, 1968. The victim had previously identified Johnson from photographs as the perpetrator of the armed robbery. He was then identified as the robber at a lineup, while represented by counsel, by the victim of still another robbery. This latter crime is the one involved in this case. The defendant entered a not guilty plea, was tried by a twelve-man jury on May 14, 1968, and convicted by a 9–3 verdict authorized by the Louisiana Criminal Code of Procedure in criminal cases in which punishment is necessary at hard labor. Johnson's arguments that he was denied due process and equal protection of the law were rejected by the Louisiana courts. Because this case was tried before *Duncan* v. *Louisiana*, 391 U.S. 145 (1968), Johnson conceded that the Sixth Amendment was not applicable to his case.

PROCEDURAL PROBLEM: Under the Louisiana Constitution and the Code of Criminal Procedure, criminal cases in which the punishment is necessarily at hard labor are tried by a jury of twelve, and the vote of nine jurors is sufficient to return either a guilty or not guilty verdict. The defendant argued that (1) in order to give substance to the proof beyond a reasonable doubt standard required by the Fourteenth Amendment, jury verdicts in criminal cases must be unanimous, and (2) state law requiring unanimous verdicts in five-man jury cases (for minor offenses in Louisiana) and in twelve-man jury cases (for capital offenses), but permitting 9–3 convictions in other cases violates the equal protection of the law clause.

THE ISSUE: Are the Louisiana provisions permitting less than unanimous verdicts in certain cases invalid under the due process and equal protection clauses of the Fourteenth Amendment?

THE ANSWER: No.

DISCUSSION: The Court held that the due process clause does not mandate a unanimous verdict in order to give effect to the requirement that guilt be proved beyond a reasonable doubt. The decision was not based on the Sixth Amendment right to a jury trial. The Court noted that jury unanimity has never been held by it to be a requisite of due process of law. Mr. Justice White, who wrote the majority opinion, rejected the argument that the nine-juror verdict undermined the reasonable doubt standard:

> *Entirely apart from these cases, however, it is our view that the fact of three dissenting votes to acquit raises no question of constitutional substance about either the integrity or accuracy of the majority verdict of guilt. [Defendant's] contrary argument breaks down into two parts, each of which we shall consider separately: first that all nine individual jurors will be unable to vote conscientiously in favor of guilt beyond a reasonable doubt when three of their colleagues are arguing for acquittal, and second, that guilt cannot be said to have been proved beyond a reasonable doubt when one or more of a jury's members at the conclusion of deliberation possesses such a doubt.* Neither argument is persuasive *[emphasis added].*

It is unlikely that the majority of jurors would simply override their colleagues without listening to them. It is far more likely that the reasoned arguments of jurors in favor of acquittal would either be answered or be persuasive enough to prevent conviction. The defendant offered no evidence that majority jurors simply ignore the reasonable doubts of their colleagues or otherwise act irresponsibly in casting their votes in favor of conviction. Before the Court would consider altering its own longstanding perceptions about jury behavior and overturn considered legislative judgment that unanimity is not essential to reasoned jury verdicts, it must have some basis for doing so other than unsupported assumptions. It concluded that as to the nine jurors who voted to convict, the State satisfied its burden of proving guilt beyond a reasonable doubt.

In discussing whether the vote of three jurors for acquittal can be said to impeach the verdict of the other nine and itself demonstrate that guilt was in fact not proved beyond a reasonable doubt, the majority concluded:

> But the fact remains that nine jurors—a substantial majority of the jury—were convinced by the evidence. In our view disagreement of three jurors does not alone establish reasonable doubt, particularly when such a heavy majority of the jury, after having considered the dissenters' views, remains convinced of guilt. That rational men disagree is not in itself equivalent to a failure of proof by the State, nor does it indicate infidelity to the reasonable-doubt standards. Jury verdicts finding guilty beyond a reasonable doubt are regularly sustained even though the evidence was such that the jury would have been justified in having a reasonable doubt . . . ; even though the trial judge might not have reached the same conclusion as the jury . . . ; and even though appellate judges are closely divided on the issue whether there was sufficient evidence to support a conviction. . . . That want of jury unanimity is not to be equated with the existence of a reasonable doubt emerges even more clearly from the fact that when a jury in a federal court, which operates under the unanimity rule and is instructed to acquit a defendant if it has a reasonable doubt about his guilt . . . cannot agree unanimously upon a verdict, the defendant is not acquitted, but is merely given a new trial. . . . If the doubt of a minority of jurors indicates the existence of a reasonable doubt, it would appear that a defendant should receive a directed verdict of acquittal rather than a retrial. We conclude, therefore, that verdicts rendered by nine out of twelve jurors are not automatically invalidated by the disagreement of the dissenting three. [Defendant] was not deprived of due process of law.

Addressing itself to the equal protection argument of the defendant the Court "perceive[d] nothing unconstitutional or invidiously discriminatory . . . in a State's insisting that its burden of proof be carried with more jurors where more serious crimes or more severe punishment are at issue. . . . As to the crimes triable by a five-man jury, if [defendant's] position is that it is easier to convince nine of twelve jurors than to convince all of five, he is simply challenging the judgment of the Louisiana Legislature. That body obviously intended to vary the difficulty of proving guilt with the gravity of the offense and the severity of the punishment. We remain unconvinced . . . that this legislative judgment was defective in any constitutional sense."

QUESTIONS

1. Does the law in your jurisdiction provide for less than unanimous verdicts? If yes, do you believe the reasons given in this case for upholding the constitutionality of the Louisiana procedure are applicable to the procedure in your jurisdiction?
2. What is meant by the proof beyond a reasonable doubt standard? preponderance of evidence standard? clear and convincing standard?
3. Formulate an argument showing that conviction by less than a unanimous verdict is an unconstitutional denial of the defendant's right to a jury trial.

Apodaca v. Oregon
406 U.S. 404, 92 S.Ct. 1628, 32 L.Ed. 2ᴰ 184 (1972)

SETTING: The defendants were convicted of various felonies by 11–1 and 10–2 verdicts, the minimum requisite vote in Oregon. The Oregon Constitution, Article 1, Section 11, provides "that in the circuit court, ten members of the jury may render a verdict of guilty or not guilty, save and except a verdict of guilty of first degree murder, which shall be found only by a unanimous verdict, and not otherwise; . . ."

PROCEDURAL PROBLEM: In their appeal to the United States Supreme Court, the defendants claimed that conviction of a crime by less than a unanimous jury verdict violates the right to a jury trial in criminal cases specified by the Sixth Amendment and made applicable to the states by the Fourteenth.

THE ISSUE: Does the Sixth Amendment require that there be a unanimous verdict to convict in a criminal case?

THE ANSWER: No.

DISCUSSION: In *Williams* v. *Florida,* 399 U.S. 73 (1970), the Court concluded that there is no constitutional mandate that there be twelve-man juries. In the current case, a 5–4 majority, four of the Justices agreed that the unanimous verdict, while of historical and traditional fixture, does not rise to the level of a constitutional requirement. The swing vote of Mr. Justice Powell was based on his belief that the state jury trial need not be identical in every respect to the federal jury trial, which mandates a unanimous verdict required by the Sixth Amendment. In his view it is the Fourteenth Amendment that imposes the jury-trial obligation on the states—thus the Sixth Amendment has no application. In his view Oregon's ten-man verdict is not violative of due process.

Justice White, after finding the legislative history of the Sixth Amendment inconclusive, observed:

> *Our inquiry must focus upon the function served by the jury in contemporary society. As we said in* Duncan, *the purpose of trial by jury is to prevent oppression by the Government by providing a "safeguard against the corrupt or overzealous prosecutor and against the complaint (sic.), biased, or eccentric judge." "Given this purpose, the essential feature of a jury obviously lies in the inter-position between the accused and his accuser of the commonsense judgment of a group of laymen. . . ."*
> *A requirement of unanimity, however, does not materially contribute to the exercise of this commonsense judgment. As we said in* Williams, *a jury will come to such a judgment as long as it consists of a group of laymen representative of a cross-section of the community who have the duty and the opportunity to deliberate, free from outside attempts at intimidation, on the question of a defendant's guilt. In terms of this function we perceive no difference between juries required to act unanimously and those permitted to convict or acquit by votes of ten to two or eleven to one. Requiring unanimity would obviously produce hung juries in some situations where nonunanimous juries will convict or acquit. But in either case, the interest of the defendant in having the judgment of his peers interposed between himself and the officers of the State who prosecute and judge him is equally well served.*

The defendants also argued that unanimity serves other purposes which are constitutionally essential to the continued operation of the jury system. Their main contention was that because the jury trial was made mandatory on the states by virtue of the due process clause of the Fourteenth Amendment, it should require a unanimous verdict in order to give substance to the reasonable doubt standard. The Court noted:

> *We are quite sure, however, that the Sixth Amendment itself has never been held to require proof beyond a reasonable doubt in criminal cases. The reasonable doubt standard developed separately from both the jury trial and the unanimous verdict. As the Court noted in the* Winship *case, the rule requiring proof of crime beyond a reasonable doubt did not*

crystallize in this country until after the Constitution was adopted. And in that case, which held such a burden of proof to be constitutionally required, the Court purported to draw no support from the Sixth Amendment.

[Defendant's] argument that the Sixth Amendment requires jury unanimity in order to give effect to the reasonable doubt standard thus founders on the fact that the Sixth Amendment does not require proof beyond a reasonable doubt at all. The reasonable doubt argument is rooted, in effect, in due process and has been rejected in Johnson v. Louisiana, *406 U.S. 356 (1972).*

QUESTIONS

1. Do you think these last three cases—*Williams, Johnson,* and *Apodaca* —will erode the right to a jury trial? Does it matter that they were all state rather than federal cases?
2. In the view of many, the federalization of state criminal procedure is about complete. Do you agree with this idea? Do the three decisions in Question 1 seem to signal a break from this trend?
3. What was Mr. Justice Powell's rationale for his holding in this case?

Ham v. South Carolina
409 U.S. 524, 93 S.Ct. 848, 35 L.Ed. 2ᴰ 46 (1973)

SETTING: Ham, a young bearded Negro, lived most of his life in Florence County, South Carolina. He was active in the civil rights movement and was well-known locally. He had never been convicted of a crime when he was arrested for and subsequently convicted of violating the South Carolina drug law for which he received an eighteen-month sentence. At the trial his basic defense was that law enforcement officers were "out to get him" because of his civil rights activities and that he had been framed on the drug charge.

PROCEDURAL PROBLEM: At the trial, the judge refused to make an inquiry of any kind as to the jurors' racial bias after Ham made a timely request. He claimed this denied him a fair trial in violation of the due process clause of the Fourteenth Amendment. Ham also argued that it was a constitutional error for the judge to refuse to inquire whether or not the jurors had a particular bias against beards. The United States

Supreme Court held that it was not a constitutional error regarding the last point.

THE ISSUE: Does the Fourteenth Amendment require a trial judge on *voir dire* examination to interrogate jurors upon the subject of racial prejudice after a timely request by the defendant?

THE ANSWER: Yes.

DISCUSSION: Justice Rehnquist, writing for seven members of the United States Supreme Court, stated that because one of the purposes of the due process clause of the Fourteenth Amendment is to insure the essential demand of fairness, and because the principal purpose of the adoption of the Fourteenth Amendment was to prohibit states from invidiously discriminating on the basis of race, "we think that the Fourteenth Amendment required the judge in this case to interrogate the jurors upon the subject of racial prejudice."

Rehnquist next addressed the problems of how many and the particular form of the questions that may be asked of veniremen regarding any racial prejudice they may harbor. Alluding to *Aldridge* v. *United States,* 283 U.S. 308 (1931), the majority voted that the "Court in *Aldridge* was at pains to point out, in a context where its authority within the federal system of courts allowing a good deal closer supervision than does the Fourteenth Amendment, that the trial court 'had a broad discretion as to the questions to be asked.' The discretion as to form and number of questions permitted by the Due Process Clause of the Fourteenth Amendment is at least as broad. In this context either of the brief general questions urged by the [defendant] would appear sufficient to focus the attention of the prospective jurors to any racial prejudice they might entertain."

Because of the trial court's refusal to make any inquiry as to racial bias on the part of the jurors after Ham's request, the judgment of the South Carolina conviction was reversed.

Justice Douglas would have held that it was an abuse of discretion for the trial judge to preclude the defendant from any inquiry by which the prospective jurors' prejudice to hair growth could have been explored. He stated, "Prejudice to hair growth is unquestionably of a 'serious character.' Nothing is more indicative of the importance currently being attached to hair growth by the general populace than the barrage of cases reaching the courts evidencing the attempt by one segment of society officially to control the plumage of another."

Justice Marshall concurred with the above and dissented on another issue.

QUESTIONS

1. Prepare a list of questions to elicit whether or not a juror is racially prejudiced.
2. Do you believe that a person who is racially prejudiced could still deliver an unbiased decision?
3. Compare question 2 above with the holdings in *Witherspoon* v. *Illinois* and *Furman* v. *Georgia* (Chapter 15). Is there a difference in rationale?

Chapter 13

Confrontation

Constitution of the United States, Sixth Amendment

In all criminal prosecutions, the accused shall enjoy the right . . . to be confronted with the witnesses against him. . . .

Constitution of Oklahoma, Article 2, Section 20

In all criminal prosecutions the accused shall have the right to . . . be confronted by the witnesses against him. . . .

Constitution of West Virginia, Article 3, Section 14

In all such trials, the accused shall . . . be confronted by the witnesses against him. . . .

Pointer v. *Texas*
380 U.S. 400, 85 S.Ct. 1065, 13 L.Ed. 2ᴰ 923 (1965)

SETTING: Accused of a $375 holdup, Pointer was hauled before a preliminary hearing in Houston, Texas. He had no lawyer and did not cross-examine his alleged victim, who then moved to California and did not subsequently appear at Pointer's trial. The State, after showing that the victim did not intend to return to Texas, offered the transcript of the victim's testimony at the preliminary hearing in evidence against Pointer. Pointer's attorney repeatedly objected to the introduction of the transcript because it was a denial of the confrontation of the witnesses against the defendant. All the defendant's objections were overruled, apparently partly because the defendant had been present at the preliminary hearing and therefore had been accorded the opportunity of cross-examining the witnesses there against him. The highest court in Texas, the Court of Criminal Appeals, affirmed the conviction of Pointer, rejecting the argument that the use of the transcript to convict him denied him rights guaranteed by the Sixth and Fourteenth Amendments.

PROCEDURAL PROBLEM: In this case Pointer did not object to the fact that he had no attorney when the victim made his statement at the preliminary hearing. However, he strongly objected that the use of the transcript of the statement at the trial denied him any opportunity to have the benefit of counsel's cross-examination of the principal witness against him.

THE ISSUES: (1) Is the Sixth Amendment right of an accused to confront the witnesses against him a fundamental right and made obligatory on the states by the Fourteenth Amendment? (2) Was the defendant denied his right to confront witnesses against him based on the facts in this case?

THE ANSWERS: (1) Yes. (2) Yes.

DISCUSSION: The Supreme Court routinely might have reversed Pointer's conviction based upon *Kirby* v. *United States* 174 U.S. 47 (1899), which held that confrontation is fundamental to a fair trial, a concept embodied in the due process guarantee of the Fourteenth Amendment. However, the majority, speaking through Justice Black, took a different tack and cited recent decisions that oblige states to observe the Fifth Amendment privilege against self-incrimination (*Malloy* v. *Hogan*, 378 U.S. 1 [1964]) and the Sixth Amendment's right to counsel (*Gideon* v. *Wainwright*, 372 U.S. 335 [1963]). Black noted:

> There are few subjects, perhaps, upon which this Court and other courts have been more nearly unanimous than in their expressions of belief that the right of confrontation and cross-examination is an essential and fundamental requirement for the kind of fair trial which is this country's constitutional goal. Indeed, we have expressly declared that to deprive an accused of the right to cross-examine the witnesses against

him is a denial of the Fourteenth Amendment's guarantee of due process of law.

Under the Court's decision, the Sixth Amendment guarantee of confrontation and cross-examination was denied Pointer. In summary, the Court declared that another Sixth Amendment right had been incorporated into the Fourteenth Amendment so as to be binding upon the states.

Due Diligence Required. Due diligence must ordinarily be shown before evidence previously taken can be read at a trial. Due diligence means that there must be a bona fide and actual search for the witness. In some states, however, if the evidence shows that the witness is outside the jurisdiction, the prosecution need not show that due diligence was exercised to insure his presence at the second trial. *People v. Hanz,* 109 Cal. App. 2^D 793 (1961).

Some state constitutions make no mention of the right to confrontation. (See *California Constitution.*) However, other provisions may provide for the taking of depositions in criminal cases in the presence of the accused and his attorney (*California Constitution,* Article I, Section 13). It might be implied, therefore, that the right of confrontation is guaranteed by such a provision. Frequently, statutory provisions provide for the confrontation of the accused by witnesses against him. See *California Penal Code,* Section 688, for an example.

QUESTIONS

1. What are the constitutional or statutory provisions in your state governing the confrontation right?
2. What is meant by the statement that the Fourteenth Amendment incorporates the Sixth Amendment's right to confrontation?
3. Define "due diligence." How is it used in your jurisdiction in respect to using transcripts of previous testimony in criminal prosecutions where the witness is unavailable?

Barber v. Page
390 U.S. 719, 88 S.Ct. 1318, 20 L.Ed. 2^D 255 (1968)

SETTING: The defendants were jointly charged with robbery, and at the preliminary hearing were represented by the same retained counsel, a Mr. Parks. During the course of the hearing, Woods, one of the defendants, agreed to waive his privilege against self-incrimination. Parks then withdrew as Woods' attorney but continued to represent Barber. Thereupon Woods proceeded to give testimony that incriminated Barber. Parks did not cross-examine Woods, although an attorney for another co-defendant did.

By the time Barber was brought to trial some seven months later, Woods was incarcerated in a federal penitentiary in Texarkana, Texas, about 225 miles from the trial court in Oklahoma. The State proposed to introduce against Barber the transcript of Woods' testimony at the preliminary hearing on the ground that Woods was unavailable to testify because he was outside the jurisdiction. Barber objected to that course on the ground that it would deprive him of his right to be confronted with witnesses against him. His objection was overruled and the transcript was admitted and read to the jury, which found him guilty. On appeal, the Oklahoma Court of Criminal Appeals affirmed his conviction.

PROCEDURAL PROBLEM: Defendant then sought federal habeas corpus, claiming that the use of the transcript of Woods' testimony in his state trial deprived him of his federal constitutional right to confrontation in violation of the Sixth and Fourteenth Amendments. His contention was rejected by the district court and on appeal the Court of Appeals for the Tenth Circuit affirmed. The United States Supreme Court granted certiorari to consider defendant's denial of confrontation claim and reversed.

THE ISSUE: Was the defendant's right to confrontation guaranteed by the Sixth and Fourteenth Amendments violated by the use of the preliminary hearing transcript even though the defendant was represented by counsel and had had the opportunity to cross-examine the witness had he so chosen?

THE ANSWER: Yes.

DISCUSSION: In *Pointer* v. *Texas*, 380 U.S. 4157 (1965), which held the right of confrontation applicable to the states through the Fourteenth Amendment, the Supreme Court noted:

> *There are few subjects, perhaps, upon which this Court and other courts have been more nearly unanimous than in their expressions of belief that the right of confrontation and cross-examination is an essential and fundamental requirement for the kind of fair trial which is this country's constitutional goal.*

The prosecution argued that there has traditionally been an exception to the confrontation requirement where a witness is unavailable and has given testimony and was subject to cross-examination at previous judicial proceedings against the same defendant. The exception has been explained as arising from necessity and has been justified on the ground that the right of cross-examination initially afforded provides substantial compliance with the purposes behind the confrontation requirement. The State argued that the introduction of the transcript was within the exception and Woods was outside the jurisdiction and therefore unavailable at the time of the trial, and, secondly, that the right of cross-examination was afforded Barber at the preliminary, although it was not utilized by him.

The Court stated that for the purposes of its decision it assumed that Barber validly waived his right to cross-examine Woods at the preliminary hearing.

The Court started with the fact that the State made absolutely no effort to obtain the presence of Woods at the trial other than to determine that he was in a federal prison outside of Oklahoma. The Court recognized the argument that there was no way to force Woods to come to Oklahoma for the trial, but stated that at the present time increased cooperation between the states themselves and the states and the federal government has largely alleviated much of the strength in the claim.

For example, in the case of a prospective witness currently in federal custody, 28 U.S.C. Section 2241(c) (5) gives federal courts the power to issue writs of habeas corpus *ad testificandum* at the request of state prosecutorial authorities. In addition, it is the policy of the United States Bureau of Prisons to permit federal prisoners to testify in state court criminal proceedings pursuant to writs of habeas corpus *ad testificandum* issued out of state courts.

In this case the state authorities made no effort to avail themselves of either of the above alternative means of seeking to secure Woods' presence at Barber's trial. The Court held that a witness is not "unavailable" for purposes of the foregoing exception to the confrontation requirement unless the prosecutorial authorities have made a good-faith effort to obtain his presence at trial. The State made no such effort here, and, as far as this record reveals, the sole reason Woods was not present to testify in person was because the State did not attempt to seek his presence. The right of confrontation may not be dispensed with so lightly.

The State argued that defendant waived his right to confront Woods at trial by not cross-examining him at the preliminary hearing. That contention is untenable. Not only was defendant unaware that Woods would be in a federal prison at the time of his trial, but he was also unaware that, even assuming Woods' incarceration, the State would make no effort to produce Woods at trial. To suggest that failure to cross-examine in such circumstances constitutes a waiver of the right of confrontation at a subsequent trial hardly comports with the Court's definition of a waiver as "an intentional relinquishment or abandonment of a known right or privilege."

Moreover, the Court would reach the same result on the facts of this case had Barber's counsel actually cross-examined Woods at the preliminary hearing. The right to confrontation is basically a trial right. It includes both the opportunity to cross-examine and the occasion for the jury to weigh the demeanor of the witness. A preliminary hearing is ordinarily a much less searching exploration into the merits of a case than a trial, simply because its function is the more limited one of determining whether or not probable cause exists to hold the accused for trial. Although there may be some justification for holding that the opportunity for cross-examination of a witness at a preliminary hearing satisfies the demand of the confrontation clause where the witness is shown actually to be unavailable, this is not, as the Court pointed out, such a case.

QUESTIONS

1. What did the Court state regarding the right to confrontation at the preliminary hearing vis-à-vis the trial?
2. What standard is used by the Court to ascertain whether a waiver of confrontation is actually acceptable?
3. Distinguish *Barker v. Page* from *Pointer v. Texas*.

Harrington v. *California*
395 U.S. 250, 89 S.Ct. 1726, 23 L.Ed. 2ᴰ 284 (1969)

SETTING: Four men were arrested and tried together for attempted robbery and first degree murder. Harrington was a Caucasian and the three other defendants Negroes. Over Harrington's objection that his trial would be severed, he was convicted of murder. Each of the three co-defendants confessed, and their confessions were introduced at the trial with instructions to the jury that it was to consider each confession only against the confessor. One of the three co-defendants, Rhone, took the stand and Harrington's counsel cross-examined him. The remaining two defendants did not take the stand.

During the trial Harrington made statements which fell short of a confession but which placed him at the crime scene. He admitted that Bosby, a co-defendant, was the trigger man, that he fled with the three, and that he attempted to alter his appearance. Several witnesses placed Harrington at the crime scene. Rhone's testimony, which was cross-examined by Harrington's attorney, placed Harrington with a gun inside the store at the time of the attempted robbery. Bosby's and co-defendant Cooper's confessions were somewhat at variance with other witnesses regarding the presence of Harrington with a loaded gun. (These two confessions were from nontestifying witnesses.)

PROCEDURAL PROBLEM: In *Bruton* v. *United States,* 391 U.S. 123 (1968) a confession of a co-defendant who did not take the stand was used against Bruton in a federal prosecution. The Supreme Court held that Bruton had been denied his rights under the Sixth Amendment's confrontation clause. Because the confrontation clause was made applicable in state trials by virtue of the Fourteenth Amendment, *Bruton* applies in this case (*Pointer* v. *Texas,* 380 U.S. 400 [1968]). Why, then, was this case granted certiorari by the Supreme Court?

THE ISSUE: Was the violation of *Bruton* v. *United States* based on special facts so as to constitute harmless error?

THE ANSWER: Yes.

DISCUSSION: The Court held in *Chapman* v. *California,* 386 U.S. 18 (1967), that before a federal constitutional error can be held harmless, the Court must be able to declare a belief that it was harmless beyond a reasonable doubt. It was also noted that "there must be some constitutional rights so basic to a fair trial that their infraction can never be treated as harmless error" but not all "trial errors which violate the Constitution automatically call for reversal."

The Court concluded that the special facts in this case in effect outweighed the lack of opportunity to cross-examine Bosby and Cooper and constituted harmless error under the *Chapman* rule.

Rhone, who was cross-examined, placed Harrington at the crime scene. Harrington admitted it. Others testified he had a gun and was an active participant. All of this evidence was cumulative. But apart from Cooper's and Bosby's confessions, the evidence against Harrington was so overwhelming that the violation of Bruton was harmless beyond a reasonable doubt.

Harrington also claimed that the conviction must be reversed if the Court could imagine a single juror whose mind could have been made up because of Cooper's or Bosby's confessions who otherwise would have remained unconvinced or in doubt. The Court rejected this claim and stated:

> *We of course do not know the jurors who sat. Our judgment must be based on our own reading of the record and on what seems to us to have been the probable impact of the two confessions on the minds of an average jury. We admonished in Chapman, 386 U.S., at 23, 87 S.Ct., at 827, against giving too much emphasis to "overwhelming evidence" of guilt, stating that constitutional errors affecting the substantial rights of the aggrieved party could not be considered to be harmless. By that test we cannot impute reversible weight to the two confessions.*
>
> *We do not depart from Chapman; nor do we dilute it by inference. We reaffirm it. We do not suggest that if evidence bearing on all the ingredients of the crime is tendered, the use of cumulative evidence, though tainted, is harmless error. Our decision is based on the evidence in this record. The case against Harrington was not woven from circumstantial evidence. It is so overwhelming that unless we say that no violation of Bruton can constitute harmless error, we must leave this state conviction undisturbed.*

QUESTIONS

1. What is "harmless error"?
2. What was the holding of *Chapman* v. *California?*
3. Do you believe that *Chapman* was diluted by the holding in *Harrington* in spite of what the Supreme Court stated?

Chapter 14

Trial Procedure and Conduct

Constitution of the United States, Eighth Amendment

In all criminal prosecutions, the accused shall enjoy the right to a public trial by an impartial jury; . . . to have compulsory process for obtaining witnesses in his favor. . . .

Constitution of Rhode Island, Article 1, Section 10

In all criminal prosecutions, the accused shall enjoy the right to . . . a public trial, by an impartial jury, . . . and to have the compulsory process for obtaining [witnesses].

Constitution of South Carolina, Article 1, Section 17

In all criminal prosecutions the accused shall enjoy the right to a . . . public trial by an impartial jury, and be fully informed of the nature and cause of the accusation; . . . to have compulsory process for obtaining witnesses in his favor. . . .

Constitution of Texas, Article 1, Section 10

. . . [T]he accused shall have a . . . public trial by an impartial jury; . . . shall have compulsory process for obtaining witnesses in his favor.

Washington v. Texas
388 U.S. 14, 87 S.Ct. 1920, 18 L.Ed. 2ᴰ 1019 (1967)

SETTING: Defendant Washington was convicted in Dallas County, Texas, of murder with malice and was sentenced by a jury to fifty years in prison. The prosecution's evidence showed that he, an 18-year-old youth, had dated a girl named Jean Carter until her mother had forbidden her to see him. The girl thereafter began dating another boy, the deceased. Evidently motivated by jealousy, defendant with several other boys began driving around the City of Dallas on the night of August 29, 1964, looking for a gun. The search eventually led to one Charles Fuller, who joined the group with his shotgun. After obtaining some shells from another source, the group of boys proceeded to Jean Carter's home, where Jean, her family, and the deceased were having supper. Some of the boys threw bricks at the house and then ran back to the car, leaving defendant and Fuller alone in front of the house with the shotgun. At the sound of the bricks, the deceased and Jean Carter's mother rushed out on the porch to investigate. The shotgun was fired by either Washington or Fuller, and the deceased was fatally wounded. Shortly afterward, Washington and Fuller came running back to the car where the other boys waited, with Fuller carrying the shotgun.

PROCEDURAL PROBLEM: Washington testified in his own behalf. He claimed that Fuller, who was intoxicated, had taken the gun from him, and that he had unsuccessfully tried to persuade Fuller to leave before the shooting. Fuller had insisted that he was going to shoot someone, and defendant had run back to the automobile. He saw the girl's mother come out of the door as he began running, and he subsequently heard the shot. At the time, he had thought that Fuller had shot the woman. In support of his version of the facts, Washington offered the testimony of Fuller. The record indicates that Fuller would have testified that defendant pulled at him and tried to persuade him to leave, and that defendant ran before Fuller fired the fatal shot.

It was undisputed that Fuller's testimony would have been relevant and material, and that it was vital to the defense. Fuller was the only person other than Washington who knew exactly who had fired the shotgun and whether defendant had at the last minute attempted to prevent the shooting. Fuller, however, had been previously convicted of the same murder and sentenced to fifty years in prison, and he was confined in the

Dallas County jail. Two Texas statutes provided at the time of the trial in this case that persons charged or convicted as co-participants in the same crime could not testify for one another, although there was no bar to their testifying for the State. On the basis of these statutes the trial judge sustained the State's objection and refused to allow Fuller to testify. Defendant's conviction followed, and it was upheld on appeal by the Texas Court of Criminal Appeals. The United States Supreme Court granted certiorari and reversed.

THE ISSUE: Is the Sixth Amendment right to have compulsory process for obtaining witnesses in his favor guaranteed in federal trials so fundamental and essential to a fair trial that it is incorporated into the due process clause of the Fourteenth Amendment?

THE ANSWER: Yes.

DISCUSSION: After discussing additional procedural rights guaranteed to a defendant, the majority emphasized that the right of an accused to have compulsory process for obtaining witnesses in his favor stands on no lesser footing than other Sixth Amendment rights, assistance of counsel, confrontation, speedy trial, and public trial, that previously had been held applicable to the states. The Court stated:

> *The right to offer the testimony of witnesses, and to compel their attendance, if necessary, is in plain terms the right to present a defense, the right to present the defendant's version of the facts as well as the prosecution's to the jury so it may decide where the truth lies. Just as an accused has the right to confront the prosecution's witnesses for the purpose of challenging their testimony, he has the right to present his own witnesses to establish a defense. This right is a fundamental element of due process of law.*

Because the right to compulsory process is applicable in this state proceeding, the question remains whether or not it was violated in the circumstances of this case. The testimony of Charles Fuller was denied to the defense not because the State refused to compel his attendance, but because a state statute made his testimony inadmissible whether he was present in the courtroom or not. The Court was thus called upon to decide whether the Sixth Amendment guarantees a defendant the right under any circumstances to put his witnesses on the stand, as well as the right to compel their attendance in court.

In concluding, the majority noted that it is very difficult to see how the Constitution would not be violated, based on an historical examination of the Sixth Amendment, by arbitrary rules that prevent whole categories of defense witnesses from testifying on *a priori* categories that presume them unworthy of belief.

The rule disqualifying an alleged accomplice from testifying on behalf of the defendant cannot even be defended on the ground that it rationally sets apart a group of persons who are particularly likely to commit perjury. The absurdity of the rule is amply demonstrated by the exceptions that have been made to it. For example, the accused accomplice may be called by the prosecution to testify against the defendant. Common sense would suggest that he often has a greater interest in lying in favor of the prosecution rather than against it, especially if he is still awaiting his own trial or sentencing. To think that criminals will lie to save their fellows but not to obtain favors from the prosecution for themselves is indeed to clothe the criminal class with more nobility than one might expect to find in the public at large. Moreover, under the Texas statutes, the accused accomplice is no longer disqualified if he is acquitted at his own trial. Presumably, he would then be free to testify on behalf of his comrade, secure in the knowledge that he could incriminate himself as freely as he liked in his testimony, inasmuch as he could not again be prosecuted for the same offense. The Texas law leaves him free to testify when he has a great incentive to perjury, and bars his testimony in situations where he has a lesser motive to lie. Condemning the arbitrary exclusion embodied in the Texas statute, Chief Justice Warren stated:

> We hold that the defendant in this case was denied his right to have compulsory process for obtaining witnesses in his favor because the State arbitrarily denied him the right to put on the stand a witness who was physically and mentally capable of testifying to events that he had personally observed, and whose testimony would have been relevant and material to the defense. The Framers of the Constitution did not intend to commit the futile act of giving to a defendant the right to secure the attendance of witnesses whose testimony he had no right to use.

QUESTIONS

1. What is meant by "a defendant is guaranteed the right to compulsory process to secure witnesses in his favor"?

2. What was the arbitrary provision of the Texas statute that the Supreme Court denounced?

3. In your estimation, is it necessary for a defendant to have available to him the compulsory processes of the court to secure witnesses in order to have a fair trial? What alternative is available to a defendant to secure witnesses if he has no compulsory process?

Illinois v. Allen
397 U.S. 337, 90 S.Ct. 1057, 25 L.Ed. 2^D 353 (1970)

SETTING: Allen was convicted of armed robbery in Illinois and sentenced to from ten to thirty years in prison. The evidence showed that he entered a tavern in Illinois and after ordering a drink took, at gunpoint, $200 from the bartender. His conviction was affirmed by the Illinois Supreme Court and the United States Supreme Court denied a petition for certiorari. Subsequently, Allen petitioned for habeas corpus in federal court claiming that because the Illinois trial judge had Allen removed from the trial, he was denied his constitutional right to remain present throughout the trial. The district court found no violation but the Court of Appeals reversed. The Supreme Court reversed the Court of Appeals.

PROCEDURAL PROBLEM: What were the facts surrounding Allen's expulsion? As the record disclosed:

> *After his indictment and during the pretrial stage, the petitioner [Allen] refused court-appointed counsel and indicated to the trial court on several occasions that he wished to conduct his own defense. After considerable argument by the petitioner, the trial judge told him "I'll let you be your own lawyer, but I'll ask Mr. Kelly [court-appointed counsel] [to] sit in and protect the record for you, insofar as possible.*
> *The trial began on September 9, 1957. After the State's Attorney had accepted the first four jurors following their voir dire examination, the petitioner began examining the first juror and continued at great length. Finally, the trial judge interrupted the petitioner, requesting him to confine his questions solely to matters relating to the prospective juror's qualifications. At that point, the petitioner started to argue with the judge in a most abusive and disrespectful manner. At last, and seemingly in desperation, the judge asked appointed counsel to proceed with the examination of the jurors. The petitioner continued to talk, proclaiming that the appointed attorney was not going to act as his lawyer. He terminated his remarks by saying, "When I go out for lunchtime, you're [the judge] going to be a corpse here." At that point he tore the file which his attorney had and threw the papers on the floor. The trial judge thereupon stated to the petitioner, "One more outbreak of that sort and I'll remove you from the courtroom." This warning had no effect on the petitioner. He continued to talk back to the judge, saying, "There's not going to be no trial, either. I'm going to sit here and you're going to talk and you can bring your shackles out and straight jacket and put them on me and tape my mouth, but it will do no good because there's not going to be no trial." After more abusive remarks by the petitioner, the trial judge ordered the trial to proceed in the petitioner's absence. The peti-*

tioner *was removed from the courtroom. The voir dire examination then continued and the jury was selected in the absence of the petitioner.*

After a noon recess and before the jury was brought into the courtroom, the petitioner, appearing before the judge, complained about the fairness of the trial and his appointed attorney. He also said he wanted to be present in the court during his trial. In reply, the judge said that the petitioner would be permitted to remain in the courtroom if he "behaved [himself] and [did] not interfere with the introduction of the case." The jury was brought in and seated. Counsel for the petitioner then moved to exclude the witnesses from the courtroom. The [petitioner] protested this effort on the part of his attorney, saying: "There is going to be no proceeding. I'm going to start talking and I'm going to keep on talking all through the trial. There's not going to be no trial like this. I want my sister and my friends in court to testify for me." The trial judge thereupon ordered the petitioner removed from the courtroom.

THE ISSUE: Can a defendant claim his constitutional right to remain in the courtroom while at the same time he engages in speech and conduct so noisy, disruptive, and disorderly that it is exceedingly difficult or wholly impossible to carry on the trial?

THE ANSWER: No.

DISCUSSION: This case dealt with the type of trial disruption which was brought to the public's attention by the chaotic trial of the "Chicago Seven." As the Court noted, one of the basic rights of a defendant, guaranteed by the confrontation clause of the Sixth Amendment and applicable to the states by virtue of the Fourteenth Amendment, is the right of the accused to be present in the courtroom at every stage of the trial. But what about the disorderly and disruptive defendant who prevents the trial from proceeding? In this case the Court specifically held that the right is lost by a defendant, who after numerous warnings, continues to act so disruptively that the trial cannot proceed with him in the courtroom.

In the reversal of the Court of Appeals holding that even under these circumstances a defendant could not be removed from his own trial, only Justice Douglas was not with the majority. Mr. Justice Black noted that trial judges must be given sufficient discretion to meet each case when dealing with disruptive, contumacious defendants. He added that no specific formula can be developed for every situation, however.

Black then went on to discuss three suggested alternatives that are available when dealing with such a defendant. He concluded that removal is sometimes the best way of handling the situation.

The first alternative is to bind and gag him, thereby keeping him present. There are inherent disadvantages in this technique. It is itself "something of an affront to the very dignity and decorum of judicial proceedings that the judge is seeking to uphold." It also defeats one of the primary purposes of the presence of one at his own trial—the opportunity to assist and communicate with counsel. Also, binding and gagging a defendant may have a significant effect on the jury.

Second, contempt will quite likely have little impact on a defendant who faces severe punishment if convicted. If a defendant is determined to prevent *any* trial, then a court is confronted with an identical dilemma in the contempt trial. An unruly defendant might be imprisoned for civil contempt and the trial discontinued until he behaves himself. This system avoids the undesirable use of gags and shackles, but it must be recognized that a defendant may conceivably, as a matter of strategy, elect a prolonged period of confinement in hopes that adverse witnesses will be unavailable.

The third technique is to remove the defendant from the courtroom and continue the trial in his absence unless he promises to conduct himself in an appropriate manner. There is nothing unconstitutional about this procedure. Justice Black observed:

> *It is not pleasant to hold that the respondent Allen was properly banished from the court for a part of his own trial. But our courts, palladiums of liberty as they are, cannot be treated disrespectfully with impunity. Nor can the accused be permitted by his disruptive conduct indefinitely to avoid being tried on the charges brought against him. It would degrade our country and our judicial system to permit our courts to be bullied, insulted, and humiliated and their orderly progress thwarted and obstructed by defendants brought before them charged with crimes. As guardians of the public welfare, our state and federal judicial systems strive to administer equal justice to the rich and the poor, the good and the bad, the native and foreign born of every race, nationality, and religion. Being manned by humans, the courts are not perfect and are bound to make some errors. But, if our courts are to remain what the Founders intended, the citadels of justice, their proceedings cannot and must not be infected with the sort of scurrilous, abusive language and conduct paraded before the Illinois trial judge in this case.*

In a concurring opinion it was emphasized that to allow the disruptive activities of a defendant like Allen to prevent his trial is to allow him to profit from his own wrong. "The Constitution would protect none of us if it prevented the courts from acting to preserve the very process which the Constitution itself prescribes." In the concurring opinion, Justice Brennan suggested that the court should make every reasonable effort to enable an excluded defendant to communicate with his lawyer and to keep him aware of the progress of the trial.

QUESTIONS

1. There was a fourteen-year lapse between the trial of Allen and this decision. Do you think that the Supreme Court should have dealt with such a state record? (See the opinion of Justice Douglas.)
2. What three techniques were suggested by the majority? Discuss.
3. If a defendant is excluded from the courtroom, our modern technology—i.e., closed-circuit television—might remove some of the severe handicaps of this procedure. Can you think of any other methods?

Estes v. Texas
381 U.S. 532, 85 S.Ct. 1628, 14 L.Ed. 2ᴰ 543 (1965)

SETTING: The evidence in this case indicated that Billie Sol Estes, through false pretenses and fraudulent representations, had induced various farmers to purchase fertilizer tanks and accompanying equipment which in fact did not exist and to sign and deliver to him chattel mortgages on fictitious property.

Estes' case was originally called for trial on September 24, 1962, in Smith County, Texas, after a change of venue from Reeves County, some 500 miles west. Massive pretrial publicity totaling eleven volumes of press clippings, which are on file with the clerk of the court, had given the case national notoriety. All available seats in the courtroom were taken and some thirty persons stood in the aisles. However, at that time a defense motion to prevent telecasting, broadcasting by radio, and news photography and a defense motion for continuance were presented, and after a two-day hearing the former was denied and the latter granted.

The initial hearings were carried live by both radio and television, and news photography was permitted throughout. The videotapes of these hearings clearly illustrate that the picture presented was not one of that judicial serenity and calm to which petitioner was entitled. Indeed, at least twelve cameramen were engaged in the courtroom throughout the hearing taking motion and still pictures and televising the proceedings. Cables and wires were snaked across the courtroom floor, three microphones were on the judge's bench, and others were beamed at the jury box and the counsel table. It was conceded that the activities of the television crews and news photographers led to considerable disruption of the hearings. Moreover, veniremen had been summoned and were present in the courtroom during the entire hearing but were later released after defendant's motion for continuance had been granted. The court also had the names of the witnesses called; some answered but the absence of others led to a continuance of the case until October 22, 1962. Though the September hearings dealt with motions to prohibit television coverage and to postpone the trial, they are unquestionably relevant to the issue before us. All of this two-day affair was highly publicized and could only have impressed those present, and also the community at large, with the notorious character of Estes as well as the proceeding. The trial witnesses present at the hearing, as well as the original jury panel, were undoubtedly made aware of the peculiar public importance of the case by the press and television coverage being provided, and by the fact that they themselves were televised live and their pictures rebroadcast on the evening show.

When the case was called for trial on October 22 the scene had been altered. A booth had been constructed at the back of the courtroom which was painted to blend with the permanent structure of the room. It had an aperture to allow cameras an unrestricted view of the courtroom. All television cameras and newsreel photographers were restricted to the area of the booth when shooting film or telecasting.

Because of continual objection, the rules governing live telecasting, as well as radio and still photos, were changed as the exigencies of the situation seemed to require. As a result, live telecasting was prohibited during a great portion of the actual trial. Only the opening and closing arguments of the State, the return of the jury's verdict, and its receipt by the trial judge were carried live with sound. Although the order allowed videotapes of the entire proceeding without sound, the cameras operated only intermittently, recording various portions of the trial for broadcast on regularly scheduled newscasts later in the day and evening. At the request of the defendant, the trial judge prohibited coverage of any kind, still or television, of the defense counsel during their summations to the jury.

Because of the varying restrictions placed on sound and live telecasting, the telecasts of the trial were confined largely to film clips shown on the stations' regularly scheduled news programs. The news commentators used the film of a particular part of the day's trial activities as a backdrop for their reports. Their commentary included excerpts from testimony and the usual reportorial remarks. On one occasion, the videotapes of the September hearings were rebroadcast in place of the "late movie."

PROCEDURAL PROBLEM: See *Discussion.*

THE ISSUE: Was Estes deprived of his rights under the Fourteenth Amendment to due process by the televising and broadcasting of his trial?

THE ANSWER: Yes.

DISCUSSION: Only four Jusices were willing to rule that televising the Estes trial was *per se* a denial of his constitutional right to a fair trial. Four Justices were unable to see any infringement of a federal right even though they deplored the practice. The fifth Justice, Harlan, made the majority decision that televising the trial violated the Fourtccnth Amendment, but he limited the ban on televising to trials that are "notorious."

Justice Clark's majority opinion stressed that no actual prejudice needs to be shown. The mere probability of unfairness is adequate. According to Clark, the use of television cannot be said to contribute materially to the objective of ascertaining the truth. It interjects an irrelevant factor into the court proceedings in which one might find numerous situations which might cause actual unfairness. Several were cited by Clark. First was the potential impact of television on the jurors. The television camera is likely to focus only on notorious trials because of the obvious commercial value. The publicity might have a conscious or unconscious effect on the juror which in all likelihood cannot be evaluated. However, experience indicates that it is not only possible but highly probable that the effect will have a direct bearing on the juror's vote as to guilt or innocence. In states that do not allow sequestration of jurors, they may see rebroadcasts of the trial on their home television sets, allowing emphasis on various parts of evidence. This may subconsciously influence the jurors more than the court testimony. In addition, new trials may be jeopardized because potential jurors often will have seen and heard the original trial when it was telecast.

Second, the quality of the testimony in criminal trials will often be impaired. The impact on a witness that he is being televised is incalculable. He may be demoralized, overly cocky, frightened, or embarrassed. It would be difficult, if not impossible, to determine the impact on a witness, but as Clark noted, experience shows that these factors do exist. Noting that there is some danger to the quality of witness testimony caused by newspaper coverage, Clark said that "the circumstances and extraneous influences intruding upon the solemn decorum of court procedure in the televised trial are far more serious than in cases involving only newspaper coverage."

The third consideration is the additional responsibilities that the presence of television places on the trial judge. He already has the difficult task of insuring that the defendant receives a fair trial. Still, when television comes into the courtroom, he must supervise it. In the case of elected judges, the political implications of the coverage may create a psychological dilemma; the possibility of a fair trial for the accused may take a back seat.

Fourth, there is the possibility of a serious impact of television on the defendant. Its presence is a form of mental harassment resembling a police lineup or the third degree. Close-ups of his expressions and features may transgress his personal sensibilities, his dignity, and his ability to concentrate on the proceedings. A defendant, in short, is entitled to his day in court—not a stadium or a national arena. Trial by television is foreign to our system of justice.

In regard to these observations Justice Clark stated:

> *The State would dispose of all these observations with the simple statement that they are for psychologists because they are purely hypothetical. But we cannot afford the luxury of saying that, because these factors are difficult of ascertainment in particular cases, they must be ignored. Nor are they "purely hypothetical." They are no more hypothetical than were the considerations deemed controlling in* Tumey, Murchison, Rideau *and* Turner. *They are real enough to have convinced the Judicial Conference of the United States, this court and the Congress that television should be barred in federal trials by the Federal Rules of Criminal Procedure; in addition they have persuaded all but two of our States to prohibit television in the courtroom. They are effects that may, and in some combination almost certainly will, exist in any case in which television is injected into the trial process.*

Will television ever be permitted in the courtroom? It may in the future, but as conditions now stand televising a trial will violate the Fourteenth Amendment.

> *It is said that the ever-advancing techniques of public communication and the adjustment of the public to its presence may bring about a change in the effect of telecasting upon the fairness of criminal trials. But we are not dealing here with future developments in the field of electronics. Our judgment cannot be rested on the hypothesis of tomorrow but must take the facts as they are presented today.*

The dissenters in this case thought that present-day television in the courtroom is extremely unwise, inviting constitutional risks and detractions from the dignity of the proceedings; however, they could find no constitutional bar to the practice. The ultimate issue is whether or not the defendant is given a fair trial.

QUESTIONS

1. What is the specific holding of this case?
2. Can you think of additional factors that weigh against having trials televised? What factors are in support of televising criminal trials?
3. Do you think that the position of the four dissenting Justices makes more sense than the unprovable, subjective dangers upon which Clark based the majority opinion?

Sheppard v. Maxwell
384 U.S. 333, 86 S.Ct. 1507, 16 L.Ed. 2ᴰ 600 (1966)

SETTING: The defendant's pregnant wife, Marilyn Sheppard, was bludgeoned to death in the upstairs bedroom of the Sheppard home in Bay Village, a suburb of Cleveland. The following story was pieced together. Marilyn and defendant were alone in their home. After dinner the defendant dozed off on the sofa and Marilyn went to bed. Hearing his wife cry out, the defendant ran upstairs and saw a "form" standing over Marilyn. The "form" and Sheppard struggled and he was struck by the "form." Regaining consciousness, Sheppard felt his wife's pulse and "felt she was gone." Sheppard heard noise downstairs and then saw a "form" running toward a nearby lake, so he chased the unidentified person. They grappled and Sheppard lost consciousness again. He subsequently came to, checked his wife again, and called a neighbor.

From the outset, suspicion focused on Sheppard and an investigation was launched by the police. Even after the police took the Sheppard home under protective custody, newspaper reporters and photographers were in and out of the premises taking pictures.

PROCEDURAL PROBLEM: The killing occurred on July 4, 1954. On July 7, the assistant county attorney, later the chief prosecutor, sharply criticized in the newspapers the Sheppard family's refusal to permit his immediate questioning. From then on, headline stories repeatedly stressed Sheppard's lack of cooperation with police officials. Over the next couple of weeks, the newspapers reported in detail stories placing the defendant in a totally unfavorable light.

On July 20, newspaper editorials against Sheppard were launched. The coroner called an inquest on July 21. It was held in a gymnasium and was covered by the newspapers, television, and radio. During the entire period, from the date of the tragedy until his indictment in August, the newspapers emphasized evidence that tended to incriminate Sheppard and point out discrepancies in his statements to authorities.

"Evidence" was continually cited by the newspapers which was not produced at the trial. The newspapers delved into Sheppard's personal life stressing his extramarital affairs as a motive for the crime. The trial testimony never showed he had any illicit relationships but one, to which he admitted during the coroner's inquest.

On July 28 and 30, headlines urged the authorities to arrest Sheppard. One editorial described him in the following language:

> *Now proved under oath to be a liar, still free to go about his business, shielded by his family, protected by a smart lawyer who has made monkeys of the police and authorities, carrying a gun part of the time, left free to do whatever he pleases. . . .*

On the evening of July 30, Sheppard was arrested. Until the trial date, two weeks before the November general election, the publicity grew in intensity. Five volumes filled with clippings similar to the quote above were collected from the three Cleveland newspapers until Sheppard was convicted in December 1954. This did not include television or radio coverage which the Supreme Court assumed was just as voluminous.

The trial judge, Judge Blythin, was a candidate to succeed himself in the November election. The selection of juror began on October 18. The news media totally covered the jury selection; prospective jurors were photographed going to and coming from the courthouse. One telecast carried a staged interview with the judge as he entered the courthouse. A rule of court prohibited picture-taking in the courtroom during actual sessions, but no restraints were put on photographers during recesses, which were taken once each morning and afternoon and over the lunch period.

The daily record of court proceedings was made available to the newspapers and the testimony of each witness was printed verbatim in local editions, along with attorneys' objections and judicial rulings. The jurors were constantly exposed to the news media. Every juror, save one, testified on *voir dire* to reading about the case in the Cleveland newspapers.

The intense publicity continued during the trial itself. There were stories that the defense counsel made an attempt at jury tampering by sampling persons on the street to ascertain their opinion of guilt or innocence in an effort to show that a change of venue was necessary. A staged, live radio debate by various newspaper reporters asserted that Sheppard had conceded his guilt by hiring a top criminal lawyer. A two-inch headline asked, "Who Will Speak for Marilyn?" The jury viewed the crime scene and hundreds of reporters, cameramen, and onlookers were there. A nationally known columnist called Sheppard a perjurer and compared the testimony of a police officer that contradicted a Sheppard statement to the confrontation between Alger Hiss and Whittaker Chambers. The defendant was compared in the newspapers to a Dr. Jekyll and Mr. Hyde, allegedly by a relative of Marilyn. No such testimony was offered at the trial. Walter Winchell broadcast a story that Sheppard had had a child by a mistress. The judge overruled a motion for a mistrial by the defense on this point after two jurors admitted to having heard the broadcast. Both indicated it would not influence their decision. Sheppard testified that the police mistreated him after his arrest. The police captain, although he was not at the trial, made headlines by his statement that Sheppard was a "bare-faced liar." The captain never testified. Finally, it was discovered that after the case was submitted to the jury and it was sequestered, members made numerous phone calls, although no records were kept of them.

THE ISSUE: Because of the factual situation and the pervasiveness of the obviously biased news media coverage, did Sheppard receive a fair trial consistent with the due process clause of the Fourteenth Amendment?

THE ANSWER: No.

DISCUSSION: The field of trial publicity is practically new. In reversing the conviction of Sheppard, the Court alluded to the publicity associated with a Roman carnival. The Court made it perfectly clear that trial judges have a duty not to allow publicity to get out of hand as it did in this case. Strong measures must be taken, given the pervasiveness and sophistication of modern communications, to prevent prejudicial publicity from confusing the minds of jurors. The balance must never be weighted against the accused.

According to the majority opinion, written by Justice Clark, there is nothing that proscribes the press from reporting events that take place in the courtroom, but where there is a reasonable chance that prejudicial news reporting will prevent a fair trial, the judge should continue the case until it abates or transfer the case to another area where the permeation of the publicity is not so great.

According to Clark, the way to cure prejudicial publicity is to take measures that will prevent it in its inception.

First, the courtroom and courthouse premises must be controlled to prevent a carnival atmosphere. There should be adequate rules governing courtroom usage, including limiting the number of reporters. The conduct of the media members must be closely regulated.

Second, the witnesses must be insulated from prejudicial news coverage. They should be protected from reading and hearing the testimony of other witnesses.

Third, the court should make some effort to control the release of leads, information, and gossip by police officers, witnesses, and counsel for both sides.

The Court concluded:

> *From the cases coming here we note that unfair and prejudicial news comment on pending trials has become increasingly prevalent. Due process requires that the accused receive a trial by an impartial jury free from outside influences. Given the pervasiveness of modern communications and the difficulty of effacing prejudicial publicity from the minds of the jurors, the trials courts must take strong measures to ensure that the balance is never weighed against the accused. And appellate tribunals have the duty to make an independent evaluation of the circumstances. Of course, there is nothing that proscribes the press from reporting events that transpire in the courtroom. But where there is a reasonable likelihood that prejudicial news prior to trial will prevent a fair trial, the judge should continue the case until the threat abates, or transfer it to another county not so permeated with publicity. In addition, sequestration of the jury was something the judge should have raised* sua sponte *with counsel. If publicity during the proceedings threatens the fairness of the trial, a new trial should be ordered. But we must remember that reversals are but palliatives; the cure lies in those remedial measures that will prevent the prejudice at its inception. The courts must take such steps by rule and regulation that will protect their processes from prejudicial outside interferences. Neither prosecutors, counsel for defense, the accused, witnesses, court staff, nor enforcement officers coming under the jurisdiction of the court should be permitted to frustrate its function. Collaboration between counsel and the press as to information affecting the fairness of a criminal trial is not only subject to regulation, but is highly censurable and worthy of disciplinary measures.*
>
> *Since the state trial judge did not fulfill his duty to protect Sheppard from the inherently prejudicial publicity which saturated the community and to control disruptive influences in the courtroom, we must reverse the denial of the habeas petition.*

QUESTIONS

1. What three steps did the Court suggest that a trial judge take to help assure that the defendant is not prejudiced by trial publicity?
2. What sanctions may a judge take to enforce his rules governing conduct of the news media?
3. Compare the factual situation and holding of this case with *Estes* v. *Texas*. Which case presents the most flagrant misuse of the power of the press? Why? Discuss.

Chambers v. *Mississippi*
410 U.S. 284, 93 S.Ct. 1038, 35 L.Ed. 2ᴰ 297(1973)

SETTING: Chambers was charged, tried, and convicted of the murder of a police officer in a jury trial in Mississippi. At the trial it developed that the defendant had a defense in that one McDonald admitted to three friends—Turner, Williams, and Carter—that he, not Chambers, had killed the policeman. Secondly, he attempted somewhat successfully to establish that he did not shoot the officer. However, proof of Chambers' defense that McDonald had killed the officer was thwarted by a strict application of two separate rules of evidence in Mississippi. Chambers' writ of certiorari to the United States Supreme Court challenging whether his trial was conducted in accord with principles of due process under the Fourteenth Amendment was granted. The conviction was reversed.

PROCEDURAL PROBLEM: The two evidentiary rules involved were the Mississippi common-law rule that a party may not impeach his own witness, and the hearsay rule. Chambers filed a pretrial motion requesting the court to order McDonald to appear. Chambers also sought at that time to be allowed to call McDonald as an adverse witness if the State did not call him. Attached to the motion were copies of McDonald's sworn confession and the transcript of his preliminary hearing, at which he repudiated the confession. The trial court granted the motion requiring McDonald to appear, but reserved a ruling on the adverse witness motion. At the trial McDonald was not called by the State; he was called by Chambers, who had McDonald's prior confession entered into evidence and read to the jury. The State on cross-examination elicited the fact that McDonald had rejected his prior confession. He also testified on cross-examination that he did not shoot the officer and that he had only confessed because of the promise of one Reverend Stokes that he would not go to jail and would receive a sizable part of a tort recovery from the town.

Upon completion of the State's cross-examination, Chambers renewed his motion to examine McDonald as an adverse witness. The trial court denied the motion, stating: "He may be hostile, but he is not adverse in the sense of the word, so your request is overruled." The State Supreme Court upheld this ruling, stating that McDonald was not an adverse witness because "[n]owhere did he point the finger at Chambers."

Because he was defeated in his attempt to directly challenge McDonald's repudiation, Chambers sought to introduce the testimony of Turner, Williams, and Carter, to whom McDonald had admitted that he had killed the officer. In each instance the State objected to the admission of the testimony because it was hearsay. The trial court sustained all three objections.

In sum, Chambers was in a serious predicament. As a consequence of the combination of Mississippi adverse witness and hearsay rules he was unable to either cross-examine McDonald or to present witnesses on his own behalf who could have discredited McDonald. Even with other evidence that Chambers presented that chipped away at McDonald's story, his defense was far less persuasive than it might have been had he been given the opportunity to subject McDonald's statements to cross-examination.

THE ISSUE: Was Chambers denied due process by not having a fair opportunity to defend against the State's accusations, to confront and cross-examine witnesses, and to call witnesses in his own behalf?

THE ANSWER: Yes.

DISCUSSION: Chambers was denied the opportunity to subject McDonald's damning repudiation and alibi to the test of cross-examination. The right of cross-examination is much more than a desirable rule of trial procedure; it is implicit in the constitutional right of confrontation. It is "an essential and fundamental requirement for the kind of fair trial which is this country's constitutional goal."

In this case, denial of Chambers' request to cross-examine McDonald was based on the Mississippi common-law rule that a witness cannot impeach his own witness. In discussing the validity of the rule, Justice Powell for the majority stated:

> *Whatever validity the "voucher" rule may have once enjoyed, and apart from whatever usefulness it retains today in the civil trial process, it bears little present relationship to the realities of the criminal process. . . . Not only was he precluded from cross-examining McDonald but as the state conceded in its oral argument, he was also restricted in the scope of his direct examination by the rule's corollary requirement that the party calling the witness is bound by anything he might say. He was, therefore, effectively prevented from exploring the circumstances of McDonald's three prior oral confessions and from challenging the renunciation of the written confession.*

Powell rejected the argument that McDonald's testimony was not "adverse" to, or "against" Chambers. The testimony tended to exculpate Chambers. "It can hardly be disputed that McDonald's testimony was in fact seriously adverse to Chambers. . . . The availability of the right to confront and to cross-examine those who give damaging testimony against an accused has never been held to depend on whether the witness was initially put on the stand by the accused or the state. We reject the notion that a right of such substance in the criminal process may be governed by that technicality or by any narrow and unrealistic definition of the word 'against.' The 'voucher' rule . . . plainly interfered with Chambers' right to defend against the State's charges."

Turning to the hearsay question, the Court noted that there are several exceptions to the hearsay rule—"Among the most prevalent of these exceptions is the one applicable to declarations against interest—an exception founded on the assumption that a person is unlikely to fabricate a statement against his own interest at the time it is made." The exception in Mississippi only applied to declarations against pecuniary interest not against the declarant's penal interest. However, the Court indicated it need not decide this case on such a technical point.

Justice Powell looked to see whether the statements of the three witnesses were made under circumstances that provided considerable assurance of their reliability. First, McDonald's statements were spontaneous and made to close acquaintances shortly after the killing. Second, each confession was corroborated in material aspects. Third, each confession by McDonald, the penal interest rationale aside, was in a real sense self-incriminatory and against his interest. Fourth, if there was any question regarding the truthfulness of the extrajudicial statements, because McDonald was in court and under oath he could have been cross-examined by the State, and his demeanor observed by the jury. Justice Powell noted that because of the persuasive assurances of trustworthiness where constitutional rights directly affecting the ascertainment of guilt are implicated, the hearsay rule cannot be mechanically applied to defeat the ends of justice.

In concluding, Powell noted:

> We conclude that the exclusion of this critical evidence, coupled with the State's refusal to permit Chambers to cross-examine McDonald denied him a trial in accord with traditional and fundamental standards of due process. . . . [W]e hold simply that under the facts and circumstances of this case, the rulings of the trial court deprived Chambers of a fair trial.

QUESTIONS

1. Define the hearsay and "adverse" witness rules.
2. Did the Court say that the hearsay rule is unconstitutional? Discuss.
3. Distinguish this case from *Pointer* v. *Texas, supra.*

Moore v. Illinois
408 U.S. 786, 92 S.Ct. 2562, 33 L.Ed. 2ᴰ 706 (1972)

SETTING: Moore was convicted in Illinois in 1964 of first degree murder. The facts in the case are important:

> A. *The victim, Zitek, operated a bar-restaurant in the village of Lansing, southeast of Chicago. Patricia Hill was a waitress there. Donald O'Brien, Charles A. Mayer, and Henley Powell were customers.*
> *Another bar called the Ponderosa Tap was located in Dolton, also southeast of Chicago. It was owned by Robert Fair. William Joyce was the bartender. One of Fair's customers was Virgle Sanders.*
> *A third bar known as Wanda and Del's was in Chicago. Delbert Jones was the operator. William Leon Thompson was a patron.*
> *The Westmoreland Country Club was in Wilmette, about 50 miles north of Lansing. The manager there was Herbert Anderson.*
> B. *On the evening of April 25 Zitek was tending bar at his place in Lansing. Shortly before 10 P.M. two men, one with a moustache, entered and ordered beer. Zitek admonished the pair several times for using profane language. They continued in their profanity and, shortly, Zitek ejected them. About an hour later a man carrying a shotgun entered. He laid the weapon on the bar and shot and killed Zitek. The gunman ran out, pursued by patrons, and escaped in an automobile.*
> C. *At the trial waitress Hill positively identified Moore as one of the two men ejected from the bar and as the one who returned and killed Zitek. She testified that she had a clear and close view from her working area at the bar and that she observed Zitek's ejection of the two men and the shotgun killing an hour later.*

D. *A second in-court identification of Moore as the man who had killed Zitek was made by the customer Powell. Powell, who at the time was playing pinochle with others, testified that he observed Moore enter the bar with a shotgun and shoot Zitek; that after the shooting he pursued Moore; and that outside the bar Moore stopped momentarily, turned, and shouted, "Don't come any further or I'll shoot you, too."*

E. *Sanders testified that on April 27, two days after the murder, he was in the Ponderosa Tap and that a customer there, whom Sanders identified as "Slick," remarked to Sanders that it was "open season on bartenders" and that he had shot one in Lansing. At the trial Sanders identified Moore as the man who was in the Ponderosa Tap on April 27. Moore was with another man who had a moustache. The two asked for a ride to Harvey, Illinois. The owner, Fair, agreed to give them the ride.*

F. *Fair testified that Moore was one of the two men who requested and were given the ride; that during the journey one of them was referred to as "Barbee"; and that one said something like, "Well, if we hadn't had that trouble with the bartender in Lansing, we'd have been all right."*

G. *The Ponderosa bartender, Joyce, testified that Sanders and Fair were in the tavern on April 27; that Moore was there at the same time; and that he arranged with Fair for Fair to give Moore and his companion a ride.*

It is thus apparent that there were positive in-court identifications of Moore as the slayer by the waitress Hill and by the customer Powell, and that there were in-court identifications of Moore as having been present at the bar in Dolton two days later by Sanders, by Fair, and by Joyce.

H. *Six months after the slaying, in the early morning hours of October 31, 1962, a Chicago police officer was shot at from a 1957 Ford automobile. Two men fled the scene. The police "staked out" the car, and several hours later Moore and a moustached man, later identified as Jerry Barbee, were arrested when they approached and entered the vehicle. The automobile proved to be owned by Barbee. A fully loaded sawed-off 16-gauge shotgun was in the car. The shotgun was introduced in evidence at Moore's trial. The State conceded that the gun so introduced was not the murder weapon, and that the State's ballistics technician, if called, would testify that the waddings taken from Zitek's body came, in his opinion, from a 12-gauge shotgun shell.*

I. *The defense called manager Anderson of the Westmoreland Country Club as a witness. He testified that Moore had been hired as a waiter there on April 24 (the day before the murder); that the club records indicated that there was a special party at the club on the evening of April 25; and that Moore was paid for working until sometime between 10 P.M. and midnight. The club's bartender testified to the same effect. Each of these witnesses nevertheless admitted that he could not remember seeing Moore at the club that night, but said that he would have known if he had been absent for any substantial period of time. The club records also indicated that Moore worked at the club the afternoon of April 27, when, according to the testimony of Sanders, Fair, and Joyce, Moore was at the Ponderosa Tap in Dolton.*

J. *O'Brien, the customer at Zitek's, testified for the defense that he observed Zitek eject two men the evening of the 25th, and that Moore was not one of them. Although he was in the restaurant at the time of the homicide, he did not see the person who shot Zitek. A police officer testified that in his opinion O'Brien was drunk at the time.*

PROCEDURAL PROBLEM: Prior to the trial the defense moved for discovery of all written statements taken by the police from any witness, to which the State agreed. At the post-conviction hearing, Moore argued that he was denied a fair trial because six items of evidence, unknown to him at the trial, were not produced but, in fact, were suppressed by the State. The first five items were statements which the State failed to produce under the original motion. The fifth was a diagram of the crime scene.

The Illinois court held that the State had not suppressed material evidence favorable to Moore. The record showed that the State presented its entire file to the defendant and no further request for disclosure was made. Moore then claimed that a specific request is not indispensable for disclosure of exonerating evidence and that the defendant could not be expected to make a request where he did not know specific evidence was in existence.

THE ISSUE: Did the suppression of the evidence amount to a denial of the defendant's discovery in the state so as to constitute a denial of due process?

THE ANSWER: No.

DISCUSSION: In *Brady v. Maryland*, 373 U.S. 83 (1963), the defendant and an accomplice were sentenced to death after having been found guilty by a jury of first degree murder. The defendant in his pretrial motion for discovery requested the prosecution to allow him to examine Brady's co-defendant's extrajudicial statement. Some of these were produced, but one statement in which the co-defendant admitted the actual killing was withheld so that Brady did not know of its existence until after his conviction. In a post-conviction proceeding, the highest court in Maryland held that the suppression of the evidence was a denial of due process "where the evidence is material either to guilt or to punishment, irrespective of the good faith or bad faith of the prosecution." The United States Supreme Court affirmed.

The *Brady* opinion established three important criteria to be ascertained:

1. Whether or not there was a suppression of evidence after a request by the defendant.
2. The favorable character of the evidence for the defense.
3. The materiality of the evidence.

Justice Blackmun, in the majority opinion, stated, "We know no constitutional requirement that the prosecution make a complete and detailed accounting to the defense of all police investigatory work on a case." The Court indicated that after reviewing the five statements the defendant claimed should have been discovered, none served to impeach in any way the positive identification of Moore as the killer. In light of all of the evidence presented at the trial, the statements were not material to the issue of guilt. In regard to the diagram, the Court was not persuaded that it contradicted the testimony of a witness and that the State had knowingly permitted false testimony of one witness to remain uncorrected. The defendant was not denied due process by the State's failure to disclose police investigative work, not contained in the prosecutor's files, that merely turned up statements either tending to confuse the defendant with another man or indicating that the defendant was not at the crime scene. The statements were, in summary, not material, nor did they impeach the defendant's positive identification.

The dissenters were primarily of the opinion that the statements were not only material but "absolutely critical" to the defendant's defense.

Both the majority and dissenting opinions reversed the death penalty based on *Furman* v. *Georgia*, 408 U.S. 238 (1972), *supra*.

QUESTIONS

1. What is meant by discovery? Is the procedure available to both the prosecution and defense? Discuss.
2. Discuss the criteria set forth in *Brady* v. *Maryland* to ascertain whether a defendant is denied due process by the State's suppression of evidence.
3. Why would it not be a good policy for the Court to establish a rule that all police investigative reports may be discovered?

Griffin v. *California*
380 U.S. 609, 85 S.Ct. 1229, 14 L.Ed. 2ᴰ 106 (1965)

SETTING: Griffin was convicted of first degree murder in a jury trial in California. He did not testify during the trial on the issue of his guilt. He did, however, testify at a separate trial on the issue of his penalty provided by California procedure. In the instructions to the jury, the trial judge stated that a defendant has a constitutional right not to testify. The judge also told the jury:

> *As to any evidence or facts against him which the defendant can reasonably be expected to deny or explain because of facts within his knowledge, if he does not testify or if, though he does testify, he fails to deny or explain such evidence, the jury may take that failure into consideration as tending to indicate the truth of such evidence and as indicating that among the inferences that may reasonably be drawn therefrom those unfavorable to the defendant are the more probable.*

In expanding on his instruction, the judge added that no such inference could be drawn respecting matters about which Griffin had no knowledge. He also stated that the defendant's failure to explain or deny the evidence of which he had knowledge did not create a presumption of guilt nor by itself warrant an inference of guilt or relieve the state of its burden of proof.

PROCEDURAL PROBLEM: The defendant had been seen with the deceased on the evening of her death. Evidence placed him in the alley where her body was found. The defendant did not testify and the prosecution made a strong closing argument regarding this failure:

> *The defendant certainly knows whether Essie Mae had this beat-up appearance at the time he left her apartment and went down the alley with her.*
>
> *What kind of a man is it that would want to have sex with a woman that was beat up if she was beat up at the time he left?*
>
> *He would know that. He would know how she got down the alley. He would know how the blood got on the bottom of the concrete steps. He would know how long he was with her in that box. He would know how her wig got off. He would know whether he beat her or mistreated her. He would know whether he walked away from that place cool as a cucumber when he saw Mr. Villasenor because he was conscious of his own guilt and wanted to get away from that damaged or injured woman.*
>
> *These things he has not seen fit to take the stand and deny or explain.*
>
> *And in the whole world, if anybody would know, this defendant would know.*
>
> *Essie Mae is dead, she can't tell you her side of the story. The defendant won't.*

THE ISSUE: Does comment on the failure to testify violate the self-incrimination clause of the Fifth Amendment made applicable in the states by the due process clause of the Fourteenth Amendment?

THE ANSWER: Yes.

DISCUSSION: Mr. Justice Douglas for the majority, in answer to the above issue, stated:

> *We think it does. It is in substance a rule of evidence that allows the state the privilege of tendering to the jury for its consideration the failure of the accused to testify. No formal offer of proof is made as in other situations; but the prosecutor's comment and the court's acquiescence are the equivalent of an offer of evidence and its acceptance.*

The Court, citing *Wilson* v. *United States,* 149 U.S. 60 (1893), ventured some reasons why a person might not want to be a witness other than fear of self-incrimination.

> *It is not everyone who can safely venture on the witness stand, though entirely innocent of the charge against him. Excessive timidity, nervousness when facing others and attempting to explain transactions of a suspicious character, and offenses charged against him, will often confuse and embarrass him to such a degree as to increase rather than remove prejudices against him. It is not everyone, however honest, who would therefore willingly be placed on the witness stand.*

The Court emphasized that comment on the refusal to testify is a remnant of the inquisitorial system of criminal justice. It is a penalty imposed by courts for exercising a constitutional privilege. The argument was also advanced that the jury will draw unfavorable inferences when a defendant does not testify anyway. To this the Court stated that it is one thing for a jury to infer without the help of the court, but for the jury to infer when the court solemnizes the silence of the accused into evidence against him is quite another.

Were this a federal case, reversible error would have been committed by the prosecutor's comment. Applying *Malloy* v. *Hogan,* 378 U.S. 1 (1964), the Court concluded "that Fifth Amendment, in its direct application to the federal government and its bearing on the States by reason of the Fourteenth Amendment, forbids either comment by the prosecution on the accused's silence or instructions by the court that such silence is evidence of guilt."

Does an accused have the right to require that the jury must be instructed that his silence must be disregarded? See *Bruno* v. *United States,* 308 U.S. 297 (1939). The Fifth Amendment gives a person a right to remain silent when another makes statements in his presence that tend to incriminate him. To use such silence as an implied admission of guilt would violate his protection. *Ivey* v. *United States,* 344 F. 2ᴰ 770 (5th Cir., 1965).

QUESTIONS

1. Do you think that the reasons given by the Court for a witness not taking the stand are realistic? Aren't all witnesses subject to the points mentioned?
2. If the "harmless error" rule were followed regarding the violation of a constitutional right, would an automatic reversal result in this case?
3. In some states the judge is permitted to comment on the weight to be given to evidence. Does the *Griffin* rule prohibit comments by the judge? What is the procedure in your jurisdiction?

Witherspoon v. *Illinois*
391 U.S. 510, 88 S.Ct. 1770, 20 L.Ed. 2ᴰ 776 (1968)

SETTING: The defendant was brought to trial in 1960 in Cook County, Illinois, upon a charge of murder. The jury found him guilty and fixed his penalty at death. At the time of his trial an Illinois statute provided:

> *In trials for murder it shall be a cause for challenge of any juror who shall, on being examined, state that he has conscientious scruples against capital punishment, or that he is opposed to the same.*

Through this provision the state of Illinois armed the prosecution with unlimited challenges for cause in order to exclude those jurors who, in the words of the State's highest court, "might hesitate to return a verdict inflicting [death]."

PROCEDURAL PROBLEM: At Witherspoon's trial, the prosecution eliminated nearly half the venire of prospective jurors by challenging, under the authority of this statute, any venireman who expressed qualms about capital punishment. From those who remained were chosen the jurors who ultimately found Witherspoon guilty and sentenced him to death. The Supreme Court of Illinois denied post-conviction relief and the United States Supreme Court granted certiorari to decide whether the Constitution permits a state to execute a man pursuant to the verdict of a jury so composed.

In the present case the tone was set when the trial judge said early in the *voir dire*, "Let's get these conscientious objectors out of the way, without wasting any time on them." In rapid succession, forty-seven veniremen were successfully challenged for cause on the basis of their attitudes toward the death penalty. Only five of the forty-seven explicitly stated that under no circumstances would they vote to impose capital punishment. Six said that they did not "believe in the death penalty" and were excused without any attempt to determine whether they could nonetheless return a verdict of death. Thirty-six veniremen, including four of the six who indicated that they did not believe in capital punishment, acknowledged having "conscientious or religious scruples against the infliction of the death penalty" or against its infliction "in a proper case" and were excluded without any effort to find out whether or not their scruples would invariably compel them to vote against capital punishment.

THE ISSUE: Is it a denial of due process of law for the State to exclude automatically all potential jurors who indicate that they are opposed to capital punishment and all who have conscious scruples against it but who are not asked whether they could never vote to impose the penalty or that they would refuse to ever consider its imposition in the case before them?

THE ANSWER: Yes.

DISCUSSION: At the outset, Justice Stewart, writing for the majority, emphasized that the issue was a narrow one which did not involve the State's assertion of a right to exclude from a jury in a capital case those who say that they could *never* vote to impose the death penalty or that they would *refuse* even to consider its imposition in the case before them.

There were two problems which the jury was to determine: (1) guilt or innocence and (2) imposition of imprisonment or death. In dismissing the defendant's argument that a jury selected in the manner it was in this case should not be permitted to bring in a guilty verdict, the majority stated that "The data adduced by the petitioner, however, are too tentative and fragmentary to establish that jurors not opposed to the death penalty tend to favor the prosecution in the determination of guilt. We simply cannot conclude . . . that the exclusion of jurors opposed to capital punishment results in an unrepresentative jury on the issue of guilt or substantially increases the risk of conviction." In light of the presently available information the Court felt it could not announce a constitutional rule that every jury selected in the way Illinois juries were selected required a reversal.

Addressing itself to the punishment aspect, the Court was much more critical of the jury selection procedure involved. The Court noted:

> [A] prospective juror cannot be expected to say in advance of trial whether he would in fact vote for the extreme penalty in the case before him. The most that can be demanded of a venireman in this regard is that he be willing to consider all of the penalties provided by state law, and that he not be irrevocably committed, before the trial has begun, to vote against the penalty of death regardless of the facts and circumstances that might emerge in the course of the proceedings. If the voir dire testimony in a given case indicates that veniremen were excluded on any broader basis than this, the death sentence cannot be carried out even if applicable statutory or case law in the relevant jurisdiction would appear to support only a narrower ground of exclusion.
>
> We repeat, however, that nothing we say today bears upon the power of a State to execute a defendant sentenced to death by a jury from which the only veniremen who were in fact excluded for cause were those who made unmistakably clear (1) that they would automatically vote against the imposition of capital punishment without regard to any evidence that might be developed at the trial of the case before them, or (2) that their attitude toward the death penalty would prevent them from making an impartial decision as to the defendant's guilt. Nor does the decision in this case affect the validity of any sentence other than one of death. Nor, finally, does today's holding render invalid the conviction, as opposed to the sentence, in this or any other case.

It is entirely possible, Stewart pointed out, that a person who opposes the death penalty, no less than one who favors it, can subordinate his personal views to abide by his oath as a juror and to obey the law of the state. In this regard the majority stated:

> But a jury from which all such men have been excluded cannot perform the task demanded of it. Guided by neither rule nor standard, "free to select or reject as it [sees] fit," a jury that must choose between life imprisonment and capital punishment can do little more—and must do nothing less—than express the conscience of the community on the ultimate question of life or death. Yet, in a nation less than half of whose people believe in the death penalty, a jury composed exclusively of such people cannot speak for the community. Culled of all who harbor doubts about the wisdom of capital punishment—of all who would be reluctant to pronounce the extreme penalty—such a jury can speak only for a distinct and dwindling minority.
>
> If the State has excluded only those prospective jurors who stated in advance of trial that they would not even consider returning a verdict of death, it could argue that the resulting jury was simply "neutral" with respect to penalty. But when it swept from the jury all who expressed conscientious or religious scruples against capital punishment and all who opposed it in principle, the State crossed the line of neutrality. In its quest for a jury capable of imposing the death penalty, the State produced a jury uncommonly willing to condemn a man to die.

QUESTIONS

1. What suggestion did the Supreme Court make in the last paragraph above?
2. What is the specific holding in this case?
3. In your jurisdiction, what procedure is used in determining whether or not a death penalty is to be imposed? Is it similar to that in Illinois? What effect, if any, does *Furman* v. *Georgia* have on this decision?

Chapter 15

Cruel
and Unusual Punishments

Constitution of the United States, Eighth Amendment

. . . [N]or cruel and unusual punishment inflicted.

Constitution of New York, Article 1, Section 5

. . . [N]or shall cruel and unusual punishments be inflicted. . . .

Constitution of Georgia of 1945, Section 2-109

. . . [N]or cruel and unusual punishment . . . inflicted. . . .

Constitution of New Jersey, Article 1, Paragraph 12

. . . [A]nd cruel and unusual punishments shall not be inflicted.

Robinson v. *California*
370 U.S. 660, 82 S.Ct. 1417, 8 L.Ed. 2^D 758 (1962)

SETTING: A California statute made it a criminal offense for a person to "be addicted to the use of narcotics."

The defendant, Robinson, was convicted after a jury trial in the Municipal Court of Los Angeles. The evidence against him was given by two Los Angeles police officers. Both testified that each had had occasion to examine the defendant's arms one evening on a street in Los Angeles some four months before the trial. The officers testified that at that time they had observed scar tissue and discoloration on the inside of the defendant's right arm, and what appeared to be numerous needle marks and a scab on Robinson's left arm. The officers also testified that Robinson ·under questioning had admitted to the occasional use of narcotics.

PROCEDURAL PROBLEM: The trial judge instructed the jury that the California statute made it a misdemeanor for a person "either to use narcotics, or to be addicted to the use of narcotics. . . . That portion of the statute referring to the 'use' of narcotics is based upon the 'act' of using. That portion of the statute referring to 'addicted to the use' of narcotics is based upon a condition or status. They are not identical. . . . To be addicted to the use of narcotics is said to be a status or condition and not an act. It is a continuing offense and differs from most other offenses in the fact that [it] is chronic rather than acute; that it continues after it is complete and subjects the offender to arrest at any time before he reforms. The existence of such a chronic condition may be ascertained from a single examination, if the characteristic reactions of that condition be found present."

The defendant was convicted and his appeal affirmed by the state courts. The state appellate court, however, had some doubt as to the constitutionality of "the crime of being a narcotic addict." The United States Supreme Court accepted the defendant's appeal specifically pertaining to the constitutionality of the state statute punishing the status of being an addict.

THE ISSUE: Is it a cruel and unusual punishment in violation of the Eighth and Fourteenth Amendments for a state to enact a statute punishing a sickness (addiction)?

THE ANSWER: Yes.

DISCUSSION: The power of the State to regulate the drug traffic was not an issue in this case. But the statute in this case was not one that punishes a person for the use of drugs, for their purchase, sale, or possession, or for antisocial or deviant behavior resulting from their administration. Rather the statute proscribes the status of narcotic addiction as a criminal offense for which the offender may be prosecuted at any time before he reforms. The California statute provided that a person is continually guilty of the offense whether or not he ever used or possessed drugs in the state and whether or not he was ever guilty of antisocial behavior there.

As Justice Stewart stated for the majority,

> It is unlikely that any State at this moment in history would attempt to make it a criminal offense for a person to be mentally ill, or a leper, or to be afflicted with a venereal disease. A State might determine that the general health and welfare require that the victims of these and other human afflictions be dealt with by compulsory treatment, involving quarantine, confinement, or sequestration. But, in the light of contemporary human knowledge, a law which made a criminal offense of such a disease would doubtless be universally thought to be an infliction of cruel and unusual punishment in violation of the Eighth and Fourteenth Amendments.
>
> We cannot but consider the statute before us as of the same category. In this Court counsel for the State recognized that narcotic addiction is an illness. Indeed, it is apparently an illness which may be contracted innocently or involuntarily. We hold that a state law which imprisons a person thus afflicted as a criminal, even though he has never touched any narcotic drug within the state or been guilty of any irregular behavior there, inflicts a cruel and unusual punishment in violation of the Fourteenth Amendment. To be sure, imprisonment for ninety days is not, in the abstract, a punishment which is either cruel or unusual. But the question cannot be considered in the abstract. Even one day in prison would be a cruel and unusual punishment for the "crime" of having a common cold.

QUESTIONS

1. What is meant that the California statute punished the "status" of being an addict?
2. What do you think the purposes of this statute were when the California legislature enacted it?
3. Is the interest of the state in prohibiting illegal drug traffic comparable to the California statute prohibiting drug addiction?

United States v. Jackson
390 U.S. 570, 88 S.Ct. 1209, 20 L.Ed. 2ᴰ 138 (1968)

SETTING: On October 10, 1966, a federal grand jury in Connecticut returned an indictment charging in count one that the defendant and two others in this case had transported from Connecticut to New Jersey a person who had been kidnapped and held for ransom and who had been harmed when liberated. The district court dismissed this count of the indictment, holding the Federal Kidnapping Act unconstitutional because it makes "the risk of death" the price for asserting the right to jury trial, and thereby "impairs . . . free exercise" of that constitutional right. The government appealed directly to the Supreme Court, and it noted probable jurisdiction. The Supreme Court reversed on the ground that the death penalty was severable.

PROCEDURAL PROBLEM: The federal kidnapping law, commonly known as the Lindbergh Act, stated in 18 U.S.C. 1201 (a):

> *Whoever knowingly transports in interstate . . . commerce, any person who has been unlawfully . . . kidnapped . . . and held for ransom . . . or otherwise . . . shall be punished (1) by death if the kidnapped person has not been liberated unharmed, and if the verdict of the jury shall so recommend, or (2) by imprisonment for any term of years or for life, if the death penalty is not imposed.*

This statute thus creates an offense punishable by death "if the verdict of the jury shall so recommend." The statute sets forth no procedure for imposing the death penalty upon a defendant who waives the right to jury trial or upon one who pleads guilty.

THE ISSUE: Was the defendant deprived of his rights under the Fifth and Sixth Amendments because the statute diluted his right not to plead guilty and his right to demand a jury trial?

THE ANSWER: Yes.

DISCUSSION: This case was not an Eighth Amendment "cruel and unusual punishment" case but it is extremely significant because it dealt a severe blow to the death penalty laws in many states that had statutes similar to the federal provisions above. The frontal assault on the death penalty as a cruel and unusual punishment gained momentum with this case.

According to the majority opinion written by Justice Stewart, a statute is patently unconstitutional if its provision has no other purpose or effect than to discourage the assertion of a constitutional right by penalizing those who opt to assert it.

The two arguments made by the government urging upholding the death penalty provision were basically that a defendant who elects to be tried by a jury cannot be put to death even if the jury so recommends—unless the trial judge agrees that capital punishment should be imposed. Moreover, the argument goes, a defendant cannot avoid the risk of death by attempting to plead guilty or waive jury trial. For even if the trial judge accepts a guilty plea or approves a jury waiver, the judge remains free, in the government's view of the statute, to convene a special jury for the limited purpose of deciding whether to recommend the death penalty. The government thus contended that, whether or not the defendant chooses to submit to a jury the question of his guilt, the death penalty may be imposed if and only if both judge and jury concur in its imposition. On this understanding of the statute, the government concluded that the death penalty provision of the Lindbergh Act did not operate to penalize the defendant who chooses to contest his guilt before a jury.

The Court noted that not once during the thirty-four-year history of the act has a jury's recommendation of death been discarded by a trial judge. In discussing convening a special jury, the majority noted:

> The Government would have us give the statute this strangely bifurcated meaning without the slightest indication that Congress contemplated any such scheme. Not a word in the legislative history so much as hints that a conviction on a plea of guilty or a conviction by a court sitting without a jury might be followed by a separate sentencing proceeding before a penalty jury. If the power to impanel such a jury had been recognized elsewhere in the federal system when Congress enacted the Federal Kidnapping Act, perhaps Congress' total silence on the subject could be viewed as a tacit incorporation of this sentencing practice into the new law. But the background against which Congress legislated was barren of any precedent for the sort of sentencing procedure we are told Congress impliedly authorized.

In concluding that the "chilling" effect of the statute rendered it unconstitutional, Stewart stated:

> Under the Federal Kidnapping Act, therefore, the defendant who abandons the right to contest his guilt before a jury is assured that he cannot be executed; the defendant ingenuous enough to seek a jury acquittal stands forewarned that, if the jury finds him guilty and does not wish to spare his life, he will die. Our problem is to decide whether the Constitution permits the establishment of such a death penalty, applicable only to those defendants who assert the right to contest their guilt before a jury. The inevitable effect of any such provision, is of course, to discourage assertion of the Fifth Amendment right not to plead guilty and to deter exercise of the Sixth Amendment right to demand a jury trial. If the provision had no other purpose or effect than to chill the assertion of constitutional rights by penalizing those who choose to exercise them, then it would be patently unconstitutional. But, as the Government notes, limiting the death penalty to cases where the jury recommends its imposi-

tion does have another objective: It avoids the more drastic alternative of mandatory capital punishment in every case. In this sense, the selective death penalty procedure established by the Federal Kidnapping Act may be viewed as ameliorating the severity of the more extreme punishment that Congress might have wished to provide.

However, the unconstitutionality of the death penalty provision did not mandate the invalidation of the Lindbergh Act in its entirety. As Justice Stewart noted, "It is clear that the clause authorizing capital punishment is severable from the remainder of the kidnapping statute and that the unconstitutionality of that clause does not require the defeat of the law as a whole." The clause is functionally independent. Its elimination in no way altered the substantive reach of the statute and left completely unchanged is basic operation. Thus "the infirmity of the death penalty clause does not require the total frustration of Congress' basic purpose—that of making interstate kidnapping a federal crime. By holding the death penalty clause of the Federal Kidnapping Act unenforceable we leave the statute an operative whole, free of any constitutional objection."

QUESTIONS

1. What is the importance of the *Jackson* case as it pertains to the development of the trend to declare the death penalty unconstitutional?
2. What is meant by the doctrine of severability as it pertains to statutory interpretation?
3. Does your jurisdiction have a "little Lindbergh Law" covering kidnapping? Are its provisions similar to the federal statute? Discuss.

Powell v. *Texas*
392 U.S. 514, 88 S.Ct. 2145, 20 L.Ed. 2ᴰ 1254 (1968)

SETTING: In December 1966, Powell was arrested, charged, and found guilty of being found in a state of intoxication in a public place in violation of Texas law. The defendant claimed that he was afflicted with the disease of chronic alcoholism and that appearing drunk in public was not of his own volition. Therefore, he should not be criminally punished for his conduct because it would be cruel and unusual to do so. The Texas trial court ruled as a matter of law that chronic alcoholism was not a defense to the charge.

Expert testimony established that Powell was a chronic alcoholic and outlined the disease concept of alcoholism. It was also claimed that alcohol is physically addicting and psychologically habituating. The expert concluded that a chronic alcoholic "loses his self-control over his drinking" and "is not able to control his behavior . . . because he has an uncontrollable compulsion to drink." Powell's expert witness also added that in his opinion jailing Powell without medical attention would operate neither to rehabilitate him nor to lessen his desire for alcohol.

Powell testified as to his many arrests for intoxication, his uncontrollable drinking, the fact that he did not become violent when drunk, and admitted that he did not even remember his arrest on the current charge.

The State did not present any expert or psychiatric evidence of its own but was content in its argument that Powell had no defense to the intoxication charge because he was "legally sane and knew the difference between right and wrong."

PROCEDURAL PROBLEM: The defense submitted and the trial court entered into evidence the following "findings of fact":

> 1. That chronic alcoholism is a disease which destroys the afflicted person's will power to resist the constant, excessive consumption of alcohol.
> 2. That a chronic alcoholic does not appear in public by his own volition but under a compulsion symptomatic of the disease of chronic alcoholism.
> 3. That Leroy Powell, defendant herein, is a chronic alcoholic who is afflicted with the disease of chronic alcoholism.

The United States Supreme Court in its opinion rejected these as "findings of fact" and stated that they are the premises of a syllogism which were obviously designed to bring this case within the scope of *Robinson* v. *California*, 370 U.S. 669 (1962). The court, in short, rejected the "syllogism."

THE ISSUE: Does the cruel and unusual punishment clause of the Eighth Amendment, as interpreted in the *Robinson* v. *California* case, apply to imprisonment for chronic alcoholism?

THE ANSWER: No.

DISCUSSION: In this case the Eighth Amendment was reached in the case of the common offense of public drunkenness. The Court, by a bare 5–4 majority, held that chronic alcoholics can be sent to jail for being drunk in public. The majority, speaking through Justice Marshall, declared that the cruel and unusual punishment clause as interpreted by *Robinson* v. *California* did not apply:

> *On its face the present case does not fall within that holding since [defendant] was convicted, not for being a chronic alcoholic, but for being in public while drunk on a particular occasion. The State of Texas thus has not sought to punish a mere status, as California did in* Robinson; *nor has it attempted to regulate [defendant's] behavior in the privacy of his own home. Rather, it has imposed upon [defendant] a criminal sanction for public behavior which may create substantial health and safety hazards, both for [defendant] and for members of the general public, and which offends the moral and esthetic sensibilities of a large segment of the community. This seems a far cry from convicting one for being an addict, being a chronic alcoholic, being "mentally ill, or a leper. . . ."*

In this same vein, Marshall commented that "If Leroy Powell cannot be convicted of public intoxication, it is difficult to see how a State can convict an individual for murder, if that individual, while exhibiting normal behavior in all other respects, suffers from a 'compulsion' to kill, which is an 'exceeding strong influence,' but 'not completely overpowering.'"

The majority opinion concluded that on the state of medical knowledge, "chronic" alcoholics in general and Leroy Powell in particular suffer from such an irresistable compulsion to drink and to get drunk in public that they are utterly unable to control their performance of either or both of these acts and thus cannot be deterred at all from public intoxication.

A second opinion by Justice White, the fifth justice in the majority, held that the Eighth Amendment would have prohibited Powell's incarceration if there was sufficient evidence to establish that he found it impossible to avoid public places when he was intoxicated. In short, the five-man majority is very tenuous. There apparently would be a 5–4 majority for applying the cruel and unusual punishment clause of the Eighth Amendment to bar punishment of a "skid row bum," who because of the compulsion to drink could not avoid drinking in public.

Two justices (Black and Harlan) in concurring opinions maintained that the public drunk is a local problem and not national. As a consequence, the local community should be permitted to handle their particularly local problems under their local rules.

The four dissenters contended that *Robinson* v. *California* is applicable and bars the conviction of a chronic alcoholic for public drunkenness. Public drunkenness is more than a mere status crime, the minority stated,

> *But the essential constitutional defect here is the same as in* Robin-

son, *where in both cases the particular defendant was accused of being in a condition which he had no capacity to change or avoid.*

QUESTIONS

1. Distinguish the holdings in *Robinson* v. *California* and *Powell* v. *Texas.* Are they factually distinguishable?
2. What kind of evidence would have satisfied Justice White?
3. Why isn't "public drunkenness" a crime of status similar to drug addiction, in the view of the majority in *Powell?*

Furman v. *Georgia*
408 U.S. 238, 92 S.Ct. 2726, 33 L.Ed. 2ᴰ 346 (1972)

SETTING: Furman was convicted of murder and rape and given the death penalty. In the state trial of Furman, the determination of whether the penalty should be death or a lighter punishment was left to the discretion of the jury. The conviction was affirmed by all the Georgia courts. The United States Supreme Court granted Furman's petition for certiorari and reversed and remanded the case for further hearings on the penalty.

PROCEDURAL PROBLEMS: See *Discussion.*

THE ISSUE: Is the death penalty as imposed in *Furman*—i.e., in the complete discretion of the jury—unconstitutional because it violates the Eighth Amendment's prohibition of cruel and unusual punishments?

THE ANSWER: Yes.

DISCUSSION: This opinion is extremely complex, with no unifying reason supporting the Court's 5–4 decision that the imposition of the death penalty in its present form is unconstitutional. Each Justice wrote his own opinion, and the conclusions added up to the opinion that the cruel and unusual punishments clause of the Eighth Amendment makes the death penalty, when imposed within the discretion of the jury, not inherently intolerable but applied "so wantonly and freakishly" that it serves no valid purpose and is therefore cruel and unusual.

Only two Justices, Brennan and Marshall, would have held the death penalty unconstitutional *per se.* Brennan said that capital punishment is inherently cruel and unusual by the application of four principles:

1. That a punishment must not be so severe as degrading to the dignity of human beings.
2. It must not be applied arbitrarily.
3. It must not be unacceptable to contemporary society.
4. The punishment must not be excessive and must serve a penal purpose more effectively than a less severe punishment.

In discussing point one, Brennan noted that it is based on several factors; pain is but one. Status punishments are degrading simply because they are punishments. In a society that strongly affirms the sanctity of life, the death penalty is unique. The punishment is continuously and progressively restricted. The only explanation for this uniqueness, according to Brennan, is its extreme severity, which renders it "unusual in its pain, in its finality, and in its enormity"; the killing by its very nature is a denial of a person's dignity and is thus human degradation.

Regarding point two, the death penalty fails because of its arbitrary application. It is no longer an ordinary punishment for any crime. It is inflicted in a miniscule number of cases in which it could be applied. This leads to the conclusion that it is arbitrary. "Indeed it smacks of little more than a lottery system," according to Brennan.

In regard to the third point, because of its severity and arbitrary application, it is likely that it is no longer accepted by contemporary society. This is borne out by various indications: crimes punishable by death have declined; death inflictions are not public spectacles; and discretionary imposition and outright ban in nine states are further indications that our society "seriously questions" its appropriateness.

Finally, the lack of demonstrated success in deterring capital crimes is a strong argument that the death penalty serves no penal purpose more effectively than does a less severe penalty. There is no evidence whatever that society's need for retribution must be satisfied by death rather than imprisonment. Brennan concluded:

> *Furthermore, it is certainly doubtful that the infliction of death by the State does in fact strengthen the community's moral code; if the deliberate extinguishment of human life has any effect at all, it more likely tends to lower our respect for life and brutalize our values.*

Justice Marshall emphasized that punishments permissible at one time may not be permissible today. This is the situation with capital punishment. Marshall stated that a punishment may be cruel and un-usual for any one of four reasons: "First, there are certain punishments which inherently involve so much physical pain and suffering that civilized people cannot tolerate them—e.g., use of the rack, the thumb screw, or other modes of torture." Second are the "unusual" punish-ments—ones "previously unknown as penalties for a given offense." Third, a penalty may be cruel and unusual because it serves no legislative purpose. Fourth, if popular sentiment abhors a punishment even though it is not excessive and does serve a legislative purpose, it may still be invalid. Marshall noted that though no prior cases strike down a penalty on this ground, "the very notion of changing values requires that we recognize its existence."

Marshall also concluded that none of the six purposes conceivably served by capital punishment—retribution, deterrence, foreclosure of recidivism, encouraging guilty pleas and confessions, eugenics, and state expenditure reductions—justify its retention. He stated that capital punishment "violates the Eighth Amendment because it is morally unacceptable to the people of the United States at this time in our history."

In Justice Douglas' opinion the Eighth Amendment, as read in light of the "English proscription against selective and irregular use of penal-ties, suggests that it is 'cruel and unusual' to apply the death penalty—or any other penalty—selectively to minorities. . . ." Douglas stated that the great amount of evidence indicates in fact that the death penalty is applied to minority groups:

> *Thus these discretionary statutes are unconstitutional in their opera-tion. They are pregnant with discrimination and discrimination is an in-gredient not compatible with the idea of equal protection of the laws that is implicit in the ban on "cruel and unusual" punishment.*

Justice Stewart, the fourth Justice for the majority, rested his opin-ion on the basis that the Eighth and Fourteenth Amendments are violated because the death penalty is incurred in a "wantonly and freakishly im-posed" manner. If the death penalty were mandatory for certain federal and state statutes, then the issue would involve whether or not a legis-lature could constitutionally set death as the penalty for certain crimes on the ground that society's interest in deterrence and retribution for such crimes wholly outweighs rehabilitation considerations. Stewart noted, "On that score . . . I cannot agree that retribution is a consti-tutionally impermissible ingredient in the imposition of punishment." Continuing, Stewart noted the rarity of the death penalty and the capricious manner in which it is imposed. There has been no legislative determination that the death penalty necessarily deters the crime on which it is imposed. He concluded, "These death sentences are cruel and unusual in the same way that being struck by lightning is cruel and unusual."

Justice White, the fifth majority member, was also of the opinion that the infrequency of the imposition of the death penalty has little if any deterrent value:

> It is also my judgment that this point has been reached with respect to capital punishment as it is presently administered under the statutes involved in these cases. Concededly, it is difficult to prove as a general proposition that capital punishment, however administered, more effectively serves the ends of the criminal law than does imprisonment. But however that may be, I cannot avoid the conclusion that as the statutes now before us are now administered, the penalty is so infrequently imposed that the threat of execution is too attenuated to be of substantial service to criminal justice.
> . . . I add only that past and present legislative judgment with respect to the death penalty loses much of its force when viewed in the light of the recurring practice of delegating sentencing authority to the jury, and the fact that a jury, in its own discretion and without violating its trust or any statutory policy, may refuse to impose the death penalty no matter what the circumstances of the crime. Legislative "policy" is thus necessarily defined not by what is legislatively authorized but by what the juries and judges do in exercising the discretion so regularly conferred upon them.

Chief Justice Burger in dissent offered some suggestions regarding legislative changes that would have to be made to allow the death penalty when imposed to insure compliance with the *Furman* decision: "The legislatures are free to eliminate capital punishment for specific crimes or to carve out limited exceptions to a general abolition of the penalty, without adherence to the conceptual strictures of the Eighth Amendment." The legislature can reassess the deterrent influence of capital punishment both as to the general idea and as affecting the commission of specific crimes. They can abolish it either totally or on a selective basis. If new evidence indicates they have acted unwisely, they can reinstate it to the extent it is warranted.

According to Burger:

> Real change could clearly be brought about if legislatures provided mandatory death sentences in such a way as to deny juries the opportunity to bring in a verdict on a lesser charge; under such a system, the death sentence could only be avoided by a verdict of acquittal. If this is the only alternative that the legislatures can safely pursue under today's ruling, I would have preferred that the Court opt for total abolition.

QUESTIONS

1. According to Justice Brennan, what tests are used to determine whether or not a punishment is cruel and unusual?
2. What was Justice White condemning in the arbitrary imposition of the death penalty? Do you think he is correct?
3. What steps can a state take to reimpose the death penalty to be in conformity with the *Furman* v. *Georgia* decision?

Chapter 16

Double Jeopardy

Constitution of the United States, Fifth Amendment

. . . [N]or shall any person be subject for the same offense to be twice put in jeopardy of life or limb; . . .

Constitution of Arizona, Article 2, Section 10

No person shall be . . . twice put in jeopardy for the same offense.

Constitution of Florida, Article 1, Section 9

No person shall be . . . twice put in jeopardy for the same offense.

Constitution of Mississippi, Article 3, Section 22

No person's life or liberty shall be twice placed in jeopardy for the same offense; but there must be an actual acquittal or conviction on the merits to bar another prosecution.

Constitution of Virginia, Section 8

He shall not be . . . put twice in jeopardy for the same offense.

Palko v. *Connecticut*
302 U.S. 319, 58 S.Ct. 149, 82 L.Ed. 288 (1937)

SETTING: Palko was indicted for first degree murder. The jury found him guilty of murder in the second degree and he was sentenced to life imprisonment. Under Connecticut procedure, the State appealed, based on alleged errors of law, and the Supreme Court of Errors of Connecticut reversed the judgment and ordered a new trial. In accordance with the Supreme Court of Errors mandate, the defendant was brought to trial again.

PROCEDURAL PROBLEM: Before the jury was impaneled and also at later stages, the defense objected that the effect of the new trial was to place Palko twice in jeopardy for the same offense and therefore violate the Fourteenth Amendment. The objections were overruled and the trial proceeded. In this trial the defendant was convicted of first degree murder and sentenced to death. The Supreme Court of Errors affirmed and the defendant appealed ultimately to the United States Supreme Court, which affirmed Palko's second conviction.

THE ISSUE: Does the Fourteenth Amendment due process clause incorporate the Fifth Amendment's guarantee that no person will be "subject for the same offense to be twice put in jeopardy of life and limb"?

THE ANSWER: No.

DISCUSSION: Palko argued that the Fourteenth Amendment made applicable in the states the Fifth Amendment requirement that no person shall twice be put in jeopardy of life and limb for the same offense. Justice Cardozo stated outright that "The execution of the sentence will not deprive [defendant] of his life without the process of law assured to him by the Fourteenth Amendment to the Federal Constitution." After reviewing the concept of due process and its fundamental nature in the criminal processes, Cardozo asked whether the defendant was subject to a hardship so acute and shocking that our polity will not endure it. "Does it violate those fundamental principles of justice which lie at the base of all our civil and political rights?" The answer was no. The Fourteenth Amendment did not incorporate the protection against double jeopardy in the Fifth Amendment.

Suppose the State's appeal had not been on alleged errors in the trial but that the jury had reached an unpopular verdict. Would double jeopardy apply? The majority members did not answer the question, but indicated they were dealing here only with the statute before them.

The Court also commented on the appeal by the State, noting that it was not attempting to wear the accused out by a multiplicity of cases with an accumulation of trials. "It asks no more than this, that the case against him shall go on until there shall be a trial free from the corrosion of substantial legal error. This is not cruelty at all, no event vexation in any immoderate degree." In summary, if the case was infected with errors adverse to the accused, he could appeal. The State has opened this avenue to the prosecution and as long as it is not abused, it is not a denial of due process.

QUESTIONS

1. Do you agree that jeopardy should not attach in this kind of case?
2. Construct an opinion holding that the Fifth Amendment prohibition against double jeopardy has been incorporated into the due process clause of the Fourteenth Amendment.
3. How did this Court define a fundamental right? Do you think double jeopardy protection fits in the definition?

Benton v. Maryland
395 U.S. 784, 89 S.Ct. 2056, 23 L.Ed. 2ᴰ 707 (1969)

SETTING: Benton was tried in the Maryland court on the charges of burglary and larceny. The jury found him innocent of larceny but convicted him of burglary. Because both the grand and petit juries in his case had been invalidly selected, Benton was given the option of reindictment and retrial on the same facts or being sentenced under the burglary conviction. He elected reindictment and retrial. At the second tiral, he was again charged with both offenses and convicted of both.

PROCEDURAL PROBLEM: Having been recharged with both larceny and burglary, Benton moved to have the larceny count dismissed on the ground that to try him again for larceny would violate the constitutional provision against double jeopardy. This motion was denied, and he was convicted of both charges. The Maryland courts upheld his convictions and the United States Supreme Court granted certiorari for the consideration of whether or not the defendant was denied his constitutional rights. The Supreme Court reversed the state courts.

THE ISSUE: Does the Fourteenth Amendment's due process clause incorporate the double jeopardy protection of the Fifth Amendment so as to make it applicable in the states?

THE ANSWER: Yes.

DISCUSSION: This case was the last of the "Warren Court" decisions that incorporated a provision of the Bill of Rights into the Fourteenth Amendment. It was also the last case to overrule an earlier landmark decision. By a 7–2 majority, it was decided that the double jeopardy prohibition of the "Fifth Amendment represents a fundamental ideal in our constitutional heritage and that it should apply to the States through the Fourteenth Amendment." According to Justice Marshall for the majority, "*Palko* represented an approach to basic constitutional rights which this Court's recent decisions have rejected."

Palko rested its denial of the Fifth Amendment right on the ground that only a denial of "fundamental fairness" taken in the overall circumstances of the conviction would cause a state violation of the Bill of Rights provision to vitiate a conviction. Marshall cited the steady cutting away of this idea and stated, "Once it is decided that a particular Bill of Rights guarantee is fundamental to the American scheme of justice, the same constitutional standards apply against both the State and Federal Government. *Palko's* roots had thus been cut away years ago. We today only recognize the inevitable." Marshall emphasized that the double jeopardy prohibition, like the right to trial by jury, is clearly "fundamental to the American scheme of justice." The validity of Benton's larceny conviction must be judged not by the watered-down standard enunciated in *Palko* but under this Court's interpretation of the Fifth Amendment's double jeopardy provision.

Maryland made a second argument that because the original indictment was void, Benton was never in jeopardy. The Court indicated that the State's claim was indeed strange because Benton could quietly have served out his burglary conviction under the "void" indictment had he not appealed the conviction. Marshall noted that "Only by accepting the option of a new trial could the indictment be set aside; at worst the indictment would seem only voidable at a defendant's option, not absolutely void."

When Does Jeopardy Attach? A defendant has been placed in jeopardy for the offense of which he is charged in the accusatory pleading as soon as a trial commences before a competent court. For jeopardy purposes, a trial begins in a jury trial when the jury is impaneled and sworn; in a court trial when the first witness is sworn; in a trial in which the cause is submitted to the court on the transcript of the evidence taken at a preliminary hearing, jeopardy probably commences when the court starts considering the evidence.

Termination of Criminal Proceedings which Bar Retrial. Retrial is barred if the trial is terminated by acquittal or conviction or:

1. If a mistrial is declared by a judge without legal cause, and the jury is discharged without the defendant's consent.
2. If a dismissal is granted without legal cause after jeopardy attaches.
3. If a joint defendant is discharged to be a witness for the state.
4. If there is a dismissal of a misdemeanor charge.

Proceedings during Trial which Do Not Bar Retrial. During the trial itself, certain conditions have come to be well accepted as not constituting jeopardy to bar retrial:

1. If a mistrial is granted at the request of the defendant, he may be tried again for the same offense.
2. If the jury is discharged through legal necessity because the jury cannot agree (hung jury) after due deliberation, the defendant may be retried.
3. If the jury is discharged because of the illness or absence of a juror, the defendant may be retried.
4. If a defendant is absent from a felony trial so as to cause the judge to declare a mistrial, he may be retried.
5. Dismissal for variance between the pleading and proof is not jeopardy.
6. Some extreme or overwhelming physical necessity will not bar retrial.
7. Some untoward accident that renders a verdict impossible does not bar retrial.

QUESTIONS

1. Compare the *Palko* and *Benton* holdings. In your opinion, why were they different? Was the *Benton* incorporation philosophy necessary to reach a decision in the case or could the philosophy that he was denied a fair trial by the Maryland procedure have been used, thereby not requiring *Palko* to be overruled?
2. What conditions during trial do not cause jeopardy to attach? Give an example of each.
3. List the times when jeopardy attaches in a criminal trial.

North Carolina v. Pearce
395 U.S. 711, 89 S.Ct. 2072, 23 L.Ed. 2ᴰ 656 (1969)

SETTING: Two cases were consolidated in this opinion. In the North Carolina case the defendant, Pearce, was convicted and sentenced to twelve to fifteen years' imprisonment. His conviction was reversed on appeal and upon a new trial he was reconvicted and sentenced to eight years which, when added to the time he had already spent in jail, amounted to a longer total sentence than that originally imposed. In habeas corpus proceedings in the federal courts it was decided that imposition of a longer sentence upon retrial was unconstitutional and void. Because the state court did not resentence Pearce, he was ordered released by the United States District Court and this was affirmed by the Court of Appeals. The United States Supreme Court granted certiorari.

In the second case, the defendant, Rice, was sentenced to ten years imprisonment on four separate charges of second degree burglary. The judgments were set aside two and a half years later because of failure to accord the defendant a right to counsel. He was retried and sentenced to prison for a total of twenty-five years. The federal district court stated that there was nothing constitutionally impermissible in imposing a harsher sentence upon retrial if there are recorded legal justifications for the increased sentence. The district court judge, however, stated that it was evident that the Alabama courts were only punishing the defendant for exercising his post-conviction rights of review. The Court of Appeals affirmed and the United States Supreme Court granted certiorari.

PROCEDURAL PROBLEM: Two separate but related issues are involved. One concerns the constitutional limitations upon the imposition of a more severe punishment after conviction of the same offense on retrial. The other is the more limited question of whether, in computing a new sentence, the federal Constitution requires that credit be given for that part of the sentence already served.

THE ISSUES: (1) Does the double jeopardy clause prevent the imposition of a harsher penalty upon retrial? (2) Is it a violation of due process for a harsher sentence to be imposed upon conviction on retrial merely because the defendant had the original conviction reversed?

THE ANSWERS: (1) No. (2) Yes.

DISCUSSION: The United States Supreme Court had some difficulty with the question of whether or not imposition of a harsher punishment after retrial was constitutionally permissible. Unable to announce a majority opinion on this question, the Court took a middle ground. Two Justices, Marshall and Douglas, favored outright prohibition. Their votes, combined with the four votes of other sitting Justices, provided a majority which stated that although neither the double jeopardy nor the equal protection clauses place an absolute restriction upon the length of a sentence imposed upon reconviction,

> In order to assure the absence of such a motivation, we have concluded that whenever a judge imposes a more severe sentence upon a defendant after a new trial, the reasons for his doing so must affirmatively appear. Those reasons must be based upon objective information concerning identifiable conduct on the part of the defendant occurring after the time of the original sentencing proceeding. And the factual data upon which the increased sentence is based must be made part of the record. . . .

In regard to credit for the time already served, Justice Stewart noted, "We hold that the constitutional guarantee against multiple punishments for the same offense absolutely requires that the punishment already extracted must be fully 'credited' in imposing sentence upon a new conviction for the same offense."

QUESTIONS

1. What standards will be applied to ascertain whether or not there is "objective information concerning identifiable conduct" that can be

used to justify a more severe sentence than previously? Give several examples.

2. Does *Pearce* have any application to those states in which the jury determines the punishment? Several courts permit jury imposition of a harsher subsequent punishment. See *Spidle* v. *Missouri,* 446 S.W. 2ᴰ 973 (1969) and "Sentence Increases on Retrial," 39 *Cincinnati Law Review* 427 (1970).

3. In your own words, what is the specific holding of *Pearce?* How does this holding correspond to the sentencing practices followed in your jurisdiction?

Ashe v. *Swenson*
397 U.S. 436, 90 S.Ct. 1189, 25 L.Ed. 2ᴰ 469 (1970)

SETTING: While six men were playing poker, three or four armed men broke into the room and robbed them. Subsequently, four persons were arrested and each was charged with seven different offenses—six for the armed robbery of each player in the room and one for the theft of an automobile belonging to one of the players which was used in the getaway. Ashe was one of those accused. He was first put on trial for the robbery of Knight, one of the players. The evidence that there had been a robbery, and that Knight was one of those robbed, was overwhelming. The evidence that Ashe was one of the defendants was weak, with a great deal of contradiction between the poker players regarding the number of robbers, let alone the identity of them.

Ashe was acquitted "due to insufficient evidence."

PROCEDURAL PROBLEM: Six weeks later, Ashe was put on trial again for the robbery of Roberts, another of the poker players. Ashe filed a motion to dismiss based on his previous acquittal. This was overruled. Between the two trials the prosecutor had bolstered his evidence of identification of Ashe and as a result the verdict was guilty. The Missouri Supreme Court rejected Ashe's plea of former jeopardy and affirmed the conviction. A collateral attack on the conviction in the state courts four years later was unsuccessful. As a result, Ashe petitioned for a writ of habeas corpus in the federal courts, which upheld the state court decision primarily on the basis of *Hoag* v. *New Jersey,* 356 U.S. 464 (1958). In the facts of that case, which were virtually identical to this case, the defendant was tried for the armed robbery of three men who were held up in a tavern. The identification evidence of Hoag was weak and he was acquitted. He was then brought to trial for the robbery of a fourth victim. This time he was convicted. When he appealed to the United States Supreme Court, the Court viewed the issue as one of due process only—whether or not the New Jersey procedure was fundamentally unfair. The Court held it was not, but did not reach the issue of whether collateral estoppel—the principle that bars relitigation between the same parties of issues actually determined at a previous trial—is a due process requirement in a state criminal trial.

THE ISSUE: Is the doctrine of collateral estoppel embodied in the double jeopardy clause?

THE ANSWER: Yes.

DISCUSSION: In this case the Court concentrated upon the doctrine of collateral estoppel which was not considered in *Hoag*. For the majority, Justice Stewart wrote that at the defendant's first trial, the single rationally conceivable issue in dispute was whether or not Ashe was one of the robbers. The jury by its verdict found that he was not. "The federal rule, therefore would make a second prosecution for robbery of [another] wholly impermissible." Because *Benton* v. *Maryland*, 395 U.S. 784 (1969), held that the Fifth Amendment's double jeopardy clause was incorporated into the due process clause of the Fourteenth Amendment, the question was not whether collateral estoppel is a requirement of due process, but whether it is, in fact, part of the Fifth Amendment's guarantee against double jeopardy. In holding that it was, the Court ruled that the defendant could not be required to "run the gauntlet" again.

Although the Court held that collateral estoppel is embodied in the former jeopardy clause, it emphasized that the two are not the same. To support a plea of double jeopardy, no more is needed than to show that the same offense was charged then and now. But collateral estoppel is claimed when the offenses are not the same. Therefore when the result of the former trial is a general verdict of not guilty, the evidence, pleadings, instructions to the jury, and all other relevant matters must be considered to determine whether a "rational jury could have grounded its verdict upon an issue other than that which the defendant seeks to foreclose from consideration."

As Stewart concluded:

> The question is not whether Missouri could validly charge the [defendant] with six separate offenses for the robbery of the six poker players. It is not whether he could have received a total of six punishments if he had been convicted in a single trial of robbing the six victims. It is simply

whether after a jury determined by its verdict that the [defendant] was not one of the robbers, the State could constitutionally hold him before a jury to litigate that issue again.

Most, if not all, states favor imposing concurrent rather than consecutive sentences for several offenses that may have been committed in a single transaction. Jeopardy does not bar successive prosecutions, but most states by statute require the prosecutor to join all the offenses into one accusatory pleading and one trial. Multiple punishment is also avoided where several crimes are perpetrated in one act by a common statutory provision in the state which bars double punishments. For example, the *California Penal Code,* section 654 provides:

> *An act or omission which is made punishable in different ways by different provisions of this code may be punished under either of such provisions, but in no case can it be punished under more than one; an acquittal or conviction and sentence under either one bars a prosecution for the same act or omission under any other.*

This type of multiple-punishment prohibition helps in carrying out the double jeopardy provisions. For example, this statement is distinct from the double jeopardy problem. Thus, where an unlawful abortion results in the death of the woman, the offender cannot be punished for both the abortion and the murder, but the conviction of abortion does not bar a conviction and punishment for murder if no punishment is imposed on the abortion conviction. See *People* v. *Tideman,* 21 Calif. Rptr. 207, 370 P. 2ᴰ 1007 (1962).

QUESTIONS

1. What is meant by the principle of "collateral estoppel?"
2. Does your jurisdiction have a statute prohibiting multiple punishment? Discuss its provisions.
3. What was the specific holding in this case?

United States v. *Jorn*
400 U.S. 470, 91 S.Ct. 547, 27 L.Ed. 2ᴰ 543 (1971)

SETTING: Jorn was originally charged with twenty-five counts of wilfully assisting in the preparation of fraudulent income tax returns. He

was brought to trial before Judge Ritter on August 27, 1968. After the
jury was chosen and sworn, fourteen of the counts were dismissed on the
Government's motion. The trial then commenced, the Government calling
as its first witness an Internal Revenue Service agent in order to put in
evidence the remaining eleven allegedly fraudulent income tax returns
the defendent was charged with helping to prepare. At the trial judge's
suggestion, these exhibits were stipulated to and introduced in evidence
without objection. The Government's five remaining witnesses were taxpayers whom the defendant allegedly had aided in preparation of these
returns.

After the first of these witnesses was called, but prior to the com-
mencement of direct examination, defense counsel suggested that these
witnesses be warned of their constitutional rights. The trial court agreed,
and proceeded in careful detail to spell out the witness' right not to say
anything that might be used in a subsequent criminal prosecution against
him and his right, in the event of such a prosecution, to be represented
by an attorney. The first witness expressed a willingness to testify and
stated that he had been warned of his constitutional rights when the
Internal Revenue Service first contacted him. The trial judge indicated,
however, that he did not believe the witness had been given any warning
at the time he was first contacted by the IRS, and refused to permit him to
testify until he had consulted an attorney.

PROCEDURAL PROBLEM: The trial judge then asked the prosecuting
attorney if his remaining four witnesses were similarly situated. The
prosecutor responded that they had been apprised of their rights by the
IRS upon initial contact. The judge, expressing the view that any warnings
that might have been given were probably inadequate, proceeded to discharge the jury; he then called all the taxpayers into court, and informed
them of their constitutional rights and of the considerable dangers of un-
wittingly making damaging admissions in these factual circumstances.
Finally, he aborted the trial so the witnesses could consult with attorneys.

The case was set for retrial before another jury, but on pretrial
motion by the defendant, Judge Ritter dismissed the information on the
ground of former jeopardy. The Government filed a direct appeal to this
Court and the United States Supreme Court noted probable jurisdiction.

THE ISSUE: Did the dismissal of the proceeding by the trial judge
deprive the defendant of his constitutional right to have his trial completed by the particular court and therefore violate the double jeopardy
clause of the Fifth Amendment and bar subsequent reprosecution?

THE ANSWER: Yes.

DISCUSSION: Justice Harlan, writing for four members of the Court, concluded that the trial judge had acted improperly in aborting the proceeding after the jury was impaneled in the first trial, and setting a date for another trial therefore constituted double jeopardy. Discussing the double jeopardy provision of the Fifth Amendment, the Court noted:

> The Fifth Amendment's prohibition against placing a defendant "twice in jeopardy" represents a constitutional policy of finality for the defendant's benefit in federal criminal proceedings. A power in government to subject the individual to repeated prosecutions for the same offense would cut deeply into the framework of procedural protections which the Constitution establishes for the conduct of a criminal trial. And society's awareness of the heavy personal strain which a criminal trial represents for the individual defendant is manifested in the willingness to limit the Government to a single criminal proceeding to vindicate its very vital interest in enforcement of criminal laws. Both of these considerations are expressed in Green v. United States, 355 U.S. 184, 187–188, 78 S.Ct. 221, 223, 2 L.Ed. 2ᴰ 199 (1957), where the Court noted that the policy underlying this provision "is that the State with all its resources and power should not be allowed to make repeated attempts to convict an individual for an alleged offense, thereby subjecting him to embarrassment, expense and ordeal and compelling him to live in a continuing state of anxiety and insecurity, as well as enhancing the possibility that even though innocent he may be found guilty." These considerations have led this Court to conclude that a defendant is placed in jeopardy in a criminal proceeding once the defendant is put on trial before the trier of the facts, whether the trier be a jury or a judge.
>
> But it is also true that a criminal trial is, even in the best of circumstances, a complicated affair to manage. The proceedings are dependent in the first instance on the most elementary sort of considerations, e.g., the health of the various witnesses, parties, attorneys, jurors, etc., all of whom must be prepared to arrive at the courthouse at set times. And when one adds the scheduling problems arising from case overloads, and the Sixth Amendment's requirement that the single trial to which the double jeopardy provision restricts the Government be conducted speedily, it becomes readily apparent that a mechanical rule prohibiting retrial whenever circumstances compel the discharge of a jury without the defendant's consent would be too high a price to pay for the added assurance of personal security and freedom from governmental harassment which such a mechanical rule would provide. As the Court noted in Wade v. Hunter, supra, at 689, 69 S.Ct., at 837, "a defendant's valued right to have his trial completed by a particular tribunal must in some instances be subordinated to the public's interest in fair trials designed to end in just judgments."
>
> Thus the conclusion that "jeopardy attaches" when the trial commences expresses a judgment that the constitutional policies underpinning the Fifth Amendment's guarantee are implicated at that point in the proceedings. The question remains, however, in what circumstances retrial is to be precluded when the initial proceedings are aborted prior to verdict without the defendant's consent.

In examination of the circumstances surrounding the mistrial declaration, Harlan concluded that the trial judge had indeed abused his discretion to insure that there was a manifest necessity for the initial dismissal of the proceedings.

The Government made the argument that there was adequate case
authority to permit reprosecution because the judge's ruling had bene-
fitted the defendant and because there was no compelling evidence showing that there had been any bad-faith prosecutorial conduct by the prosecution aimed at triggering a mistrial in order to get another day in court.
To this claim Justice Harlan noted that, "In sum, we are unable to conclude on this record that this is a case of a mistrial made 'in the sole
interest of the defendant.'" Going further, he held that "Reprosecution
after a mistrial has unnecessarily been declared by the trial court obviously subjects the defendant to the same personal strain and insecurity
regardless of the motivation underlying the trial judge's action."

In conclusion, Harlan stated:

> *Applying these considerations to the record in this case, we must
> conclude that the trial judge here abused his discretion in discharging
> the jury. Despite assurances by both the first witness and the prosecuting
> attorney that the five taxpayers involved in the litigation had all been
> warned of their constitutional rights, the judge refused to permit them to
> testify, first expressing his disbelief that they were warned at all, and
> then expressing his views that any warnings that might have been given
> would be inadequate. In probing the assumed inadequacy of the warn-
> ings that might have been given, the prosecutor was asked if he really
> intended to try a case for willfully aiding in the preparation of fraudulent
> returns on a theory that would not incriminate the taxpayers. When the
> prosecutor started to answer that he intended to do just that, the judge
> cut him off in midstream and immediately discharged the jury. It is
> apparent from the record that no consideration was given to the possi-
> bility of a trial continuance; indeed, the trial judge acted so abruptly in
> discharging the jury that, had the prosecutor been disposed to suggest a
> continuance, or the defendant to object to the discharge of the jury, there
> would have been no opportunity to do so. When one examines the cir-
> cumstances surrounding the discharge of this jury, it seems abundantly
> apparent that the trial judge made no effort to exercise a sound discretion
> to assure that, taking all the circumstances into account, there was a
> manifest necessity for the sua sponte declaration of this mistrial. United
> States v. Perex, 9 Wheat., at 580. Therefore, we must conclude that in
> the circumstances of this case, appellee's reprosecution would violate the
> double jeopardy provision of the Fifth Amendment.*

Chief Justice Burger concurred with the Harlan approach, "not without reluctance, however, since the case represents a plain frustration of
the right to have this case tried, attributable solely to the conduct of the
trial judge." Justices Black and Brennan were of the opinion that the

Court lacked jurisdiction to hear the appeal but they nevertheless joined the majority in the opinion.

In dissenting, Justices Stewart, White, and Blackmun were of the opinion that "abuse of discretion" was not in itself "adequate to resolve double jeopardy questions of this kind." In citing *Gori* v. *United States*, 376 U.S. 364 (1961), Stewart wrote that "The real question is whether there has been an 'abuse' of the trial process resulting in prejudice to the accused, by way of harassment or the like, such as to outweigh society's interest in the punishment of crime. It is in this context, rather than simply in terms of good trial practice, that the trial judge's 'abuse of discretion' must be assessed in deciding the question of double jeopardy. . . . Even assuming that the trial judge's action was plainly improper by any standard of good trial practice, the circumstances under which the mistrial was declared did not involve 'abuse' of a kind to invoke the constitutional guarantee against double jeopardy."

QUESTIONS

1. Do you support the majority opinion or the dissent? What are the strong points in each?
2. Define the phrase "judge's abuse of discretion." Can it be defined with any degree of certainty?
3. Distinguish this case from the preceding one, *Ashe* v. *Swenson*. Which makes more sense to you?

Chapter 17

Sentencing

Williams v. *Illinois*
399 U.S. 235, 90 S.Ct. 2018, 26 L.Ed. 2ᴰ 586 (1970)

SETTING: Williams was convicted of petty theft and received one year imprisonment and a $500 fine, the maximum allowable. He was also taxed $5 for court costs. The state law provided that after serving the one year if the defendant was in default of the fine and court costs he would remain in jail to "work off" his obligations at a rate of $5 per day. In effect, the sentence imposed added an additional 101 days of confinement because Williams could not pay the $505.

PROCEDURAL PROBLEM: While incarcerated, the defendant petitioned the sentencing judge to vacate the court order requiring him to remain in jail beyond one year because of nonpayment of the fine and court costs. The defendant alleged that he was indigent, and he should be released in order to "be able to get a job and earn funds to pay the fine and costs." The State did not dispute the factual allegations, but the trial court dismissed the petition on the State's motion. The Illinois Supreme Court subsequently held that there was "no denial of equal protection of the law when an indigent is imprisoned to satisfy payment of the fine."

Before the United States Supreme Court the defendant argued

primarily that the equal protection clause of the Fourteenth Amendment prohibits imprisonment of an indigent beyond the maximum term authorized by the statute governing the substantive offense when that imprisonment flows directly from his present inability to pay a fine and court costs.

THE ISSUE: May a defendant be continued in confinement beyond the maximum term specified by the statute because of his failure to satisfy the monetary provisions of the sentence?

THE ANSWER: No.

DISCUSSION: The United States Supreme Court said that the Fourteenth Amendment equal protection clause is violated in this type of situation because such a procedure constitutes impermissible discrimination between those defendants able to pay and those unable to pay. The Court also recognized that in prior cases the Court had tacitly approved incarceration to work off unpaid fines—*Hill* v. *Wampler,* 298 U.S. 460 (1936). It was also explained that traditionally commitment for failure to pay a fine was not viewed as a part of the punishment or as an increase in the penalty; rather it was viewed as a means of enabling the court to enforce collection of money that a convicted defendant was obligated by the sentence to pay. The additional confinement could always be avoided, so the argument went, by payment of the fine.

Chief Justice Burger, who wrote the majority opinion, reasoned that "once the State has defined the outer limits of incarceration necessary to satisfy its penological interests and policies, it may not then subject a certain class of convicted defendants to a period of imprisonment beyond the statutory maximum solely by reason of indigency."

The Court emphasized that its holding did not deal with a judgment of confinement for nonpayment of a fine in the familiar pattern of alternate punishments, such as "$10 or 10 days." (See *Tate* v. *Short,* following.) It also stated that it did not decide whether a state is precluded in any circumstances from holding an indigent accountable for a fine by use of a penal sanction. "We hold only that the Equal Protection Clause of the Fourteenth Amendment requires that the statutory ceiling placed on imprisonment for any substantive offense be the same for all defendants irrespective of their economic status."

It was also noted that the State is not powerless to enforce judgments against those financially unable to pay; "Indeed, a different result would amount to inverse discrimination since it would enable an indigent to avoid both the fine and imprisonment whereas other defendants must always suffer one or the other conviction."

QUESTIONS

1. What two issues, as noted by Justice Burger, did this decision leave unanswered?
2. Does your jurisdiction permit imposition of a fine and court costs to be "worked off"? How has this been interpreted by your state courts?
3. Does this decision, in effect, encourage judges to sentence defendants for the maximum term allowed by law? Explain your reasons and conclusion.

Tate v. *Short*
401 U.S. 395, 91 S.Ct. 668, 28 L.Ed. 2ᴰ 130 (1971)

SETTING: The defendant accumulated fines of $425 on nine convictions in the Corporation Court of Houston, Texas for traffic offenses. He was unable to pay the fines because of indigency and the Corporation Court, which otherwise has no jurisdiction to impose prison sentences, committed him to the municipal prison farm according to the provisions of a state statute and municipal ordinance which required that he remain there a sufficient time to satisfy the fines at the rate of $5 for each day; this required that he serve eighty-five days at the prison farm. After twenty-one days in custody, defendant was released on bond when he applied to the County Criminal Court of Harris County for a writ of habeas corpus. He alleged that "Because I am too poor, I am, therefore, unable to pay the accumulated fine of $425." The county court held that "legal cause has been shown for the imprisonment," and denied the application. The Court of Criminal Appeals of Texas affirmed, stating: "We overrule appellant's contention that because he is too poor to pay the fines his imprisonment is unconstitutional." The United States Supreme Court granted certiorari, and reversed on the authority of *Williams* v. *Illinois*, 399 U.S. 235 (1970).

PROCEDURAL PROBLEM: The Illinois statute involved in *Williams* authorized both a fine and imprisonment. Williams was given the maximum sentence for petty theft of one year's imprisonment and a $500 fine, plus $5 in court costs. The judgment, as permitted by the Illinois statute, provided that if, when the one-year sentence expired, Williams had not paid the fine and court costs, he was to remain in jail a sufficient length of time to satisfy the total amount at the rate of $5 per day. The Supreme Court held that the Illinois statute as applied to Williams worked an invidious discrimination solely because he was too poor to pay the fine, and therefore violated the equal protection clause. Although the *Tate* case involved offenses punishable by fines only, the issue arose whether defendant's imprisonment for nonpayment constituted the same unconstitutional discrimination as condemned in *Williams*.

THE ISSUE: Does the equal protection clause bar a state from automatically converting a fine to imprisonment for those who are unwilling to pay forthwith, while limiting punishment to the payment of a fine for those who are able to pay?

THE ANSWER: Yes.

DISCUSSION: The Court, speaking through Justice Brennan, adopted the view previously stated in *Morris* v. *Schoonfield*, 399 U.S. 508 (1970):

> *[T]he same constitutional defect condemned in* Williams *also inheres in jailing an indigent for failing to make immediate payment of any fine, whether or not the fine is accompanied by a jail term and whether or not the jail term of the indigent extends beyond the maximum term that may be imposed on a person willing and able to pay a fine. In each case, the Constitution prohibits the State from imposing a fine as a sentence and then automatically converting it into a jail term solely because the defendant is indigent and cannot forthwith pay the fine in full.*

The Court was careful to point out, however, that it was not barring the imprisonment of a defendant who is able but unwilling to pay. The Court also did not forbid imprisonment as a method of enforcement when alternate means fail despite the defendant's reasonable efforts to satisfy the fine by those means. One method recognized by the Court was payment of fine by installment payments.

Justice Blackmun, in a concurring opinion, thought that the majority holding "may well encourage state and municipal legislatures to do away with the fine and to have the jail term as the only punishment for a broad range of traffic offenses." Such a course would eliminate any equal protection problems, but perhaps would open Eighth Amendment considerations. As Blackmun concluded, "If, as a nation, we ever reach that happy point where we are willing to set our personal convenience to one side and we are really serious about resolving the problems of traffic irresponsibility and the frightful carnage it spews upon our highways, a development of this kind may not be at all undesirable."

QUESTIONS

1. Distinguish this case from *Williams* v. *Illinois*. Is the result in this case desirable? Discuss.
2. In addition to installment payments, what are other methods which you can suggest for an indigent to pay a fine? What are the practical difficulties involved in each of your solutions?
3. Because of high administrative costs in collecting small fines, do you think that under the *Tate* holding, judges will be inclined to impose short jail sentences rather than fines?

Chapter 18

Juvenile Proceedings

Kent v. United States
383 U.S. 541, 86 S.Ct. 1045, 16 L.Ed. 2ᴰ 84 (1966)

SETTING: Kent, 16 years old, was arrested by the police in Washington, D.C. for entering a woman's apartment, taking her wallet, and raping her. He was taken to a juvenile receiving home. Kent had an attorney who believed that the juvenile court judge might waive jurisdiction and permit Kent to be tried as an adult. Because of this the defendant's attorney filed a motion for a hearing on the question of waiver of jurisdiction.

PROCEDURAL PROBLEM: The District of Columbia's Juvenile Court Act gives the juvenile court exclusive jurisdiction over a juvenile charged with a violation of law, except that it authorizes the juvenile judge to waive jurisdiction and transfer the case to the United States District Court "after full investigation in case of any child sixteen years of age or older who is charged with an offense that would amount to a felony if committed by an adult."

The juvenile court judge did not rule on the motion, did not hold a hearing, and did not confer with Kent's counsel or parents. He nevertheless entered an order that after a full investigation he was waiving jurisdiction, and directed that Kent be held for trial as an adult in the district court. Kent was subsequently found guilty and sentenced to

389

from thirty to ninety years in prison. This conviction was affirmed by the Court of Appeals, but the United States Supreme Court reversed and remanded the case to the district court for a hearing *de novo* on the issue of waiver.

THE ISSUE: Was the purely arbitrary decision of the juvenile court judge waiving jurisdiction in violation of the plain requirements of the statute?

THE ANSWER: Yes.

DISCUSSION: This was the first case in which the United States Supreme Court reviewed the actions of a juvenile court and portended future court activity in this area. Although the statute in this case authorized the juvenile court judge to waive jurisdiction over a juvenile of 16 years of age if he is charged with a felony, this does not permit a completely arbitrary procedure as used by the judge. There is no place in our system of law for reaching a decision of such great consequences without formality—hearing, notice, counsel, and reasons for charges. The Court refused to recognize that a juvenile proceeding is criminal and requires the full complement of procedural safeguards in a criminal trial or even an administrative hearing, but the five-man majority held that the proceedings must measure up to the essentials of due process and fair treatment.

Kent did lay down several specific requirements for the future:

1. There must be a hearing on the waiver issue.
2. The child has a right to be represented by an attorney.
3. The attorney may discover the court's records and reports that are used in reaching a waiver decision.
4. The judge must give his reasons for the waiver decision in writing.

In raising the basic questions involving due process in juvenile proceedings, the Court left little doubt that state juvenile court procedure will be subject to attack on due process grounds.

Justice Fortas, speaking for the majority, attacked the idea that because juvenile proceedings are "civil in nature and not criminal," procedural rights guaranteed in criminal cases should be denied in juvenile cases:

> *While there can be no doubt of the original laudable purpose of juvenile courts, studies and critiques in recent years raise serious ques-*

tions as to whether actual performance measures well enough against theoretical purpose to make tolerable the immunity of the process from the reach of constitutional guaranties applicable to adults. There is much evidence that some juvenile courts, including that of the District of Columbia, lack the personnel, facilities, and techniques to perform adequately as representatives of the State in a parens patriae capacity, at least with respect to children charged with law violation. There is evidence, in fact, that there may be grounds for concern that the child receives the worst of both worlds: that he gets neither the protections accorded to adults nor the solicitous care and regenerative treatment postulated for children.

This concern, however, does not induce us in this case to accept the invitation to rule that constitutional guaranties which would be applicable to adults charged with the serious offenses for which Kent was tried must be applied in juvenile court proceedings concerned with allegations of law violation. The Juvenile Court Act and the decisions of the United States Court of Appeals for the District of Columbia Circuit provide an adequate basis for decision of the case, and we go no further.

The Court disposed of this case on a very narrow ground:

In these circumstances, considering particularly that decision as to waiver of jurisdiction and transfer of the matter to the District Court was potentially as important to petitioner as the difference between five years' confinement and a death sentence, we conclude that, as a condition to a valid waiver order, petitioner was entitled to a hearing, including access by his counsel to the social records and probation or similar reports which presumably are considered by the court, and to a statement of reasons for the Juvenile Court's decision.

QUESTIONS

1. The decision in this case was narrow. What was it? What is meant by a waiver of jurisdiction in this case?
2. In your estimation, what is the purpose of a juvenile proceeding?
3. Distinguish between "civil" and "criminal" proceedings. What is meant by *parens patriae?*

In re Gault
387 U.S. 1, 87 S.Ct. 1428, 18 L.Ed. 2ᴰ 527 (1967)

SETTING: Gault, 15 years old, was taken into custody by the Gila County, Arizona sheriff on the complaint of a woman who said Gault and another boy had made an obscene phone call to her. His parents were not told he was being taken into custody. He was then taken to detention and his mother was orally notified that he was in detention for making an obscene phone call and that the next afternoon a juvenile court hearing would be held. At the hearing, the complainant did not appear, no one was sworn, no transcript or recording was made, and the juvenile officer stated that Gault had admitted making the lewd remarks after questioning, out of the presence of Gault's parents, and without being advised of his right to remain silent. Neither the boy nor his parents were advised of the boy's right to remain silent, to be represented by counsel, and of the right to appointed counsel if they could not afford one.

At the conclusion of the hearing, the juvenile court committed the boy as a juvenile delinquent to the Arizona State Industrial School "for the period of his minority [that is, until age 21] unless sooner discharged by due process of law." Had Gault been 18, the maximum punishment would have been two months.

PROCEDURAL PROBLEM: On appeal to the United States Supreme Court, due process was claimed to have been violated because of the denial of (1) notice of charges, (2) right to counsel, (3) right to confrontation and examination, (4) privilege against self-incrimination, (5) right to a transcript of the proceedings, and (6) right to appellate review. The question of appellate review was not answered by the Court in this case.

THE ISSUE: Do procedural due process considerations apply to juvenile delinquency proceedings that may lead to commitment to a state institution?

THE ANSWER: Yes.

DISCUSSION: This opinion was very wide and far-reaching because it was not concerned with only a single constitutional right of an accused but with several. The Court included the rights to be given sufficient notice to make a defense preparation, to be advised of the right to counsel, to have counsel appointed if unable to afford one, to remain silent, and to confront and cross-examine witnesses in juvenile proceedings that could lead to detention of juveniles as delinquents.

Justice Fortas was careful to point out that the Court was not concerned with the proceedings or constitutional rights applicable to the pretrial stages of the juvenile process, nor did the Court direct its attention to the post-adjudicative or dispositional process. The Court was only concerned with those proceedings at which a juvenile is adjudicated to be a delinquent as a result of alleged misconduct for which he may be committed to a state institution.

Justice Fortas, after tracing the history and development of juvenile procedures, sketched a plan for future proceedings. He emphasized that the procedural safeguards announced in this case did not in any way repudiate the basic idea of juvenile legislation. It is quite proper to consider a juvenile hearing as something quite different and apart from a criminal trial. The adjudicated delinquent is someone much different from the convicted criminal. The emphasis remains heavily on rehabilitation rather than punishment. The highest motives and enlightened impulses have led to a system peculiar for juveniles. But the theoretical and constitutional basis for the present system is nevertheless debatable. In its results the system of juvenile justice has been far from satisfactory. It has demonstrated in its history that unbridled, arbitrary discretion, however well-meaning, is often a poor substitute for careful procedures and principles. As Fortas noted:

> It is claimed that juveniles obtain benefits from the special procedures applicable to them which more than off-set the disadvantages of denial of the substance of normal due process. As we shall discuss, the observance of due process standards, intelligently and not ruthlessly administered, will not compel the States to abandon or displace any of the substantive benefits of the juvenile process. . . . Further, we are told that one of the important benefits of the special juvenile court procedures is that they avoid classifying the juvenile as a "criminal." The juvenile offender is now classed as a "delinquent." There is, of course, no reason why this should not continue. . . .

In summary, the minimum safeguards which must be afforded to meet the due process demands are that:

1. The juvenile and his parents must have timely notice in advance of the hearing of the specific issues that they must meet.

2. The juvenile and his parents must be notified of the child's right to be represented by counsel retained by them, or if they are unable to afford counsel, that the court will appoint counsel for the representation of the juveniles.

3. The court must advise the juvenile of his privilege against self-incrimination, and his right to counsel. The court may not consider his confession or admission unless such admonition is given.

4. The juvenile and his parents have a right to confront and cross-examine witnesses against the juvenile. In other words, there cannot be a commitment to a state institution in the absence of sworn testimony which has been subjected to the opportunity for cross-examination.

QUESTIONS

1. Explain the due process safeguards that must be found in a juvenile proceeding as stated in *In re Gault*.
2. Discuss the effect that *Gault* will have on police work with juveniles.
3. What are additional constitutional issues which the Court did not reach in this case? What evidentiary problems are likely to crop up as a result of *Gault*?

In re Winship
397 U.S. 358, 90 S.Ct. 1068, 25 L.Ed. 2ᴰ 368 (1970)

SETTING: Winship, a 12-year-old-boy, stole $112 from a woman's pocketbook. This act, if committed by an adult, would have constituted larceny. Winship was found to be delinquent and was committed to the boys' training school for possibly as long as six years. The various state courts affirmed the commitment.

PROCEDURAL PROBLEM: A New York statute authorized determination of juvenile delinquency based on a preponderance of evidence. The hearing judge acknowledged that his finding of delinquency was based on a preponderance of evidence and rejected the claim that due process required proof beyond a reasonable doubt.

THE ISSUE: Is proof beyond a reasonable doubt among the essentials of due process and fair treatment required during the adjudicatory stage when a juvenile is charged with an act that would constitute a crime if committed by an adult?

THE ANSWER: Yes.

DISCUSSION: Justice Brennan, writing for five justices, held that the due process clause requires that a conviction of a criminally accused be based on proof of guilt beyond a reasonable doubt:

> *Lest there remain any doubt about the constitutional stature of the reasonable doubt standard, we explicitly hold that the Due Process Clause protects the accused against conviction except on proof beyond a reason-*

able doubt of every fact necessary to constitute the crime with which he is charged.

The Court stated that the same standard applies to the adjudicatory stage of a juvenile court delinquency proceeding in which a youth is charged with an act that would be a crime if committed by an adult.

The State argued that because this proceeding was "civil" in nature and not criminal, the preponderance of evidence requirement was not invalid. Brennan stated in response to this argument that "We made clear in that decision [*Gault*] that civil labels and good intentions do not themselves obviate the need for criminal due process safeguards in criminal courts for '[a] proceeding where the issue is whether the child will be found to be a delinquent and subject to the loss of his liberty for years is comparable in seriousness to a felony prosecution.'"

Brennan noted that numerous Supreme Court decisions "indicate that it has long been assumed that proof of a criminal charge beyond a reasonable doubt is constitutionally required." This standard "plays a vital role in the American scheme of criminal procedure and 'provides' concrete substance for the presumption of innocence."

Answering the argument that to afford juveniles the protection of proof beyond a reasonable doubt would risk destruction of the beneficial aspects of the juvenile process, the majority stated:

> *Use of the reasonable-doubt standard during the adjudicatory hearing will not disturb New York's policies that a finding that a child has violated a criminal law does not constitute a criminal conviction, that such a finding does not deprive the child of his civil rights, and that juvenile proceedings are confidential. Nor will there be any effect on the informality, flexibility, or speed of the hearing at which the factfinding takes place. And the opportunity during the post-adjudicatory or dispositional hearing for a wide-ranging review of the child's social history and for his individualized treatment will remain unimpaired. Similarly, there will be no effect on the procedures distinctive to juvenile proceedings that are employed prior to the adjudicatory hearing.*
>
> *We conclude, as we concluded regarding the essential due process safeguards applied in Gault, that the observance of the standard of proof beyond a reasonable doubt "will not compel the States to abandon or displace any of the substantive benefits of the juvenile process."*

In the dissenting opinion, the main fear was that juvenile courts were being pushed one step closer toward becoming full-fledged criminal courts. The decision, in the view of the dissenters, takes one more element of flexibility from the courts in dealing with the problems of youthful offenders. Justice Black, in a separate dissenting opinion, thought that the federal Constitution does not expressly require proof of guilt beyond a reasonable doubt and therefore reading it into the due process clause of the Fourteenth Amendment is incorrect.

QUESTIONS

1. *Gault* left a number of constitutional issues regarding the fact-finding processes open. Which one did *In re Winship* decide?
2. Define the standard of proof beyond a reasonable doubt; preponderance of evidence. Can they really be distinguished and understood by the layman?
3. Does the position of the dissenters that the juvenile court is moving more and more toward becoming a criminal court with advocates for both the State and defendant seem to be sound? Discuss this idea pro and con.

McKeiver v. *Pennsylvania*
403 U.S. 528, 91 S.Ct. 1976, 29 L.Ed. 2ᴰ 647 (1971)

SETTING: McKeiver, 16 years old, was accused of robbery, larceny, and receiving stolen goods. These acts were declared to be delinquent acts in a Pennsylvania juvenile court proceeding, although the acts were felonies under Pennsylvania law. In another case, a boy, age 15, was charged with acts of juvenile delinquency in the form of assault, battery, and conspiracy, all misdemeanors. In separate proceedings, counsel's request for a jury trial was denied. The Pennsylvania appellate court upheld the denial of the request for a jury trial.

In a third case, several juveniles in North Carolina were declared to be delinquent in a juvenile proceeding and were placed on probation. The public was excluded from these hearings over counsel's objection and counsel's request for a jury trial was denied. The juvenile court's decision was affirmed by the North Carolina appellate courts.

The United States Supreme Court considered the cases together.

PROCEDURAL PROBLEM: The problem was to ascertain some of the constitutional protections that inhere to juveniles as a result of the *Gault* breakthrough.

THE ISSUE: Does the due process clause of the Fourteenth Amendment assure the right to a jury trial in the adjudicative phase of a state juvenile court delinquency proceeding?

THE ANSWER: No.

DISCUSSION: The right to a jury trial guaranteed by the Sixth Amendment is not among the constitutional safeguards that the due process clause requires at the juvenile delinquency adjudicatory phase. Justice Blackmun, in announcing the judgment of the Court, noted the greatly increased number of rights accorded to juveniles facing commitment on juvenile delinquency charges. He also insisted "that these successive decisions do not spell the doom of the juvenile court system, or even deprive it of its 'informality, flexibility, or speed.'" According to Blackmun, imposition of the jury trial requirement as a constitutional precept "will remake the juvenile proceeding into a fully adversary process." It will tend to place the juvenile court squarely in the routine of criminal process and seriously discourage State efforts to experiment and to seek the elusive answers to the problems of the young.

The 1967 Presidential Commission on Law Enforcement and the Administration of Justice, *Task Force Report: Juvenile Delinquency and Youth Crime,* emphasized:

> The imposition of the jury trial on the juvenile court system would not strengthen greatly, if at all, the fact-finding function, and would, contrarily, provide an attrition of the juvenile court's assumed ability to function in a unique manner. It would not remedy the defects of the system. Meager as has been the hoped-for advance in the juvenile field, the alternative would be regressive, would lose what has been gained, and would tend once again to place the juvenile squarely in the routine of the criminal process.

Blackmun noted that there is nothing to prevent a juvenile court judge in a particular case in which he feels there is a need, from using an advisory jury.

Does the fact that some states do follow the practice of permitting a jury trial in a juvenile adjudicatory proceeding indicate that the practice accords due process? The judgment announced by Blackmun indicated that though not conclusive, it is certainly worth "considering in determining whether the practice 'offends some principle of justice so rooted in the traditions and conscience of our people as to be ranked as fundamental.' It therefore is of more than passing interest that at least 29 States and the District of Columbia by statute deny the juvenile a right to a jury trial in cases such as these. The same result is achieved in other States by judicial decision. In 10 States statutes provide for a jury trial under certain circumstances."

Justice Harlan agreed with the result, but on the theory that the Constitution does not require a jury in any state case under the Sixth Amendment. He also was unsure that the discrimination between adults and juveniles can be justified because the juvenile process has now become so close to a criminal trial. Justice Brennan joined the plurality's conclusion that these cases are not within the meaning of the Sixth Amendment's safeguard. He was of the opinion that a jury trial is not required so long as there is some means of keeping the juvenile process open to the public's scrutiny.

Justice White concurred, stating that juvenile proceedings are entirely different from adult criminal prosecutions. He also emphasized Blackmun's point that the states are free to adopt the jury trial concept in juvenile proceedings if they think it is wise.

The dissenters—Marshall, Black, and Douglas—maintained that the Bill of Rights made applicable to the states by the Fourteenth Amendment, mandates a jury trial.

QUESTIONS

1. Discuss the pros and cons of having a jury trial to adjudicate delinquency. Does the fact that a juvenile court may waive jurisdiction over a juvenile to allow him to be tried in a criminal court in effect guarantee a juvenile a right to a jury trial?
2. Because there was no majority opinion in this case, do you think the decision is likely to stand under a concerted attack?
3. Through this decision, what constitutional safeguards have been afforded to juveniles? What important ones in your opinion have been neglected?

Chapter 19

Corrections

Morrissey v. *Brewer*
408 U.S. 471, 92 S.Ct. 2953, 33 L.Ed. 2ᴰ 484 (1972)

SETTING: Morrissey was convicted of false drawing or uttering of checks in 1967 pursuant to his guilty plea, and was sentenced to not more than seven years' confinement. He was paroled from the Iowa State Penitentiary in June 1968. Seven months later, at the direction of his parole officer, he was arrested in his home town as a parole violator and incarcerated in the county jail. One week later, after review of the parole officer's written report, the Iowa Board of Parole revoked Morrissey's parole and he was returned to the penitentiary, which was located about 100 miles from his home. Morrissey asserts he received no hearing prior to revocation of his parole.

The parole officer's report on which the Board of Parole acted shows that defendant's parole was revoked on the basis of information that he had violated the conditions of parole by buying a car under an assumed name and operating it without permission, giving false statements to police concerning his address and insurance company after a minor accident, and obtaining credit under an assumed name and failing to report his place of residence to his parole officer. The report states that the officer interviewed Morrissey, and that he could not explain why he did not contact his parole officer despite his effort to excuse this on the ground that he had been sick. Further, the report asserts that Morrissey admitted buying the car and obtaining credit under an assumed name and also admitted having been involved in the accident. The parole officer recommended that his parole be revoked because of "his continual violating of his parole rules."

A second case was consolidated with the Morrissey decision which also involved revocation of parole. The state courts affirmed revocation of probation in both cases.

PROCEDURAL PROBLEM: The procedural problem in this case is important because of the virtually unanimous opinion of the United States Supreme Court that the due process clause indeed affects procedures regarding the revocation of parole.

THE ISSUE: Does the due process clause of the Fourteenth Amendment require that a state afford an individual some opportunity to be heard prior to revoking his parole?

THE ANSWER: Yes.

DISCUSSION: After reviewing the function of parole in the correctional process, Chief Justice Burger for the majority announced that the due process clause entitles a state parolee facing revocation of his probation to a hearing to determine whether he did in fact violate his parole, and if he did, what should be done about it. Noting that the liberty of a parolee, although indeterminate, includes many of the core values of unqualified liberty and that its termination is a grievous loss for the parolee and others, the Court stated that depriving a person of liberty is important and must be evaluated within the protections of the Fourteenth Amendment. "Its termination calls for some orderly process, however informal."

Burger acknowledged that a parolee is frequently said to be in custody, but even here, the elements of liberty accorded to him cannot be summarily treated by the state procedure. A simple factual hearing can in no way interfere with the revocation of parole and will certainly not interfere with the exercise of a state's discretion to remand a person to prison if the facts of violation are established.

What due process protections must be accorded to a parolee who is about to face recommitment? The Chief Justice went into some detail outlining the due process requirements. A "preliminary hearing" should be held at or reasonably near the place where the parolee is arrested, and as promptly as convenient after the arrest to determine whether "there is probable cause or reasonable grounds to believe that the arrested parolee has committed the acts which would constitute a violation of parole conditions." The determination of the grounds should be made by someone who is not directly involved in the case.

For this preliminary hearing, the parolee should be given notice of the place and purpose of the hearing and of what violations are alleged. The parolee must be given the opportunity to appear personally, offer evidence relevant to the issue, and to confront persons who have given adverse information on which the parole revocation is based. If the hearing officer determines that revealing the identity of the informant would subject him to risk of harm, he need not subject him to confrontation and cross-examination.

In addition, the hearing officer must keep an informal record of what transpires at the hearing. The summary must include the substance of the evidence in support of the revocation and the position of the parolee. The hearing officer then has the obligation to determine whether there is probable cause to revoke the parole. The hearing officer need not be a judicial officer.

A second hearing then determines whether there will be a revocation of parole. This hearing must be before a "neutral and detached" hearing body such as the traditional parole board, the members of which do not need to be judicial officers or lawyers. In addition to all the protections of the preliminary hearing, there must be written notice of the alleged violations of parole. At the conclusion of this hearing there must be a written statement as to the evidence on and the reason for revocation of the parole.

The Chief Justice emphasized that there is no intent to "create an inflexible structure for parole violation procedures." The majority decision further stated that:

> The few basic requirements set out above, which are applicable to future revocations of parole, should not impose a great burden on any State's parole system. Control over the required proceedings by the hearing officers can assure that delaying tactics and other abuses sometimes present in the traditional adversary trial situation do not occur.

The Court expressly did not decide the question of whether or not the parolee is entitled to the assistance of retained counsl or to appointed counsel if he is indigent. In his concurring opinion, Justice Brennan thought that the parolee must be afforded the right to retain a lawyer if he desires to do so. "The only question . . . is whether counsel must be furnished the parolee if he is indigent."

Mr. Justice Douglas, in dissent, would have held that a parolee should be entitled to counsel.

QUESTIONS

1. What are the rights a parolee must be afforded at the preliminary hearing made after the arrest to determine whether or not there is probable cause to believe that the parolee committed the acts which would constitute a violation of the parole conditions?
2. What protections must be present at the parole revocation hearing?
3. What right normally found in the concept of due process was not given to the parolee in this case? What reasons can you give for this decision?

Gilmore v. Lynch
319 F. Supp. 105 (N.D. Cal., 1970)

SETTING: In California, state prison inmates contested the validity of a prison regulation which limited law books to be made available in prison libraries. Another regulation also prohibited one inmate from possession of legal documents pertaining to the case of another inmate.

PROCEDURAL PROBLEM: The prisoners alleged that the above rules, individually, are arbitrary and unreasonable and, collectively, deny indigent prisoners and their jailhouse lawyers the legal expertise necessary if access to the courts is to be meaningful in any way. The argument of the defendant (the State) was based on precedent which indicated that state authorities do not have an obligation "to provide library facilities and opportunities" for inmates to look for legal loopholes for which only a lawyer is trained to search. In short, the argument indicated that providing law books in a prison library is a matter of privilege which can be withheld by the State. The problem was whether or not the State has an obligation to provide legal research materials to indigent prisoners.

THE ISSUE: Under the equal protection clause of the Fourteenth Amendment, must a state make available to indigent prisoners enough legal research materials to insure that their access to legal advice and to the Courts is equal to that of more affluent prisoners?

THE ANSWER: Yes.

DISCUSSION: The California federal District Court stated:

> *The rights invoked by plaintiffs herein have been given considerable emphasis by past and present case law. Reasonable access to the courts is a constitutional imperative which has been held to prevail against a variety of state interests. Similarly, the right under the equal protection clause of the indigent and uneducated prisoner to the tools necessary to receive adequate hearing in the courts has received special re-enforcement by the federal courts in recent decades.*

The district court emphasized that access to the courts is a very large concept which

> *encompasses all the means a defendant or petitioner might require to get a fair hearing from the judiciary on all charges brought against him or grievances alleged by him.*

The district court noted that this has been interpreted to include, among other things, court-appointed counsel for indigents, free transcripts, process-serving privileges, and *in forma pauperis* filing privileges.

The California solution until this case was, according to the district court, a "patchwork." The affluent are guaranteed the right to communicate with private counsel and to buy personal law books without any restrictions except for space requirements. According to the California procedure, "The indigent, however, are relegated to seeking out fellow inmates with legal knowledge, and to the resources of the prison law library, the contents of which are severely limited under the regulations now under attack." Thus the reforms in the California system aided the more affluent prisoners in having access to legal advice and the courts. The lot of the indigent inmates, however, was neglected. "This neglect of one class, when contrasted with the attention paid to the rights of others, raises serious equal protection questions. . . . Further, . . . [the] plaintiffs' very clearly defined right to reasonable access to the courts is seriously infringed by the highly restrictive nature of the book list set forth in Prison Regulation 300.041, even if that list is theoretically supplemented by the State Law Library." The inadequacy of the law books argument withstood the State assault that there was a need for economy in book purchases and that the need for discipline in the institution justified the regulations.

In concluding, the Court enjoined the enforcement of the prison regulation, but did not undertake the task of devising a system in which indigents were given adequate means of access to the legal expertise necessary to obtain judicial consideration of alleged grievances cognizable by the courts. "The Department of Corrections will therefore, decide whether to expand the present list of basic codes and references . . . or whether to adopt some new method of satisfying the legal needs of its charges."

In summary, the State's obligation under the Fourteenth Amendment's equal protection clause to make available to indigent inmates sufficient legal research materials to insure their access to the courts is at least equal to that of more affluent prisoners.

In *Younger* v. *Gilmore*, 404 U.S. 15 (1971), a two-paragraph *per curiam* opinion affirmed the California District Court ruling and also found that it has jurisdiction to entertain an appeal by the State.

QUESTIONS

1. What is meant in this case that the California regulation violated the equal protection clause of the Fourteenth Amendment?
2. What did the district court hold in this case?
3. Give some of the considerations that must be present when the California Federal District Court decides to determine that the law books available to prisoners are adequate.

Jackson v. Indiana
406 U.S. 715, 92 S.Ct. 1845, 32 L.Ed. 2ᴰ 435 (1972)

SETTING: Jackson was a mentally defective deaf-mute who could not read, write, or virtually otherwise communicate; he was charged with two criminal offenses and was committed under the Indiana statute governing commitment of mentally defectives. The doctors' report showed that Jackson's condition precluded his understanding of the nature of the charges against him or participating in his defense, and their testimony showed that the prognosis was "rather dim." Even if Jackson were not a deaf-mute he would still be incompetent to stand trial. His intelligence was not sufficient to enable him ever to develop the necessary communication skills. According to a deaf-school interpreter's testimony, the State had no facilities that could assist Jackson in learning minimal communication skills. After finding that Jackson "lack[ed] comprehension sufficient to make his defense," the court ordered him committed until such time as the health department could certify his sanity to the court. Jackson's counsel filed a motion for a new trial, which was denied. The State Supreme Court affirmed.

PROCEDURAL PROBLEM: The Indiana commitment statute for incompetent criminal defendants provides that if at any time before submission of the case to the court or jury, the trial judge has reasonable ground to believe that the defendant is insane, he must appoint two examining physicians and schedule a competency hearing which is heard by the court alone without a jury. The testimony of the doctors plus other evidence is produced on this issue of incompetency. If the court finds that the defendant does not understand the proceedings and cannot make his defense because of lack of comprehension, the trial is delayed or continued and the defendant is remanded to the state mental health agency to be confined in an appropriate psychiatric institution. When the defendant regains his sanity, the institution superintendent certifies him to the court, which shall order him to be brought to trial. The statute has no provision for periodic review by the court or mental health authorities of the defendant's condition. Although Jackson had an attorney, the statute does not give the defendant the right to counsel at the competency hearing. The evidence in this case showed little hope for improvement of the defendant's mental condition. Counsel argued that commitment under the above statute amounted to a commitment for life. This deprived Jackson of equal protection, counsel contended, because, without the criminal charges pending against him, the State would have had to proceed under other statutes generally applicable to all other citizens: either the commitment procedures for feebleminded persons or those for mentally ill persons. Counsel argued that under these other statutes (1) the decision to commit would have been made according to a different standard, (2) if commitment were warranted, applicable standards for release would have been more lenient, (3) if committed as feebleminded, defendant could have been assigned to a special institution affording appropriate care, and (4) he would then have been entitled to certain privileges not now available to him.

THE ISSUE: May a mentally incompetent defendant be committed to an institution for an indefinite period simply on account of his incompetency to stand trial on the charges filed against him without violation of equal protection and due process clauses of the Fourteenth Amendment?

THE ANSWER: No.

DISCUSSION: The deaf-mute defendant, committed and confined as criminally insane, could not, consistent with the due process clause, be confined indefinitely on the basis that he was incompetent to stand trial. The criminal commitment statute for insanity mentioned above and under which Jackson was confined is quite different in its impact from two civil commitment statutes in Indiana. In several very important provisions, the criminal insanity statute makes commitment much easier and release much more difficult. There is no requirement that the person committed receive therapeutic care or treatment. Probably more important is the fact that an individual committed civilly as "feebleminded" is eligible for release when his condition justifies it or under the second civil commitment statute "when the superintendent or administrator shall discharge such person or [when] cured of such illness." Thus, under either civil statute, when the individual no longer requires custodial care or treatment or detention, or when the department of mental health believes the person's best interests would be served, he may be released. Under the civil commitment standards, Jackson might have been eligible for release according to the evidence presented. On the other hand it is unlikely that, based on the criminal commitment statute, he would ever be released because the statute provided for no release unless there was a substantial change in his condition.

Justice Blackmun, writing the majority opinion for a unanimous Court (Justice Douglas concurred in a separate opinion), referred to *Baxstrom* v. *Herold*, 383 U.S. 107 (1966), which held that a state prisoner committed civilly at the end of a criminal prison sentence was denied equal protection when deprived of a jury trial that other civilly committed persons received. With this in mind, Blackmun concluded that "If criminal conviction and imposition of sentence are insufficient to justify less procedural and substantive protection against indefinite commitment than that generally available to all others, the mere filing of criminal charges surely cannot suffice."

The Supreme Court found the State's argument that the detention of the defendant was only temporary to be unpersuasive. Psychiatric testimony established that Jackson's chances of recovery were dim and even if he could improve, it was unlikely that he would be able to understand the proceedings against him or aid his counsel because of his deficiency. The Court further indicated that there was no constitutional argument with an *ex parte* order committing a defendant for a period of observation to determine whether or not he is a defective.

The Court also flatly rejected the State's argument that defendant's confinement was analogous to punishment for civil contempt arising from a refusal to cooperate in the evaluation proceedings. The Court emphasized that if there is to be confinement that can rest on a theory of civil contempt, then a hearing must be held to determine if the defendant's behavior amounts to contempt in fact.

In its closing summary, the Court stated:

> We need not address these broad questions here. It is clear that Jackson's commitment rests on proceedings that did not purport to bring into play, indeed did not even consider relevant, any of the articulated bases for exercise of Indiana's power of indefinite commitment. The State statutes contain at least two alternative methods for invoking this power. But Jackson was not afforded any "formal commitment proceedings addressed to [his] ability to function in society," or to society's interest in his restraint, or to the State's ability to aid him in attaining competency through custodial care or compulsory treatment, the ostensible purpose of the commitment. At the least, due process requires that the nature and duration of commitment bear some reasonable relation to the purpose for which the individual is committed.
>
> We hold, consequently, that a person charged by a State with a criminal offense who is committed solely on account of his incapacity to proceed to trial cannot be held more than the reasonable period of time necessary to determine whether there is a substantial probability that he will attain that capacity in the foreseeable future. If it is determined that this is not the case, then the State must either institute the customary civil commitment proceeding that would be required to commit indefinitely any other citizen, or release the defendant. Furthermore, even if it is determined that the defendant probably soon will be able to stand trial, his continued commitment must be justified by progress toward that goal. In light of differing state facilities and procedures and a lack of evidence in this record, we do think it appropriate for us to attempt to prescribe arbitrary time limits. We note, however, that petitioner Jackson has now been confined for three and one-half years on a record that sufficiently establishes the lack of a substantial probability that he will ever be able to participate fully in a trial.

QUESTIONS

1. What is meant by the term "civil" commitment? "criminal" commitment?
2. Does your jurisdiction provide for a procedure to commit a defendant until he is mentally competent to stand trial? What are the provisions of the statute? Do they square with the standards set up by this case?
3. In Justice Douglas' concurring opinion, he saw a self-incrimination basis for his decision in striking down the Indiana criminal commitment statute. What do you think his rationale for such a position is?

Johnson v. *Avery*
393 U.S. 483, 89 S.Ct. 747, 21 L.Ed. 2ᴰ 718 (1969)

SETTING: The defendant, serving a life sentence in the Tennessee State Penitentiary was transferred to the maximum security building in the prison for a violation of a prison regulation which states:

> *No inmate will advise, assist, or otherwise contact or aid another, either with or without a fee, to prepare Writs or other legal matters. It is not intended that an innocent man be punished. When a man believes he is unlawfully held or illegally convicted, he should prepare a brief or state his complaint in letter form and address it to his lawyer or a judge. A formal Writ is not necessary to receive a hearing. False charges or untrue complaints may be punished. Inmates are forbidden to set themselves up as practitioners for the purpose of promoting a business of writing Writs.*

PROCEDURAL PROBLEM: Six months after being transferred to the maximum security building, the defendant filed a motion in the federal district court for law books and a typewriter, and seeking relief from his confinement in the maximum security building. The district court treated the motion as a petition for a writ of habeas corpus and ordered him released from disciplinary confinement and restored to the status of an ordinary prisoner. The regulation was held to be void because it barred illiterate prisoners from access to federal habeas corpus. Subsequently, the State appealed and the Sixth Circuit Court of Appeals reversed, concluding that the regulation did not unlawfully interfere with the federal right of habeas corpus. The Court of Appeals reasoned that limiting the practice of law to lawyers and the need for preserving prison discipline justified the need for the regulation.

THE ISSUE: Did the Tennessee regulation deny a prisoner, in the absence of adequate outside assistance, the opportunity to secure federal habeas corpus assistance?

THE ANSWER: Yes.

DISCUSSION: Justice Fortas for the majority noted that the Supreme Court has constantly emphasized the fundamental importance of the writ of habeas corpus in our constitutional scheme because its basic purpose is to enable those who are unlawfully in confinement to obtain their freedom. Therefore it is fundamental that prisoners have access to the courts to present their complaints.

In response to the State's argument that regulation is justified as part of the discipline system, Fortas recognized this justifiable interest, but said that in this case the interest must yield to the prisoner's habeas corpus right:

> There can be no doubt that Tennessee could not constitutionally adopt and enforce a rule forbidding illiterate or poorly educated prisoners to file habeas corpus petitions. Here Tennessee has adopted a rule which, in the absence of any other source of assistance for such prisoners, effectively does just that. The District Court concluded that "[f]or all practical purposes, if such prisoners cannot have the assistance of a 'jail-house lawyer,' their possibly valid constitutional claims will never be heard in any court." The record supports their conclusion.

Fortas emphasized that because Tennessee does not provide an available alternative to the assistance provided by other inmates, it will just have to live with "jail-house lawyers."

Two points of interest for the future were not addressed by the majority in this case. First, it did not make clear whether a prisoner's access to habeas corpus is based on the Constitution or upon the federal habeas corpus statute. Second, the issue of whether the availability of access to "jail-house lawyers" is or is not a matter of right to prisoners seeking post-conviction relief, was left unanswered.

In its concluding remarks the Court noted:

> Even in the absence of such alternatives, the State may impose reasonable restrictions and restraints upon the acknowledged propensity of prisoners to abuse both the giving and the seeking of assistance in the preparation of applications for relief: for example, by limitations on the time and location of such activities and the imposition of punishment for the giving or receipt of consideration in connection with such activities. But unless and until the State provides some reasonable alternative to assist inmates in the preparation of petitions for post-conviction relief, it may not validly enforce a regulation such as that here in issue, barring inmates from furnishing such assistance to other prisoners.

QUESTIONS

1. What is the specific holding of this case? Does a prisoner have the right to counsel and a hearing to challenge a decision to move him to isolation or a more severe disciplinary process? What is the rule in your jurisdiction? For an interesting article, see "Prison Discipline

and Inmate Rights," 5 *Harvard Civil Rights–Civil Liberties Law Review* 227 (1970).

2. In a dissent by Justices White and Black, they emphasized the evils that would result from permitting jail-house lawyers to set up business. What, in your estimation, are some of these evils?

3. The idea has also been put forth that the permissible use of jail-house lawyers might conceivably ease problems involving prison discipline. How is this possible? Discuss fully.

Wilwording v. *Swenson*
404 U.S. 249, 92 S.Ct. 407, 30 L.Ed. 2ᴰ 418 (1971)

SETTING: This case was a *per curiam* decision of the Supreme Court. The defendants challenged only their living conditions and disciplinary measures while confined in maximum security in the Missouri State Penitentiary, and did not seek their release. Their state habeas corpus petitions were dismissed in the state courts. The federal district court and Court of Appeals affirmed the dismissal because there were other alternative avenues of relief open to the defendants in the state.

PROCEDURAL PROBLEM: The federal statute requiring exhaustion of state remedies before removal to the federal courts is merely an accommodation to the federal system designed to give the states the first opportunity to pass on and correct in the state courts alleged violations of a prisoner's federal rights. The statute does not expect impossible or successive barriers to the invocation of federal habeas corpus.

THE ISSUE: Does the "exhaustion of state remedies" rule require that every state remedy must be pursued when at the outset the defendant cannot intelligently select the proper way and in the end finds that none of the available remedies is effective or appropriate?

THE ANSWER: No.

DISCUSSION: Under the procedure in many states, innumerable procedural roadblocks are set up in the appellate process. This *per curiam* addressed itself to this specific problem. In addressing this issue, the Court stated that a person is not required to file repetitious applications in the state courts. The mere possibility of success in additional state proceedings also does not bar removal to federal courts. In this case it was a matter of conjecture whether the State would have heard the defendant's claims under any of the state procedures. Furthermore, the United States Supreme Court noted: "We are not referred to a single instance, regardless of the remedy invoked, in which the Missouri Courts have granted a hearing to state prisoners on the conditions of their confinement. In these circumstances, section 2254 (U.S.C.) did not require [defendants] to pursue the suggested alternatives as a prerequisite to taking their claims in federal court."

The Court also emphasized that although cognizable in federal habeas corpus, the defendant is entitled to have his complaints treated as claims for relief under the Civil Rights Acts for deprivation of constitutional rights by prison officials. The remedy provided by these acts "is supplementary to the state remedy, and the latter need not be first sought and refused before the federal one is invoked." State prisoners, according to the opinion, are not held to a stricter statement of exhaustion than other civil rights plaintiffs.

The Supreme Court reversed the judgment of the Court of Appeals and remanded the case for further proceedings.

QUESTIONS

1. What is meant by a *per curiam* opinion?
2. What did this *per curiam* opinion hold regarding whether or not the living conditions were bad or the discipline was too harsh in the Missouri State Penitentiary?
3. What is meant by saying that a defendant must exhaust his remedies under state law before removal to the federal courts?

United States v. *Muniz*
374 U.S. 150, 83 S.Ct. 1850, 10 L.Ed. 2ᴰ 805 (1963)

SETTING: Muniz was a prisoner in the federal correctional institution in Danbury, Connecticut. On August 24, 1959, when Muniz was outside one of the buildings at the institution, he was struck by one of the inmates and then chased into another dormitory by twelve other inmates. A prison guard, choosing to confine the attack instead of interceding, locked the dormitory. The twelve inmates set upon Muniz and beat him unconscious. He suffered a fractured skull and partial loss of vision in his right eye.

PROCEDURAL PROBLEM: Muniz alleged that the prison officials were negligent in failing to provide sufficient guards to prevent the assaults leading to his injuries. He also alleged that they were also negligent by letting prisoners, some of whom were mentally abnormal, intermingle without adequate supervision. Muniz and another in this suit brought their litigation seeking damages for personal injuries suffered during their confinement in federal prison. The federal district court dismissed the case on the ground that the suit was not permitted by the Federal Tort Claims Act (F.T.C.A.), 28 U.S.C. sec. 1346(b). The Court of Appeals, Second Court, reversed and the United States Supreme Court granted certiorari. The Supreme Court held that suits by prisoners are permissible under the F.T.C.A. for injuries sustained while in a federal prison.

The Act provides that the "United States shall be liable, respecting the provisions of this title relating to tort claims, in the same manner and to the same extent as private individuals under the same circumstances." The various exceptions provided by Congress do not preclude suits by federal prisoners for injuries sustained in prison. Whether or not a claim could be made would depend on whether a private person would be liable under state law, but prisoners are permitted to sue.

THE ISSUE: Can a person sue under the Federal Tort Claims Act to recover damages from the United States government for personal injuries sustained during confinement in a federal prison, because of the negligence of a government employee?

THE ANSWER: Yes.

DISCUSSION: Former Chief Justice Warren, upon examination of the legislative history of the F.T.C.A., concluded that Congress intended to permit suits such as those in this case. First, Congress wished to avoid injustice to those having meritorious claims that were barred by the doctrine of sovereign immunity and to eliminate the burden of having Congress investigate and pass private bills seeking relief. Second, an exception barring federal prisoners from suing was eliminated from the F.T.C.A. from past tort claims acts, thereby reflecting a deliberate congressional choice not to exempt prisoners from the act. Third, congressional committee history referred to several state acts allowing tort actions in derogation of sovereign immunity. In one of the states, New York, it was well settled that a state prisoner could sue. Congressional equanimity in the face of such liability further strengthened the conclusion that Congress intended to permit suits by federal prisoners.

Answering the Government's argument that the impact of liability would seriously impair the person, discipline, and administration of the prisons, Warren stated:

> We also are reluctant to believe that the possible abuses stemming from prisoners' suits are so serious that all chance of recovery should be denied. It is possible, as the Government suggests, that frivolous suits will be brought, designed only to harass or, more sinister, discover details of prison security useful in planning an escape. And it is possible that the Government will be subjected to the burden of pretrial preparation, discovery, and trial, even though it prevails on the merits. This seems an inescapable concomitant of any form of liability. It is also possible that litigation will damage prison discipline, as the Government most vigorously argues. However, we have been shown no evidence that these possibilities have become actualities in the many States allowing suits against jailers, or the smaller number allowing recovery directly against the States themselves.

The majority noted that the government is not defenseless. It is relieved from liability—"Any claim based upon an act or omission of an employee of the Government; exercising due care, in the execution of a statute or regulation, whether or not such a statute or regulation be valid, or based on the exercise or performance or the failure to exercise or perform a discretionary function or duty on the part of a federal agency or an employee of the Government, whether or not the discretion of the employee is abused."

Also, the government is not responsible for intentional torts of its employees, for which prisoners might be especially tempted to initiate retributive litigation. In Warren's conclusion for the majority:

> The Federal Tort Claims Act provides much needed relief to those suffering injury from the negligence of government employees. We should not, at the same time that state courts are striving to mitigate the hardships caused by sovereign immunity, narrow the remedies provided by Congress. As we said in Rayonier, Inc. v. United States, supra (352 U.S. at 320), "There is no justification for this Court to read exemptions into the Act beyond those provided by Congress. If the Act is to be altered that is a function for the same body that adopted it."

QUESTIONS

1. What is the doctrine of sovereign immunity? Is it a "relic of a bygone era?"

2. Does your jurisdiction have a tort claims law similar to the federal statute? What are its provisions regarding suits by prisoners?

3. What reasons did Justice Warren give as indicating that Congress did not intend to exclude federal prisoners from suing for injuries sustained during their time in prison?

Appendix

---

* Enacted by the Omnibus Crime Control and Safe Streets Act of 1968, § 802.

§ 2510. DEFINITIONS

As used in this chapter—

1. "Wire communication" means any communication made in whole or in part through the use of facilities for the transmission of communications by the aid of wire, cable, or other like connection between the point of origin and the point of reception furnished or operated by any person engaged as a common carrier in providing or operating such facilities for the transmission of interstate or foreign communications;

2. "Oral communication" means any oral communication uttered by a person exhibiting an expectation that such communication is not subject to interception under circumstances justifying such expectation;

3. "State" means any State of the United States, the District of Columbia, the Commonwealth of Puerto Rico, and any territory or possession of the United States;

4. "Intercept" means the aural acquisition of the contents of any wire or oral communication through the use of any electronic, mechanical, or other device.

5. "Electronic, mechanical, or other device" means any device or apparatus which can be used to intercept a wire or oral communication other than—

a. Any telephone or telegraph instrument, equipment or facility, or any component thereof, (i) furnished to the subscriber or user by a communications common carrier in the ordinary course of its business and being used by the subscriber or user in the ordinary course of its business; or (ii) being used by a communications common carrier in the ordinary course of its business, or by an investigative or law enforcement officer in the ordinary course of his duties;

b. A hearing aid or similar device being used to correct subnormal hearing to not better than normal;

6. "Person" means any employee, or agent of the United States or any State or political subdivision thereof, and any individual, partnership, association, joint stock company, trust, or corporation;

7. "Investigative or law enforcement officer" means any officer of

the United States or of a State or political subdivision thereof, who is empowered by law to conduct investigations of or to make arrests for offenses enumerated in this chapter, and any attorney authorized by law to prosecute or participate in the prosecution of such offenses;

8. "Contents," when used with respect to any wire or oral communication, includes any information concerning the identity of the parties to such communication or the existence, substance, purport, or meaning of that communication;

9. "Judge of competent jurisdiction" means—

a. A judge of a United States district court or a United States court of appeals; and

b. A judge of any court of general criminal jusisdiction of a State who is authorized by a statute of that State to enter orders authorizing interceptions of wire or oral communications;

10. "Communication common carrier" shall have the same meaning which is given the term "common carrier" by section 153(h) of title 47 of the United States Code; and

11. "Aggrieved person" means a person who was a party to any intercepted wire or oral communication or a person against whom the interception was directed.

§ 2511. INTERCEPTION AND DISCLOSURE OF WIRE OR ORAL COMMUNICATIONS PROHIBITED

1. Except as otherwise specifically provided in this chapter any person who—

a. Willfully intercepts, endeavors to intercept, or procures any other person to intercept or endeavor to intercept, any wire or oral communication;

b. Willfully uses, endeavors to use, or procures any other person to use or endeavor to use any electronic, mechanical, or other device to intercept any oral communication when—

i. Such device is affixed to, or otherwise transmits a signal through, a wire, cable, or other like connection used in wire communication; or

ii. Such device transmits communications by radio, or interferes with the transmission of such communication; or

iii. Such person knows, or has reason to know, that such device or any component thereof has been sent through the mail or transported in interstate or foreign commerce; or

iv. Such use or endeavor to use (A) takes place on the premises of any business or other commercial establishment the operations of which affect interstate or foreign commerce; or (B) obtains or is for the purpose of obtaining information relating to the operations of any business or other commercial establishment the operations of which affect interstate or foreign commerce; or

v. Such person acts in the District of Columbia, the Commonwealth of Puerto Rico, or any territory or possession of the United States;

c. Willfully discloses, or endeavors to disclose, to any other person the contents of any wire or oral communication, knowing or having reason to know that the information was obtained through the interception of a wire or oral communication in violation of this subsection; or

d. Willfully uses, or endeavors to use, the contents of any wire or oral communication, knowing or having reason to know that the information was obtained through the interception of a wire or oral communication in violation of this subsection;

shall be fined not more than $10,000 or imprisoned not more than five years, or both.

2. a. i. It shall not be unlawful under this chapter for an operator of a switchboard, or an officer, employee, or agent of any communication common carrier, whose facilities are used in the transmission of a wire communication, to intercept, disclose, or use that communication in the normal course of his employment while engaged in any activity which is a necessary incident to the rendition of his service or to the protection of the rights or property of the carrier of such communication: *Provided,* That said communication common carriers shall not utilize service observing or random monitoring except for mechanical or service quality control checks.

ii. It shall not be unlawful under this chapter for an officer, employee, or agent of any communication common carrier to provide information, facilities, or technical assistance to an investigative or law enforcement officer who, pursuant to this chapter, is authorized to intercept a wire or oral communication.

b. It shall not be unlawful under this chapter for an officer, employee, or agent of the Federal Communications Commission, in the normal course of his employment and in discharge of the monitoring responsibilities exercised by the Commission in the enforcement of chapter 5 of title 47 of the United States Code, to intercept a wire communication, or oral communication transmitted by radio, or to disclose or use the information thereby obtained.

c. It shall not be unlawful under this chapter for a person acting under color of law to intercept a wire or oral communication, where such person is a party to the communication or one of the parties to the communication has given prior consent to such interception.

    d. It shall not be unlawful under this chapter for a person not acting under color of law to intercept a wire or oral communication where such person is a party to the communication or where one of the parties to the communication has given prior consent to such interception unless such communication is intercepted for the purpose of committing any criminal or tortious act in violation of the Constitution or laws of the United States or of any State or for the purpose of committing any other injurious act.

    3. Nothing contained in this chapter or in section 605 of the Communications Act of 1934 (48 Stat. 1143; 47 U.S.C. 605) shall limit the constitutional power of the President to take such measures as he deems necessary to protect the Nation against actual or potential attack or other hostile acts of a foreign power, to obtain foreign intelligence information deemed essential to the security of the United States, or to protect national security information against foreign intelligence activities. Nor shall anything contained in this chapter be deemed to limit the constitutional power of the President to take such measures as he deems necessary to protect the United States against the overthrow of the Government by force or other unlawful means, or against any other clear and present danger to the structure or existence of the Government. The contents of any wire or oral communication intercepted by authority of the President in the exercise of the foregoing powers may be received in evidence in any trial hearing, or other proceeding only where such interception was reasonable, and shall not be otherwise used or disclosed except as is necessary to implement that power.

§ 2512. MANUFACTURE, DISTRIBUTION, POSSESSION, AND ADVERTISING OF WIRE OR ORAL COMMUNICATION INTERCEPTING DEVICES PROHIBITED.

    1. Except as otherwise specifically provided in this chapter, any person who willfully—

    a. Sends through the mail, or sends or carries in interstate or foreign commerce, any electronic, mechanical, or other device, knowing or having reason to know that the design of such device renders it primarily useful for the purpose of the surreptitious interception of wire or oral communications;

b. Manufactures, assembles, possesses, or sells any electronic, mechanical, or other device, knowing or having reason to know that the design of such device renders it primarily useful for the purpose of the surreptitious interception of wire or oral communications, and that such device or any component thereof has been or will be sent through the mail or transported in interstate or foreign commerce; or

c. Places in any newspaper, magazine, handbill, or other publication any advertisement of—

i. Any electronic, mechanical, or other device knowing or having reason to know that the design of such device renders it primarily useful for the purpose of the surreptitious interception of wire or oral communications; or

ii. Any other electronic, mechanical, or other device, where such advertisement promotes the use of such device for the purpose of the surreptitious interception of wire or oral communications,

knowing or having reason to know that such advertisement will be sent through the mail or transported in interstate or foreign commerce,
shall be fined not more than $10,000 or imprisoned not more than five years, or both.

2. It shall not be unlawful under this section for—

a. A communications common carrier or an officer, agent, or employee of, or a person under contract with, a communications common carrier, in the normal course of the communications common carrier's business, or

b. An officer, agent, or employee of, or a person under contract with, the United States, a State, or a political subdivision thereof, in the normal course of the activities of the United States, a State, or a political subdivision thereof, to send through the mail, send or carry in interstate or foreign commerce, or manufacture, assemble, possess, or sell any electronic, mechanical, or other device knowing or having reason to know that the design of such device renders it primarily useful for the purpose of the surreptitious interception of wire or oral communications.

§ 2513. CONFISCATION OF WIRE OR ORAL COMMUNICATION INTERCEPTING DEVICES.

Any electronic, mechanical, or other device used, sent, carried, manufactured, assembled, possessed, sold, or advertised in violation of section 2511 or section 2512 of this chapter may be seized and forfeited to the United States. . . .

§ 2514. IMMUNITY OF WITNESSES.

[This section provided for transactional immunity for witnesses required to testify about violations of this chapter. It is superseded by the general immunity statute, 18 U.S.C. § 6001 et seq.]

§ 2515. PROHIBITION OF USE AS EVIDENCE OF INTERCEPTED WIRE OR ORAL COMMUNICATIONS.

Whenever any wire or oral communication has been intercepted, no part of the contents of such communication and no evidence derived therefrom may be received in evidence in any trial, hearing, or other proceeding in or before any court, grand jury, department, officer, agency, regulatory body, legislative committee, or other authority of the United States, a State, or a political subdivision thereof if the disclosure of that information would be in violation of this chapter.

§ 2516. AUTHORIZATION FOR INTERCEPTION OF WIRE OR ORAL COMMUNICATIONS.

1. The Attorney General, or any Assistant Attorney General specially designated by the Attorney General, may authorize an application to a Federal judge of competent jurisdiction for, and such judge may grant in conformity with section 2518 of this chapter an order authorizing or approving the interception of wire or oral communications by the Federal Bureau of Investigation, or a Federal agency having responsibility for the investigation of the offense as to which the application is made, when such interception may provide or has provided evidence of—

a. Any offense punishable by death or by imprisonment for more than one year under sections 2274 through 2277 of title 42 of the United States Code (relating to the enforcement of the Atomic Energy Act of 1954), or under the following chapters of this title: chapter 37 (relating to espionage), chapter 105 (relating to sabotage), chapter 115 (relating to treason), or chapter 102 (relating to riots);

      b. A violation of section 186 or section 501(c) of title 29, United States Code (dealing with restrictions on payments and loans to labor organizations), or any offense which involves murder, kidnapping, robbery, or extortion, and which is punishable under this title;

      c. Any offense which is punishable under the following sections of this title: section 201 (bribery of public officials and witnesses), section 224 (bribery in sporting contests), subsection (b), (e), (f), (g), (h), or (i) of section 844 (unlawful use of explosives), section 1084 (transmission of wagering information), section 1503 (influencing or injuring an officer, juror, or witness generally), section 1510 (obstruction of criminal investigations), section 1511 (obstruction of State or local law enforcement), section 1751 (Presidential assassinations, kidnapping, and assault), section 1951 (interference with commerce by threats or violence), section 1952 (interstate and foreign travel or transportation in aid of racketeering enterprises), section 1954 (offer, acceptance, or solicitation to influence operations of employee benefit plan), section 1955 (prohibition of business enterprises of gambling), section 659 (theft from interstate shipment), section 664 (embezzlement from pension and welfare funds), sections 2314 and 2315 (interstate transportation of stolen property), section 1963 (violations with respect to racketeer influenced and corrupt organizations) or section 351 (violations with respect to congressional assassination, kidnapping and assault);

      d. Any offense involving counterfeiting punishable under section 471, 472, or 473 of this title;

      e. Any offense involving bankruptcy fraud or the manufacture, importation, receiving, concealment, buying, selling, or otherwise dealing in narcotic drugs, marihuana, or other dangerous drugs, punishable under any law of the United States;

      f. Any offense including extortionate credit transactions under sections 892, 893, or 894 of this title; or

      g. Any conspiracy to commit any of the foregoing offenses.

      2. The principal prosecuting attorney of any State, or the principal prosecuting attorney of any political subdivision thereof, if such attorney is authorized by a statute of that State to make application to a State court judge of competent jurisdiction for an order authorizing or approving the interception of wire or oral communications, may apply to such judge for, and such judge may grant in conformity with section 2518 of this chapter and with the applicable State statute an order authorizing, or approving the interception of wire or oral communications by investigative or law enforcement officers having responsibility for the investigation of the offense as to which the application is made,

when such interception may provide or has provided evidence of the commission of the offense of murder, kidnapping, gambling, robbery, bribery, extortion, or dealing in narcotic drugs, marihuana or other dangerous drugs, or other crime dangerous to life, limb, or property, and punishable by imprisonment for more than one year, designated in any applicable State statute authorizing such interception, or any conspiracy to commit any of the foregoing offenses.

§ 2517. AUTHORIZATION FOR DISCLOSURE AND USE OF INTERCEPTED WIRE OR ORAL COMMUNICATIONS.

1. Any investigative or law enforcement officer who, by any means authorized by this chapter, has obtained knowledge of the contents of any wire or oral communication, or evidence derived therefrom, may disclose such contents to another investigative or law enforcement officer to the extent that such disclosure is appropriate to the proper performance of the official duties of the officer making or receiving the disclosure.

2. Any investigative or law enforcement officer who, by any means authorized by this chapter, has obtained knowledge of the contents of any wire or oral communication or evidence derived therefrom may use such contents to the extent such use is appropriate to the proper performance of his official duties.

3. Any person who has received, by any means authorized by this chapter, any information concerning a wire or oral communication, or evidence derived therefrom intercepted in accordance with the provisions of this chapter may disclose the contents of that communication or such derivative evidence while giving testimony under oath or affirmation in any proceeding held under the authority of the United States or of any State or political subdivision thereof.

4. No otherwise privileged wire or oral communication intercepted in accordance with, or in violation of, the provisions of this chapter shall lose its privileged character.

5. When an investigative or law enforcement officer, while engaged in intercepting wire or oral communications in the manner authorized herein, intercepts wire or oral communications relating to offenses other than those specified in the order of authorization or approval, the contents thereof, and evidence derived therefrom, may be disclosed or used as provided in subsections (1) and (2) of this section. Such contents and any evidence derived therefrom may be used under subsection (3)

of this section when authorized or approved by a judge of competent jurisdiction where such judge finds on subsequent application that the contents were otherwise intercepted in accordance with the provisions of this chapter. Such application shall be made as soon as practicable.

§ 2518. PROCEDURE FOR INTERCEPTION OF WIRE OR ORAL COMMUNICATIONS.

1. Each application for an order authorizing or approving the interception of a wire or oral communication shall be made in writing upon oath or affirmation to a judge of competent jurisdiction and shall state the applicant's authority to make such application. Each application shall include the following information:

a. The identity of the investigative or law enforcement officer making the application, and the officer authorizing the application;

b. A full and complete statement of the facts and circumstances relied upon by the applicant, to justify his belief that an order should be issued, including (i) details as to the particular offense that has been, is being, or is about to be committed, (ii) a particular description of the nature and location of the facilities from which or the place where the communication is to be intercepted, (iii) a particular description of the type of communications sought to be intercepted, (iv) the identity of the person, if known, committing the offense and whose communications are to be intercepted;

c. A full and complete statement as to whether or not other investigative procedures have been tried and failed or why they reasonably appear to be unlikely to succeed if tried or to be too dangerous;

d. A statement of the period of time for which the interception is required to be maintained. If the nature of the investigation is such that the authorization for interception should not automatically terminate when the described type of communication has been first obtained, a particular description of facts establishing probable cause to believe that additional communications of the same type will occur thereafter;

c. A full and complete statement of the facts concerning all previous applications known to the individual authorizing and making the application, made to any judge for authorization to intercept, or for approval of interceptions of, wire or oral communications involving any of the same persons, facilities or places specified in the application, and the action taken by the judge on each such application; and

f. Where the application is for the extension of an order, a statement setting forth the results thus far obtained from the interception, or a reasonable explanation of the failure to obtain such results.

2.   The judge may require the applicant to furnish additional testimony or documentary evidence in support of the application.

3.   Upon such application the judge may enter an ex parte order, as requested or as modified, authorizing or approving interception of wire or oral communications within the territorial jurisdiction of the court in which the judge is sitting, if the judge determines on the basis of the facts submitted by the applicant that—

a.   There is propable cause for belief that an individual is committing, has committed, or is about to commit a particular offense enumerated in section 2516 of this chapter;

b.   There is probable cause for belief that particular communications concerning that offense will be obtained through such interception;

c.   Normal investigative procedures have been tried and have failed or reasonably appear to be unlikely to succeed if tried or to be too dangerous;

d.   There is probable cause for belief that the facilities from which, or the place where, the wire or oral communications are to be intercepted are being used, or are about to be used, in connection with the commission of such offense, or are leased to, listed in the name of, or commonly used by such person.

4.   Each order authorizing or approving the interception of any wire or oral communication shall specify—

a.   The identity of the person, if known, whose communications are to be intercepted;

b.   The nature and location of the communications facilities as to which, or the place where, authority to intercept is granted;

c.   A particular description of the type of communication sought to be intercepted, and a statement of the particular offense to which it relates;

d.   The identity of the agency authorized to intercept the communications, and of the person authorizing the application; and

e.   The period of time during which such interception is authorized, including a statement as to whether or not the interception shall automatically terminate when the described communication has been first obtained.

An order authorizing the interception of a wire or oral communication shall, upon request of the applicant, direct that a communication common carrier, landlord, custodian or other person shall furnish the applicant forthwith all information, facilities, and technical assistance necessary to accomplish the interception unobtrusively and with a minimum of interference with the services that such carrier, landlord, custodian, or person is according the person whose communications are to be intercepted. Any communication common carrier, landlord, custodian or other person furnishing such facilities or technical assistance shall be compensated therefor by the applicant at the prevailing rates.

5. No order entered under this section may authorize or approve the interception of any wire or oral communication for any period longer than is necessary to achieve the objective of the authorization, nor in any event longer than thirty days. Extensions of an order may be granted, but only upon application for an extension made in accordance with subsection (1) of this section and the court making the findings required by subsection (3) of this section. The period of extension shall be no longer than the authorizing judge deems necessary to achieve the purposes for which it was granted and in no event for longer than thirty days. Every order and extension thereof shall contain a provision that the authorization to intercept shall be executed as soon as practicable, shall be conducted in such a way as to minimize the interception of communications not otherwise subject to interception under this chapter, and must terminate upon attainment of the authorized objective, or in any event in thirty days.

6. Whenever an order authorizing interception is entered pursuant to this chapter, the order may require reports to be made to the judge who issued the order showing what progress has been made toward achievement of the authorized objective and the need for continued interception. Such reports shall be made at such intervals as the judge may require.

7. Notwithstanding any other provision of this chapter, any investigative or law enforcement officer, specially designated by the Attorney General or by the principal prosecuting attorney of any State or subdivision thereof acting pursuant to a statute of that State, who reasonably determines that—

a. An emergency situation exists with respect to conspiratorial activities threatening the national security interest or to conspiratorial activities characteristic of organized crime that requires a wire or oral communication to be intercepted before an order authorizing such interception can with due diligence be obtained, and

b. There are grounds upon which an order could be entered under this chapter to authorize such interception,

may intercept such wire or oral communication if an application for an order approving the interception is made in accordance with this section within forty-eight hours after the interception has occurred, or begins to occur. In the absence of an order, such interception shall immediately terminate when the communication sought is obtained or when the application for the order is denied, whichever is earlier. In the event such application for approval is denied, or in any other case where the interception is terminated without an order having been issued, the contents of any wire or oral communication intercepted shall be treated as having been obtained in violation of this chapter, and an inventory shall be served as provided for in subsection (d) of this section on the person named in the application.

8. a. The contents of any wire or oral communication intercepted by any means authorized by this chapter shall, if possible, be recorded on tape or wire or other comparable device. The recording of the contents of any wire or oral communication under this subsection shall be done in such way as will protect the recording from editing or other alterations. Immediately upon the expiration of the period of the order, or extensions thereof, such recordings shall be made available to the judge issuing such order and sealed under his directions. Custody of the recordings shall be wherever the judge orders. They shall not be destroyed except upon an order of the issuing or denying judge and in any event shall be kept for ten years. Duplicate recordings may be made for use or disclosure pursuant to the provisions of subsections (1) and (2) of section 2517 of this chapter for investigations. The presence of the seal provided for by this subsection, or a satisfactory explanation for the absence thereof, shall be a prerequisite for the use or disclosure of the contents of any wire or oral communication or evidence derived therefrom under subsection (3) of section 2517.

b. Applications made and orders granted under this chapter shall be sealed by the judge. Custody of the applications and orders shall be wherever the judge directs. Such applications and orders shall be disclosed only upon a showing of good cause before a judge of competent jurisdiction and shall not be destroyed except on order of the issuing or denying judge, and in any event shall be kept for ten years.

c. Any violation of the provisions of this subsection may be punished as contempt of the issuing or denying judge.

d. Within a reasonable time but not later than ninety days after the filing of an application for an order of approval under section 2518(7) (b) which is denied or the termination of the period of an order or extensions thereof, the issuing or denying judge shall cause to be served, on the persons named in the order or the application, and such other parties to intercepted communications as the judge may determine in his discretion that is in the interest of justice, an inventory which shall include notice of—

1. The fact of the entry of the order or the application;

2. The date of the entry and the period of authorized, approved or disapproved interception, or the denial of the application; and

3. The fact that during the period wire or oral communications were or were not intercepted.

The judge, upon the filing of a motion, may in his discretion make available to such person or his counsel for inspection such portions of the intercepted communications, applications and orders as the judge determines to be in the interest of justice. On an ex parte showing of good cause to a judge of competent jurisdiction the serving of the inventory required by this subsection may be postponed.

9. The contents of any intercepted wire or oral communication or evidence derived therefrom shall not be received in evidence or otherwise disclosed in any trial, hearing, or other proceeding in a Federal or State court unless each party, not less than ten days before the trial, hearing, or proceeding, has been furnished with a copy of the court order, and accompanying application, under which the interception was authorized or approved. This ten-day period may be waived by the judge if he finds that it was not possible to furnish the party with the above information ten days before the trial, hearing, or proceeding and that the party will not be prejudiced by the delay in receiving such information.

10. a. Any aggrieved person in any trial, hearing, or proceeding in or before any court, department, officer, agency, regulatory body, or other authority of the United States, a State, or a political subdivision thereof, may move to suppress the contents of any intercepted wire or oral communication, or evidence derived therefrom, on the grounds that—

i. The communication was unlawfully intercepted;

ii. The order of authorization or approval under which it was intercepted is insufficient on its face; or

iii. The interception was not made in conformity with the order of authorization or approval.

Such motion shall be made before the trial, hearing, or proceeding unless there was no opportunity to make such motion or the person was not aware of the grounds of the motion. If the motion is granted, the contents of the intercepted wire or oral communication, or evidence derived therefrom, shall be treated as having been obtained in violation of this chapter. The judge, upon the filing of such motion by the aggrieved person, may in his discretion make available to the aggrieved person or his counsel for inspection such portions of the intercepted communication or evidence derived therefrom as the judge determines to be in the interests of justice.

b. In addition to any other right to appeal, the United States shall have the right to appeal from an order granting a motion to suppress made under paragraph (a) of this subsection, or the denial of an application for an order of approval, if the United States attorney shall certify to the judge or other official granting such motion or denying such application that the appeal is not taken for purposes of delay. Such appeal shall be taken within thirty days after the date the order was entered and shall be diligently prosecuted.

§ 2519. REPORTS CONCERNING INTERCEPTED WIRE OR ORAL COMMUNICATIONS.

1. Within thirty days after the expiration of an order (or each extension thereof) entered under section 2518, or the denial of an order approving an interception, the issuing or denying judge shall report to the Administrative Office of the United States Courts—

    a. The fact that an order or extension was applied for;

    b. The kind of order or extension applied for;

    c. The fact that the order or extension was granted as applied for, was modified, or was denied;

    d. The period of interceptions authorized by the order, and the number and duration of any extensions of the order;

    e. The offense specified in the order or application, or extension of an order;

    f. The identity of the applying investigative or law enforcement officer and agency making the application and the person authorizing the application; and

    g. The nature of the facilities from which or the place where communications were to be intercepted.

2. In January of each year the Attorney General, an Assistant Attorney General specially designated by the Attorney General, or the principal prosecuting attorney of a State, or the principal prosecuting attorney for any political subdivision of a State, shall report to the Administrative Office of the United States Courts—

    a. The information required by paragraphs (a) through (g) of subsection (1) of this section with respect to each application for an order or extension made during the preceding calendar year;

    b. A general description of the interceptions made under such order or extension, including (i) the approximate nature and frequency of incriminating communications intercepted, (ii) the approximate nature and frequency of other communications intercepted, (iii) the approximate number of persons whose communications were intercepted, and (iv) the approximate nature, amount, and cost of the manpower and other resources used in the interceptions;

     c. The number of arrests resulting from interceptions made under such order or extension, and the offenses for which arrests were made;

     d. The number of trials resulting from such interceptions;

     e. The number of motions to suppress made with respect to such interceptions, and the number granted or denied;

     f. The number of convictions resulting from such interceptions and the offenses for which the convictions were obtained and a general assessment of the importance of the interceptions; and

     g. The information required by paragraphs (b) through (f) of this subsection with respect to orders or extensions obtained in a preceding calendar year.

     3. In April of each year the Director of the Administrative Office of the United States Courts shall transmit to the Congress a full and complete report concerning the number of applications for orders authorizing or approving the interception of wire or oral communications and the number of orders and extensions granted or denied during the preceding calendar year. Such report shall include a summary and analysis of the data required to be filed with the Administrative Office by subsections (1) and (2) of this section. The Director of the Administrative Office of the United States Courts is authorized to issue binding regulations dealing with the content and form of the reports required to be filed by subsections (1) and (2) of this section.

§ 2520. RECOVERY OF CIVIL DAMAGES AUTHORIZED.

Any person whose wire or oral commumnmication is intercepted, disclosed, or used in violation of this chapter shall (1) have a civil cause of action against any person who intercepts, discloses, or uses, or procures any other person to intercept, disclose, or use such communications, and (2) be entitled to recover from any such person—

     a. Actual damages but not less than liquidated damages computed at the rate of $100 a day for each day of violation or $1,000, whichever is higher;

     b. Punitive damages; and

     c. A reasonable attorney's fee and other litigation costs reasonably incurred.

A good faith reliance on a court order or legislative authorization shall constitute a complete defense to any civil or criminal action brought under this chapter or under any other law.